CONTENTS

INVESTIGATING THE LEISURE AND TOURISM INDUSTRIES

Introduction

It has been said that people's lifestyles, their needs and wants are changing faster than ever before. What was yesterday's desire is today's need. What was acceptable five years ago or less holds very little interest for us today. People have greater expectations. They demand improved services, better quality, affordable prices and when it involves their leisure and holiday they want all this and more.

No industries are as dynamic as the leisure and tourism industries. Together they are recognized as the world's largest industry. Over the last thirty years both have been the major growth industries of the world. In the UK they employ millions of people and earn the country billions of pounds in revenue. Consumer spending on leisure and tourism for 1995 was predicted as being £101 billion or approximately 25 per cent of all expenditure. Not surprising that their importance to the UK economy, jobs market and general well-being of the country has made the subject a major talking point.

This unit will begin to explore the many talking points of this subject by:

- Investigating the structure and scale of the UK leisure and tourism industries
- Exploring the UK leisure and recreation industry and its development
- Exploring the UK travel and tourism industry and its development
- Investigating the impact of the UK leisure and tourism industries.

Element 1.1 Investigate the structure and scale of the UK leisure and tourism industries

Performance criteria

1 Describe the structure of the UK leisure and recreation industry, giving examples of its facilities.
2 Describe the structures of the UK travel and tourism industry, giving examples of its facilities.
3 Assess the scale of the leisure and tourism industries nationally.
4 Explain the role of the public sector, giving examples of public sector organizations from both industries.
5 Explain the role of the private sector organizations, giving examples of private sector organizations from both industries.
6 Explain the role of the voluntary sector organizations, giving examples of voluntary sector organizations from both industries.
7 Investigate the relationship between the sectors.

Before we begin, it is interesting to note that not all people see leisure and tourism as two separate industries. Some commentators see tourism simply as a part of a wider leisure pursuit. As such, we will start by reviewing and defining what leisure and tourism is really about.

Leisure recreation and tourism defined

Leisure, recreation and tourism are words that everyone will have heard or used many times. Leisure for most of us is to do with leisure time, while recreation refers to leisure activities that people choose to carry out in their spare time. The word 'tourism' is often thought of in terms of travel, holidays and sightseeing. Many of us have seen visitors at some time, in our own areas or elsewhere, whom we may have thought of as tourists, when in fact they may have been local visitors enjoying a recreational activity.

Let's look at each of these terms separately.

Leisure

A dictionary definition of the word 'leisure' states that this is:

time at one's own disposal

Unfortunately, this only goes a little way towards describing what leisure actually means to everyone. For example, leisure time may mean the time when you can go and do what you wish. Consider your own situation at school or college, when the bell rings for the end of the teaching session. Does this signal a leisure break in the day's lessons? You might spend the time talking with friends, or just kicking a ball around the schoolyard – basically doing what you want in the time available. Of course, besides lessons at school there are many other things that we all perform through our daily lives, such as going to work, sleep, eating, doing homework, or domestic chores.

A better definition of leisure therefore could be:

The time available to an individual when the disciplines of work, sleep and other basic requirements have been met!

Recreation

Recreation has been referred to as the leisure activities that people choose to carry out in their spare time. The types of activities are very wide-ranging, but can be broadly categorized as those carried out in our local neighbourhood or at home, and those which are carried out some distance away from home, as shown in Figure 1.1.

Neighbourhood/ Home-Based	Away from the Home
Watching TV and videos Gardening Model building Needlework Painting Listening to music Reading and writing, talking Computer games DIY	Educational/cultural – going on an education exchange trip, visiting a major heritage attraction or national museum
Home maintenance Car Playing games in the garden, park or local sports facility Going to the local library, theatre, cinema, pub, club, museum, watching local football/rugby team Shopping Learning new skills at local college (e.g. languages)	Social – day trip to the seaside, visiting friends and relatives, going on holiday

Sport – going to away games to watch your favourite football team. Swimming gala in another town

Nature and environment – walking, camping and caravanning, youth hostelling association, birdwatching

Business trips – travelling to visit a client or to attend an exhibition or trade show |

Figure 1.1   Types of recreation

Task 1.1

Try and add other recreation activities to the above list.

Tourism

The major difference between leisure recreation and tourism recreation is that tourism is about conducting activities elsewhere or away from the home for a period of time, and to be elsewhere requires travel. The definition that best sums up this idea and is probably the most commonly used states:

Tourism is the temporary short-term movement of people to destinations outside the places in which they normally live and work and their activities during their stay at these destinations

Tourist Society, 1976

Think about the things that would need to be in place for you to describe yourself as a tourist.

1 You would have to be away from home or your normal place of work.

2 Your visit would be temporary in that you intend to return home in a short space of time (i.e. day, week, month, etc.).

3 The purpose of your visit would be enjoyment, possibly business.

It is important to note that distance or time clearly indicates as to whether we consider ourselves as tourists. As such, tourism means that we should include people who travel to another place, even in their own country, as tourists. For example, if someone travels 100 miles from Carlisle to Edinburgh for a weekend, then they become tourists while they are travelling and while they are in Edinburgh. 'Day trippers' will also fall within this category, since they also visit tourist attractions such as Alton Towers and use tourist information centres for advice.

It is worth noting here that the word 'tourist' refers to both UK residents (i.e. domestic tourists) and overseas visitors travelling to and/or around the UK. There are basically two major reasons why people travel: either for leisure or business.

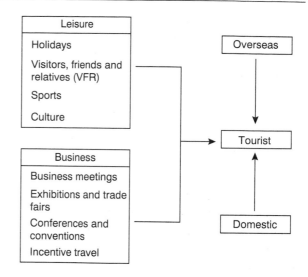

Figure 1.2 Tourism activities

Figure 1.2 highlights the different types of tourism activity under each of these category headings.

However, it should be noted that there are several tourism activities that do not fit neatly under either category. These include education, religion and health.

Figure 1.3 provides examples of these tourism activities.

Combining them all together, recreation has been described as those activities carried out by people in their spare time, and so relates to both leisure and tourism.

The difficulties of determining which is a leisure recreation activity and which is a tourism recreation activity relate to the many overlapping areas of interest that exist between them. The link that separates them relates to the purpose of the activity chosen and the geographical range or distance travelled.

Figure 1.4 identifies these broad recreational activities, but positions those activities that are predominantly home- or neighbourhood-based under leisure while those relating to activities further away from the home requiring transport under tourism.

Business tourism

Business Meetings – Business people often travel to meet each other to discuss business, for example:
A tour representative drives to London to meet an overseas client on a stopover to New York

Exhibition or trade fair – Such an event is organized on behalf of the travel trade for them to show off their tourism products and services in the hope of attracting buyers, for example:
The World Travel Market – London, Camping and Caravanning Exhibition, NEC, Birmingham

Conferences and conventions – Groups of people use conferences or conventions as a venue to discuss a range of topics of interest to them. An example could include:
The Tory Party Conference in Brighton

Incentive travel – Travel incentives have become a major inducement in getting companies as well as individuals to achieve set targets, for example:
A weekend break in Edinburgh for being the top salesperson of the month

Leisure tourism

Leisure tourism involves travel for the following purposes:

Holidays	– A week's cruise on the Norfolk Broads
Sport	– A day out at the Grand National
VFR	– Staying the weekend with a friend in another town
Culture	– Attending a music festival such as an Eisteddfod in Wales

Other tourism

Education	– An Indian student attending a college in London for a month to learn English
Religion	– A disabled person travels to Lourdes in France in search of a miracle cure
Health	– A professional footballer takes a trip to New York to see an orthopaedic specialist

Figure 1.3 Examples of tourism activity

Task 1.2

Below is a list of recreational activities. Read them carefully and then identify:

1 Which are leisure and which are tourism activities.

2 Categorize the tourism activities by the different types of business and leisure tourism.

3 For each tourism category identified, suggest a further example of your own.

- *A bonfire party at a friend's house*
- *A fourteen-day trip to the Costa del Sol*
- *Attending a wedding anniversary in the next town*
- *A retail distributor flies to the Far East to buy goods*
- *A visit to a stately home*
- *A fishing weekend in Scotland*
- *A timeshare villa in Spain offered to customers who purchase a set amount of goods through the year*
- *A local football match in the park*
- *A weekend in London to visit Buckingham Palace, the British Museum and the Tate Gallery*
- *A visit to the Camping and Caravan Show at G Mex, Manchester*
- *A meal out in a restaurant*
- *Ford organizes a sales convention in Florida for its overseas car distributors.*

The structure of the UK leisure and recreation industry

The leisure and recreation industry is comprised of organizations from the public, private and voluntary sectors of the economy. Such a diverse industry provides a host of leisure and recreational services, from the private surrounds of our own homes to the public gallery of a theatre to the quiet reflections in a library to the noisy and energetic pursuits on a playing field or in a discothèque. The components of the leisure and recreation industry are shown in Figure 1.5.

Arts and Entertainment

Arts and entertainment can be considered a massive industry on its own. The major sectors of the leisure industry covered by arts and entertainment include:

- TV
- Radio
- Books

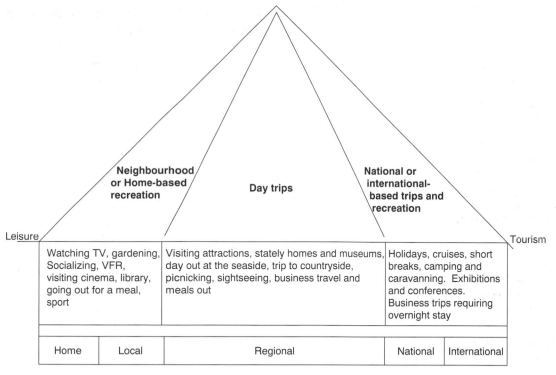

	Neighbourhood or Home-based recreation	Day trips	National or international-based trips and recreation		
	Watching TV, gardening, Socializing, VFR, visiting cinema, library, going out for a meal, sport	Visiting attractions, stately homes and museums, day out at the seaside, trip to countryside, picnicking, sightseeing, business travel and meals out	Holidays, cruises, short breaks, camping and caravanning. Exhibitions and conferences. Business trips requiring overnight stay		
Home	Local	Regional		National	International

Leisure — Tourism

Geographical range

Figure 1.4 The recreation continuum

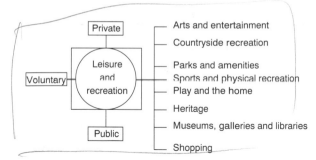

Figure 1.5 The structure of the leisure and recreational industry

- Hi-fi
- Film and cinema
- Theatre and drama
- Concerts
- Opera and ballet
- Festivals and events
- Dance
- Cabaret, casinos
- Pubs and clubs
- Amateur and community arts

Many of the above services are provided by private sector organizations such as Carlton, Granada or the Rank Organization. The services they provide can be seen to be either home-based or those that take place in public venues. However, the voluntary sector also plays a major role, for example, over 1 million people are estimated to participate in amateur music and drama. This figure does not take account of the members of amateur bands, dance classes, film and video workshops or youth theatre. In addition, the public sector of education, with its many artistic activities at school, college and university, expands these figures greatly.

Countryside recreation

Until the mid-1960s the recreational use of the countryside in Britain was very limited in scale and use. However, with the Access to the Countryside and National Parks Act of 1949, demand for countryside recreation has grown and grown. The English Tourist Board estimates show that upwards of 500 million day trips to the countryside are made every year in England alone (based on 1994–95 figures).

Parks and amenities

'Parks' is a term that most people understand to mean a certain area of open space which is given over to leisure and pleasure. 'Park' in this context refers to urban parks – a feature of Victorian England that was designed to allow for passive and recreational activities. However, today parks and amenities could be extended to include much wider provision, such as:

- Gardens
- Sports grounds
- Golf courses
- Cycleways
- Zoos
- Festivals
- Shows and exhibitions

Sports and physical recreation

Approximately 200 sports and physical recreation activities have been documented, ranging from hare coursing to golf, from angling to running, from football to snooker, which highlights the diversity of the activities. Most sports facilities are provided by the public sector, either the local authority or from funding provided by the Sports Council. Most paying spectator sports are provided by the private sector.

Participation in sport is on the increase, particularly for golf, hiking, rambling, skiing, keep-fit and cycling. However, participation in team sports is seen to be in decline, particularly those in the voluntary and schools sector.

Play and the home

Play has been described as a universal process, most evident in the young, which involves enjoyment of social, physical, imaginative and emotional activity for its own sake. It has been said that without play there would be no sports, no arts, no games, and, as such, no age limit should be attached to it.

Play involves play centres, adventure playgrounds, often school, and youth clubs such as Cubs, Brownies, even holiday play schemes. However, the vast majority of play takes place in or near the home. Interestingly, home-based leisure is set to become the major recreation industry of the 1990s. The development of electronic games, interactive CD and multi-media is expected to make the world of play even more home-based.

Heritage

Heritage is a term which we apply to historic buildings, ancient monuments, stately homes and gardens, castles and churches, even heritage centres. The term 'heritage' distinguishes it from museums, galleries and libraries in seeking to offer the visitor an experience rather than merely an educational or pleasurable visit.

Museums, galleries and libraries

Millions of people visit museums and galleries each year seeking knowledge, enjoyment and understanding of times gone by. Millions more continue to read. All are attractive venues, despite the competition from other major leisure activities.

Museums and galleries represent a wide assortment of leisure activities, many of which are today managed and run by non-public organizations such as private companies, national industries, educational institutions, charitable trusts, voluntary organizations, even private individuals. Many, of course, are managed and run by the public sector which stems from the 1850 Libraries Act which permitted local authorities to spend their money on creating and administering museums and libraries. In fact, the 1964 Libraries and Museums Act passed a duty on local authorities to provide an efficient, free lending service to the public which has led to a network of approximately 2500 public libraries covering the whole country.

Shopping

Although not always considered a pleasurable experience, most would agree that it is an activity that we all indulge in in our leisure time. Changes to the Sunday trading and licensing laws, coupled with the growth of out-of-town leisure centres where retail shops are combined with restaurants, cafés and bowling alleys, cinemas, clubs and pubs, have further developed the concept of leisure shopping.

The private sector has a virtual monopoly in this area.

The structure of the UK travel and tourism industry

The fragmented nature of the travel and tourism industry has led to it being supplied by many thousands of small as well as some large organizations which provide a vast array of tourism products and services for domestic and overseas tourists.

There are generally three categories of organizations involved in the structure of the tourism industry:

- The promoters of tourism destinations
- The producers of tourism products
- The distributors of tourism products.

These are shown below in Figure 1.6.

The structure is designed to meet tourist needs in terms of:

- Where to go.
- How to get there.
- Where to stay.
- What to do.

These core features of the industry are provided by a mixture of public and private sector organizations such as British Airways and rail companies, Holiday Inns and even local authorities which provide leisure facilities and tourist information centres.

The products and services are made available by a number of intermediaries or distributors, such as travel agents and tour operators, who buy and sell the producers' products and services. The

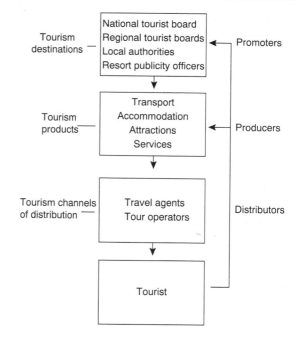

Figure 1.6 The structure of the UK travel and tourism industry

producers of tourism products and services can also sell direct to the tourist, bypassing the distributors.

Tourism destinations

The main reason why people travel is to go to a particular destination. There are five different types of tourist destinations in Britain. These are:

- A holiday resort or seaside region, e.g. Scarborough
- A cultural or historic town or region, e.g. Bath
- A national feature, such as a special part of the country, e.g. Land's End
- A major tourist attraction, e.g. Windsor Castle
- A business facility, e.g. Olympia, London or NEC, Birmingham.

The public sector, represented by the national and regional tourist boards and the local authority, plays a key role in co-ordinating the activities of all concerned to promote their regions as national as well as international tourist destinations. There are four national tourist boards (NTBs): England, Wales, Scotland and Northern Ireland. Each seeks to promote its own region of the UK. We will briefly review a few of the activities of the English tourist board, as the other three boards operate along similar lines.

The English Tourist Board (ETB) provides publications for the trade and the public. For example, it produces a travel trade guide which lists hotels, self-catering accommodation, coach operators, etc. throughout the country. It also produces where to stay and what to do guides for tourists when visiting England. Tourism advice is offered to local authorities and the private and voluntary sectors which can be booked by direct financial assistance for suitable major tourism projects in the form of loans and grants.

Case study

Regional Tourist Boards (RTBs)

The national tourist boards are supported at a local level by regional or area tourist boards, whose job it is to market and promote their own areas. There are eleven regional tourist boards in England, three tourism councils in Wales and thirty-two area boards in Scotland supported by the Highlands and Islands Development Board and the three councils of Edinburgh, Kirkcaldy and Moray.

The RTBs are generally seen as destination organizations in that their activities are all geared towards making tourists aware of their destination and encouraging them to visit. Their activities include:

- Advice to the national boards on applications for financial assistance
- Approval of grants of up to £100 million for tourism development projects
- Advice to commercial operators within their areas
- Liaison with local authorities over matters of tourism planning and management
- Supply of statistical information for the national tourist boards, undertaking their own surveys and research and providing more detailed local information

- Co-ordination of promotional campaigns via the product of a variety of regional tourism guides, exhibitions, events and shows.

The RTBs would argue that each destination within a country and outside it compete with one another. Places as far apart as Norfolk and Northern Ireland, London and New York, Blackpool and Barbados all compete for a piece of the total tourism spend. Getting tourists to visit a destination is therefore a highly competitive business and is very much dependent on the destination's image and how it is promoted in stimulating the tourist to choose that destination rather than another.

Tourism products

Transport

Transport can represent the main reason for taking a trip, from a journey on a canal boat or an ocean-going cruiser to a sightseeing trip on a London bus to view the capital's attractions. It also provides a means of access in travelling to and around destinations. Having a good transport network is therefore essential for a country or region if it is to develop its potential for travel and tourism.

Land transport represents the major form of travel within the UK. The car is the most popular of all land transport, accounting for 57 per cent of all UK holiday trips, and when hire cars, bus and coach travel are included, this figure rises to 73 per cent (Insights, 1995). In contrast, as car ownership has increased, so tourist traffic on the railways has fallen – a situation which has accelerated since the 1990s.

UK airports have expanded rapidly since the 1960s, and are seen as the main gateways for providing access to overseas tourists.

Accommodation and catering

There are basically two things that tourists always need and often refer to when they have been away – somewhere to stay and something to eat and drink. Accommodation and catering are clearly important components of the tourism industry – if these two components are not right the visit will not be seen as a success.)

Most accommodation and catering are provided by the commercial private sector, although the non-commercial public and voluntary sectors are represented through such facilities as outdoor activity centres or university lodging (operated by local authorities or educational institutions) to Cub camps and the Youth Hostel Association (operated by voluntary groups). Let us not forget that the VFR (visiting friends and relatives) market is a substantial and growing sector of the accommodation base in the tourism industry. Also, there is a wide variety of other forms of private accommodation used by tourists, including second homes, canal boats, yachts and timesharing apartments and villas.)

The accommodation sector offers widely different forms of sleeping and catering facilities. These, however, can be broadly categorized as either serviced or self-catering.

- *Serviced* – generally refers to the provision of catering, but also includes other services during a person's stay, such as bar facilities, housekeeping, cleaning rooms and changing towels
- *Self-catering* – although there is always an element of service in self-catering, it generally means that tourists cater for themselves and do their own housekeeping.

A feature of the industry is that as mass tourism has developed so, too, has the size of the organizations in the industry. The hotel sector in particular is now dominated internationally as well as at home by a few major companies. Their expansion has often involved franchising, which is where a hotel or motel is operated by individual franchisees who pay royalties to the main company for the use of its name and its marketing skills. This has proved a great success for both the largest hotel and fast-food groups in the world – Holiday Inn and McDonald's.

Attractions

It is often claimed that the major reason for choosing a destination is because of its attractions. This could be represented by the proximity of the accommodation to the sea, countryside, mountains, parks, historic monuments, sports facilities and entertainment. In fact, a definition of attractions could be:

All those things that draw visitors to a particular place

A fuller definition of attractions is given by the Travel and Tourism Society as:

A designated permanent resource which is controlled and managed for the enjoyment, amusement, entertainment and education of the visiting public.

There is a vast array of visitor attractions in the UK, the range of which has more than doubled over the last ten years. Most can be categorized as either man-made or occurring naturally, as indicated in Figure 1.7.

Tourism channels of distribution

The term 'channel of distribution' is used to describe the methods by which tourism products, and, in particular, travel services, are distributed from the producer to the consumer.

The distribution link that brings the producers of tourism products and services together to satisfy tourist needs is provided by:

- Principals
- Brokers
- Tour operators
- Travel agents.

Principals

A large proportion of UK domestic tourism is supplied direct by the producers, who sell their products and services through their own offices or retail outlets. The remainder, including virtually all outgoing (British holidaymakers abroad) as well as incoming tourism (overseas tourists

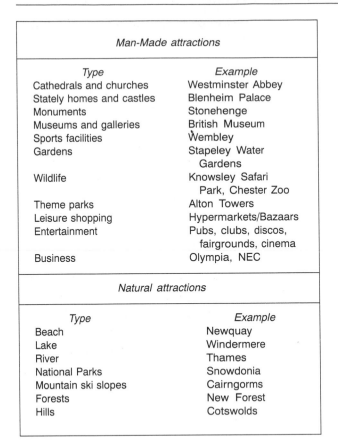

Man-Made attractions	
Type	*Example*
Cathedrals and churches	Westminster Abbey
Stately homes and castles	Blenheim Palace
Monuments	Stonehenge
Museums and galleries	British Museum
Sports facilities	Wembley
Gardens	Stapeley Water Gardens
Wildlife	Knowsley Safari Park, Chester Zoo
Theme parks	Alton Towers
Leisure shopping	Hypermarkets/Bazaars
Entertainment	Pubs, clubs, discos, fairgrounds, cinema
Business	Olympia, NEC

Natural attractions	
Type	*Example*
Beach	Newquay
Lake	Windermere
River	Thames
National Parks	Snowdonia
Mountain ski slopes	Cairngorms
Forests	New Forest
Hills	Cotswolds

Figure 1.7   Types of attractions in the UK

visiting Britain), is supplied by a number of intermediaries who buy up the individual component tourism products and sell them either direct or, more traditionally, through retail outlets. These alternative channels of distribution are illustrated in Figure 1.8.

Brokers

These are agents who generally involve themselves in the distribution of airline seats, although they could equally become involved in bulk purchase of hotel beds or other services. By buying in bulk they are able to negotiate much lower prices for airline seats or hotel beds, which they then sell direct to the consumer or through travel agents.

Tour operators

Like brokers, they also buy in bulk, the difference being that the tour operator packages together the various tourism products of transport,

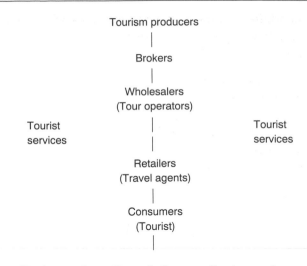

Figure 1.8   The tourism channels of distribution

accommodation and services into a single product often termed the *packaged holiday*. These products often include:

- Flight, ferry or train crossing
- Accommodation
- Coach transfers on arrival at the tourist destination
- Travel services, including holiday insurance, medical and financial arrangements, car hire, as well as a tour representative.

These packages are promoted through a variety of holiday brochures which are offered direct to the consumer or distributed via travel agents for sale to the general public. The travel agent receives commission for the sale of a package holiday from the tour operator of approximately 10 per cent off the cost of the holiday.

Travel agents

The role of the travel agent is that of a retailer in that it provides a place where the public can buy individual tourism products and/or packaged holidays. It differs from other retailers in that it generally does not take ownership of the products but simply provides an outlet for the distribution and display of the various travel products available for the consumer to purchase.

In addition to the above, travel agents sell a wide variety of other travel-related products and services, such as:

- Airline tickets
- Train tickets
- Ferry tickets
- Bus and coach travel
- Car hire
- Theatre tickets
- Accommodation reservation
- Travel insurance
- Currency exchange
- Sightseeing tours.

Travel agents are generally classified as being either:

- *Retail travel agents* – dealing with travel arrangements of the general public

- *Business travel agents* – they sometimes operate out of clients' own premises and are therefore also referred to as business house agencies. Their primary role is to serve the needs of industrial or commercial organizations, although they may also deal with personal holiday needs. The major business travel agents belong to GBTA, the Guild of Business Travel Agents

- *Others* – there are a number of other organizations involved in the distribution of travel and tourism products. These include:

    - *Ground handlers/Incoming tour operators*
      Incoming tours of the UK are organized by ground handlers. These organizations handle on the ground arrangements in the UK for foreign visitors on behalf of overseas tour operators. Ground arrangements cover all aspects of the tour except the flight into and out of the country. Most ground handlers are based in London.

    - *Conference organizers*
      The conference business is of great importance to the hotel accommodation sector. Conferences improve occupancy rates and greatly add to the tourism receipts of the host country. The British Tourist Authority (BTA) estimates that a third of tourism spend comes from business travel, and much of this is generated through conferences.
      Conference organizers are often involved in selecting the accommodation and arranging the catering as well as organizing the event. This can involve booking the hotels, organizing delegate mailings, registrations to actually running the conferences and finalizing the bills.

Tourism services

Many tourism services depend on the movement of tourists, such as customs and passport control, and yet are not considered part of the industry. Other services, while peripheral to the industry, nevertheless play an important role in providing services for the tourists themselves and to the suppliers of tourism, such as:

- Guiding services
- Tourist information services
- Financial services
- Marketing.

Guiding services

Many travel and tourism organizations provide guiding services. The service entails guiding, informing and sometimes interpreting information for tourists. Two types of service are offered:

- *Couriers* – Also known as tour escorts or leaders, these services are generally offered by tour operators and coach companies. The couriers supervise and shepherd groups of tourists to or around their tourist destination, often giving a commentary on the local features of the area and what to look for.

- *Guides* – Guides in this context are often specialists on a particular area, possibly local historians or interpreters. The information they provide to tourists on the places or areas visited is often much more detailed, and may be delivered in a foreign language.

Tourist information services

The national and regional tourist boards around the country will provide tourism information on their areas over the phone or through the post. However, with major support from the local authorities, the local tourist organizations fund a national network of tourist information centres (TICs). There are over 700 TICs throughout the UK whose job it is to collect and impart information on a wide range of subjects. Enquiries received can range from queries about bus or train timetables or where to stay or eat, to when the next meeting of the local birdwatchers' club takes place on what are the main industries offering employment in the area. Most enquiries are, however, about accommodation and what to do or visit. The ETBs 'Where to Stay' and 'Where to Go' guides are made available, as are regional tourist board guides from around the country.

Financial services

The two major services offered here relate to insurance and currency or credit exchange:

● *Insurance* – This is an important and, in many cases, necessary service relating to a tourist's travel arrangements. Insurance will often be required to cover:

  – cancellation of holiday
  – medical care
  – personal loss or accident
  – baggage loss or delay
  – trailer or caravan.

  Insurance services are provided by a raft of independent insurance companies, but are also provided by tour operators and travel agents. The commission received on insurance can be as high as 30–50 per cent, so most travel agents and tour operators endeavour to sell insurance as part of their normal range of services.

● *Currency exchange* – There is a wide selection of ways to pay for services and goods today in this country and abroad. However, at some stage where overseas travel is involved sterling will have to be exchanged for another currency.

The main means of exchanging currency include:
  – changing sterling for foreign currency or travellers' cheques at a bank or building society
  – arranging for advance transfer of funds to a specific foreign bank
  – Eurocheques (supported by a Eurocheque card) allow the holder to pay for items or draw cash in European currencies
  – credit cards such as Visa and Access (known as MasterCard) can be used to buy goods or services or obtain cash advances
  – some travel agents, particularly business travel agents, deal in travellers' cheques, while some of the larger ones, such as Thomas Cook and American Express, issue their own cheques.

Trade press

Weekly trade publications, such as *The Grocer*, *Hotel & Catering*, the *Travel Trade Gazette* and *Travel News*, provide an invaluable source of information to the industry. Employees can keep up-to-date on up-and-coming new products or services on offer, while major events can be publicized nationally.

Marketing services

Many organizations provide marketing support for the promoters, producers and distributors of travel and tourism products. These range from marketing consultants, research organizations to brochure and exhibitions designers, printers, public relations and advertising agencies.

The scale of the leisure and tourism industries nationally

The leisure and tourism industries are among the largest and fastest growing industries in the UK and around the world. Both are multi-million-pound industries employing millions of people. Their economic importance is highlighted by the government-published national accounts, which show that leisure and tourism accounts for over £100 billion per year.

Leisure expenditure, as indicated above, represents approximately 25 per cent of the UK's total consumer spending. Some may regard this as an overstatement of its importance and size, since it includes such categories as catering (including accommodation) and all forms of travel. Others may see it as an understatement, since such items as tobacco and sportswear are not included. Nevertheless it is clear that, while a large proportion of the expenditure – approximately £70 billion – is on leisure, it is also true to say that there is a significant non-leisure portion of around £30 billion, such as hotel and transport expenditure, much of which can be classified as tourism.

Consumer spending on leisure

Overall, UK average weekly leisure expenditure is increasing, as can be seen from Figure 1.9. In 1986 average weekly expenditure was £40.06, but by 1993 the figure had reached £46.01, an increase of 14 per cent. What these figures do not show, however, is the shift in leisure expenditure between leisure activities. Figures published by leisure consultants and illustrated in Table 1.1,

however, provide a fuller picture of the size and shift in leisure expenditure over a ten-year period, 1990 to 2000.

Between 1985 and 1995 the UK leisure market has grown rapidly. In value terms, it is estimated that we now spend around 150 per cent more on leisure than in 1985, despite the fact that the amount of leisure time has remained fairly static over the same period. However, compared with the 1980s, the growth in leisure spending has slowed considerably in the 1990s, mainly owing to the continued economic recession.

Although encouraged by some of the lowest inflation rates since the Second World War,

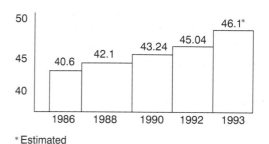

* Estimated

Figure 1.9 Average weekly UK leisure expenditure (*Source*: Adapted from *Social Trends*)

Table 1.1 Leisure spending (1990–2000)

Consumer spending	1990	1991	1992	1993	1994	1995	1996	1997	1998	1999	2000
Reading	4.71	4.49	4.40	4.49	4.56	4.60	4.66	4.72	4.76	4.79	4.83
Home entertainment	8.41	8.73	9.60	10.53	11.58	12.70	13.36	14.03	14.40	14.85	15.38
House and garden	6.73	6.45	6.67	7.04	7.37	7.55	7.84	8.18	8.45	8.67	8.91
Hobbies and Pastimes	5.06	5.12	5.31	5.27	5.30	5.40	5.60	5.84	6.02	6.18	6.35
In the home	24.91	24.80	25.99	27.33	28.82	30.26	31.46	32.77	33.63	34.49	5.47
Eating out	18.42	16.64	16.77	17.32	17.46	18.09	18.72	19.44	20.10	20.74	21.41
Alcoholic drink	21.36	20.57	19.71	19.65	20.38	20.75	21.05	21.47	21.66	21.72	21.82
Eating and Drinking	39.78	37.20	36.48	36.97	37.84	38.83	39.77	40.92	41.76	42.46	43.23
Local entertainment	2.46	2.36	2.26	2.32	2.25	2.23	2.28	2.36	2.40	2.42	2.44
Gambling	3.11	2.95	2.94	3.06	3.22	5.28	5.38	5.59	5.74	5.84	5.97
Active sport	4.30	3.97	3.54	3.46	3.45	3.51	3.61	3.72	3.81	3.88	3.96
Neighbourhood leisure	9.87	9.28	8.74	8.84	8.92	11.02	11.27	11.68	11.9	12.14	12.36
Sightseeing	0.43	0.42	0.42	0.43	0.46	0.48	0.50	0.53	0.55	0.57	0.59
Holidays in UK	6.13	6.19	6.19	6.13	6.28	6.96	6.67	6.81	6.84	6.83	6.83
Holidays overseas	9.40	9.84	11.01	11.19	13.10	13.63	14.38	15.31	15.99	16.54	17.16
Holidays and tourism	15.96	16.45	17.62	17.76	19.85	21.07	21.56	22.65	23.38	23.94	24.58
Away from home	65.61	62.93	62.85	63.57	66.61	70.92	72.60	75.24	77.08	78.53	80.17
All leisure	90.52	87.73	88.83	90.90	95.43	101.18	104.05	108.01	110.71	113.02	115.64

Source: Leisure Consultants

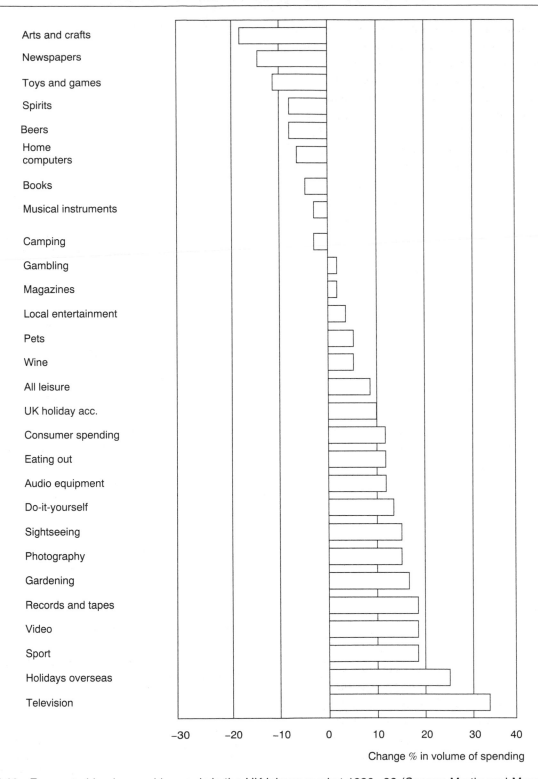

Figure 1.10 Forecasted leaders and laggards in the UK leisure market 1990–96 (*Source*: Martin and Mason Leisure Consultants)

consumer spending on leisure is not expected to take off until such time as the job market becomes more stable or people become accustomed to more flexible working patterns. This is reflected by the fact that there has been no growth in the amount spent in the major leisure fields of catering and drinking between 1990 and 1995. Given the large increases in prices over the last five years, this reflects a significant fall in numbers of people going out to eat and drink. Most of the increase in consumer spending on leisure has been spent on in-house activities, such as computer games, TV and video.

The major growth and decline sectors in the 1990s are compared in Figure 1.10 below.

Travel and tourism worldwide

Travel and tourism is the world's biggest industry. According to the World Travel and Tourism Council, the industry:

- Provides direct and indirect employment worldwide for more than 150 million people
- Accounts for approximately 11 per cent of all consumer spending worldwide, 10.8 per cent of all capital invested and 7 per cent of all government spending.

Its rate of growth has been phenomenal since the Second World War. In terms of international tourism arrivals, Figure 1.11 reflects the continued increase in world tourism.

Europe continues to dominate the international travel scene, accounting for over 60 per cent of all international arrivals and just over half of all tourism expenditure (receipts). The easing of border controls through Eastern Europe may give even greater prominence in statistical terms, while the combination of the Channel Tunnel and the deregulation of Europe's airlines is expected in the long term to reinforce this prediction. However, Japan has shown how quickly a developing nation can become a major tourism player, having overtaken Britain and moved strongly into third place, behind West Germany and the USA respectively. That being said, with

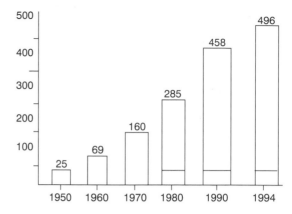

Figure 1.11 World international tourism arrivals (millions) 1950–1994 (*Source*: World Travel Organization)

the exception of Japan, the only countries to be found among the world's top ten generators of international tourism are located in Western Europe and North America.

The UK travel and tourism market

According to figures published by the BTA, tourism in Britain is forecast to reach £40 billion by the turn of the century, making it the fastest growing industry in the UK. The value of UK tourism in 1994 was given as £34 billion, a breakdown of which is provided in Figure 1.12.

Note: Of the £34 billion spent in 1994, £18,310 million was spent by outgoing British tourists travelling abroad.

Tourism and the economy

UK tourism generated an income of £24,316 million in 1994 for the UK economy. Figure 1.13 illustrates the split between holiday/visiting

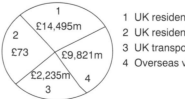

1 UK residents staying overnight
2 UK residents on day trips
3 UK transport of overseas visitors
4 Overseas visitors in the UK

Figure 1.12 Breakdown of UK travel and tourism market 1995

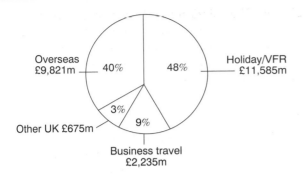

Figure 1.13 UK tourism earnings 1994 (*Source*: Insights 1995/96)

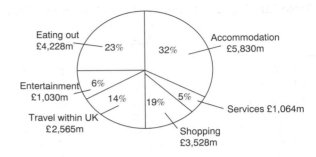

Figure 1.14 Tourism spending breakdown (*Source*: BTA 1993)

friends and relatives (VFR), business travel, other travel and income from overseas tourists.

1994 was a good year for Britain's tourism industry. The number of overseas visitors went up to 21 million, and they spent a record £9.8 billion, up 6 per cent on 1993. Unfortunately, the growth in world tourism still outstripped the UK's performance, leading to a fall in world market share.

Nevertheless, domestic and incoming tourism is up significantly for the eleven months ended November 1995, and with the anticipated price rises in overseas holidays for the 1996 summer season, coupled with the good weather of 1995, 1996 is expected to be another record year for domestic and incoming tourism.

While UK travel and tourism is clearly increasing, so is the number of UK residents travelling abroad. Most people tend to think of tourism only in terms of travelling abroad, which is not surprising given the extent of British travel. The figures show that the number of outgoing trips has increased by a third, to 33 million, over the last ten years, reflecting the high priority given to overseas travel by the British.

Consumer spending on tourism

Tourism accounts for about 7–8 per cent of consumer spending in Britain. However, it should be recognized that the UK is not only a major generator of international and domestic tourism but also a world destination in its own right.

The largest part of all tourist expenditure is spent on accommodation. Together with catering (eating out) it represents over half of all tourist spending. Figure 1.14 provides an outline of the key spending areas.

Consumer spending on tourism continues to rise as the UK market for tourism, both domestic and from overseas, increases. Table 1.2 shows the increasing scale of the UK tourism market in terms of the number of trips made, the number of overnight stops and the amount spent.

Incoming tourism

Our well-developed tourism industry is highly dependent on visitors from overseas. In 1990 the number of international visits into Britain was over 18 million, but by 1994 this stood at over 21 million, an increase of 17 per cent. The USA still generates the greatest number of overseas tourists to the UK, but there is an increasing trend for greater numbers of visitors from other long-haul markets, such as Australia and Japan, as well as from Europe.

Table 1.2 UK tourism market 1990–1994

	Trips		*Nights*		*Spend**	
	1990	1994	1990	1994	1990	1994
Domestic	96m	110m	399m	417m	£10460m	£14495m
Incoming	18m	21m	198m	194m	£ 7865m	£ 9919m
	114m	131m	597m	611m	£18325m	£24457m
Outgoing	25m	28m	?	288m	?	£18310m

(*The above figures do not include travel costs.)

Source: Insights 1995/96

Table 1.3 Top ten generators of tourists to Britain 1994

	Arrivals	Spend
1 USA	3.0 m	£ 1,800 m
2 France	2.8 m	£ 478 m
3 Germany	2.5 m	£ 788 m
4 Ireland	1.7 m	£ 581 m
5 Netherlands	1.2 m	£ 299 m
6 Belgium	1.0 m	£ 198 m
7 Italy	0.8 m	£ 406 m
8 Spain	0.7 m	£ 317 m
9 Japan	0.6 m	£ 410 m
10 Canada	0.6 m	£ 266 m

Source: International Passenger Survey 1994/95

Table 1.3 shows the top ten generating countries for incoming tourism into Britain.

The majority (90 per cent) of all overseas tourists visit England, and most of those visit London. For approximately 60 per cent of overseas tourists, London is *the* destination to visit. Although it is one of the world's largest cities, tourist activity is concentrated within a relatively small part of it, in one square mile of the City of London and in Westminster. Although tourism spills over into other boroughs of London, such as Kensington, Chelsea, Wimbledon and Richmond, a greater proportion of visitors travel within the UK to the 'honey pot' historic towns and places such as Stratford upon Avon, York, Edinburgh, the Lake District and Chester.

Domestic tourism

In 1989 the four national tourist boards of England, Scotland, Wales and Northern Ireland launched the United Kingdom Tourism Survey (UKTS). This replaced the separate surveys carried out by each of the boards to measure the level of domestic tourism and to allow comparison across different parts of the UK. However, due to lack of comparability of the new survey with those of previous years, it is difficult to assess the performance of tourism in 1989 and beyond with the years prior to 1989. Evidence does, however, strongly suggest that tourism continues to increase, particularly in terms of spending.

The majority of tourism trips made by UK residents are to destinations within the UK. In 1994 domestic tourism accounted for 80 per cent of all tourism trips, 59 per cent of all nights' accommodation and 44 per cent of all expenditure, as can be seen from Table 1.4 below.

Table 1.4 Distribution of domestic tourism

	UK resident tourism 1994/95					
	1994	% change on 1993	1994	% change on 1993	1994	% change on 1993
All destinations	136.7	+20%	704.4	+12	32805	+19
UK	109.8	+21	416.5	+11	14495	+17
England	90.8	+24	328.8	+14	11650	+21
Scotland	8.5	−6	37.6	−10	1310	−8
Wales	9.8	+27	40.1	+13	1075	+14
Northern Ireland	1.2	−8	4.8	−15	180	+20
Non−UK	27.5	+17	287.8	+14	18310	+21
Rest of European Union (ex UK)	19.6	+21	180.6	+20	10535	+29
Elsewhere (Non UK)	8.2	+8	107.2	+5	7775	+12
Total European Union (including UK)	128.9	+2	597.2	+3	25030	+22

Source: Insights, September 1995/96

Domestic tourism contrasts sharply with incoming tourism in that it invariably involves fewer nights away and a lower level of spending. In 1994 the average length of stay for domestic trips was four nights, with an average spend of £150. For overseas visitors, the corresponding figures were 9.2 nights and £467 (*Note*: The average length of stay for overseas visitors has fallen steadily since 1979 when it was at around 12.4 nights, albeit the average spend has more than doubled over the same period).

Unlike overseas tourists, who prefer the heritage and entertainment of the nation's towns and cities, UK residents generally seek out the idyllic scenery and mild climate of the south coast. The UKST survey of 1994 showed that the West Country continued to be Britain's top holiday destination, accounting for 23 per cent of all holiday trips. Southern England was next in popularity, with 9 per cent, followed closely by East Anglia and Yorkshire and Humberside.

Task 1.3

Identify ten UK tourist destinations and list the reasons why overseas or domestic tourists are attracted to these.

The role of the public sector in leisure and tourism

The state, which includes central and local government organizations, provides recreation activities and facilities in the public sector. The facilities they provide exist in essence to provide support for the community. These activities and facilities include, for example:

- Libraries and museums
- Heritage centres and galleries
- Parks, children's play areas and sports grounds
- Local authority sports centres
- Municipal swimming baths
- Visitor attractions
- Tourist information centres
- Music festivals.

Central government

Central government is seldom directly involved in the provision of leisure and tourism activities in the UK. However, it does support leisure and tourism via the organizations that it forms, the law and the grants that it provides to local authorities, quangos and other leisure organizations.

Prior to the 1990s there were over twenty different government departments which had some direct or indirect influence or control over the leisure and tourism industry. Today there are just five, as shown below in Figure 1.15

Many of the staff of the other departments were transferred in April 1992 to a new department, set up to co-ordinate many of the diverse activities of the leisure and tourism industry in the UK. Its name, which heads up the list of government departments, is the Department of National Heritage (DNH). These diverse activities range from broadcasting, sport, tourism and the arts to

Figure 1.15 Government departments involved in leisure and tourism

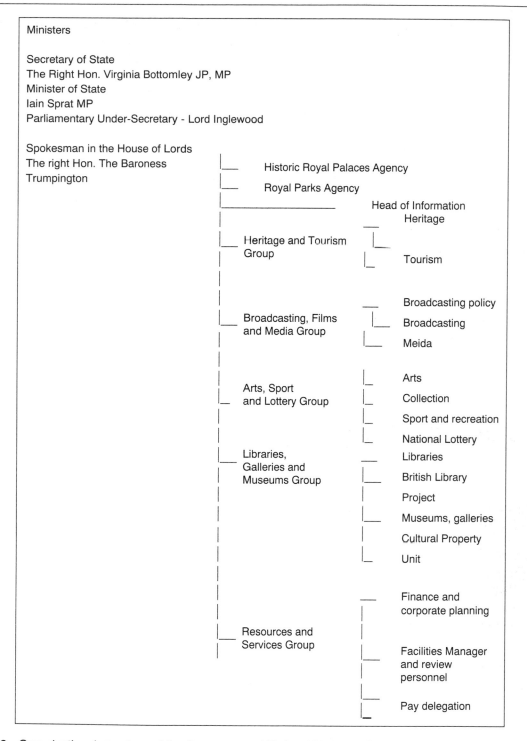

Figure 1.16 Organizational structure of the Department of National Heritage (*Source*: DNH Annual Report 1994)

national heritage and the film industry. It also includes what is called a Millennium Fund, which is money raised for projects to celebrate the start of the twenty-first century. The structure of the DNH includes five directorates, which have responsibility for a number of leisure and tourism activities, as shown below in Figure 1.16.

As can be seen from Figure 1.16 there are a number of public bodies grant-funded directly by the DNH as well as other government departments. When linked directly to government departments, these are known as quasi-autonomous non-governmental organizations or quangos. In theory, quangos are independent of the government, being allowed to manage their own affairs free of political bias. In practice, this is somewhat difficult to apply.

In addition to quangos, the government also owns and controls several nationalized industries that are extremely important in the provision of leisure and tourism, such as British Rail, the BBC and the Post Office. For example, British Rail supports the leisure and tourism industry by way of providing access to various destinations, perhaps as part of a day out, a business trip or a holiday. As a major landowner, British Rail is also concerned with environmental and conservation issues which affect a host of leisure activities, such as birdwatching and rambling.

The BBC is a major promoter of leisure and tourism interest for the UK population as it televises and serializes radio and TV programmes on different themes, such as sport, culture, natural history and holidays.

Task 1.4

In what ways could the Post Office become involved in leisure and tourism?

Case study

The Arts Council of Great Britain

The Arts Council was established under Royal Charter in 1946. As a national body, its aims are:

- To develop and improve the knowledge, understanding and practice of the arts
- To increase the accessibility of the arts to the public throughout Great Britain
- To advise and co-operate with departments of government, local authorities and other bodies.

Prior to 1994 the Council was made up of a chairperson and nineteen other members appointed by the Secretary of State for National Heritage, which delegated its responsibilities in Scotland and Wales to the Scottish and Welsh Arts Councils respectively. However, today each of these Councils including England, have become autonomous bodies, directly accountable to their own Secretaries of State.

Funding

The Arts Council is part of the funding structure under the auspices of the Department for National Heritage, which also includes the Crafts Council, the Scottish and Welsh Councils, the British Film Institute and the Regional Arts Council, as shown in Figure 1.17 below.

The Arts Council for Northern Ireland is funded directly by the Northern Ireland Department of Education.

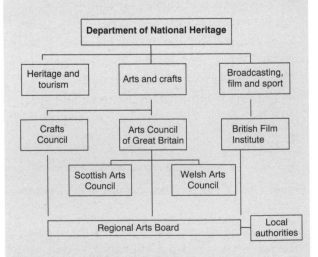

Figure 1.17 Funding structure for the arts in Great Britain

The Regional Arts Boards (RABs) have objectives which are similar to those of the Arts Council, but their involvement in crafts and film gives them a wider brief. The RABs work closely with the Arts Council, local authorities, the British Film Institute, the Crafts Council and many voluntary arts and community organizations. The governing bodies of the RABs reflect this partnership approach, and bring together representatives from different interested groups.

Case study

The Sports Council

The Sports Council is an independent body established by Royal Charter in 1972, replacing the Advisory Sports Council (ASC) as well as absorbing part of the structure of the Central Council of Physical Recreation (CCPR). Although its remit covers all British sport, it is mainly concerned with English matters, there being separate councils for Wales, Scotland and Northern Ireland.

The Sports Council has four main aims:

- To increase participation in sport and physical recreation
- To increase the quality and quantity of sports facilities
- To raise standards of performance
- To provide information for and about sport.

Funding

The Sports Council is the central part of a funding structure which includes the Scottish, Welsh and Northern Ireland Councils, nine regional offices which work closely with the ten Regional Councils for Sport and Recreation and other governing bodies of sport (see Figure 1.18).

Figure 1.18 Sports Council structure for funds and advice

Funding for the Sports Council comes largely from the Department for National Heritage, although additional funds are generated through sponsorship, training and coaching. The Council receives an annual grant from government, the levels of findings of which have increased year on year up to 1995/96, when there has been a slight reduction in real terms as shown in Figure 1.19 below.

Participation, facilities and standards

The Council has an extensive programme to increase participation in sports nationally. Part of this programme has been to:

- Provide grants to the regional councils to help develop a range of sporting activities in their areas

1972–73	3.6	million	1986	30.1	million
74	5.0	million	87	37.3	million
75	6.57	million	88	37.1	million
76	8.32	million	89	38.4	million
77	10.2	million	90	41.8	million
78	11.5	million	91	44.7	million
79	15.2	million	92	46.0	million
80	15.5	million	93	47.6	million
81	19.2	million	94	50.6	million
82	20.9	million	95	49.8	million
83	28.0	million	96	49.8	million (estimated)
84	27.1	million			
85	28.6	million			

Figure 1.19 Sports Council funding 1972/73–1995/96 (*Source*: Sports Council)

- Organize promotional programmes such as 'Action Sport'
- Run campaigns to persuade people to get involved in sport.

Despite tremendous progress in the development of facilities including swimming baths, gymnasia and multi-purpose sports halls, more has yet to be done. However, the Council also believes that existing facilities could be better used by:

- Opening up more school facilities for use by the local community
- Providing lighting
- Introducing artificial surfaces.

The Council's programme of action includes:

- Actively encouraging the development of new or improved sports facilities through advice and, if appropriate, financial assistance, especially in areas of need
- Researching and preparing efficient and economical standard design solutions for sports buildings and systems
- Designing, building and testing inventory facilities and systems, including artificial playing surfaces, heating/ventilation techniques and computerized administration.

Standards of performance are promoted via:

- Six national centres for excellence at:
  Bisham Abbey Sports Centre, Buckinghamshire
  Crystal Palace Sports Centre, London
  Lilleshall Sports Centre, Shropshire
  Plas Y Brenin Sports Centre, North Wales
  Holme Pierrepoint Sports Centre, Nottingham
  National Cycling Centre, Manchester
- Financing the National Coaching Foundation (NCF)
- Offering support to the governing bodies of sport as well as encouraging sponsorship of sport in the private sector.

The Council is the country's main service of information and data about sport. It also acts as a focal point for the collection, exchange and dissemination of knowledge from other sources, both nationally and internationally.

In 1988 the British International Sport Committee (BISC) was established to co-ordinate the work of the British Olympic Association, the Sports Councils and the CCPR in seeking to promote Britain as a venue for major international sporting events.

Local government

The largest area of government provision in leisure and tourism is local authority leisure services. The facilities and services provided by local government are:

1 Those suitable for mass or public recreation which are not provided by the private or voluntary sectors owing to cost or lack of profit potential.
2 Those facilities and services which it has a legal duty to provide, such as education and libraries.

The administration of local government operates on three levels:

- County council
- District council
- Parish council.

At each level there are elected councillors who provide their services on a voluntary basis. Their job is to represent the views and wishes of the local people in deciding which local amenities, public services and facilities to support financially to enhance their social life. The councillors work alongside salaried local government officers who carry out the decisions of the ruling council. The issues to be decided on differ, depending on the type of council involved.

Parish council

A parish is a small rural area of England and Wales, usually centred around a village. Its leisure and tourism role is limited to the area it serves in deciding on such matters as:

- The type of recreational activities that should take place on common pasture land
- Maintenance of local gardens
- Fees to charge for use of playing fields
- Advice on the routing of local footpaths, bridleways or the opening of a new nearby leisure centre.

District council

A district is an area which exists within a county boundary. It is much larger than a parish and will often encompass many villages, urban communities or even towns. As such, a district council can be a town council, a city council, or a borough council. Its main role is to do with local issues regarding:

- Refuse collection
- Rent
- Council tax
- Housing
- Public health
- Improvement grants.

However, from a leisure and tourism standpoint, it can also be directly involved in providing swimming baths, indoor and outdoor sports facilities, tourist information centres, parks and open spaces, museums and libraries.

County council

A county is an administrative area within England and Wales. County councils were created by the 1977 Local Government Act.

The role of the county council compared with that of the district council is not always as straightforward as it may at first appear. The county council's role generally involves broad issues relating to the provision of:

- Education
- Social services
- Planning
- Environmental health

- Highways and transportation
- The police.

Local authorities have a legal duty to provide educational and recreational opportunities for schools, colleges and libraries, although in practice they usually take their obligations much further. As a means of sharing the burden, county councils often share responsibility with district councils for the upkeep and provision of libraries, museums, playing fields, sports centres, swimming pools, art galleries, even tourism, and will often provide grants to various private and voluntary organizations involved in the leisure and tourism industry.

The funding of leisure and tourism in the public sector

Central government funding

The public sector raises funds (i.e. money) by taxing individuals and businesses in order to pay for facilities and services for the population. There are two types of taxation:

- *Direct tax* – this tax is collected by the Inland Revenue and is levied on income and capital, such as personal income tax, corporation tax, capital gains tax, transfer tax (i.e. gifts) and stamp duties
- *Indirect tax* – this tax is collected by Customs and Excise and includes, for example, excise duty on tobacco, alcohol, petrol and betting. Value added tax (VAT) is also an indirect tax.

A major new contributor to government coffers is the National Lottery. In the first year of operation the Lottery has raised £1322 million for good causes, £2360 million in prize money and a further £567 million in government tax.

All revenues collected are allocated to different government departments in order to pay for the supply of services, such as education, health, transport, national parks, historic buildings and monuments. Local government receives a major share of their own budgets from central government via the Central Government Grant.

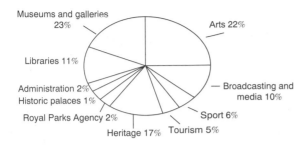

Figure 1.20 Expenditure plans for DNH 1996/97

Grants and subsidies are also provided to quangos and other leisure and tourism bodies. The expenditure plans for the DNH for 1995/96 illustrates this, as shown in Figure 1.20.

Of a total allocation of £3.5 billion from the Treasury, the lion's share (60 per cent) was earmarked for the arts, museums, galleries and libraries, with only 5 per cent going directly into tourism.

Local government funding

Local authorities raise their funds in several ways:

- Central government grant
- Council tax
- Uniform Business Rate
- Municipal trading
- European funding.

- *Central government grant* – All local authorities are heavily dependent on central government for a major share of their revenue. Up to 60 per cent of local authority funds are provided this way, although in recent years the level of central government grants has fallen in real terms to as low as 40 per cent, and so to maintain leisure and tourism provision local authorities must look elsewhere for their funding.
- *Council tax* – Council tax (previously known as the poll tax or rates) is levied on each property within the local authority area. Council tax varies by area, depending on the spending requirements of the local authority.
- *Uniform Business Rate* – Business organizations in the local area, such as shops, cinemas, theatres, cafe's and bars, have to pay a uniform business rate or tax and, as with council tax, this varies from area to area.
- *Municipal trading* – Many local authorities apply charges or fees for services they provide, such as car parks, swimming baths, sports centres, library fines, etc. In recent years, there has been greater emphasis placed on charging more through entrance and user fees.
- *European Union (EU)* – Some local authorities, as well as public bodies such as colleges and universities, bid for EU funds for specific projects which often include leisure and tourism because of economic and social benefits to the community. The main sources of the EU funding are the European Social Fund and the European Regional Development Fund.

Case study

The National Lottery

The first draw of the National Lottery took place on week ending 14 November 1994, paying out over £8 million to the first prizewinner. The biggest winners of all, however, were the five good causes earmarked to receive around 27 per cent of all monies staked on the Lottery. The five specific areas identified in the National Lottery Act of 1993 were:

- The arts
- Heritage
- Sport
- Charities
- Millennium projects to mark the twenty-first century.

The management of the Lottery

The Lottery is managed by the Camelot Group Plc, which is a consortium of private companies including G-Tech, Racal, ICL, De La Rue and Cadbury Schweppes. It operates under a licence issued by the Office of the National Lottery (OFLOT), itself responsible to the DNH.

OFLOT has a statutory responsibility under the 1993 Act to ensure that:

- The Lottery is run with due propriety
- The interests of all participants in the National Lottery are protected
- The maximum amount possible is raised for the five good causes.

Where the money goes

In 1995, the first full year of operation, the National Lottery raised £3.4 billion. When added to the amount raised by instant scratchcards, which were introduced in March 1995, the total rose to £4.7 billion. The total proceeds for 1995 are provided in Table 1.5 below:-

Prizes take the lion's share of the proceeds, with 50.7 per cent, the government takes 12 per cent in duty, while 10 per cent is paid out in operating and management costs split 50/50 between retailer commission, 5 per cent, and Camelot, 5 per cent. That leaves 27 per cent to be paid out in good causes, which in 1995 was £1322 million (see Table 1.6). After deduction of the costs of running the five committees set up to distribute the money, this meant a huge influx of funds for the arts, sport and heritage developments.

Of the £1.8 billion, each of the five good causes will receive approximately £260 million each

Table 1.5 Pattern of National Lottery sales in 1995

£ m in 1995	On-line National Lottery £	Instant scratchcards £	Total £
Quarter 1	750 m	10	760
Quarter 2	872 m	526	1398
Quarter 3	936 m	425	1361
Quarter 4	869 m	333	1203
	3427 m	1294	4721

Source: Camelot

Table 1.6 Allocation of Lottery revenue 1995

	%	£m
Prizewinners	50.7	2360
Duty	12.0	567
Retail commission	5.1	236
Camelot	5.2	236
Good causes	27.0	1322
Total Lottery revenues	100.0	4721

Source: Leisure Consultants estimates based on Camelot data

year. In the case of the arts, the £260 million will be divided according to the population in each of the four home countries.

The biggest arts project to benefit from Lottery funds is the Royal Opera House, London, which has been earmarked to receive over £50 million as part of a major refurbishment project.

How are the proceeds distributed?

Under the direction of the DNH there are five bodies set up to distribute the Lottery money. These are:

- The arts – the Arts Council in each of the home countries
- Heritage – the National Heritage Memorial Fund
- Sport – the Sports Council in each home country
- Charities – the National Lottery Charities Board
- Millennium projects – the Millennium Commission.

The Lottery money has so far only been given to fund capital projects that have a large proportion of partnership funding. The projects have been described as being for the public good, not for private gain. However, recent announcements by the Secretary of State suggest that future Lottery proceeds may be used for maintaining and running certain selected projects.

Task 1.5

Camelot's own research shows current average sales of on-line Lottery ticket at around £2.35 per household per week. However, the potential for further expansion is great, given Camelot's plans to increase the number of outlets selling Lottery tickets from 2500 to 3600 by the end of 1996, possibly including a mid-week draw. There are, however, a number of prominent people, notably the Church, who have expressed grave concern as to whether the whole venture has been socially undesirable or even an economic success.

In preparation for a class discussion in groups of three, decide:

1 Who are the main subscribers to the two lotteries?
2 Are people spending more because of the lotteries, or are they shifting their expenditure around, and, if you decide on the latter, who is losing out?
3 If money is required for good causes, is gambling the most appropriate way to fund them?
4 Large amounts of lottery money are being used to support projects which many of the ordinary people of the UK may never use or appreciate. How do you think the money should be distributed?.

Note: You may be interested to know that the poorer sections of our community, often described as C2, D, E households, contributed up to 60 per cent of on-line tickets and substantially more on the scratchcards.

The role of the private sector in leisure and tourism

The private sector includes all businesses, big and small, who supply recreational goods and services. It is the dominant sector in the supply of leisure and tourism opportunities since most of the revenue generated comes from the commercial sector. This sector also provides an interesting dimension to leisure and tourism provision since their survival is dependent on them being able to compete in gaining and keeping customers through adapting to changing fashion and trends.

Types of private sector business in the leisure and tourism industry

Private sector businesses in the leisure and tourism industry can be categorized by their legal status under one of the following headings:

- Sole trader
- Partnerships
- Private limited company
- Public limited company
- Co-operative.

Sole trader

A sole trader is an individual who runs and controls a business. Often the individual has worked in the leisure and tourism industry, but decides to leave his job because he can make a better living for himself on his own, free from the bureaucracy of a large organization.

The person provides all the capital and takes all the risks, but keeps all the profits (or bears all the losses). Most sole traders are small businesses, and there are lots of them in the leisure and tourism industry. They often provide the professional or support services for larger organizations such as sports trainers (e.g. coaching staff or instructors), caterers, transport hire, retailers of leisure and sportswear, and cafe's, etc.

Partnership

A partnership involves a group of individuals who own and control a business. By law there must be between two and twenty people to form a partnership. The partners are subject to unlimited liability which means that, like the sole trader, they accept all the risks but in return keep all the profits. An exception to this is a sleeping partner, who does not become involved in the management of the business.

Because there are more people involved, the likelihood is that the partnership will be bigger than a sole trader. Examples of partnerships include pubs, clubs, restaurants, guest houses, catering and leisure consultants.

Private limited company

All organizations in leisure and tourism who have Ltd after their name are private limited companies. The word 'limited' means that a company's investors (i.e. shareholders) are only liable for that amount of company debt for which they have invested. It is quite different from a sole trader, particularly as the company has a legal identity of its own separate from its owners.

Capital is raised by selling shares in the business, often initially among family and friends, but as the business grows this is often extended to include others to provide more capital. Not surprisingly, most private limited companies are family businesses.

Public limited company

As large private companies continue to grow, they find the attraction of becoming public limited companies very compelling because, as a Plc, a company can sell its own shares on the Stock Exchange in order to raise finance. To trade as a public limited company, a company must have a minimum of two directors (private companies need only one), a share capital of at least £50,000, a Trading Certificate issued by Companies House, and the term 'Plc' must follow after their name. Ownership and control are divided between the company's shareholders. Again, liability is limited to the money they have invested in it. Directors are voted in by shareholders to run the company and in turn hire managers and staff. Being publicly owned means that other companies can make takeover bids by offering to buy shareholders' shares at favourable prices.

Most Plcs are large, employing many hundreds, even thousands of people. Some of the largest leisure organizations listed on the Stock Exchange include Grand Metropolitan Plc, Rank Organization Plc, Granada Plc, Ladbrokes Plc, Mecca Plc.

Co-operatives

'Co-operative' is a term applied to a trading group. There are basically two types:

- *Retail co-operative society* – The retail co-operative movement began in Rochdale in 1844 as a retailing organization trading on co-operative principles. Even in the mid-1990s, the retail co-operative movement as an entity is still one of Britain's largest retailers.

  The company structure, as with a private company, is similarly based on shareholders owning the company, the difference being that membership is voluntary and open and there is only one vote per shareholder rather than one vote per share. In turn, all workers vote in managers, who in turn manage the business on behalf of the workers, making the co-operative principles by which the organization operates far more democratic.
- *Co-operative groups* – In the leisure and tourism industry co-operative groups are often quite small and community-related. Such organizations as local art galleries, drama societies or street theatre entertainment may be organized by such co-operatives.

The funding of leisure and tourism in the private sector

The sources of funding for the private sector leisure and tourism organizations include:

- Funds provided by owners of the business, called capital
- Funds borrowed from external sources, called liabilities
- Funds provided by profits
- Sponsorship
- Public sector grants or loans.

Capital

For a sole trader or partnership, this type of finance (funding) may come from private savings or from colleagues. However, a large public company will raise funds by selling shares on the Stock Exchange to individuals or other organizations.

Liabilities

A business may borrow money from a number of sources, such as banks, finance houses and creditors.

- *Banks* – Most leisure and tourism organizations will approach the high street banks when seeking to borrow money. Banks can provide funds in a variety of forms, such as overdrafts (short-term credit made available to cover everyday business expenses); loans, which are long-term in nature (up to ten years) and often used to purchase some capital item such as a new van or sports equipment; and mortgages, which, with a typical twenty-five-year payback period, are generally used to purchase land and property.
- *Finance houses* – These are often owned by banks. The funding services available include:
  - leasing. Here the business pays a rental to the finance house to secure the use of certain assets, such as vehicles, computer reservation screens and systems, bar or restaurant facilities, etc.
  - hire purchase (HP). Using HP the business can acquire an asset by putting down an initial deposit and then paying the balance with interest over an agreed period of time.
- *Creditors* – The suppliers of a company provide a business with funding by allowing companies to buy stock on credit. A restaurant may buy its food from wholesalers who require payment in a month's time, which is the equivalent of lending money to the business.

Profits

Once a business is up and running, it is hoped that the value of its sales will exceed its costs and so it will make profits. Some of the profits will be taken by sole traders or partners as part of their living expenses, while for limited companies profits will need to be paid to shareholders in the form of a dividend. However, profits can and generally are ploughed back into the business and

often form the single most important source of funding. Some businesses within the leisure and tourism industry will receive a percentage or commission on the total price of the product or service sold. Travel agents, for example, receive a commission from the operators (usually 10 per cent) on the cost of the holidays that they sell.

Sponsorship

For some private leisure and tourism organizations, sponsorship is an extremely important source of funding. Most amateur as well as professional sports rely heavily on the funding they receive from individual sponsors, from the local sports shop paying for the kit of a local rugby team to Sky Television's sponsorship of the Rugby League.

Public sector grants and loans

Private sector leisure and tourism organizations can apply for grants or loans from a variety of public sector bodies. Government quangos will often provide assistance for the improvement or development of facilities. Such institutions include:

- Arts Council
- Sports Council
- Countryside Commission
- English Heritage
- Forestry Commission
- English Nature
- National Tourist Board.

Local authorities in turn will often work closely with private sector organizations and support them with finance to provide leisure and tourism facilities where it is seen to be in the interests of their local community.

The role of the voluntary sector in leisure and tourism

The voluntary sector is made up of groups of people who agree to give up their free time to form and run organizations not generally provided by either the public or private sector. Most of these organizations are created to meet the needs of local people, for example, a group forms a tennis, cricket or football club to provide the opportunity for the community to take part in these sports.

There is a vast array of voluntary organizations, which vary in size from small local groups with fewer than twenty-five members (for example, a local drama group) to large organizations such as the National Trust and the Youth Hostel Association. The majority of voluntary organizations are local ones, including charities involved in:

- Sport and physical recreation, e.g. local sports clubs, football associations
- Adventure organizations, e.g. Outward Bound, Duke of Edinburgh Award Scheme and Operation Raleigh
- Youth organizations, e.g. YMCA, Scouts and Guides and the National Association of Youth Clubs
- Community activities, e.g. local action groups
- Heritage conservation and protection, e.g. National Trust, Royal Society for the Protection of Birds
- Animals and pets, e.g. Pony Clubs, Cats Protection League.

Most voluntary groups rely entirely on the freely given services of local people to run the day-to-day activities of the organization. For example, Cubs and Brownies' leaders undertake the organization for the personal satisfaction they receive from the task they take on board. However, larger organizations, such as the National Trust, employ large numbers of specially trained people at their offices around the country to work alongside volunteers in managing the affairs of the organization.

Whether operating a small informal voluntary organization or a large formal organization, the structure of that voluntary organization will generally require it to be made up of a minimum of:

- A chairperson
- A treasurer
- A secretary.

Other members can be co-opted to take on such roles as membership secretary or social secretary or team captain, utilizing their particular skills and experiences or because they were daft enough to allow themselves to be elected! All will serve and be accountable to the members, and will in turn need to seek re-election, normally every year at an annual general meeting.

Three types of members represent the club. These are:

- *Ordinary members* – members of the general public who pay a subscription to the organization in return for membership
- *Honorary members* – people held in certain esteem by the organization for past services or favourable contributions and who are invited to join the organization
- *Patron members* – voluntary organizations sometimes invite people who may be quite famous to head up their organization (i.e. as a figurehead), and so lend an air of prestige to the organization. Many members of the Royal Family are figureheads for voluntary groups; for example, the Queen is patron of the YHA, as is Princess Diana of the London Festival Ballet.

Case study

The National Trust

The National Trust is a voluntary organization which exists for the benefit of the public and holds buildings and countryside in England, Wales and Northern Ireland in trust for the future generations of people in this country. The National Trust for Scotland is a separate organization which operates independently of the English-based National Trust.

At the time of writing, the National Trust was 100 years old, having been founded in 1895. The importance of the Trust's work was recognized by the government as early as 1907, when the Trust was incorporated by an Act of Parliament, its purpose to promote the permanent preservation, for the benefit of the nation, of lands and tenements, including buildings of beauty and historic interest. This mandate was extended in 1937 to include country houses and their contents, the outcome of which was that families could donate their houses and contents to the Trust with a financial endowment to maintain it in perpetuity. In return, the donor could go on living in the property subject to public access and measures to maintain its original character.

The Trust prefers this arrangement, seeking to preserve houses as homes, not museums. Places owned by the Trust include:

- Houses
- Medical buildings
- Archaeological sites
- Follies
- Chapels
- Dovecotes
- Gardens and landscaped parks
- Industrial monuments
- Coast and country
- Villages
- Buildings of useful interest.

Some of its properties are associated with famous people, such as Thomas Hardy, Sir Francis Drake and Beatrix Potter.

Today the National Trust is Britain's third largest landowner, protecting over 230 historic houses, 100 gardens, 600 000 plus acres of countryside as well as 530 miles of unspoilt coastline.

Last year the Trust played host to over eleven million visitors to its buildings and gardens, while millions more freely enjoyed the coastline and countryside which the Trust preserves for us all.

Structure

The Trust is governed by a ruling council of fifty-two members, half of which are nominated

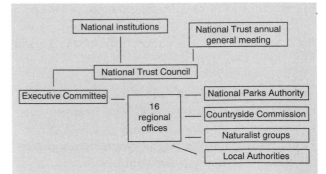

Figure 1.21 The structure of the National Trust and its relationships with other bodies

by such bodies as the British Museum, the Ramblers Association and the Royal Horticultural Society, the other half being nominated by members at its annual general meeting. The Council will appoint a twenty-eight-strong Executive Committee, which in turn appoints a number of voluntary regional committees, the members of which have expert knowledge of subjects concerned with the Trust's work, such as fine arts, architecture, conservation and horticulture (see Figure 1.21).

The day-to-day activities of the Trust are carried out by some 170 full-time administrative staff who work in the Head Office in London and at the sixteen regional offices around the country. These offices work closely with other national and local bodies concerned with conservation and planning in order to try to ensure that their work is beneficial to the future well-being of the nation.

The relationship between public, private and voluntary sectors

The traditional leisure and tourism services that are provided for us today have not always existed in their current form, and the relationship between the various sectors of leisure and tourism provision has undergone substantial change. Less than 200 years ago, public funding for leisure services hardly existed, and it was not until the 1969 Development of Tourism Act that the public sector became involved in tourism at all. The 1990s, however, are proving a challenging time for leisure and tourism provision. Within the last five years alone the economic and political environment has forced the public, private and voluntary providers to critically assess their aims and objectives. Public facilities have become privatized and are now open to private management through competitive tendering. Private companies have developed interests in a wide variety of leisure and tourism concerns and have sought partnership agreements with the public sector, while many voluntary and public bodies now make use of commercial sponsorship.

N. Barret, in an article entitled 'Sport or Physical Recreation', highlighted the inter-relationship of such partnerships, a version of which is illustrated in Figure 1.22.

Although much of the relationship between the three sectors has been discussed in the previous sections of the unit, there are several key areas in which all three share common objectives regarding greater efficiency and more economic and effective use of their resources and facilities. These are:

- Multi-use and joint provision
- Compulsory Competitive Tendering (CCT)
- Partnerships.

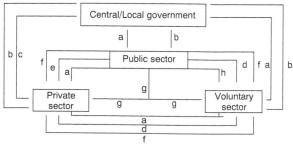

Key
a Sponsorship and patronage to the voluntary and public sectors
b Taxation, excise duty, VAT returns, rent to local/central government
c Planning gain, and partnership agreements
d Grants or loans
e Rescue or support programmes
f Provision of facilitities and activities to support tourism
g Mutual aid partnership agreement
h Administrative support, research, publications and training

Figure 1.22 The relationship between the private, public and voluntary sectors

Multi-use and joint provision

In today's society it is crucial to make the most effective use of facilities and opportunities. The provision and use of facilities are closely related to the process of good management. This process is often called multiple or dual use and joint provision.

Multiple use has been defined as:

The longer term regular use on an organized basis of facilities (particularly those financed by public funds) used by the general public either as members of groups or clubs or as individuals for whom the facility was not primarily intended.

Schools and colleges are the main bodies involved, but multiple use can be extended to include facilities belonging to the Ministry of Defence, nationalized industries and even private clubs. Basically, facilities are shared by all sectors; for example, adult education evening classes are held in schools and offered to local residents during term-time. The local football or athletics club hires the school gymnasium for training in the evenings and the playing fields at weekends. This activity provides for greater use of the facilities, but often the interests of the school and the members of the public conflict.

Joint provision has been described as:

The joining of two or more groups to design and construct a facility for mutual benefit.

This concept has proved, and continues to prove, very popular with some local authorities. It often involves a local authority working closely with another local authority or private organization in providing certain facilities; for example, two neighbouring local authorities may each wish to build a leisure centre in their local area, but, even with funding from the Sports Council, because of other pressing commitments and priorities, such as health, roads or housing, cannot afford to build and run the centre. However, by choosing to build one, possibly larger, leisure centre located, so as to be able to serve both communities, both

Figure 1.23 Sports hall attached to a school

authorities may be able to benefit from sharing the cost.

The private sector can also help here. Let's suppose a private developer, say P & O Developments, is seeking planning permission to build a new leisure hotel complex in the area. The plans submitted do not include a swimming pool. However, with some negotiation and persuasion offering public sector support there may be scope for the construction and management of a swimming pool which could be made available for public as well as private use. In this relationship both parties gain, in that the private sector gains its planning permission and the public sector gains a swimming pool. Schemes such as these have enabled areas of the country to have new facilities even when the local authorities' resources are limited.

A good example of this was the building of the Aston Villa Recreation Centre. Constructed in 1989, the centre was developed and purpose-built by Asda Stores as a condition of being allowed to build a supermarket on the adjacent site. The facility, which is run by Birmingham City Council, is used by schools, the community and Aston Villa Football Club. Other examples include the Sandcastle complex in Blackpool, which was jointly provided by Sunley Leisure and the local council, while Sealand Road, home of Chester Football Club, was redeveloped in 1993 by Morrisons, who in return built a new stadium for them just outside the town.

Compulsory Competitive Tendering (CCT)

Under the 1988 Local Government Act, the government passed its Compulsory Competitive Tendering legislation, which required that certain services that were traditionally provided by local authorities, for example, refuse collection, catering and ground maintenance, as well as the management of local authority sports and leisure facilities, should be open for competition. This meant that individuals or groups could bid against each other to obtain a contract to manage a sports or leisure facility. Since August 1993, all such local authority facilities have been put out for private tender. The facilities and management activities involved in such tenders are illustrated in Figure 1.24.

Often current employees of the local authority formed what are known as direct labour organizations (DLOs) to compete for the contract which usually extend for a period of five years. Many have been successful in obtaining the contracts, so preserving their own jobs. Where they have not been successful, they have often been taken on by the private organization who has won the contract, or they could be redeployed by the local authority to another department within the council.

The argument in favour of CCT is to do with competition. Greater competition is seen to enable a local authority to make considerable savings and offer better services, thus achieving better value for money and benefits for the community. The major argument against is that the quality and range of services provided is often reduced once CCT is applied and the price of the services offered is invariably increased. While costs are clearly reduced, this is seen simply as a job-cutting exercise, which is contrary to local authority objectives to provide jobs in their locality.

The evidence to date suggests that, while costs and jobs have been cut, there have been more services provided, not less. The jury is still out on CCT, however, because although services generally have improved, prices in turn have risen considerably since 1992, reflecting what central government terms a fairer economic price – but whether it is value for money is up to the public to decide.

Partnerships

Partnerships within leisure and tourism are an essential feature of the industries' development. The underlying principle is that partnerships between two or more sectors lead to developments that would be difficult to achieve by one sector alone. Such partnerships are essential in the management and funding of leisure and tourism projects across the whole spectrum of the industry, from sport and physical recreation to the arts and from countryside to tourism development.

Examples similar to those given under multiple use and joint provision include:

- Partnership agreements which provide for 'planning gain'. A commercial developer is permitted to build offices, hotels, shops or private residences, provided the recreation facilities for the public form part of the provision. An example is the partnership between Broadlands District Council and IHS, a Swiss-based leisure developer, to provide Norwich Sports Village. The scheme incorporates indoor tennis, squash, health and

Facilities	Management activities involved
Pitches for team games	Taking bookings
Cycle tracks	Collection of fees and charges
Golf courses and putting greens	Cleaning and maintenance
Gymnasia	Supervising activities
Bowling alleys	Instruction
Badminton, squash, tennis courts	Catering
Swimming baths	Hire of sports and other equipment
Leisure and sports centres	Security
Artificial ski slopes	Marketing and promotion

Figure 1.24

fitness and a large multi-purpose sports hall, alongside a 150-bed hotel. The council provided £1.05 million and leased the land to IHS over 150 years, with a fixed annual rent alongside a profit-sharing agreement which operates only after IHS received an agreed return on its investment.

- The Indoor Tennis Initiative (ITI) is a partnership agreement between the Lawn Tennis Association, the Sports Council and the All England Tennis Club, each of which has committed funds over a five-year period to pump prime initiatives so that investment is stimulated in partnership with the private sector. An outcome of this, for example, has seen the opening of the Bidston Indoor Tennis Centre on the Wirral, Merseyside, which opened in 1994 as a result of co-operation between the ITI, Wirral Borough Council and the developers. The land for the Centre was provided by the Council, and the construction costs were split between ITI and the developers.

▪ Assignment 1.1 ▪

By completing this assignment it leads to coverage of Element 1.1 PCs 1, 2, 3, 4, 5, 6, and 7 and Core skills may include communication 3.1; 3.2; 3.3; and 3.4 and IT 3.1; 3.2; 3.3; 3.4.

Scenario

You are trainee managers in a large leisure organization. As part of your training programme you have been asked to work together to produce a report which will be presented to the senior management team.

Task 1

Within your group decide on examples of facilities in leisure and recreation and travel and tourism. You will also need to discuss public and private sector organizations and the voluntary sector.

Each of these areas will need investigation, so split the work between the people in your group to make sure that the work is evenly shared.

Task 2

Having decided on how you are going to split up the work, prepare letters of enquiry or decide how you are going to research the topic. Remember, you are not likely to receive answers to every letter you send, so you may need to prepare a few.

If you have completed a work placement, you may be able to use information you have gained there.

Task 3

Having carried out your research and collected some information, you then need to decide what to include. Remember to share the different aspects of the information with the rest of your group.

Describe the structure of UK leisure and recreation, travel and tourism industries and give examples.

Explain the role of public, private and voluntary sectors and again give examples and investigate the relationship between the sectors.

Task 4

Present your information in report format and submit to your tutor for marking.

Element 1.2 Explore the UK leisure and recreation industry and its development

Performance criteria

1 Describe the major steps in the development of the UK leisure and recreation industry
2 Explain the factors which have influenced the development of the UK leisure and recreation industry
3 Describe, with examples, leisure and recreation products and services in the UK and give reasons for their distribution.
4 Investigate leisure and recreation products and services in a locality.

Introduction

Throughout history leisure has been seen as a symbol of wealth and status. It has been strongly influenced by religion and many of its activities can trace their origins to religious festivals. Leisure has also developed, as a direct result of improvement in technology, rapid and efficient transport systems that have enabled people to travel for education and pleasure.

The major steps in the development of leisure and recreation

1700s   Paid employment and regulated working hours

1800s   Government becomes involved in leisure through the provision of sewers, public baths and open spaces

1860   Invention of the bicycle made independent travel possible for the masses

1870   60-hour working week became the standard and a half-day holiday per week was introduced on a Saturday afternoon, creating what was later to be termed the weekend

1870   Bank Holiday Act

1885   Invention of the motor car

1900s   Transport vastly improves (sea, rail, road and air)

         The introduction of cinemas

1938   Holiday with Pay Act

1950   TV becomes widely popular across the UK

1960s   The introduction of the 37-hour working week

1964   The first National Sports Centre constructed at Crystal Palace
         Public Libraries and Museums Act

1968   Countryside Act, leading to the development of countryside recreation and conservation activities, including provision of country parks and picnic sites

1972   Local Government Act, providing
and   permissive powers to local authorities to
1976   provide support for cultural festivities such as going to the theatre and art centres, as well as support for non-cultural recreation facilities such as sports centres and leisure centres, etc

1980s   Leisure technology in the home takes off.

The history of leisure

People often think of leisure as a modern phenomenon. The truth is that many of today's leisure pursuits have their origins in the past, tied through religion and warfare. Of course, it's hard to imagine living in a world without electricity, motor cars, supermarkets or leisure centres. These are the products of the industrial society. We take these things for granted, and yet in primitive times people lived without such products.

Primitive society

Primitive society was based on people hunting and gathering food. The leisure opportunities that did present themselves were usually associated with festivals and celebrations such as weddings, the birth of children, or the harvesting of food. Like today, most of the recreational activities involved playing musical instruments, singing and dancing.

The Greeks and Romans

In ancient times, to enjoy leisure was seen as a mark of social status. Civilizations such as the Greeks and Romans demonstrated tremendous interest in the arts and in athletic competitions, but these were restricted only for free-born citizens such as

- The nobility
- The military
- Religious leaders.

The purpose of the competitions, which included boxing, wrestling, javelin and discus throwing to name just a few, was to test and improve military skills. The outcome of such events led to the start of the original Olympic Games, itself a forerunner of the modern-day track and field athletics.

In Roman times, leisure generally meant entertainment. By AD 354 there were 200 public holidays, including 175 days of games. The Romans built public facilities for the mass entertainment and enjoyment of its citizens. Rome itself had over 800 public baths for use by the public free of charge.

Travel became faster and more convenient as the Romans built roads in order to conquer and trade with other nations. The most famous of Rome's leisure and recreational facilities – the Coliseum – benefited from improved transport, attracting crowds of up to 300 000, many of which travelled from towns across the empire. Although

many of these people would be visiting friends and relatives, a lot more of them needed somewhere to stay and eat and something to do. The provision of catering and accommodation witnessed the birth of a leisure industry comprising tourism, hospitality and entertainment.

Task 1.6

Conduct a library search to discover what other leisure/recreational activities were pursued by the Greeks and Romans.

The Middle Ages

The fall of the Roman Empire had a major impact on leisure. The period between AD 400 and AD 1000 was known as the Dark Ages and, as the name suggests, these were hard times, with few leisure opportunities. Those leisure activities that were practised, such as jousting, hunting, music and dance, were generally restricted to the feudal lords of the day. For the majority of the people, the rise of Christianity led to leisure being associated more with holy days, with worship and religious festivals. In Medieval Britain, such religious festivals were focused around key times of the agricultural year such as:

- Christmas (Mid-Winter Feast)
- Easter (Spring Festival)
- Autumn (Harvest Festival)
- Saints', and holy days, such as Sundays.

Renaissance and reformation

The end of the Middle Ages saw a period of major advancement in literature and art, known as the Renaissance. Between AD 1300 and AD 1500 there was a rebirth in the arts and learning in

Europe, particularly in Italy. Paintings by such figures as Michelangelo, Leonardo da Vinci and Raphael led the way, while in Britain literary figures such as Shakespeare, Milton and Marlowe plied their trade.

The work ethic of the Protestant Church, however, hardened attitudes towards leisure. This Reformation period attacked the excesses of the rich and severely limited leisure and recreational activities for the masses. Even today, certain leisure activities are restricted in some societies, especially on Sundays.

Task 1.7

Can you identify which leisure and recreational activities are frowned upon in our society if conducted on a Sunday?

The Industrial Revolution

The greatest impact on the development of the leisure and recreation industry was the Industrial Revolution. Many changes followed in its wake, not least the rapid growth of towns and cities as people moved away from what was a self-sufficient agriculture-based economy to a rapidly developing mechanized economy based on mass production and paid employment.

For the people of this era, it meant a different style of living and great social and economic changes.

However, for those who managed the factories it created wealth, which they used to buy and own possessions and to entertain their friends and relatives. Trips in the summer season were often made by these people to the spa towns of Bath, Buxton and Tunbridge Wells, which had become fashionable resorts for the wealthy and the up-

and-coming sector of society – later to be called the middle classes.

The population of the countryside declined as new farming methods and machines meant that fewer people were required on the land. People sought work in the new towns to earn money, often for the first time and so have a better life. The reality was that the towns were overcrowded and the people had to work 70–100 hours per week for very little money, while living in housing which was later to be described as slums. Unlike in the countryside, time spent at work in the towns was regulated, and so dictated the time left over for leisure interests and activities.

The Victorian Age

In Victorian industrial society the work ethic was still very dominant and leisure was, for the most part, restricted to the better-off. Nevertheless, the period between the mid-1800s and the twentieth century was when many of today's leisure activities were developed.

At the start of the age, the towns had become so overcrowded, with open sewers, unclean drinking water and disease, that they had become unhealthy places to live. Pressure was put on the government to improve living conditions, and by the end of the 1800s most urban areas had proper sewers, running water, public baths, parks and open spaces. By the 1880s the Ministry of Health was assisting local authorities to build pools, public baths and working boys' clubs in areas across the country. Parks and gardens emerged, as did libraries and museums. Even the working week was reduced to around 60 working hours. By seeking to improve the health and quality of life of its people, this, then, was government's first direct involvement in leisure.

The establishment of the British Empire over this period meant that more people travelled to far-away places for trade, but also for education. The construction of the railway network in 1830 opened up the countryside and the coastal regions. Trains originally designed for carrying goods were adapted to carry passengers. The trend of travel to the seaside, although originating with the nobility in the Georgian era, really took off once the general public were given access to affordable travel on the trains. As soon as new railway lines were constructed to the nearest coastal point, seaside towns such as Brighton, Clacton, Scarborough and Blackpool developed rapidly.

Later changes in the Victorian era included the setting aside of land by local authorities for playing fields, recreation areas and gymnasia. Large stadia were built by the private sector on the outskirts of towns as leisure became more profitable. Saturday afternoon, or Saturday half-day as it was called, was accepted by the employers as a time set aside for the workers' leisure and recreation. Many of today's sporting events were conceived and played at this time, for example:

1846   Rugby became a regulated sport

1863   Football Association founded

1873   County cricket inaugurated

1877   International Lawn Tennis Championship at Wimbledon

1886   Hockey Association founded

1888   Football League formed

1895   Rugby League formed

1906   Olympic Games resurrected (after a gap of 2000 years).

Coupled with these developments in sports and public facilities, the late nineteenth century heralded the introduction of the music hall show, cabaret and the dance halls.

Twentieth-century developments in leisure and recreation

At the turn of the twentieth century leisure and recreation were coming to be seen as an integral feature of everyday life. Their importance to society was emphasized following two World Wars (1914–18 and 1939–45). The violence and loss of life to many millions of ordinary people worldwide made the public more determined than ever to enjoy life to the full. This culminated in great importance being attached to such leisure

pursuits as socializing, entertainment and enjoyment.

The interwar years of 1918–1939 saw a return to many of the leisure pursuits of the Victorian age, such as walking, cycling, climbing and generally keeping fit outdoors. This was actively encouraged by the government, who realized, after the First World War, that the British people were generally unfit and undernourished. This preoccupation with the keep-fit routine led to a massive expansion of the Boy Scout and Girl Guide movements, which were founded in 1908 and 1910 respectively, and to the provision of milk by the government for children at school. By 1934 the National Playing Fields Association was established and government allowed the playing of games in public parks, while in 1937 the government founded the National Fitness Council, which provided sports grants to voluntary bodies.

The post-war boom following the Second World War created many more jobs than ever before, which meant more money for people to spend. Much of this new-found wealth was spent on buying new homes and a host of new consumer labour-saving devices, such as washing machines, vacuum cleaners and electric irons. For women in particular, this meant that more time was available for leisure pursuits.

A post-war baby boom led to a youth culture in the 1960s, 1970s and 1980s that was dominated by fashion, music and dancing. With it came changing attitudes towards leisure and greater opportunities for participation in all sorts of recreational activities, such as painting, acting, playing football to spectating or watching a show.

The great outdoor activities of the early twentieth century seem to be giving way to the great indoors in the latter half of the century. The growth of social clubs and commercial leisure centres which linked sport with socializing is an important feature of this era; so, too, is entertainment. Television, videos and personal computers (PCs) have become a powerful alternative source of entertainment, to the detriment of cinemas and theatres.

Since the Victorian age the concept of class had declined in importance as most leisure pursuits became available to all. However, from the 1994 Family Expenditure Survey it is clear that there still exists a clear connection between expensive leisure pursuits such as hang-gliding, yachting, three-day eventing, ballooning and flying and the rich minority. As through history, the more wealth and status one has, the greater the amount of leisure one enjoys would appear to be repeating itself in the 1990s.

Task 1.8

Make a list of all the leisure and recreational activities that you are generally involved with. Then interview your parents, grandparents and older relatives to find out what types of leisure and recreational activities they pursued at a similar age to you now. Compare the lists and highlights the changes, giving your reasons why.

Influencing factors affecting leisure and recreation activities and their distribution

Much of what we know or expect in life is inherited from traditions, knowledge and attitudes formed over periods throughout our history. There are, however, six broad areas of influence over a person's enjoyment of leisure, illustrated below in Figure 1.25.

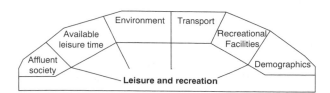

Figure 1.25

Affluent society

The more affluent a society in terms of economic, education and political stability, the more leisure and recreation it is likely to encounter. In 1872 Disraeli was quoted as saying that 'increased means and increased leisure are the two civilizers of man'.

In such societies, certain recreational activities may be restricted by cost or time to the rich, but people on low incomes will be afforded concessions to encourage them to participate in leisure and recreational activities.

Leisure time

A key influencer is the amount of time available to spend on leisure. People in work generally have more money to spend on leisure, but less time. Their hours are generally regulated, and although differences in work patterns occur between jobs, nevertheless the time available for leisure and recreation for the majority is squeezed between 5.00 p.m. and 10.00 p.m. midweek and at weekends. People with no paid employment can usually choose when to complete their tasks and have greater flexibility over their leisure time, but less choice on the activities they can afford. In the UK it is not surprising to note that retired people have the most leisure time, which in 1993 was averaging upwards of 90 hours per week.

Environment

The physical surroundings of a country or even an area in which you live, either natural or man-made facilities, generally influences the leisure and recreational pursuits followed. People in cold and wet climates may seek more indoor activities, while those in sunny and drier climates may seek more outdoor activities. People who live in cities generally take advantage of spectator or passive activities, such as watching a sporting event, going to the theatre or eating out. Those in the countryside, by a lake or at the seaside are more likely to engage in walking, climbing or sailing activities.

Transport

The importance attached to personal mobility in affording people the opportunities to reach and so partake of leisure and recreational activities cannot be overstated. Car ownership has risen dramatically in the UK since the 1950s in response to the desire for independent travel. The effect on the industry has led to a whole new form of accommodation and catering establishments such as motels, lodges, caravan and camping parks, roadside cafés and restaurants being developed, while hotels and attractions in more isolated areas away from public transport routes have welcomed a growing market of private motorists.

Recreational facilities

The greater the number of leisure and recreational facilities, the better off society is in terms of leisure provision and the greater the choice that will be on offer. Many of today's facilities have been made available over the last thirty years. In determining the range of facilities available in an area you should consider:

- Those facilities that are in the private, public and/or voluntary sector
- The cost or price of each activity provided
- The necessity or availability of special clothing or equipment or instruction in order to participate.

Clearly, the more varied the above, the more opportunities available for people to take advantage of leisure and tourism.

Demographics

Factors such as age, sex, education, even the size of the population, can influence leisure and recreation participation. The 1995 Census of Population Survey showed that the population of the UK is growing older. No longer does the youth culture dominate the leisure activities of this country. As a nation we now have a higher number of senior citizens in society then ever before. Table 1.7 identifies the numbers of people in different age groups and projected changes.

Table 1.7 UK population (in thousands) 1981–2031

	1971	1976	1981	1986	1988 Base	1991	1996	2001	2011	2021	2031
Persons all ages	55,927	56,216	56,352	56,763	57,065	57,533	58,462	59,201	59,989	60,823	61,200
0–4	4553	3721	3455	3642	3747	3914	4136	3973	3594	3837	3740
5–9	4684	4483	3677	3467	3619	3656	3918	4140	3686	3708	3852
10–14	4232	4693	4470	3690	3394	3484	3666	3928	3987	3610	3844
15–19	3862	4244	4735	4479	4250	3707	3499	3681	4164	3712	3722
20–24	4282	3881	4284	4784	4728	4496	3724	3517	3960	4019	3628
25–29	3686	4239	3828	4237	4495	4746	4469	3700	3675	4157	3721
30–34	3284	3629	4182	3787	3892	4200	4702	4430	3458	3899	3972
35–39	3187	3225	3589	4158	3847	3771	4170	4669	3643	3619	4099
40–44	3325	3136	3185	3561	4005	4132	3742	4133	4379	3420	3858
45–49	3532	3262	3090	3142	3209	3518	4079	3691	4585	3586	3566
50–54	3304	3423	3179	3023	3055	3080	3450	3997	4014	4256	3333
55–59	3365	3151	3271	3055	3000	2919	2980	3339	3519	4389	3433
60–64	3222	3131	2935	3055	2940	2873	2756	2817	3681	3719	3956
65–69	2736	2851	2801	2641	2865	2759	2614	2516	2913	3091	3867
70–74	2029	2260	2393	2364	2166	2267	2379	2272	2263	2988	3041
75–79	1356	1499	1708	1837	1860	1853	1816	1920	1798	2118	2259
80–84	803	849	968	1132	1196	1265	1306	1313	1354	1374	1825
85+	485	538	602	709	796	894	1056	1166	1315	1313	1484

Source: General Household Survey 1989, HMSO

Task 1.9

1 Briefly describe the trends in age structure, indicating which age groups are continuing to increase and which are declining.
2 Describe the effect these changes may have on the planning for leisure provision.

In addition to the above, changes in the make-up of the family, including higher numbers of one-parent families, changing patterns of employment, etc., will impact on the leisure and recreation industry.

UK leisure and recreation, products and services

Are leisure and recreation products and services the same?

The answer is no. Products are things that we can touch or see – they are tangible, such as magazines, sunglasses, a drink or a meal at a café. We buy them, own them, use them. Services, on the other hand, are intangible products. We hire them, use them, but we do not take ownership of them. Services often support the sale of a product, such as serving customers in a shop, in a restaurant, behind a bar, providing coaching lessons or entertaining in a theatre.

Leisure and recreation resources

The range of leisure resources in any area is often very extensive. Look around your own area and consider the variety and range of facilities and recreational activities provided. Most of you will find that there is a park or play area, a youth club or leisure centre. If you live near the sea, lake or river, is there a fishing or boating club nearby? Let's not forget such resources as hills, fields, parks, woodlands or mountains where you can play sports, ride a mountain bike, climb or simply enjoy a walk or drive.

Most of the leisure and recreation products and services we buy or use are man-made. However, from the above there are also a number which are provided by natural resources. This element looks at the range of leisure and recreation products and services available in the UK, but first focuses on the natural resources which influence the distribution of these products and services.

Natural resources

Britain's natural resources include, for example:

- Climate
- Mountains
- Hills
- Seaside
- Rivers
- Lakes.

Variations in climate across the UK, with the north generally experiencing colder winters and the south warmer summers, often affects the type, variety and location of leisure and recreation products. The south and southwest obtains the most sunshine hours which, coupled with its temperate climate, attracts the largest numbers of holidaymakers in the summer season. Activities such as camping and caravanning, sunbathing, surfing, boating and yachting are much more prevalent in the south compared with the north.

The topography of the country, with the greater number of hills and mountains in the north such as Snowdonia, the Pennines, Lake District and West of Scotland, attracts many activities, including climbing, fell running, walking, rambling and sightseeing, even skiing. This terrain produces more rivers and lakes, which again encourages fishing, windsurfing and powerboating.

Countryside leisure and recreation

The countryside provides a major natural resource for leisure and recreational activities. A national survey of countryside recreation produced for the Countryside Commission showed the top ten activities and their popularity in percentage terms as follows:

Type of activity	%
1 Drives, outings, picnics	19
2 Long walks	18
3 Visiting friends and relatives	14
4 Visits to the coast	8
5 Informal sport	12
6 Organized sport	7
7 Pick-your-own	4
8 Historic buildings	4
9 Country parks	4
10 Spectator sports	3
11 Others	7
	100

Owing to increasing interest in health and fitness, many passive forms of recreation are increasingly giving way to people searching for more active pastimes, for example, climbing, fishing, walking and riding. In fact, after gardening, trips to the countryside are the most popular of all outdoor recreation pursuits.

Future forecasts on the slowing down of overseas trips in favour of staying at home, coupled with the growth in overseas visitors, will, it is believed, contribute to a growing demand for the countryside. In fact, 38 million people are estimated to make at least one trip to the countryside each year, the majority of which are made in the summer. Continued development in countryside leisure provision is therefore likely to continue. Ironically, the reasons given for people wishing to visit the countryside, such as scenery, beauty and relative peace and quiet, are likely to be the very things threatened by an expansion of such leisure and recreational activities.

Task 1.10

Produce a map and promotional leaflet for a walk in an area of the countryside with which you are familiar. Your leaflet should describe the main natural attractions and activities available. Information should also be provided on access to the area and a description of the flora and fauna.

Entertainment and the arts

Entertainment and the arts encompasses a vast range of leisure and recreational activities, ranging from ballet to disco dancing, the opera to pop music, watching TV soaps to seeing a Shakespeare play. It is probably useful to think of these activities in terms of those which are conducted in the home and those conducted outside the home, for example:

In the home	*Outside the home*
Watching a video	Taking in a live show
Reading a book/magazine	Attending an exhibition
Listening to the radio	Visiting an art gallery
Painting, drawing, writing	Going to the cinema
Watching TV	Going to the theatre
Playing on the computer	Listening to a concert

As can be seen, entertainment and the arts operates on many different levels. Its facilities, which are all man-made, are provided by the three sectors of the leisure and recreation industry – public, private and voluntary. There are so-called cultural industries of broadcasting, film, video, music and publishing sections, which are controlled by such organizations as the BBC, News International and Rank Industries, and there are venues for live programmes and for the visual arts, provided by theatres, galleries, concert halls, clubs, pubs and civic centres. Some of these recreational products and devices will be reviewed below.

In the home:

- *Television* – The BBC Television Service was first founded in 1936, and since then the growth in TV has been spectacular. Independent television was launched in 1954, followed by BBC2 in 1964 and Channel 4 in 1982. Breakfast TV was introduced in 1983, followed almost immediately by ITV's TV-AM. Between 1981 and 1990 cable TV came on line, while in 1988 the Astra Satellite went into orbit, offering what is best known as Sky Television. A fifth terrestrial channel covering the majority of the country was planned for 1993, but has yet to get off the ground.

  A breakdown of the terrestrial TV regions is given in Figure 1.26.

MAP OF ITV AREAS

NET ITV INDIVIDUALS

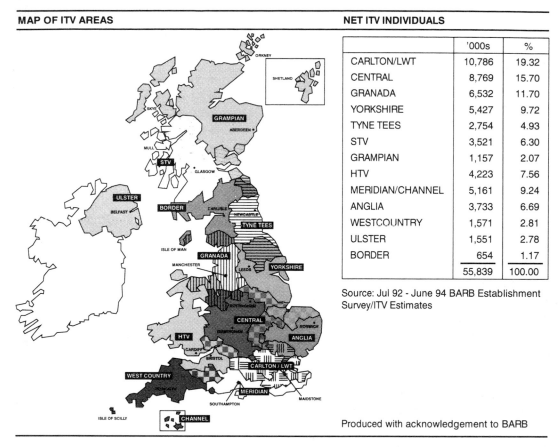

	'000s	%
CARLTON/LWT	10,786	19.32
CENTRAL	8,769	15.70
GRANADA	6,532	11.70
YORKSHIRE	5,427	9.72
TYNE TEES	2,754	4.93
STV	3,521	6.30
GRAMPIAN	1,157	2.07
HTV	4,223	7.56
MERIDIAN/CHANNEL	5,161	9.24
ANGLIA	3,733	6.69
WESTCOUNTRY	1,571	2.81
ULSTER	1,551	2.78
BORDER	654	1.17
	55,839	100.00

Source: Jul 92 - June 94 BARB Establishment Survey/ITV Estimates

Produced with acknowledgement to BARB

Figure 1.26 Map of ITV areas (courtesy of BARB)

Today upwards of 98 per cent of all households own a TV set and, in many cases, two or three. On average, each person spends three and a half hours per day watching TV, making it the single largest leisure activity in the UK. For this reason, restrictions are planned on all public service broadcasting, requiring all companies to present programmes of high quality for the public good. The service should inform and educate as well as entertain and should reflect a proper balance and range of subject matter.

Interestingly, cable TV has less rigid regulations and satellite TV is currently unregulated, albeit this is now being looked at by the government.

● *Books* – Despite the growth and popularity of the media, electronic games, computers and CDs, books have never been so popular, and continue to capture a significant proportion of

the public's leisure time. Like the radio, reading books can be enjoyed in as well as outside the home, such as in a library, at work or even on a train. A Market and Opinion Research Institute (MORI) poll for the *Sunday Times* revealed that half the population read ten or more books a year. Seventy per cent of all books read are fiction, the largest sector being romantic novels, which are nearly all purchased by women. Crime thrillers were the next popular, followed by historical, war/adventure and science fiction books.

Interestingly, as the number of public libraries in the UK has declined in recent years, so the number of books sold and read, as well as the number of bookshops, has been increasing. The British book trade is vast, and despite the inequalities of size it is estimated that the UK book industry produces and sells as many books per year as the USA.

Outside the home:

- *Theatre* – In 1990 the *British Theatre Directory* listed 130 professional theatres in the UK; the majority (ninety-six) were located in or around Greater London, of which fifty were actually situated in the West End. This concentration of professional theatres in the UK is generally owing to the type of audiences attracted to them – these being affluent people, business organizations and overseas visitors. The distribution of such theatres is compounded, however, by the fact that London also houses the two National Theatre Companies: the Royal Shakespeare Company (RSC) at the Barbican and the Royal National Theatre on the South Bank, as well as a host of major national and international attractions.

In addition to the above, there are a further 470 non-professional theatres in other regions of the country as well as another thirty-six small clubs and lunchtime theatres in London. This list includes some city centre civic halls, but does not include the multitude of venues used by touring companies, such as leisure centres, village halls, community centres or schools.

It should be noted that theatre does not mean just drama. Increasingly, theatres are used for a wide range of performing arts, such as concerts, cabaret and light entertainment. It will not surprise you to learn that the theatre audience in the UK is around eleven million visitors, with the most popular shows being musicals. However, unlike most passive leisure activities, this area has remained static, with little or no increase in its visitor numbers over the past ten years.

- *Cinema* – Once the great entertainment of this century, the cinema's popularity has been in rapid decline since the launch of television in the 1950s. However, the General Household Survey of 1987 showed the cinema to be the most popular audience-type recreation activity (See Table 1.8).

In recent years there has been a minor resurgence of interest in the cinema. Cinema visits had dropped to an all-time low of 53 million in 1984, but by 1994 this figure went up to an estimated 112 million, an annual increase of 11 per cent per annum. These

Table 1.8 Popularity of audience type recreation activities

Activity	%
Cinema	11
Theatre	7
Opera	5
Ballet	4
Others	73

Source: General Household Survey 1987

Figure 1.27 Glyndebourne

increases in attendance are not due to corresponding growth in cinema sites, which since 1984 have remained fairly static, at around 1300 screens on 650 sites; rather, the growth has coincided with the development of the multiplex. The multiplex cinema is a purpose-built entertainment facility which contains up to fourteen screens offering the latest film releases. Located on the edge of town, multiplexes are often part of a larger entertainment complex, including arcades, bowling alleys, clubs and restaurants, and so become a major attraction, especially for the young.

Figures provided by the Cinema and Video Audience Research shows that 64 per cent of all people aged 7 and over had visited the cinema at least once in 1994. The biggest sector of the

population to visit the cinema was the 7–24-year-olds, 90 per cent of whom claimed to have made a visit within the last twelve months (See Table 1.9). This makes the cinema very popular with, as well as dependent on, a young audience.

- *Opera, Ballet and concerts* – These should be seen as minority forms of entertainment. They are expensive to produce, and highly dependent on Arts Council subsidies for their survival. Although they receive what some commentators would suggest is a disproportionate amount of art funding, it nevertheless only allows them to maintain seven opera companies five ballet, companies and nine national symphony orchestras. These are listed below in Figure 1.28.
  - **Opera** The major home for opera in the UK is the Royal Opera House (ROH) at Covent Garden which is shared with the Royal Ballet. The ROH has consistently received the single largest grant from the Arts Council, which has recently been backed with a grant of £50 million from the National Lottery for major refurbishment work.
  - **Ballet** Like opera, the UK's major ballet company the Royal Ballet, is based at the Royal Opera House, which is also shared with Sadlers Wells Royal Ballet. The latter is

Table 1.9 Attendances at cinemas 1984–1994

Age	1984	1986	1988	1990	1994
7–4	73	87	84	86	91
15–24	59	82	81	87	89
25–34	49	65	64	79	77
35–44	45	60	61	70	64
45 and over	13	25	34	41	40
All persons aged 7 and over	38	53	56	64	69

Source: Cinema and video audience research

Opera London	Ballet London	Concerts London
Royal Opera House (ROH) Covent Garden English National Opera (ENO) Coliseum	Royal Ballet Covent Garden Sadlers Wells Royal Ballet	London Philharmonic Orchestra London Symphony Orchestra Philharmonia Royal Philharmonic Orchestra
Regional	*Regional*	*Regional*
Scottish Opera Welsh National Opera Opera North Opera 80 Glyndebourne Productions	English National Ballet National Ballet Scottish Ballet	The Halle, Manchester Royal Liverpool Philharmonic City of Birmingham Symphony Orchestra Bournemouth Symphony Orchestra Scottish National Orchestra

Figure 1.28 National classical music and dance organizations

exclusively concerned with touring to other cities around the UK. In addition to ballet, there are several other contemporary dance companies that should be noted – The Rambert Dance Company and its London Contemporary Dance Theatre, the Extemporary Dance Theatre and the Palace Theatre – all of which are situated in or around London.

– **Concerts** Together with the major orchestras listed, there are approximately 150 symphony and chamber orchestras and thousands of performances. Unlike theatres, where programmes run for several days or weeks, concerts are, more often than not, one-off events. Not surprisingly, there are few concert halls that specialize exclusively in one form of music. The Barbican, home of the London Symphony Orchestra, not only promotes classical concerts and pop music, but also doubles as a conference centre.

● *Museums* – There are approximately 500 museums in the UK, of which nearly three-quarters are in the private sector. Over half of this total number of museums are housed in listed buildings, themselves a source of public interest. That interest extends to 110 million visits to museums each year, with a further 60 million visits to the historic houses.

Every county in the UK has some form of museum provision, but the distribution is very much skewed towards the south. Around 50 per cent of all museums are located in the southern counties, while the northwest, South Wales and the Strathclyde region of Scotland have very poor provision. This is disappointing, particularly in light of the fact that museums have never been so popular overall. Moreover, this interest has coincided with the opening of newer museums. In fact, more than half of all museums today opened after 1971.

Type of Museum	Example
National	British Museum, London, National Museum of Art and Design
Local history	Colchester City Museum
Science and technology	Museum of Science and Technology, Manchester, Catalyst Museum, Widnes, Cheshire
Fine arts	Victoria and Albert Museum, London, Barber Institute, Birmingham
Film and photography	Museum of Moving Images, London and Bradford
Industrial heritage	Wigan Pier, Ironbridge Gorge Museum
Historical	Howarth Parsonage, West Yorkshire, Captain Cook's Birthplace Museum, Washington
Archaeology	Corinium Museum, Cirencester
Ethnography	Pitt Rivers Museum, Oxford, Museum of Mankind, London
Natural History	Natural History Museum, London
Maritime	Portsmouth Maritime Museums, British Maritime Museum, Merseyside Maritime Museum
Transport	National Railway Museum, York, Great Western Railway Museum, Swindon, National Motor Museum, Beaulieu

Figure 1.29 Types of museums in the UK

Task 1.11

It has often been argued that the Arts Council places too much emphasis upon sponsoring the cultural activities favoured by the few, such as ballet, opera and orchestras, and not enough on arts and entertainment for the masses.

Write to the Arts Council or your Regional Arts Council and ask for details on their funding arrangements and who and what they subsidize. Make notes from the information obtained for a class discussion on the role of the Arts Council and the future contribution it should make to the popular mass arts.

The type of museums available to the UK public is very wide and varied, as can be seen from the list in Figure 1.29.

Parks and amenities

A list of the main providers of parks and amenities was given by the Institute of Leisure and Amenity Management as:

- Local authorities
- Regional and National Parks
- Countryside Commission
- Nature Conservancy Council
- Water companies
- Sports Council
- The National Trust
- The Forestry Commission.

The range of facilities provided by these organizations is enormous, and includes parks (urban and regional), sports grounds, golf courses, artificial sports pitches, cycleways, zoos, shows and exhibitions, even allotments and cemeteries. A brief summary of several of these leisure and recreational products and services is provided below.

- *Urban parks* – The Industrial Revolution witnessed the introduction of urban parks. Many such parks were given over to the local community by public benefactors as a way of improving the health and fitness of their town's workforce. Such parks would generally be designed with a large expanse of grassland intertwined with walkways, alongside which would be shrubberies and a central bandstand. The first municipal urban park was Birkenhead Park situated on the Wirral, which was designed by Joseph Paxton, head gardener for the Duke of Devonshire at Chatsworth in Derbyshire.
- *Gardens* – Gardening is one of the most popular forms of recreational activity in the UK. It involves all sections of the community, from passive visits to garden shows to active gardening at home. Visits to gardens account for an important part of the UK tourism market. The coastal resorts of Torquay, Paignton, Brighton and Bournemouth have always paid a great deal of attention to the quality and presentation of their garden displays. Many more large garden centres, such as Stapeley Water Gardens in Cheshire, today

are seen as major attractions, particularly for day trips out for the family.

- *Golf courses* – Although golf has been around for several centuries, it has only really taken off as a sport over the last thirty years, both as an active and passive leisure pursuit. Although not as popular as other participative activities such as walking, or organized sports such as soccer, it nevertheless has a huge passive following, which is demonstrated by the large gathering which attended last year's Open Tournament at St Andrews, attracting 20 million people over four days and a further 150 million TV viewers worldwide.
- *Zoos* – The original idea and emphasis behind the zoo was to have a living museum or collection of live animal species as opposed to presenting these creatures in a real-life setting. Today's zoos are quite different, however, from those of the recent past. Cages have given way to field-like enclosures which, wherever possible, are designed to resemble the natural habitat of each animal. Despite the changes, attendances at zoos have continued to decline, mainly owing to the negative attitudes people hold with regard to keeping animals in captivity. London Zoo almost closed at the beginning of the 1990s because of falling attendances and lack of support or sponsorship. In order to survive, modern zoos have become more commercialized, offering a much more varied leisure experience by developing, for example:

  - zoological garden and education courses, as at Chester Zoo
  - a chairlift and miniature railway, as at Dudley Zoo, West Midlands
  - themed attractions, as at Flamingo Land, North Yorkshire.

Sport and physical recreation

Over the last thirty years there has been a major change in the pattern and provision of sporting and physical recreation facilities in the UK. People's expectations in these areas have increased in line with increased leisure time and money to spend. Today's swimming pools are expected to have wave machines, water slides and viewing galleries, while leisure centres are expected to provide a wide selection of sporting facilities, together with non-sporting facilities for holding parties, discos, bars and restaurants.

Today sport and physical recreation forms a major part of the leisure and recreation industry. Up to 60 per cent of the adult population of the UK take part in some form of sport or physical recreation at least once a month, reflecting the importance attached to this activity.

However, as with art and entertainment, this activity can be split between sports participation and sports spectating.

- *Sport's participation* – The types of sports and recreation products and services available are

Outdoor	In-door
Playing field	Swimming pool
Cycle track	Gymnasium
Golf course	Sports hall
Bowling green	Ice rink
Sports stadium	Leisure centre
Boating lake	Bowling alley
Artificial ski slope	Badminton, squash, tennis courts
Tennis court	Shooting range
Riding centre	
Go-kart track	

Figure 1.30 List of outdoor and indoor sporting products and services

best listed under the heading of outdoor and indoor sports. Although not an exhaustive list, a number of these are listed in Figure 1.30.

Figure 1.31 Sporting activity

Table 1.10 Adult sports participation 1995

Sports	Numbers participating (millions)
Walking	20.2
Swimming	4.4
Snooker, pool, billiards	3.1
Keep-fit, yoga	7.2
Cycling	2.3
Darts	1.3
Golf	4.7
Ten pin bowling	1.1
Running, jogging	1.9
Soccer	7.2

Source: General Household Survey 1995

The General Household Survey for 1995 shows that walking, with 65 per cent of all adults participating, continues to be the most popular recreational activity in Britain. Next in popularity is swimming, which is experiencing a resurgence in interest with the improvement and availability of pools. A full list is provided in Table 1.10.

Participation continues to increase overall, with greater involvement from casual sport rather than from organized sport through the governing bodies. There are some concerns about the level of team sports, which at best has remained static but in some areas has declined significantly over the last fifteen years. While team sports in the voluntary sector continue to flourish, team sports in the public sector at school or college has witnessed a corresponding decline.

- *Spectator sports* – Most spectator sports are run by the public sector in conjunction with related governing bodies of sport. However, where sporting events attract large numbers of spectators, whether at a venue or through the medium of television, the commercial interests are never too far away. The attendances at Association Football matches make it the most popular spectator sport in the UK, twice that of the theatre and generating the equivalent revenue to that received at cinemas.

However, attendances at football matches, while on the up, are only half of what they were in the mid-1970s, as Table 1.11 shows.

Table 1.11 Average attendance at football matches

	Football Association Premier League 1, 2 (000s)	Football Division 1 (000s)	Scottish Football Premier Division (000s)
1961/63	26,106	16,132	1178
1971/72	31,352	14,652	5228
1981/82	22,556	10,282	9467
1991/92	21,622	10,525	11,970
1994/95	17,476	11,476	13,371

Source: Social Trends 1995

Task 1.12

Conduct a survey of sport and recreation in your area, and identify the more popular activities. Produce a report on the importance of these activities to the local leisure service, detailing which sectors of the leisure industry provide them.

▪ Assignment 1.2 ▪

PC	1,2,3,4,
Core skills	
Communication	3.1. 1,2,3,4,5
	3.2. 1,2,3,4,5,
	3.4. 1,2,3,4
I.T.	3.1. 1,2,3,4
	3.2. 1,2,4,5
	3.3. 1,2,3,4,5,6

Explore the UK leisure and recreation industry and its development scenario.

You are employed by a local authority leisure and tourism department. You have been asked to produce a report on the development of the leisure and recreation industry nationally and to focus on a particular locality and report back on the industry within this area.

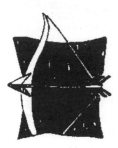

Task 1

Produce a report describing, in general terms, the factors which have influenced the development of the UK leisure and recreation industry, and describe the major steps in this industry's development. Describe the leisure and recreation products and services available nationally, including one example from each of the following:

- *Arts and entertainment facilities*
- *Sports participation*
- *Outdoor facilities*
- *Heritage sites*
- *Play schemes*
- *Catering facilities*
- *Accommodation facilities.*

Give reasons for the variation in distribution of these products and services across the UK.

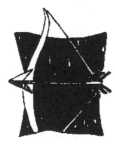

Task 2

Select a particular locality within the area you live in or within an area with which you are familiar. Produce a report on the products and services available in this locality and give reasons for their availability at this particular location.

Element 1.3 Explore the UK travel and tourism industry and its development

1 Explain the factors which have influenced the development of the UK travel and tourism industry.
2 Describe the major steps in the development of the UK travel and tourism industry.
3 Describe, with examples, the products and services available through the UK travel and tourism industry.
4 Investigate the products and services available in selected travel and tourism facilities.

Introduction

It is the travel and tourism industry that looks after tourists, so before discussing the industry's development it is important to understand what it is tourists need, since it is the satisfaction of these needs that go to make up the travel and tourism industry.

In Element 1.1 we discovered that people who travel and stay one or more nights away from their home or normal place of work are called tourists. Whether these people spend their time on business or pleasure, they all basically require and need:

- The means of travel
- Somewhere to stay
- Something to eat and drink
- Something to do.

In providing for these needs, the travel and tourism industry is seen to be made up of three key elements called the three As:

- *Access* – Transport
- *Amenities* – Accommodation/Catering
- *Attractions* – Something to do.

Figure 1.32 highlights the formation of the three As by tracing the major steps in the development of the UK travel and tourism industry.

The rise and development of travel and tourism

Early origins

Tourism involves being elsewhere, and to be elsewhere requires travel. The earliest forms of travel and tourism date back many centuries. Excluding travel for the purpose of work, tourism can be said to take two forms:

1670	The start of the Grand Tour
1821	First regular cross-channel ferry crossing between Dover and Calais
1830	The start of the railways
1837	Start of hotel constructions at railway stations
1840	Cunard introduces passenger cruises to North America
1841	Organized travel introduced by Thomas Cook
1855	Thomas Cook organizes the first overseas packaged tour to Paris
1871	The Bank Holiday Act created, four public holidays a year
1890s	Major hotel development in London to accommodate wealthy European and British visitors (e.g. Claridges, Savoy) Half-day closing introduced in some local areas
1901	Factories Act passed, giving women and young people six days' holiday a year
1913	The war years led to major advances, particularly in aircraft technology. People became much more aware of other countries, and with widespread car ownership people sought greater freedom to travel when on holiday
1936	Britain's first holiday camp at Skegness opened by Billy Butlin
1938	Holiday with Pay Act
1950	Vladimir Raitz of Horizon introduced first 'packaged holiday'
1957	Transatlantic air travellers exceed number travelling by sea for the first time
1958	Introduction of the wide-bodied Boeing 707 jet aircraft
1969	Development of Tourism Act and the setting up of BTA, the national tourist boards of Great Britain
1983	Three-quarters of British workers have four or five weeks' holiday a year
1992	Department of National Heritage formed
1994	A record million overseas visitors came to Britain

Figure 1.32 Major steps in the development of the UK travel and tourism industry

- Travel for business
- Travel for religion.

Merchants throughout history have travelled extensively in order to trade, but were often restricted owing to inadequate roads and transport. The Romans were noted merchants, and as their empire expanded through conquest so, too, did their need for better communications and transport throughout Europe, North Africa and the British Isles. The Romans built first-class roads, with staging inns to help feed and accommodate the traveller on his way. This led to the start of foreign tourism, as the more wealthy Romans sought to use these new transport facilities to visit their friends and relatives stationed throughout Italy, Greece, Egypt, even Britain.

In Britain today, there are remains of Roman fortress towns such as Chester, Colchester, York and many others. The Romans left a legacy of good roads and a strong communication network which was to become the bedrock for the future UK traveller and trader in the Middle Ages. Of course, with the exceptions of trade and holy pilgrimages, travel was always highly restricted – that was, until the mid-seventeenth century – the Renaissance period and the start of the Grand Tour.

The Grand Tour circa sixteenth and seventeenth century

The Grand Tour was an outcome of the freedom of and quest by the aristocracy to travel to Europe in order to broaden their education. The tour took in all the major cultural centres of Europe, including, for example, Rome, Strasbourg, Berlin and Paris. The practice was later adopted by many wealthy traders of the day, and was recognized as the education for gentlemen.

In the eighteenth century travel for health became important, and so the resurgence of the spa towns such as Leamington Spa, Bath, Harrogate and Scarborough, first developed by the Romans, became popular again. In the latter half of this century, fuelled by the writings of Dr Richard Russell on the health-giving properties of sea-water, many people sought to visit the sea and many hamlets on the coast were transformed into the seaside resorts we know today. Much of this travel was made possible with the arrival of the stage-coach, which, although itself not noted for its comfort, at least allowed people other than the rich to travel. Over time, much of the character of both the spa and the seaside resorts changed, as pleasure rather than health became the prime motivator for visitors.

The Victorian Age

This was the era when tourism really began to develop, particularly for the masses. Prior to the nineteenth century, travel was something that was endured rather than enjoyed.

Three major factors had a profound effect on the development of the travel and tourism industry at this time. These were:

- The advancement of steam power
- The introduction of organized travel
- The impact of seaside resorts.

The advancement of steam power

The development of steam power affected travel and tourism through the introduction of the railways as well as passenger steamships.

- *Railways* – Following the introduction of a rail link between Liverpool and Manchester in 1830, a huge programme of railway construction commenced. What got railways going, however, as a major form of passenger transport were certain entrepreneurs such as Thomas Cook and Sir Rowland Hill, who hired the trains from the railway companies and then sold the seats to their friends and the public in general.

  At first the railways linked all the major towns and cities, but because of the exploits of Thomas Cook these were soon extended to the resorts, so that travel was purchased for both business and pleasure.

- *Steamships* – Increasing trade worldwide, especially with the USA, meant that ever faster, more reliable forms of communication were required. As with the railways, so the technological advances in steam power led to a whole new generation of ships. A regular cross-channel ferry service between Dover and Calais was established in 1821 and by 1937 the Peninsular and Oriental Steam Navigation Company, better known as P & O, had a long-distance, deep-sea steamship service to India and the Far East. Cunard Steamship Company was not far behind, running regular deep-sea service mail links with the USA by 1840.

The introduction of organized travel

Thomas Cook was accredited with the first organized excursion between Leicester and Loughborough for his Temperance Association in 1841. So successful was the trip that he was asked to repeat the exercise many times over. Within ten years he was leading a whole new form of travel called the organized tour, often involving complicated excursions for the day including train, boat and accommodation. His fame quickly spread, to the extent that in 1851 Prince Albert asked him to organize the travel arrangements for the Great Exhibition, which took place in Hyde Park in London. Over 160 000 people were transported via Cooks Tours, which included organizing accommodation in hotels, guest houses and dormitories. He even provided hot water bottles on the train to keep his passengers warm and, best of all, couriers and guides to help them get the most from their visit.

The Paris Exhibition of 1855 gave Cook the opportunity to further the industry's development by organizing trips abroad. He also organized the first excursion to the USA in 1866, and followed this up in 1872 with a round the world trip taking in Hong Kong, Singapore and India which lasted nearly a year. Other travel organizers, such as the Cyclist Touring Club, imitated Cooks Tours, albeit that, rather than focus on pleasure, they put more emphasis on education and health. Sir Henry Lunn followed this up with the first tours of Greece as well as the first skiing holidays to Switzerland.

Seaside resorts

The new-found interest in sea bathing at this time meant that the expanding railway network tended to follow the developing resorts, accelerating their growth. The importance attached to the family by the Victorians also led to the emphasis being placed on family holidays, for which the seaside resorts were ideally suited By 1870, a typical holiday for a family would be a day trip to the seaside. This was further aided in 1871 with the passing of the Bank Holidays Act, which gave every employee four public holidays each year.

As the railways developed, so the seaside resorts flourished. However, many of the new railway centres could not cope with the demand for accommodation and amenities, and so a period of hotel construction commenced.

Railway hotels were constructed at each railway terminal, which played a significant role in the development of hotels over the next 100 years. The high cost of land led to the early formation of hotel chains, which took the place of sole-proprietor hotels. Some resorts also benefited from the introduction of steamboat services in the early nineteenth century which, it is believed, led to the construction of many of the seaside piers.

Travel and tourism in the twentieth century

There were several key events in the twentieth century which greatly affected the development of the travel and tourism industry:

- The two World Wars
- The Holiday with Pay Act
- The introduction of holiday camps
- Advances in jet aircraft technology
- The start of the packaged holiday
- The Tourism Development Act.

The two World Wars

The early twentieth century saw an increase in travel and tourism due to a more stable travel network, coupled with better healthcare in Central Europe which made the possibility of illness whilst abroad a less daunting prospect. The outbreak of the First World War slowed down this increase in the immediate war years, but in the longer term actively assisted its development. The outbreak of the war brought about greater control of people moving between different countries, and it was for this reason that passports were introduced. Prior to this, foreign travellers did not require passports to travel in Europe. (Note: A passport is an official document issued by the

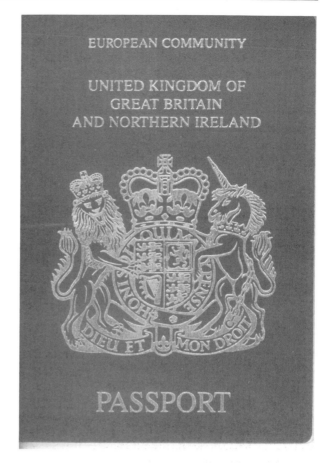

Figure 1.33 A passport

government, certifying the holder's identity and citizenship and entitling the holder to travel under its protection to and from other countries.)

The period between the First and the Second World Wars saw an increase in both domestic and European holidays. Like the crusaders, the returning British soldiers had travelled extensively and brought home tales of battle as well as wonderment at the regions they had visited. However, the Great Depression of the early 1930s did curtail the development of overseas travel for a number of years as unemployment increased to an all-time high, as did the number of businesses that failed. Domestic holidays, however, flourished, with the traditional seaside resorts of Brighton, Scarborough and Blackpool seeing new competition from Llandudno, Skegness, Clacton-on-Sea and Great Yarmouth. Many of the tourists who visited these resorts were dependent on the railways for their travel, but the advent of the motor car was about to turn the transportation industry on its head, and would have done sooner if it were not for the outbreak of the Second World War.

Travel within the war years was mainly for mobilizing troops and the transportation of government officials and journalists covering the war campaign. Those civilians who did travel stayed well away from the European and transatlantic routes between Britain and the USA. Travel by air was seen as a newer and safer alternative to sea travel and expansion of overseas routes developed rapidly. Military expansion, with new aeroplanes for bombing and troop movements, led to the development of large transport-carrying planes, and it was this innovation that was going to change overseas transportation for Britain in the post-war years.

The Holiday with Pay Act

The British Travel and Holiday Association was established by the government in 1929 in recognition of the growing importance of tourism to the British people. Moreover, in 1938 the government recognized the importance of holidays in maintaining the health and efficiency of the nation's workforce through the Annulee Report. The Report led to the Holiday with Pay Act being passed in the same year, encouraging employers to give a period of paid annual holiday leave to their employees. The concept of the two-week annual holiday developed very quickly, and for the first time the bulk of the population could afford to holiday together as a family.

The introduction of the holiday camp

The holiday camp was first introduced by Sir Billy Butlin in 1936 with the opening of a Butlins Holiday Camp in Skegness. Aimed at the growing mass of low-income families, the camps not only gave the opportunity for whole families to take a holiday away together, but offered a standard of comfort not previously available at the seaside boarding house. Accommodation and food were

provided, together with 24-hour entertainment, all at an affordable, all-inclusive price. The holiday camp was a forerunner of what people have today become accustomed to expect from packaged holidays. Its constant success, however, did not go unnoticed, and in turn led to a spate of similar camps, such as Pontins and Warners, being built all over the country.

Popular even today, albeit in a different form, Butlins and Warners Holidays dominate the market. No longer called camps, but holiday villages or holiday centres, they have developed to include large undercover leisure areas including such attractions as tropical fun pools and wave machines. Moreover, the family image has changed somewhat to also appeal to adults only, the young and the elderly, such as Pontins Holiday Centres.

Advances in aircraft technology

The period 1930–1950 saw largely domestic tourism. For example, in Britain 26 million UK residents took a long holiday in 1950 while only five and a half million took a foreign holiday. It was at this time that the seaside resorts were at their zenith. However, one outcome of the Second World War was the development of the jet aircraft, and this greatly affected holiday-taking patterns and led to the demise of the steamships.

In the immediate post-war years there was a surplus of military aircraft, which entrepreneurs such as Freddie Laker used to expand air travel to the masses. This was aided by the arrival of the wide-bodied Boeing 707 Jets in 1950, which overtook sea cruises as the main means of overseas travel. Destinations could be reached in a fraction of the time, and very quickly the business traveller converted to scheduled flights. Although expensive to begin with, tourist and economy fares were soon introduced. However, these were often beyond the reach of the average person. In trying to attract a mass market, private airlines broke new ground with the development of chartered flights, which ultimately led to the package holiday.

Packaged holidays

Vladimir Raitz from Horizon Holidays is credited with the first ever modern package holiday to Corsica in 1950. A 32-seater DC3 aircraft was chartered, and by filling every seat instead of trying to commit to a block of seats he was able to make huge savings in the cost of the air transport and therefore the overall cost of the holiday.

This type of operation was quickly seized upon by other operators who began to develop tour operations across Europe, but particularly to Spain. By the early 1960s mass package holidays were a major phenomenon of European travel, with upwards of six million overseas holidays being taken by the British by 1970. Competition became fierce and prices tumbled. Such developments led to an imbalance between the numbers of British citizens travelling abroad and the number of overseas tourists travelling to Britain. A real economic battle was developing in trying to keep the British spending more of their time and money at home rather than abroad. So important was the outcome of this battle that the government became directly involved through the Development of Tourism Act.

Development of Tourism Act 1969

Often called a 'Charter for Tourism', the introduction of the Development of Tourism Act in 1969 signalled a new government policy directed towards tourism. The Act established a new framework for public sector tourism, taking into account the industry's importance to the national economy.

Recognizing the failure in other countries, notably Spain, to control the growth of tourism in terms of conservation, consumer rights and the quality of the tourist product, successive governments at home began to plan to control the supply and demand of tourism in the UK. The Act itself sought to set up:

- The BTA and the national tourist boards of Great Britain
- The hotel development and incentive scheme
- Registration of Tourism Accommodation.

- *National tourist organizations (NTOs)* – With the passing of the Act the following national tourist organizations were formed:

  - The British Tourist Authority, which is concerned with encouraging incoming tourism from overseas visitors

  - The four tourist boards of Britain: English Tourist Board (ETB)

    Scottish Tourist Board (STB)

    Welsh Tourist Board (WTB)

    Northern Ireland Tourist Board (NITB) (formed in 1974)

  - The Tourism Committees of the States of Jersey, Guernsey and the Isle of Man.

- *Hotel development and incentive schemes* – Designed in the short term to improve the quality and number of hotel accommodation in order to meet the demand and overcome lack of bedspace, particularly in London. Grants and loans under section 4 were administered by the NTOs up until 1974 when the money ran out. Highly successful though it was for London, it did not have sufficient impact for the rest of the country.

- *Registration of tourism accommodation* – This part of the Act was designed to include rights of inspection by government officials similar to what is common in Europe. Unfortunately, it has never been fully implemented. The industry preferred to follow a voluntary registration of classification and grading of tourist accommodation with revised success. This is covered in more detail under Accommodation.

Task 1.13

1 *Review the promotion activities of the BTA and decide which of these activities are primarily concerned with:*

- *making visitors aware of new tourism products/services in the UK*
- *providing information to alter (or reinforce) visitors' attitudes or perceptions of the UK*
- *encouraging visitors to visit the UK.*

  Give your reasons why.

2 *What would you consider to be the main advantages and disadvantages for a domestic tourist taking a holiday in the UK? If you were the marketing manager for ETB, how would you go about promoting these advantages to the residents of the UK?*

Case study

Four national tourist boards (NTBs) have been set up to promote tourism throughout Great Britain. These are the English Tourist Board (ETB), the Scottish Tourist Board (STB), the Welsh Tourist Board (WTB) and the Northern Ireland Tourist Board (NITB). Their job is to provide information to persuade the domestic tourist to visit their areas of the country. They do this by providing promotional leaflets and brochures on different tourist destinations and events, and are supported in their efforts by a number of local area and regional tourist boards.

The British Tourist Authority (BTA) was set up in 1969 to oversee the NTBs and to act as an umbrella organization for consolidating their efforts when promoting the UK abroad. How the BTA does this is by having sales offices in many countries abroad, including, for example, the USA, Germany, France, Austria, Saudi Arabia, Australia and Ireland. These offices consolidate and distribute the promotional leaflets and brochures of the national and regional tourist boards across the UK. In addition, they liaise with overseas travel agents and tour operators by organizing seminars, exhibitions and travel trade shows.

A very effective way of promoting the UK is to invite overseas journalists and travel trade customers to visit various parts of the UK on what are called familiarization trips. Although co-ordinated by the BTA, very often it is the national and regional tourist boards and their public and private sector partners, who are engaged in leisure and tourism, who actually provide the accommodation, travel arrangements, catering and entertainment. The major benefits obtained from this arrangement are that it provides enormous scope for the facilities that can be offered and is a way of sharing the cost of the trips. Similarly, the BTA will sponsor stand space at the world's largest tourism exhibitions, such as the World Travel Market London, ITB Berlin and MITCAR Paris, at which the authority will share space and costs with its partners.

UK travel and tourism products and services

Transport

Without transport there would be no travel or tourism. Its importance to tourism can be summed up in three ways:

- A means of travel to a destination
- A means of getting around a destination
- A major feature of the tourist trip.

Transport provides the means of travel to a destination from the tourist place of origin and back again. Once tourists have arrived, it also provides the means of travelling around a destination, for example, the use of a taxi or bus to visit a major attraction such as the Houses of Parliament or Buckingham Palace. Finally, transport can be the major reason for taking a trip, such as a train journey on the Orient Express. On other occasions, transport is seen as an integral part of the holiday experience, such as a fly-cruise package tour, a flight on Concorde or a cruise on the QE2. In total, BTA estimates that in 1994 £158 million was spent on travel within the UK, accounting for 6% of all domestic and overseas tourist expenditure.

Transportation for both UK as well as overseas tourists can be divided into land, water and air travel.

Land transport

Land transport includes travel by:

- Train
- Car
- Bus and coach.

- *Train* – Despite nationalization in 1947 the railways have continued to decline in the later half of this century, due mainly to the increasing ownership of private cars and the rapid expansion of freight transport by road. British Rail sought to resolve the fall in traffic by huge reductions in their route operations, which resulted in many smaller resorts and tourist destinations being no longer accessible by train.

  Innovations such as the development of the high-speed 125 train operating on Intercity routes and packages for short-break holidays have helped stem the decline, but for the most part travel by train has lost its popularity with all tourists. Interestingly, though, most first class travel and over one third of all travel on the trains is for business purposes, suggesting that there is a hard core of loyal rail travellers. This should be reviewed however, against the fact, that the larger part of tourist trips today represent only 15 per cent of the 1950 level.

  The opening of the Channel Tunnel has already begun to see an increase in train travel, especially between London and the important business centres such as Paris and Brussels.

However, much of the expected increase in traffic by train is not expected to arrive until after the year 2005, when it is anticipated that the now agreed high-speed rail link between London and Folkestone will be completed. Until it is, most travellers are seeking to disembark and use their own cars on exiting the Tunnel.

In 1993/4 a new rail authority called Railtrack was established by the government as part of its privatization Bill. Railtrack currently owns and manages the rail network which operates along approximately 7800 miles of track carrying somewhere in the region of 750 million passengers. Selected passenger and freight service routes on the railways are starting to be franchised in 1996, which may signal the end of British Rail as we now know it.

Another major growth area in train travel has been the re-emergence of private steam railways. In Britain there are some forty-five such lines in operation.

- *Channel Tunnel* – Despite fierce competition, the Euro train tunnel attracted 41,050 passengers in its first year of operation, and is expected to increase this by 14% by the year 2000. The overall impact of the Tunnel's opening has been to increase the demand for car and coach travel and general rail passenger traffic between Britain and the Continent and vice versa.
- *Car* – The increase in car ownership is given as the major reason for the decline of the railway system in many countries, not just Britain. Figure 1.34 shows the increasing importance of the car as the main means of holiday travel in the UK, compared with other land transport over the last forty years.

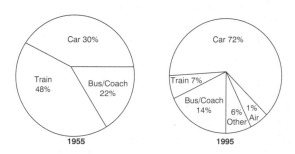

Figure 1.34 Modes of transport used for holiday travel in the UK (*Source*: Travel trade estimates)

The car has two great advantages, in that it provides:

- Independence, in allowing tourists to travel as and when they want
- Convenience and the means to explore and travel around destinations which might otherwise be inaccessible.

Not surprisingly, today the car accounts for over two-thirds of all holiday travel within the UK.

Car hire is also popular, especially among business travellers. Tourists often use car hire as a means of travelling to their resorts from stations or airports or, again, as a means of exploring a destination, such as fly-drive holidays. It is also often possible to hire a car in one location and return it to the same car hire company in another location.

- *Bus/Coaches* – Coach operators offer a wide choice of tourist services by way of:
  - Private hire service
  - Express trunk routes for domestic and international travel
  - Tours and excursions
  - Transfers from, for example, airports to tourist destinations.

Although not particularly popular with business travellers, this form of travel is sought after by the young and the elderly since it offers one of the most convenient (i.e. local pick-up and direct delivery right to the resort) and cheapest means of travel. New express coaches seek to attract other users by way of providing a much wider range of services, including such extras as on-board toilets, reclinable seats, telephone, video, as well as snack bar refreshments, even stewardesses.

Local bus services, too, are often used by visitors in large towns and cities. London Transport has estimated that over 20 per cent of all passengers on its famous red London buses are tourists.

Water transport

Water transport is available in the UK in four forms:

- Ocean liners
- Cruising
- Ferry services
- Inland waterways and lakes.

- *Ocean liners* – Since 1950 and the advent of the jet aircraft, ocean line voyage services offering passengers transport between various ports of call have greatly declined. Unable to compete on speed or cost, the business traveller was first to 'jump ship', followed soon after by the tourist. Today hardly any line voyage services survive, and where they do it is only on a seasonal basis. For example, the QE2 still operates a service between Southampton, Cherbourg and New York in the summer months, but for the rest of the year it cruises round the world.

- *Cruising* – Since the 1950s the passenger shipping industry has moved steadily away from line voyages and towards cruises. The cruise ship is not only important as a means of getting from one place to another, but also comprises all the three As in providing accommodation, meals and entertainment as well as, or simply a place to relax on the sundeck. In some respects, therefore, the cruise ship is the tourist destination, albeit allowing the tourist to disembark at various points along the route to explore the destinations at which the ship calls. Popular cruises include those sailing around the Caribbean and the Mediterranean. However, more luxurious cruises could include the QE2, which will travel to far more distant places.

- *Ferry services* – Since the early nineteenth century tourists have regularly crossed the English Channel between Britain and France. Britain is today linked by several regular ferry services to all European countries with North Sea coasts and with Ireland, as shown in Figure 1.35.

Between 1975 and 1995 operators saw a six-fold increase in coach traffic, while over 3 million of the 16 million car owners in Britain took their cars abroad.

The major ferry operators include P & O Brittany Ferries, North Sea Ferries, Stena and Sally Line. These operators offer new, soft, play areas, restaurants and bars. They have also linked up with several coach operators in

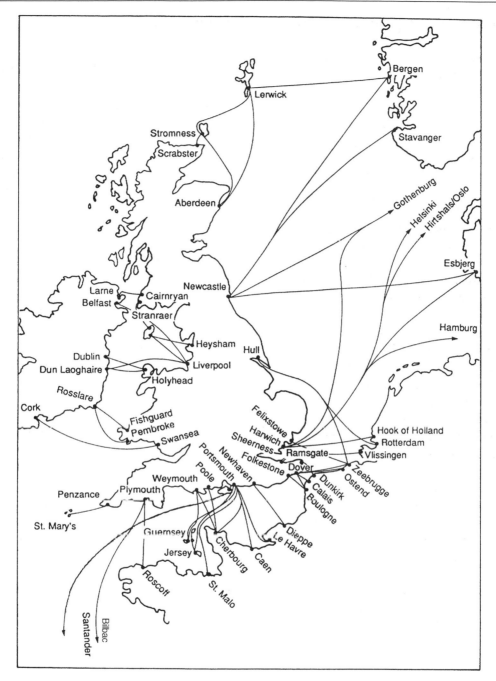

Figure 1.35 Major ferry services to Western Europe and Scandinavia

expanding their long-distance intra-European service offering package tours to more distant continental destinations. These arrangements are, however, particularly at risk with the opening of the Channel Tunnel. Owing to the high cost of short sea services it is felt that in the longer term the ferry operators will concentrate their activities more on a seasonal basis, as did ocean-going liners with the advent of the jet aircraft.

● *Inland waterways and lakes* – Many countries, including Britain, have a network of rivers, canals and lakes along which tourists travel or cruise at a leisurely pace in a variety of boats. The UK is fortunate in having an extensive network of such waterways, which provide

Key

Navigable canals and rivers

Unnavigable canals and rivers

Canals and rivers not administered by British Waterways

British Waterways regional boundaries

1 Scotland

2 North West

3 North East

4 Midlands/South West

5 Southern

WATFORD
Head Office

Leeds
Regional Office

▲ Waterway Office

● Towns

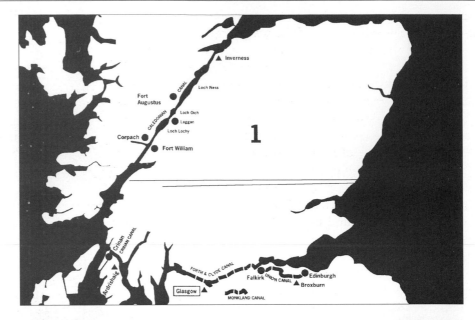

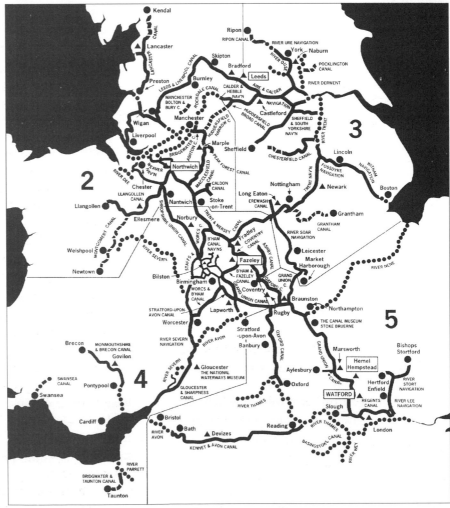

Figure 1.36 Britain's inland waterways network (Courtesy of British Waterways)

many water-based recreation and tourism experiences. The popularity of the waterways has been enhanced by the renovation of many former inner city canals and derelict docks. Cruising on such waterways is based on the idea of moving from place to place on a floating home and disembarking to explore some village or town along the way. There are many different types of boats involved, but the most popular are the narrowboats, which are ideal for canal cruising, and the cabin cruisers, which are wider but shorter in length and are often found on rivers and lakes. Many of the boats for hire today are equipped with all the comforts of home and are capable of accommodating up to twelve people. Most popular of the cruising areas of Britain are the Norfolk Broads, the River Thames and the canals and rivers of central and northern Britain, as shown in Figure 1.36.

Air travel

By far the largest number of overseas trips, both outward and inward to the UK, are by air. International passenger statistics suggest that upwards of 85 per cent of all holidaymakers prefer to travel to their overseas destination by this method.

There are some twenty-seven airlines, excluding air taxi companies based in or operating from the UK. In addition, there are thirty-three UK airports handling passenger traffic, the major airport group being British Airways Authority (BAA), which owns Heathrow, Gatwick, Stansted, Southampton, Glasgow, Edinburgh and Aberdeen Airports.

Figure 1.37 gives the passenger throughput for the top ten UK airports.

There are three broad headings under which air transport can be categorized:

- Scheduled air services
- Non-scheduled or charter services
- Air taxi services.

- *Scheduled air services* – Scheduled air services or scheduled flights are so called because they

Airport	Total passenger throughput (m)
1 Heathrow	44.9
2 Gatwick	19.8
3 Manchester	12.4
4 Glasgow	4.6
5 Birmingham	3.5
6 Edinburgh	2.5
7 Belfast	2.3
8 Stansted	2.3
9 Aberdeen	2.1
10 Luton	1.9

Figure 1.37 Top ten UK airports 1992 (*Source*: Airport authorities)

regularly operate specific domestic or international routes according to published timetables or schedules which are fixed in advance. The routes are operated under license granted by the countries over which they fly or serve and operators must fly in accordance with the schedule, whether or not there are enough passengers (i.e. load factor) to make a profit, in much the same way as a local bus or train service operates to its timetables. Because of this, operating loads are generally set out at around 30 per cent of an aircraft's seating capacity, which has the effect of making scheduled fares very expensive. Most airlines offering scheduled flights are national airlines carrying the name and flag of the country in which they have their headquarters, for example, American Airlines, Emirates Airlines, Air France and British Airways. Other carriers are known as second or third force airlines according to their relative importance and size, while those providing a network of local or regional services are referred to as feeder airlines. Apart from British Airways, there are three other UK scheduled carriers, these being Virgin Atlantic, British Midland and Air UK.

- *Charter air services* – Chartered flights are services organized to meet travel needs at specific times, are not fixed to a specific timetable and can be altered or cancelled if passenger numbers fall off. All charter flights seek 100 per cent capacity, although in practice the load factor is probably an average of around 90 per cent, which has the effect of keeping prices low.

Most charter flights are usually organized by tour operators for the purpose of transporting holidaymakers, and for this reason the majority of the flights are organized in the summer to holiday destinations such as the Mediterranean. In recent years, tour operators have taken over or formed their own charter airlines. If a tour operator cannot sell enough seats on a particular flight it can cancel the flight, but more often than not seeks to combine those passengers with passengers on another flight to the same destination.

- *Air taxi services* – Air taxi services are generally offered by small private charter companies, who carry upwards of eighteen passengers to specific destinations. Being small, these aircraft can often utilize the runways of small as well as large airports. As such, they are of particular interest to business executives in that, for example, they allow the passengers to fly out to a meeting in a specific location and fly back the same day.

Accommodation and catering

Accommodation is an important component of the tourism product, because all tourists require somewhere to stay and something to eat. No tourist destination can ever hope to attract large numbers of tourists if it doesn't have an adequate range of accommodation and catering facilities. Its importance is emphasized by British Hospitality Association figures which indicate that in 1994 2.4 million people were employed directly or indirectly (as well as hotels and restaurants, this also includes pubs, clubs, retail, healthcare and education) in the hotel and catering sector.

Types of accommodation

As previously identified, there are many forms of accommodation, ranging from commercial city centre hotels, motels, farms, boarding/guest houses, flats, villas and holiday centres to non-commercial establishments, such as youth hostels, residence clubs, time-share villas, tents, caravans, while not forgetting visiting friends and relatives. Most of these forms of accommodation are categorized by whether they are serviced or non-serviced (i.e. self-catering). A list of serviced and self-catering accommodation is provided in Figure 1.38.

A breakdown of the most frequently used accommodation on holidays of four nights or more in the UK is shown below in Table 1.12.

The difference between serviced and self-catering is that serviced accommodation includes meals and housekeeping services, such as making beds and general cleaning, while self-catering does not. Meals provided by serviced accommodation can range from supply of breakfast only to a range of meals throughout the day, as indicated below:

- Bed and breakfast – breakfast only
- Half board – breakfast plus one meal (lunch or dinner)
- Full board – breakfast plus two meals.

However, the difference between serviced and self-catering is not always as clear today as it used to be, since with many self-catering or self-service establishments there is the opportunity for the tourist to have meals provided via on-site restaurants, cafés or bars.

Table 1.12 Holiday accommodation in the UK 1991–93

| | 4+ nights' holiday | | 1–3 nights' holiday |
	1971 (%)	1993 (%)	1993 (%)
Licensed hotel/motel	17		25
Unlicensed hotel/boarding house	18	19	25
Friend's/relatives' house	27	29	41
Caravan	19	22	15
Rented accommodation	10	19	4
Holiday camp/village	6	6	2
Camping	8	5	5
Paying Guest and private guest houses	4	2	4
Others	4	3	4
Total	113	105	100

Source: Hospitality Yearbook 1996

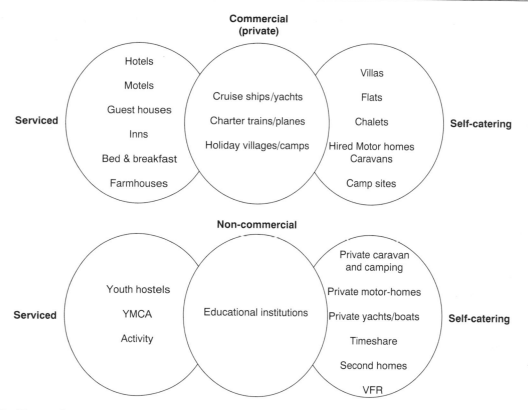

Figure 1.38 Types of tourist accommodation

Serviced accommodation

Although difficult to assess accurately the availability of accommodation in the UK, trade estimates suggest that there is a stock of around 100 000 serviced accommodation establishments throughout Britain. The majority of these establishments are privately owned, and over 50 000 are hotels, of this figure there are 23 500 registered hotels in Great Britain. A breakdown by region is provided in Figure 1.39.

In addition to this hotel stock, the trade estimates that a further 30 000 farm/guest houses, boarding houses and bed and breakfast; establishments can be added to the total service stock of accommodation.

The type of service offered in serviced accommodation will vary according to the needs of the tourist it is likely to attract. For example, a guest house will provide a room, bathroom and communal lounge and the service will include meals, depending on what tariff you can afford:

Region	Total
Cumbria	972
Northumbria	782
N W England	3156
Yorkshire & Humberside	2158
Heart of England	1469
East Midlands	1366
East Anglia	1384
London	457
West Country	3674
Southern England	2213
S E England	1442
Total England	19073
Total Scotland	2876
Total Wales	1438
Northern Ireland	122
Total UK	23509

Figure 1.39 Number of registered hotels in Great Britain by region 1994 (*Source*: ETB, WTB, STB, NITB)

bed and breakfast bed, breakfast and evening meal; or full board.

A hotel or motel, however, may be able to provide a bedroom, bathroom ensuite with shower or jacuzzi, TV, trouser press, telephone and tea- and coffee-making facilities. The types of service offered will vary according to the size and category of hotel, but could include:

- Room service with meals
- Dining room
- Coffee shop
- Leisure suite
- Function room
- Conference centre
- Secretarial services.

The provision offered will vary in price, and will depend further on whether the service requirement is weekday or weekend. Hotels often sell weekend breaks for tourists which are cheaper than the normal business rate during the week. Leisure facilities in hotels may be available to non-residents, as this helps spread costs over the year.

Within the hotel industry there have been significant changes in the ownership of the major hotel groups within the UK. A listing of the top ten UK hotels as at the end of 1995 is provided in Table 1.13.

It should be noted that many of the hotels in the major groups are themselves not registered for

Table 1.13 Top ten UK hotel groups in 1995

Hotel group	Hotels in UK	Not listed	Rooms in UK
1 Forte*	350	220	30687
2 Thistle and Mount Charlotte	105	25	13834
3 Whitbread Hotels	155	110	10023
4 Queens Moat Hotels	86	—	9716
5 Hilton UK	42	25	8684
6 Stakis Hotels	42	42	4991
7 Jarvis Hotels	61	38	4549
8 Macdonald Hotels	52	—	3124
9 Acarr UK	29	3	4413
10 Swallow Hotels	35	—	4379

*includes 127 Travelodge hotels acquired by Granada early 1996

Source: Hospitality Yearbook 1996

inspection purposes (see Classification of accommodation, below).

Self-catering accommodation

Although upwards of 60 per cent of all UK residents generally stay in some form of serviced accommodation when holidaying abroad, less than 30 per cent do so when vacationing at home. Self-catering offers the British holidaymaker the freedom of choice and value for money which families with young children particularly find convenient as well as affordable.

Most self-catering takes the form of rented accommodation such as a flat, chalet, country cottage or villa. Rented accommodation often appeals to tourists who prefer to live in a real home or who, because of necessity (i.e. large family), can only afford this type of accommodation.

Self-catering rented accommodation has grown in importance in Britain as more and more people have become car owners. The greater access afforded by private car ownership has led to the countryside becoming more popular for weekend breaks and longer holidays in farm dwellings or holiday apartments.

Many tourist destinations in Britain and abroad have specifically built blocks of holiday apartments, villas and holiday villages, which have then been sold to UK or overseas residents under timeshare arrangements. Timesharing is a name given to an arrangement involving the purchase of a period of time (usually in blocks of weeks) in a furnished property, which allows the purchaser to use that property over the same period each year. Not surprisingly, the most popular weeks of July and August cost a lot more than a week in January, unless, of course, the timeshare was in a popular skiing resort.

Holiday centres such as Butlins Holiday World and Pontins have offered serviced accommodation for many years, but in response to customer demand now offer a combination of both self-catering as well as serviced accommodation. Much has been done in this sector to improve the old holiday camp image portrayed by the television programme 'Hi-di-Hi'. Over the last ten years Butlins has invested over £100 million in upgrading its five holiday centres and expects to attract in the region of 1.5 million tourists each year. Center Parcs, a Dutch company, has taken the holiday centre or village into a new era by providing an all-weather, sub-tropical swimming paradise in each of its fourteen centres around Europe. Three such villages have recently been opened in Britain at Sherwood Forest, Nottinghamshire, at Thetford, on the Norfolk/Suffolk border and at Longleat, Cambridge.

Camping and caravanning, like weekend breaks in the country, have mushroomed with the growth in car ownership. Between them, camping and caravanning accounted for 27 per cent of all holidays in the UK in 1992, with caravanning taking the lion's share with 23 per cent. Facilities at caravan and camp sites have greatly improved in Britain over the last twenty years. The sites themselves have become more luxurious, often providing a wide range of facilities, such as shops, restaurants, pubs, sports and leisure centres and all kinds of entertainment. The sites often hire six- to eight-berth caravans, which has proved very popular with families as an alternative form of self-catering accommodation.

Task 1.14

In groups of three or four, conduct a survey of different types of accommodation in your local area or town. Try to ascertain whether the accommodation is registered and which classification grading scheme it uses. Prepare your details for a class discussion of the type, availability and quality of accommodation in your area.

Different groups can survey different types of accommodation (e.g. serviced and self-catering, hotels, guest houses, B and B, boarding houses, camping and caravanning).

Classification of accommodation

Tourists need to know what standard of facilities to expect when booking accommodation. For this reason, many countries operate a classification scheme, which groups accommodation according to the facilities offered, so the greater the number of facilities (for example, room with en-suite, trouser press, tea- and coffee-making facilities), the higher the class. In most European countries such classification schemes are compulsory in order to maintain and improve standards. They are enforced by representatives of the Ministry of Tourism, who visit and inspect the provision of facilities and make a classification award.

In 1969 the Development of Tourism Act made provision for the first major classification of hotels compulsory throughout the UK. This was resisted by the industry, and the BTA made no attempt to impose it, preferring instead to rely on a system of voluntary registration which was only introduced in 1975. The classification scheme adopted, based on 'crowns', categorized suitable accommodation by type, physical features, such as the number of bedrooms, and graded the quality of the facilities and services provided as shown below:

Category	Classification	Grading
Hotel	Listed	Approved
Guest house	One crown	Commended
Boarding house	Two crowns	Highly commended
Bed & breakfast	Three crowns	Deluxe
Farmhouse	Four crowns	
	Five crowns	

All tourist boards in Britain have adopted the crown scheme for hotels, guest houses, bed and breakfast and farmhouse accommodation. However, since the scheme is voluntary a large proportion of accommodation remains unclassified.

An annual fee is charged by the tourist board, who in turn will send out its inspectors, unannounced, to inspect premises. Those participating in a classification scheme are entitled to display the classification awarded and to use the classification in any of their advertising material.

The ETB has adopted a similar scheme for non-serviced accommodation based on 'keys'. Over half of all self-catering establishments are expected to have applied for a key rating by 1995. In addition, a system of ticks is now in operation for all caravan parks and camp sites, again using similar classification criteria as for the crowns. Examples of such classification symbols are provided in Figure 1.40 below. In addition to the crowns, we should also mention what for many are probably the best known private classification schemes, operated by the RAC and AA motoring organizations. These provide for star ratings of hotels, the AA's assessment being based on three characteristics:

- Statements of fact as to the nature of the premises and services provided
- The number and extent of the premises and services
- The subject assessment of their quality.

With the harmonization and standardization of laws and regulations throughout Europe taking place, it is probable that new EC legislation will soon come into effect, forcing Britain to adopt a compulsory form of accommodation registration.

Task 1.15

Prepare notes for and against the argument that:

- *All hotels should be compulsorily registered and graded*
- *All types of commercial accommodation should be registered and graded.*

 **DE LUXE**

HIGHLY COMMENDED

COMMENDED

APPROVED

 **LISTED**

Figure 1.40 Hotel classification symbols in Britain

Attractions

Having travelled to a destination and acquired suitable accommodation, the next thing on the tourist's agenda, whether for pleasure or business, is something to do. Attractions give tourists something to do and, as such, are the third important component in the tourism mix of products and services. Its importance to the travel and tourism industry is such that in 1995 the BTA estimated that 35 million people visited a tourist attraction in Britain, with a total of 350 million visits in all, in the course of which £147 million was spent on British tourist attractions, 50 per cent of which was admission fees.

Attractions are the very reason why tourists visit a destination, and with such large sums of expenditure attached to them it will probably come as no surprise to learn that the number of attractions in Britain has more than doubled in the last ten years. Most of the attractions on offer today are relatively new, with examples ranging from theme parks, educational museums to sealife centres and butterfly farms. Other attractions have been around for quite some time, and include, for example, cathedrals and churches, historic houses and monuments, parks and coastal and countryside areas.

The BTA estimates that there are approximately 2400 attractions in the UK, receiving 10 000 visitors or more per year. Most of these attractions can be categorized as either man-made or occurring naturally, as illustrated in Element 1.1.

Although this section is primarily concerned with man-made attractions, the natural attractions of Britain, including its Heritage Coasts, National Parks and Areas of Outstanding Natural Beauty, are major attractions in their own right.

Natural attractions

For such a small country Britain has a wealth of natural attractions, from the mountain landscapes of Scotland and Wales to the beautiful coastline of the West Country. The meandering rivers of the Norfolk Broads contrast sharply with the striking contours of the Lake District, as do the picturesque South Downs with the rugged moorland of North Yorkshire. The combined pulling power of such attractions is such that the ETB estimates that upwards of 550 million day visits are made to the countryside each year. On a good Sunday it is suggested that upwards of 18 million trips will be made alone. The popularity of certain natural attractions is, in fact, put at risk by the sheer volume of these visits. The natural environment in which these attractions exist needs to be protected in order to conserve the very thing which attracts the visitors in the first place. In recognition of this fact, and to ensure access to the countryside while providing protection to the most scenic parts of England and Wales, the 1947 National Parks and Access to the Country Act was passed. The Act gave powers to the Countryside Commission to set up and maintain three key areas of the countryside:

- National Parks
- Areas of Outstanding Natural Beauty (AONB)
- Heritage Coasts.

The countryside covered by these three areas is highlighted in Figure 1.41.

- *National Parks* – Ten National Parks of England and Wales were designated by the Countryside Commission. By being declared a National Park the characteristic beauty of the landscape of the area is strictly protected and existing wildlife and historic buildings preserved. The parks are highlighted in Figure 1.42.

  The National Parks are very popular, attracting over 80 million visits in any one year, the most popular of all being the Peak District, which attracts over 20 million visitors. Although no new parks have been created, in 1987 both the Norfolk Broads as well as the New Forest in Hampshire have become National Parks in all but name.

  No National Parks exist in Scotland or Northern Ireland, although the Countryside Commission for Scotland has recently been pressing for the Cairngorms, Ben Nevis, Glencoe area and the Loch Lomond and Trossachs area to be designated as such.
- *Areas of Outstanding Natural Beauty (AONB)* – There are currently forty-one AONB

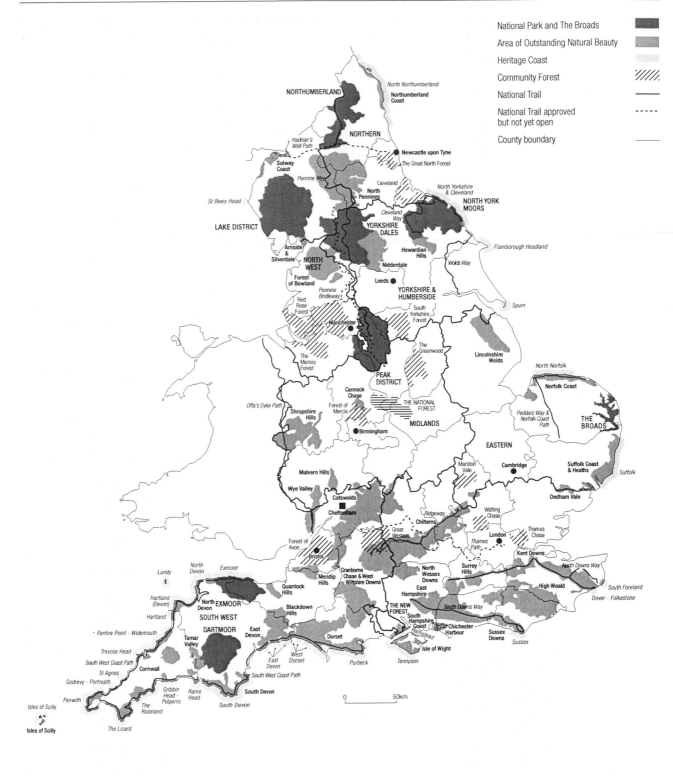

National Park and The Broads
Area of Outstanding Natural Beauty
Heritage Coast
Community Forest
National Trail
National Trail approved
but not yet open
County boundary

COUNTRYSIDE
COMMISSION

Figure 1.41   The countryside commission's designated and defined interests

	Established	Area (sq km)
Dartmoor	1951	945
Lake District	1951	2280
Peak District	1951	1404
Snowdonia	1951	2170
North Yorkshire Moors	1951	438
Pembrokeshire Coast	1952	583
Exmoor	1954	686
Yorkshire Dales	1954	1761
Northumberland	1956	1031
Brecon Beacons	1957	1350

Figure 1.42 National Parks of England and Wales

covering approximately 13 per cent of England and Wales, while in Scotland the Countryside Commission has designated a further forty National Scenic Areas (NSA), as shown in Figure 1.43.

Although often popular destinations for leisure and tourism, these areas are designated as such for conservation rather than recreation.

- *Heritage coasts* – There are forty-five heritage coasts covering 1460 kilometres or 33 per cent of the coastal areas of England and Wales. Some of the individual coastal areas are tremendously popular tourist attractions. The Great Orme at Llandudno, North Wales, with its scenic coastal walks, bob sleigh and ski slopes – not forgetting its two-mile chairlift – attracts many thousands of visitors each year. St Michael's Mount in Cornwall attracts over 200 000 visitors annually, while in Northern Ireland the single most visited tourist attraction (next to Crawfordsburn Country Park) is the Giant's Causeway, which attracts around 350 000 visitors each year.

Of all the heritage coastal attractions, Land's End is by far the most popular and best known. Situated at the very end of the Cornish peninsula, the coastal site has now been turned into a theme park incorporating a miniature model area of Cornwall, exhibition hall, small farm and hotel.

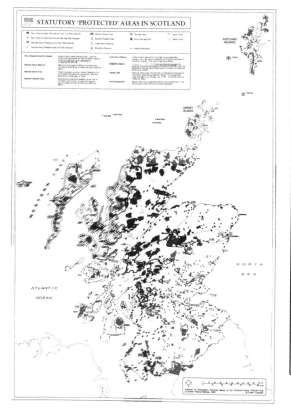

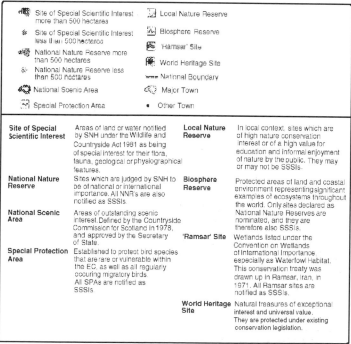

Figure 1.43 National Scenic Areas in Scotland (*Source*: Scottish Natural Heritage)

Task 1.16

Working in pairs, each group to select one organization from the list below or another that you are familiar with:

Public	Private	Voluntary
Countryside Commission	*National Caravan Council*	*Youth Hostel Association*
National Parks	*British Homes and Holiday*	*Outward Bound Trust*
Sports Council	*Parks*	*National Trust*
British Waterways Board	*Rank Organization*	*Ramblers Association*
Department of National	*Mecca Organization*	*Central Federation of*
Heritage	*Granada Group*	*Physical Recreation*
Nature Conservancy	*First Leisure*	
Council	*Brent Walker*	
London Zoo		

Research and write a detailed report, exploring the objectives, roles and activities of the organization you have selected.

Man-made attractions

Besides natural attractions, Britain has developed a vast array of man-made attractions for the prime purpose of providing education, fun and entertainment. The popularity of such attractions in terms of visitor numbers is often sub-divided into attractions that allow free entry, such as museums, and those that charge admission, such as theme parks. Figure 1.44 lists the top ten UK tourist attractions (free and paid admission).

Attractions which offered free admission generally were more frequently visited than those which had to be paid for. Blackpool Pleasure Beach and Alton Towers remain Britain's top tourist attractions. The performance of Madame Tussauds, however, is particularly noteworthy, given the size and number of the major free attractions available in London.

Several of the key visitor attractions are discussed opposite.

Free Admission		Paid Admission	
Attraction	**No of Visitors**	**Attraction**	**No of Visitors**
1 Blackpool Pleasure Beach	7,200,000*	Alton Towers	3,011,000
2 British Museum, London	5,896,692	Madame Tussauds	2,631,538
3 Albert Dock, Liverpool	5,300,000*	Tower of London	2,407,115
4 Strathclyde Country Park	4,380,000*	St. Pauls Cathedral	1,900,000
5 National Gallery, London	4,301,656	Natural History Museum	1,625,000
6 Palace Pier, Brighton	3,500,000*	Chessington World of Adven.	1,614,000
7 Funland & Laserbowl	2,500,000*	Blackpool Tower	1,305,000
8 Canterbury Cathedral	2,250,000*	Science Museum, London	1,235,000
9 Tate Gallery, London	2,226,399	Thorpe Park Surrey	1,235,000
10 Westminster Abbey	2,200,000*	Drayton Manor, Staffs.	1,104,000
*Estimated visitor numbers			

Figure 1.44 Top ten UK attractions (free and paid admission) 1994 (Adapted from BTA Tourist Attraction Survey May 1995)

Theme parks

Theme parks are primarily outdoor entertainment attractions which offer a wide variety of different activities, including white knuckle rides, safari parks, boats, live entertainment, shops and refreshments. Although considered a comparatively new type of attraction, having been developed in the USA by Walt Disney, the term 'theme and leisure park' is often more loosely used to cover a much wider range of attractions, from funfairs such as Blackpool Pleasure Beach to novelty parks such as Chessington World of Adventures.

Thorpe Park, which opened in 1979, is regarded as the first of the modern leisure theme parks in Britain. The main difference between the original funfair theme park and the new leisure-type theme park is really to do with size. Leisure theme parks extend over many areas or even many miles of land. Unlike funfairs, which are free to enter but which charge for each ride, theme parks generally charge a fixed entry price for the whole day and all rides thereafter are free.

The biggest theme parks attract millions of people each year, which in the summer season results in queues at peak times of the day. To get visitors to repeat their visits they need to invest in even newer, more terrifying rides which are very costly to create. In its efforts to remain Britain's No. 1 paid tourist attraction, Alton Towers invested approximately £12 million on its Nemesis ride, which was the only one of its kind when installed. Not surprisingly, the high cost of constructing such spectacular rides has meant that theme parks are only a feature of the developed countries of the world.

Historic houses and monuments

Historic or stately homes and castles, while often thought of together, are different, in as much as the word 'castle' means 'fortified building' while 'stately home' means 'large, magnificent house'. Both, however, are tied by history and culture in attracting large numbers of visitors. Castles are preserved as ancient monuments, the most visited of all being the Tower of London, attracting nearly

2 500 000 visitors per annum. Most monuments are either publicly owned or voluntarily managed, unlike historic houses which, according to the Historic Houses Association, are predominantly still owned by families with long-standing connections with the house.

The top ten historic houses and monuments by number of visits is given in Figure 1.45.

Cathedrals and churches

The word 'cathedral' is derived from the Greek word 'cathedra', meaning 'seat'. Cathedrals are churches which contain the seat or throne of a bishop. Most cathedrals date back to the Middle Ages, although Truro, Coventry and Liverpool Cathedrals were built over the last two centuries. In total there are eighty-two cathedrals in the UK, the most popular with visitors being St Paul's Cathedral, London, Canterbury Cathedral and Westminster Abbey, each of which benefits from their close proximity to the capital as a worldwide tourist destination.

The top ten cathedrals and churches in the UK are listed in Figure 1.46.

With the exception of St Paul's, few, if any, of the other cathedrals or churches throughout the country charge admission, and yet in many cases it is the churches of the towns and villages that are the best preserved and offer the most interesting buildings to view.

Historic house/Monument	No. of Visitors
1 Tower of London	24,077,115
2 Windsor Castle, Berkshire	1,090,668
3 Edinburgh Castle	992,078
4 Roman Baths and Pump Room, Bath	871,308
5 Warwick Castle	755,670
6 Stonehenge, Wiltshire	696,605
7 Shakespeare's Birthplace, Stratford	591,205
8 Hampton Court Palace	543,061
9 Leeds Castle, Kent	537,965
10 Blenheim Palace, Oxfordshire	449,755

Figure 1.45 Top ten UK historic houses/monuments 1994 (*Source*: BTA Tourist Attraction Survey 1995)

Cathedral/Church	No. of Visitors
1 St Paul's Cathedral	2,600,000
2 Canterbury Cathedral	2,500,000
3 Westminster Abbey	2,300,000
4 York Minster	2,000,000
5 Chester Cathedral	1,000,000
6 Salisbury Cathedral	600,000
7 Worcester Cathedral	590,000
8 Norwich Cathedral	530,000
9 Buckfast Abbey	450,000
10 Exeter Cathedral	400,000

Figure 1.46 Top ten UK cathedrals and churches 1994 (*Source*: BTA Tourist Attraction Survey 1995)

Museums and galleries

Museums and galleries have always been popular places to visit for educational purposes. The distribution of many of the country's national museums and galleries is unfortunately based in one location – in London, as can be seen in Figure 1.47.

Despite the predominance of London there are several notable museums and galleries outside the capital, such as the Tate Gallery in Liverpool; Beaulieu National Motor Museum; Glasgow Museum and Art Gallery; Royal Museum of Scotland, Edinburgh; Wigan Pier, Lancashire; and the National Museum of Photography, Bradford.

Many new styles of museum are developing to widen the appeal to the younger market.

Museums and galleries	No. of visitors
1 British Museum, London	5,896,692
2 National Gallery, London	4,301,656
3 Tate Gallery, London	2,226,399
4 Natural History Museum, London	1,625,000
5 Victoria and Albert Museum, London	1,440,334
6 Service Museum, London	1,268,839
7 National Portrait Gallery, London	1,044,149
8 Royal Academy, London	952,472
9 Glasgow Art Gallery and Museum	930,680
10 National Museum of Photography, Bradford	737,096

Figure 1.47 Top ten UK museums and galleries 1994 (*Source*: BTA Tourist Attraction Survey 1995)

Children's museums are becoming ever more popular, particularly with regard to science and technology. Craftspeople have been brought into the museums and galleries to enable the public to watch processes they would not normally see. 'Hands-on' experiences, with lots of buttons to push and things to touch and see, are used to bring education to life. The Jorvik Viking Centre at York, the new Royal Armouries Museum in Leeds, Tales of Robin Hood, Nottingham and the Eureka Children's Museum in Halifax are examples of a new kind of museum in action, while Ironbridge Gorge Museum, Beamish Museum, Wigan Pier and the National Maritime Museum in Liverpool are examples of museum sites which recreate historical times so that visitors can witness the sights, sounds and smells of times gone by.

Case study

This jewel in the crown moves North

The name outside says 'Royal Armouries Museum' – not the most catchy, fun-sounding place, but do not be misled; museums are no longer places with lots of old guns and stuffed owls in glass cases.

Here things move. Falcons hunt, craftsmen make suits of armour and the visitor can even take part in some of the decisive battles of the past.

Here you sit down at a computer terminal, check the battle statistics, the scenario and take military decisions, even change the course of a battle.

If the computer software is extended to include the Battle of Waterloo, it will be possible to re-write that affair.

And you can do more than re-shape the destiny of the world – watch knights fight with swords and poleaxes, see hunting dogs at work, see leather workers make boots, saddles, the buff coats of the English Civil Wars, discover how a crossbow works, and assess, under strict supervision, your own shooting skills.

The Museum has been created on the canal banks at Leeds, where a kind of repeat of the massive Albert Dock restoration at Liverpool has been going on. The Museum is a massive tourism boost for the north, and divides Britain's vast collection of military treasures of the past between three centres.

The Royal Armouries artillery is now outside Portsmouth. Tower of London pieces are in the famous White Tower. The Royal Armouries Museum at Leeds has 44 000 pieces in one of the finest collections in the world.

The creation of the Armouries Museum outside London has led to some sniffy criticism from academics who feel that such national treasures should remain in the capital at the Tower of London.

The re-arrangement, however, makes it possible to put far more on display. As it was, only 10 per cent was on public view. 'Tragic', said a museum spokesman. The figure is now up to 25 per cent.

Also, more British people will now be able to see their heritage. The reply to those who complain about the shifting out of military pieces from London is that only 20 per cent of those who go to the Tower are from Britain anyway.

More than five million British people live within one hour's drive of the Museum at Leeds. Few overseas visitors to London are likely to miss what has been moved north and, if they are really keen, will find that Leeds is not at the end of the world, but on the M1. 'Anyway, we are giving to the British people a great collection', says a spokesman.

It has cost £42.5 m and has been funded by public and private money, a finance deal which is seen as a template for other projects. Those engaged on assessing the likely cash return have found that the visitors are likely to include more women than men.

This is odd to those who think military museums and guns mean men. But then, this is not just a traditional museum with a magnificent collection, but a huge experience in social history across countries and centuries.

Beyond the glass cases there are galleries devoted to the tournament, hunting, oriental, war and self-defence.

Hunting links the early needs to find food to hunting as a challenge to courage as preparation for war. Self-defence deals with the threats to the medieval citizens of London to contemporary women armed with noxious sprays in their handbags to defend themselves.

This museum is so big, so packed with things to see and hear, that a visit needs time, food and lots of energy. Beyond the galleries and the live displays from animals, birds and humans, there are five hours of films.

The whole experience is brought to life with the modern wonders of computers, lights, sights and sounds.

Researchers expect visitors to increase to a million a year. The first big boost comes this Easter. 'How many do you expect?' I asked the museum man. 'Lots', he replied.

The museum costs £6.95 before 3.00 p.m. and £2 less after 3.00 p.m. – telephone 0113 220 1999 for more details.

Reproduced by kind permission of Harold Brough and the *Daily Post*.

Task 1.17

London has been shown to have an abundance of leisure and tourist attractions.

1 Carry out some research and identify the size and scale of the leisure and tourism attractions in London compared with the rest of the country.

2 Make notes arguing for and against London continuing to dominate the UK market for leisure and tourism.

Gardens

Britain is fortunate in having a vast array of gardens open to the public. Many country houses, palaces and castles have beautiful grounds that attract millions of visitors each year.

Most of the country's most prestigious gardens are owned and managed by the government. The National Trust owns some fifty historic gardens, while the National Trust for Scotland owns a further twenty-three. Many privately owned gardens operate as garden centres, which have become highly popular venues for the public to visit. The top ten most popular visited gardens are shown in Figure 1.48.

Gardens	No. of visitors
1 Tropical World, Roundhey Park, Leeds	1,236,521
2 Hampton Court, London	1,000,000*
3 Stapeley Water Gardens, Cheshire	1,000,000*
4 Kew Gardens, London	988,801
5 Royal Botanic Gardens, Edinburgh	788,119
6 Botanic Gardens, Belfast	600,000
7 RHS Wisley, Surrey	586,829
8 Botanic Gardens, Glasgow	350,000
9 University of Oxford Botanic Gardens	306,000
10 Duthie Park Winter Gardens, Aberdeen	260,792

*Estimated visitor numbers

Figure 1.48 Top ten UK gardens 1994 (*Source*: BTA Tourist Attraction Survey 1995)

Wildlife attractions

Wildlife attractions are an increasingly popular section of the tourism market and offer a range of products in the UK, from zoos, safari parks and sealife centres to bird sanctuaries, butterfly and trout farms and seal sanctuaries. Several of these are discussed below.

● *Zoos* – According to the Zoo Licensing Act 1981, zoos are establishments where wild animals are kept for exhibition to the public.

  The word 'zoo' is an abbreviation of the term 'zoological garden' and is an appropriate term in that all UK zoos (most of which are privately owned) need to exhibit their wildlife in order to raise funds to stay in business. All except a few are self-sufficient; the remainder survive only by attracting government grants and sponsorship.

  Towards the later half of the twentieth century, their role has changed to one of conservation rather than exhibition, particularly in the case of endangered species. Conventional zoos have been having a difficult time in terms of attracting visitors, partly because of the competition from a new type of zoo – the safari park – but also because of changing attitudes towards keeping animals in captivity, even for breeding purposes.

● *Safari parks* – Safari parks are designed to allow animals to wander free in a much wider enclosure or countryside area. Visitors can drive through the countryside and view the animals from the safety of their car or bus. The first safari park to be set up in Britain was in the grounds of Longleat House in 1966. Since then, a number of safari parks have opened around the country, the most notable being Windsor Safari Park and Knowsley Safari Park on Merseyside.

● *Wildlife sanctuaries* – Wildlife sanctuaries or reserves are managed by such organizations as the Wildfowl Trust and the Royal Society for the Protection of Birds (RSPB). These areas are designated as special reserves for the breeding of birds and wildfowl, especially endangered species, and are also used to educate the public

Wildlife reserves	No. of visitors
1 Slimbridge, Gloucestershire	200,000
2 Martin Mere, Lancashire	180,000
3 Leighton Moss Nature Reserve, Lancashire	90,000
4 Arundel Wildfowl Wetlands, Sussex	87,346
5 Washington Wildfowl, Tyne and Wear	77,000
6 Risley Moss Nature Reserve, Warrington	74,428
7 Quoile Nature Reserve, Northern Ireland	56,220
8 Britain's Wildlife Reserve, Staffordshire	54,000
9 Peakirk Wildfowl Trust, Cambridgeshire	45,000
10 Welney Wildfowl and Wetlands, Cambridgeshire	28,408

Figure 1.49 Top ten UK wildlife reserves 1994 (*Source*: BTA Tourist Attraction Survey 1995)

about them. Over 900 000 paying tourists visited the major reserves in 1994, as shown in Figure 1.49.

- *Farms* – Many farms are today turning to tourism. The paying public are keen to experience life on a working farm. However, the word 'farm' in this context includes a number of activities not necessarily related to simply raising crops or animals. Trout farms, for example, although normally set up for commercial reasons, nevertheless attracted 130 000 visitors in 1990. Butterfly farms have proved particularly attractive to tourists, including Butterfly World at Stockton-on-Tees; Edinburgh Butterfly and Insect World; Butterfly Centre in Newent and the Tropical Butterfly Gardens at Cleethorpes.

Towns and shopping

Although much of the domestic tourism in Britain has tended to be based around seaside resorts or countryside attractions, overseas tourism, on the other hand, is often town- or city-based.

London, for example, attracts around 60 per cent of all incoming tourists. It is particularly popular for its heritage, but is also strongly supported by the shops. Millions of visitors are simply attracted by the diversity of the shops available, particularly around Oxford Street and Regent Street, which are home to some of the world's most famous store names, including Harrods, Liberty's, Selfridges, Hamley's and Marks & Spencer.

The most popular places for overseas visitors to stay in order of rank are:

- London
- Edinburgh
- Oxford
- York
- Birmingham
- Glasgow
- Manchester
- Chester
- Stratford
- Cambridge.

Many overseas visitors embark on what is termed the 'milk run' heritage tour of Britain, which seeks to take in most, if not all, the above, including stopovers in the Lake District and Canterbury.

▪ Assignment 1.3 ▪

By completing this assignment it leads to coverage of PCs 1, 2, 3 and 4 and Core Skill coverage of communication 3.1 PCs 1, 2, 3 and 4, 3.2 PCs 1, 2, 3 + 4, 3.4 PCs 1, 2, 3 and 4 and IT 3.1 PCs 1, 2, 3 and 4, 3.2 1, 2, 3 and 4 and 3.3 PCs 1, 2, 3 and 4.

Scenario

You are employed by a travel organization which is offering seminars for travel and tourism students. You have been asked to research the UK travel and tourism industry and its development and to produce material which could be used in the delivery of the seminars.

Task 1

Produce a report on the travel and tourism industry and its development.

1 Explain, in general terms, the factors which have influenced the development of the UK travel and tourism industry and describe the major steps in the development of this industry.

2 Within the report describe the products and services available through the UK travel and tourism industry. Support your description with the use of three examples of tourism products/services, one from each of the following:

- Leisure travel
- Business travel
- Visiting friends and relations

and six examples of tourism products/services from the following:

- Holidays
- Tours
- Activities at destination
- Accommodation
- Catering
- Transport
- Agency and information services
- Guiding services
- Currency exchange.

Between them the examples should cover domestic, outgoing and incoming travel and tourism.

Task 2

Select two facilities, one from the tourism industry and the other from the travel industry. Produce a report identifying and describing the products and services for each of these facilities.

Element 1.4 Investigate the Impact of the UK leisure and tourism industries

Performance criteria

1 Investigate the economic impact of the leisure and tourism industries.
2 Investigate the social impact of the leisure and tourism industries.
3 Investigate the environmental impact of the leisure and tourism industries.
4 Evaluate the impact of leisure and tourism industries on a locality and summarize the findings.

Introduction

The rapid growth of leisure and tourism in the latter half of the twentieth century has created many opportunities but also problems on a major scale for the UK. Successive governments have come to realize that leisure and tourism not only impacts on the wealth of the nation but also attracts negative long-term problems in terms of social disorder or a changing environment which needs to be planned for, if it is not to get out of control.

There are three major types of impact that leisure and tourism can have on the UK. These are:

- Economic impacts
- Social impacts
- Environmental impacts.

The effects of each of these impacts will be discussed separately.

Economic impacts

All industries impact on the economy of the areas in which they operate – the leisure and tourism industry is no different. Economic impacts can be categorized under three headings:

- Income
- Employment
- Investment.

Income

Income is the money generated through wages and salaries, rent and profits, even taxation of leisure and tourism activities, such as VAT on travel services, hotel accommodation or on a meal out. The sum total of all incomes in a country is called the national income, and the importance of leisure and tourism to a country's economy can be assessed by looking at how much income is generated by leisure and tourism.

The economic importance of leisure and tourism is illustrated by the government-published National Accounts.

Leisure and tourism's contribution to the income of an area is, however, often greater than is at first apparent because of the concept known as the multiplier effect. Economic researchers are convinced that the amount spent by visitors in an area is recirculated many times in the local economy by way of wages, transport hire, money being saved and spent on goods and services. For example, money spent by visitors on a weekend break is received by the hotel and attractions owners, who then pay tax on profits, save some (or invest) and spend the rest. Much of what they spend will go on buying services, food and drink from local suppliers within the area, who in turn will pay taxes, save and spend. The money circulates round and round and would go on doing so indefinitely if it were not for the fact that money is taken out of the area by way of central taxes and the purchase of goods and services made outside the area. In economic terms, this is known as 'leakage' from the local economy. In general, however, for every £1 spent on leisure and tourism in an area the multiplier effect more than doubles the amount.

At the international level, leisure and tourism also makes a major contribution to the country's balance of payments. This is a statement of incoming and outgoing currency flows between particular countries. Overseas tourists who buy UK tourist or leisure services are paying for what are called invisible items on the country's balance of payments. For example, if a UK resident goes to Greece there is an invisible payment on the UK's tourism balance account with that country, while if an Italian tourist visits Britain the UK's tourism balance gets an invisible receipt. The total of receipts, minus payments, during a year is the balance of payments on the government's tourism account. Figure 1.50 shows Britain's overall balance of payments between 1970 and 1993.

Since 1981 Britain's balance of payments has been in a deficit situation, reflecting the growth of overseas holidays taken by UK residents. The pressure has been on the government to try to attract as many overseas tourists as possible so that they purchase the invisible leisure and tourism services of this country. In addition, with the help of tourist boards, it has tried very hard to persuade its own people, through various promotions, to stay at home and take their holidays within the UK. Where all else fails, governments can, and have in the past, resorted to placing restrictions on overseas travel via taxation limitations and availability of foreign currency, or even refusal to grant exit permits to certain countries.

Employment

The creation of income from leisure and tourism is closely bound up with employment. Leisure and tourism creates a significant number of jobs in the UK in the private, public and voluntary sectors. Very few industries can match these two for the variety and numbers of jobs on offer, from working in a travel agency, with a tour operator or reservation agency in the generating area, to working in a hotel, catering or services, excursion booking clerk, coach or tour operator, to being a security guard, curator or cleaner in a stately home or museum.

For many, this is the primary economic benefit that a country or area gains from leisure and tourism. However, it should be noted that a very large number of these jobs are seasonal or part-time, and that what the industry contributes in terms of full-time employment is often considerably less than its contribution to the total numbers of job hours worked. This is particularly true of tourism, which can greatly impact on the job prospects of people at different times of the year. For example, in places such as the

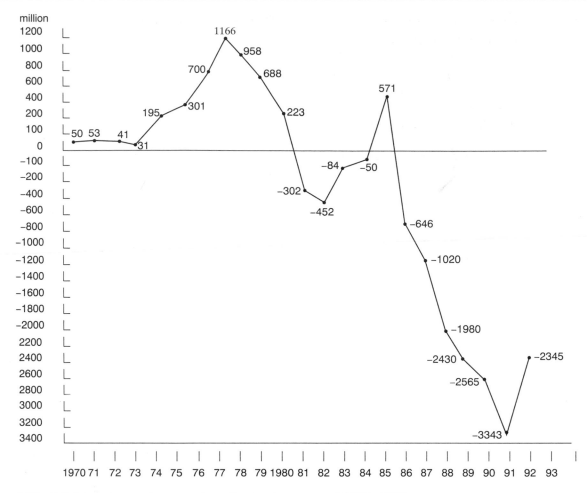

Figure 1.50 Britain's balance of payments on the tourism account 1970–1993

countryside, seaside or mountain resorts there are few alternative employment opportunities, and so government and private organizations invest millions of pounds in trying to extend the season and so keep people fully employed. Blackpool Council, in co-operation with local businesses, tries to extend the holiday season at the seaside resort through the autumn with the added attraction of the Blackpool Lights.

Figures provided by the Department of Employment offer a breakdown of the employment sector of the UK leisure and tourism industry:

Employment sector	%
Public houses and bars	22.3
Hotels and other tourist accommodation	20.6
Restaurants, cafés	20.5
Nightclubs and clubs	9.4
Museums and galleries, sports and other leisure activities	27.2
	100.0%

From the above, it is clear that the vast majority of jobs are to be found in the accommodation, catering and hospitality sectors of the industry. In addition, it is estimated that a further 20 000 self-employed people, such as guides, travel operators and consultants, are also involved in the leisure and tourism industry.

The multiplier effect on employment is likely to be the same as that on income, assuming that jobs with average wage rates are created. If visitors stay in a destination, jobs are directly created in the leisure and tourism industry there. These jobs support families, who in their turn require their own goods, which gives rise to indirect employment in the area for shops, pubs, clubs, sports facilities, etc. However, being a service industry it is labour-intensive and, as such, tends to reflect the seasonality of the business, with many more jobs available in the summer holiday months compared with the off-peak months in the winter.

- Transport (airlines, airports, coach operators, tours)
- Travel services (travel agencies, operators)
- Accommodation (farms, camping and caravanning)
- Catering (restaurants, cafés and bars)
- Attractions (theme parks, licensed entertainment, conference and exhibition centres).

Recent developments in technology have tended to reduce or change the labour requirements in leisure and tourism. For example, computer reservation systems have reduced the need for booking clerks by tour operators, airlines and hotels. The increased popularity of technology-based leisure activities such as CDs, TV and video and computer games has created new jobs, for example in manufacture and the media, at the expense of others, such as in theatres, cinemas and spectator sports.

Task 1.18

Carry out a survey of your local area, identify and then describe the job opportunities that are available in the leisure and tourism industry. This information may be best presented in the form of a table.

Job roles	Qualifications	Skills	Suitability

Career opportunities

There are many job opportunities in the leisure and tourism industry, as can be seen from those listed below:

- *Outdoors* – Maintaining gardens, historical sites, countryside parks and forest areas, or caring for animals in a safari park or zoo.
- *In an office* – Planning the travel arrangements for a package holiday for a tour operator or running the reception area for a caravan park or holiday village.
- *Overseas* – As a resort representative on an exchange from a hotel, training as anything from chef to receptionist to lounge waiter.
- *In a theatre* – In charge of the lighting or scenery or marketing and publicity for the theatre.
- *In a seaport* – Co-ordinating the activities of a roll-on-roll-off ferry terminal or working in the terminal as a hire car receptionist.
- *In an exhibition centre* – Providing help and assistance for conference delegates or visitors to an exhibition.
- *In a town centre* – Working in the Tourist Information Office, helping visitors to make their arrangements for accommodation, travel, entertainment.
- *In a museum* – Helping to build exhibit stands or covering for exhibits and paintings, assisting visitors, both local and foreign, with information.
- *In the air* – Working as a cabin-crew member, assisting passengers as a steward or stewardess.
- *On the ground* – As an airport receptionist working on behalf of an airline, taking bookings, issuing tickets and checking in passengers before their flights.
- *In a sports centre* – In the office, planning events, managing activities and staff, or in the sports hall, weights room and swimming pool, supervising activities and maintaining the safety of customers and clients.

It is practically impossible to list all the hundreds of jobs we find in leisure and tourism, but over the next few pages we will look at some of them.

However, for reasons of space only brief details will be given.

Hotels, catering and licensed trade

Depending on your chosen area of this part of the industry and the qualifications and experience you possess, it is possible to work as a:

- Chef
- Conference and banqueting manager
- Hotel manager
- Hotel porter
- Receptionist
- Restaurant manager
- Room attendant
- Waiter or waitress.

Popular catering

- Call order chef
- Crew member (McDonald's, Wimpy, Burger King).

Licensed trade

Not everyone will play a part here, as no person under 18 years of age will normally work in an area dispensing alcohol, but jobs include:

- Cellar management
- Cocktail bar person
- Lounge waiter
- Wine waiter or sommelier.

The jobs mentioned can lead to you being a publican or licensee of your own public house, wine bar or brasserie.

Travel

- *Air* – Most people immediately think of the air steward or stewardess. The vast majority of people see these staff as airbound waiters, which is not the case. Air stewards need to be able to handle any kind of emergency and initiate the appropriate safety procedures straight away. First aid skills, social skills and initiative are all qualities required by cabin staff.

    Other aspects of air travel will include jobs such as:

  - Airline manager
  - Airline sales representative
  - Airport manager.

- *Sea* – Apart from the captain, navigators and engineers who are paramount to the running of the ship or ferry, staff in the following areas are needed:

  - Bar person
  - Cabin waiter or steward
  - Chef
  - Entertainments manager
  - Housekeeper
  - Lounge waiter
  - Purser.

- *On-shore* – Ferry and hovercraft managers are required to observe the entrance and exit of vehicles onto their vessels in port and also to ensure that activities in the terminals run smoothly.

- *Road* – Coach operators generally provide three types of supervisory role within the company:

  - Private hire manager
  - Tour manager
  - Traffic manager.

    National carriers, such as National Express, will also have:

  - Stewards to serve food and refreshments to passengers
  - Coach drivers – a skilled job requiring a Public Service Vehicle (PSV) licence to drive.

- *Rail* – Jobs here would include:

  - Buffet car waiter
  - Dining car chef
  - Guard
  - Pullman Class stewards and stewardesses
  - Ticket inspector/conductor.

    Some of the above roles would be interchangeable. In general, the conductor and steward are seen as senior staff.

- *Travel agency staff* – Travel staff work in agencies. This means that a company acts as a link between the general public and a service. Travel agencies then link prospective travellers with tour operators, transport services, such as airlines, coaches and trains, and other businesses offering travel services, such as hotels. Travel agency staff include:

- Tour operator
- Business travel operator
- Incoming tour operator
- Reservations staff
- Couriers
- Resort representative
- Tour guide.

Leisure facilities and entertainment

This area provides the most diverse range of job roles available and requires staff with a different range of experience and qualifications.

- *Cinema staff*

  - Bar staff
  - Cashiers

- Cinema manager
- Projectionists
- Sales staff (confectionery, drinks, etc.)
- Usherettes.

The multiplex cinemas have created a heavy demand for such personnel.

- *Theatre staff*

  - Cashiers, box office manager
  - Lighting technicians
  - Manager
  - Sales and marketing officer
  - Scenery assistants.

- *Museums and art galleries* – The advent of 'working museums' and museums of science and technology with working exhibits has brought about an expansion in this area. Museums geared towards children, such as 'Eureka' at Halifax in Yorkshire and 'Catalyst' in Widnes, Cheshire, have resulted in families, groups and individuals visiting in greater numbers.

Figure 1.51   Interactive exhibit at the Catalyst Museum, Widnes, Cheshire

Staff who work in these areas include:

- Managers (sometimes referred to as curators, keepers or directors)
- Attendants
- Catering staff
- Sales and marketing staff
- Sales staff
- Security staff.

Historical property management – This is not the easy life that the tranquil surroundings of a heritage property and its lovely gardens might lead you to imagine. The manager is responsible for co-ordinating:

- Catering facilities
- Customer care
- Function facilities
- Health and safety
- Increasing visitor numbers
- Maintenance of the property, including the gardens
- Publicity
- Security.

Staff include:

- Caretakers
- Cleaners
- Marketing and publicity staff
- Office staff
- Security staff.

Zoos and wildlife parks – Animals need care and attention 365 days of the year – a challenging job for anyone. These operations require:

- Carers
- Marketing and publicity staff
- Sales staff.

Theme parks and tourist attractions – Major investment has been made in this area of leisure, with companies recruiting staff in areas such as:

- Catering
- Customer liaison
- Entertainment
- Grounds maintenance
- Health and safety
- Maintenance

- Planning
- Publicity and marketing
- Security.

Sport and Recreation – Again, a very wide range of job roles in areas such as:

- Athletic stadiums
- Beauty therapy clinics
- Coaching centres
- Health and fitness clubs
- Health farms
- Local authority sports clubs
- Private sector
- Saunas and solariums
- Sports barns
- Swimming pools
- Tennis centres
- Weight training centres

to name a few!

Entry into this area of work, as with other areas, requires very specific qualifications before you may even be considered. Some of the qualifications and attributes are provided in Table 1.14.

Investment

Investment in any area can provide short-term gains for the local area in terms of jobs for constructing and managing the new facilities, as well as the money brought in by purchasing things such as accommodation, goods, petrol, etc. However, the longer-term impact is that investment encourages other businesses and government agencies to invest more in an area they view as successful. The overall effect is self-perpetuating, provided a positive image of the area is maintained.

Rapid expansion in an area because of leisure and tourism often leads to more investment in both leisure and tourism and in other industries – this phenomenon is known to economists as the accelerator concept. For this reason, local and central government have used and continue to use leisure and tourism investment as a springboard for regenerating run-down areas of towns and cities. The International Garden Schemes of the 1980s were such an investment, as government

Table 1.14

Job Title	Background	Attributes
Sports centre attendant	• First point of entry into sport and recreation centres • Usually local authority • Activities would include assisting swimmers, cleaning pool and surrounds, supervising changing areas, moving and laying out equipment	• Minimum age 18 years, need to be a strong swimmer possessing or working towards Pool Life Guard Bronze Award • Must be prepared to work unsocial hours
Sales assistant – public sector leisure and tourism	• Persons wishing to start out in leisure and tourism sales would be working in the local office of the council, assisting with mailing, dealing with customers, staffing the TIO (Tourist Information Office)	• 17+ years, in receipt of GNVQ Intermediate qualification, ability to word process, good social skills
Travel agency clerk	• A courier in travel often starts here, organizing stationery for clients, organizing the display shelves, undertaking duties required by the manager and occasionally assisting in the foreign currency unit	• 17+ years, GNVQ Intermediate, including some specific option or additional units, such as Researching Tourist Destinations and Travel Geography, good social skills and ability to work on your own
Gallery attendant	• Most museums and art galleries run by local councils require attendants to move and arrange exhibits	• 17+ years, an interest in the arts, fit and able to work without supervision
Adventure holidays assistant	• These jobs may be seasonal and will be undertaken in Europe and North America • Most companies will require employees to supervise young children or teenagers in sport and other leisure activities whilst in their care	• 18+ years, GNVQ Intermediate, with some GCSE grades. A language qualification is also an advantage – especially if working in France. Some companies require a driving licence, good leadership qualities, fitness and ability to work without supervision
Countryside rangers assistant	• This job may involve you working locally or away from home • Country parks require constant maintenance and tending of natural resources such as ponds, lakes and coastal pathways • Essentially it is an outdoor job, but may involve an employee undertaking clerical or office duties as required	• 18 years, driving licence, GNVQ or City and Guilds qualification, preferably a conservation skill, such as stone wall building, fencing and/or paving included within the course, fit and with an interest in environmental and conservation issues
Events management (trainee)	• An increasing number of companies are now involving themselves in organizing sports and leisure events to include exhibitions – occasionally a vacancy exists for a trainee. Here the employee would be involved in a lot of fetching and carrying duties, but with the opportunity of observing more senior staff in operation, e.g. sales, planning and design • Staff enthusiasm and motivation plus undertaking other qualifications whilst in employment creates good opportunities in an expanding business	• 28+ years, driving licence essential, GCSE grades plus GNVQ Intermediate level qualification or equivalent. Good social skills, initiative and prepared to work unsocial hours. A liking for travel abroad would be required as some jobs will be out of your local area

sought to redevelop old, run-down areas of the country around such cities as Glasgow, Liverpool, Stoke-on-Trent and Cardiff. Other investment schemes have included inner city developments such as the Docklands Project, London, Castlefield, Manchester and the Albert Dock, Liverpool.

Case study

Calderdale in West Yorkshire is an area rich in both industrial heritage and beautiful scenery. Leisure and tourism has been used by the local authority to regenerate some of the area's mill towns, such as Hebden Bridge and Todmorden.

The success of the scheme is such that today approximately one and a half million day visits are made to the area, generating an estimated £24 million in tourism income and supporting nearly 2000 jobs. Supported through government investment and voluntary aid, many of the old mill buildings have been renovated and other environmental improvements, such as planting of trees, have been carried out.

According to the Pennine Heritage Trust, tourism has capitalized on the character of the area, and care has been taken to offer visitors a genuine experience while at the same time improving the local economy and environment.

Although many public sector investment schemes are designed to generate the economic benefits of increased income and employment there are, however, some negative effects that need to be considered:

- Land prices often rise as a result of leisure and tourism developments, which can prevent local people from buying their own homes or even drive them away from the areas in which they were brought up. This is proving a particular problem in the countryside and in some inner city areas. The buying of second homes throughout the more picturesque areas of

Britain, many of which are used only for a short period of time, has left many villages deserted and the young local population dispersed.
- The effect of such changes on local business has led to the closure of local shops for staple foods, postal services, garages and pubs, etc. because of lack of all-year-round demand for their services. Conversely, areas that have proved very popular with tourists may lose their local shops in favour of retail outlets geared to the particular needs of the tourist, such as cafés and souvenir and gift shops.
- Many traditional jobs may suffer or even disappear in areas where leisure and tourism are particularly strong, offering better pay and conditions. This can greatly affect working areas where the skills of the working population are not passed on through succeeding generations.
- Charges may be levied through council as business taxes on the local community to pay for the provision and upkeep of certain facilities which may be primarily used by visitors – for example, the management of tourist information centres, heritage visitor centres, even attractions such as museums, historic houses and swimming pools.

Social impacts

The social impact of leisure and tourism refers to changes in the quality of life of residents who are affected by leisure and tourism developments. The development of leisure and tourism in an area or country acts as a vehicle for economic modernization, which itself inevitably leads to changes in the structure of society. These changes have brought with them both positive and negative aspects.

Some of the positive aspects have already been discussed, but can be summarized as:

- Greater income
- Education
- Employment
- Improvements in infrastructure and services, such as a wider range of shops, theatres and museums.

Some of the negative aspects, however, include:

- Changes in traditional social and family values
- Cultural practices may be adopted by the host community to suit the needs of visitors, such as late night opening, Sunday trading, excessive noise, drinking, smoking and gambling, even the way we dress or speak to each other.

Leisure and tourism and social changes

There is a threshold of tolerance by the host community towards all leisure and tourism visitors. Provided the number of visitors and their commutative activities remain below a critical level, while the economic benefits are positive, the presence of visitors is usually acceptable. However, once that threshold has been exceeded, negative feelings of discontent arise. These negative feelings are brought about when:

1 The social or cultural distance between the visitor and the host community is great. For example, opening a rave discothèque or all-night bowling alley in the centre of a retirement estate may prove too great a divergence.
2 The size of the leisure and tourism destinations (i.e. shopping centre, arcade or resort) is physically not big enough to absorb the visitors without squeezing out the local activities. For example, in large cities like London, Glasgow or Birmingham many millions of visitors are absorbed by the sheer size of these places each year – unlike places like Clovelly, a picturesque village in Devon, or Bowness, a small town at the centre for watersports activities on Lake Windermere, where visitor arrivals in the summer greatly exceed the size and activities of the local population. In these circumstances, resentment is caused owing to:

- Overcrowding
- Restrictions on access to facilities put aside for visitors, such as private beaches, off-limit areas, restricted use of waterways
- Increased crime
- Unsociable behaviour, such as vandalism, drunkenness

- Local language under-used – a criticism often levied by Welsh-speaking communities.

On a positive note, leisure and tourism has led to the revitalization of areas through the rekindling of interest in local crafts and architecture. The revival of many local customs in rural England, such as Morris dancing, owes much to tourism, something which the national tourist boards have been quick to pick up on and to try to exploit by promoting traditional cuisine through their publications *A Taste of England*, *A Taste of Scotland* and *A Taste of Wales*.

Environmental impacts

A healthy leisure and tourism industry is vital for Britain's well-being not only in terms of its contribution to the economy and to employment but also because of the part it plays in enriching our lives by bringing pleasure and enjoyment. That said, an OECD report on the impact of tourism and the environment stated:

A high quality environment is essential for tourists. On the other hand, the quality of the environment is threatened by tourism development itself which is promoted because of its economic importance.

In this context, the more successful leisure and tourism is, the more it provides in terms of economic and social benefits and the more likely it is to eventually destroy itself.

Leisure, tourism and the environment are closely linked, in that the former relies on the environment to provide beautiful countryside and coastlines, historic houses and cities, sports centres and theatres for its survival, but in turn without leisure and tourism the UK's ability to conserve its heritage and maintain its environment would be weakened. The restoration of industrial buildings, as in Wigan and Bristol, and the transformation of derelict sites into beautiful gardens, as in Glasgow, Cardiff and Liverpool, are just a few positive examples.

Nevertheless, the advances in technology and the complexity of twentieth-century living have led to various environmental problems, the major ones of which include:

- Overcrowding
- Traffic congestion
- Physical erosion
- Pollution
- Inappropriate developments.

Overcrowding

Local people who reside at popular tourist destinations are often overwhelmed by large numbers of visitors. Cornish seaside villages such as Polperro or Tintagel may feel that their privacy – even within their very homes – is invaded by prying eyes.

Overcrowding is not usually continuous, but occurs spasmodically. For example, a leisure centre is often empty during the day and crowded in the evenings. Westminster Abbey experiences a surge of visitors every morning before the 'Changing of the Guard' ceremony at Buckingham Palace.

The major problem with overcrowding is to do with the risk of damage at a site owing to wear and tear or accidental damage. People's movements or views may become restricted because of the sheer numbers of visitors at a location, as is often the case in the Shambles at York or the Lanes in Brighton. The aesthetic beauty of the place may be spoilt if, say, countryside walks are cluttered with ramblers or the peace and quiet of a lake is broken by the thunderous sounds of speedboats.

Traffic congestion

Most leisure and tourism travel is by private car, although sizeable numbers also arrive by coach. Many historic towns and cities suffer from traffic congestion. Often the medieval street patterns of the towns are unsuited to the size and volume of such traffic, while the fabric of the buildings degenerates with the constant vibrations. Car and coach parks are expensive to provide and sites in the town difficult to find.

The National Parks of England and Wales also come under particular pressure. Places such as Dovedale in the Peak District, Flatford Mill in Essex and Slaughter Houses in the Cotswolds are unable to accommodate the huge numbers of car visitors on peak summer days. Narrow country lanes become clogged up, and traffic jams occur even on the major roads leading to the destinations.

Physical erosion

Physical damage to the countryside through the erosion of paths and vegetation by walkers, cyclists or cars is a constant threat to the environment. The erosion of river banks and lake shores by the wash of boats is also prominent in areas such as the Lake District and the Norfolk Broads.

Cathedrals and historic houses and monuments also suffer from wear and tear caused by visitors. Paintings and tapestries can be damaged by exposure to humidity and light. Monuments are often broken, vandalized, even stolen.

For example, just over two million people visit Westminster Abbey each year. Most enter by the West Door, causing the ledges in the nave to become worn away, while the thirteenth-century Cosmat pavement in front of the High Altar is now starting to degenerate. Likewise, the eighteenth-century floor at Canterbury Cathedral has worn away by $1\frac{1}{4}$ inches in places.

Pollution

This refers not only to pollution of water and air (i.e. noise pollution) but also to litter. Combined pollution and litter are two of the most common problems concerning leisure and tourism, particularly in urban areas. Local authorities in popular resorts spend millions of pounds of local taxpayers' money each year on removing the litter and providing the street cleansing and public facilities such as toilets for incoming visitors. In Windsor, for example, it is estimated that the Borough Council spends over £1 million each year providing services to visitors to the town. But even outside towns, litter and pollution generally in fields and waterways are natural eyesores as well as hazards to the natural wildlife. Plastic bags from picnics or barbecues continue to lead to the death of young animals.

Inappropriate development

With increased numbers of visitors to an area there are pressures for new developments to serve and capitalize on their needs by way of providing shops, restaurants, cafés, hotels, kiosks, toilets, parking, signs and visitor centres. All too often, however, the development of such facilities is not always in keeping with the setting or character of the destination which was the very reason that first attracted the visitor.

Large-scale accommodation complexes in the countryside or shopping malls in a historic town can and do change the character of the area. Moreover, they can seriously damage the habitat for local residents, and even affect the flora and fauna of the area. In this regard, the size and scale of all developments need to be in keeping with the area and sensitive to the needs of the local residents.

Task 1.19

Write a letter to Center Parcs in Sherwood Forest, Alton Towers in Staffordshire or an attraction near you, requesting information on how the design of their facility has helped the local environment to absorb people, their cars and visitor facilities with minimal impact on the wider landscape.

Tackling the problem

Some of the measures being taken to address these problems include:

- Capacity restrictions
- Transport
- Marketing and information

- Conservation
- Control and design of developments.

Capacity restrictions

Every visitor destination has an optimum capacity in terms of numbers of people (and cars). Exceeding these numbers will be seen as leading to a deterioration in the quality of the visitor experience. At one extreme, access to a destination may be denied or severely restricted. For example, in the case of Stonehenge, visitors to the site are no longer allowed inside the circle of stones because of the gradual erosion caused by touching the monument. Restricted access may, however, prove beneficial for safety reasons. Allowing 50 000 spectator's into the Anfield Football stadium, while possible several years back, is today seen as both unsafe as well as unsatisfactory in terms of the spectators' experience. The stadium is now all-seater, and access is restricted to 33 000 at present.

Transport

Most visitors reach their destination by private car. Today many local authorities and regional tourist boards are actively involved in re-routing traffic away from sensitive sites by way of better signposting, closure of roads to vehicles and more yellow lines to prevent parking and congestion.

Historic cities and towns such as Oxford, Chester, Bath and York have been very active in promoting park and ride schemes. At Ironbridge Gorge Museum a minibus service links the various museum sites and visitors are encouraged to use it.

Marketing and information

Better marketing is being used to spread demand for leisure and tourism destinations over longer periods to encourage greater use of the facilities outside the peak times. However, in some cases the solution has been not to promote a popular site at all, rather to promote an alternative destination.

Figure 1.52   Stonehenge

Figure 1.53   Examples of visitor information signage

Tourist information centres (TICs) and visitor centres have also played a key role here in providing tourists with information on the range of attractions on offer and in directing visitors to them.

Conservation

Wear and tear is inevitable at destinations, but damage can be minimized if visitors are properly supervised. For example, the use of wardens and guides to help supervise and guide visitors as to where to go can reduce unnecessary damage, vandalism, even theft. Many National Trust properties use volunteer guides to direct people around their gardens and buildings.

Task 1.20

Visit your local Department of Tourism and Leisure Services and find out what information is available for European visitors to the area. Also try and find out if the area is being promoted in Europe, and if so, how and where.

Protective coverings can also be placed over fragile surfaces to prevent/reduce wear and tear. Pathways can be reinforced and visitors encouraged not to wear high-heeled shoes or use flashlights on their cameras. Some items are encased in glass – whole rooms have been installed with humidity and temperature controls to protect sensitive items.

Control and design of development

Planning, whether by central or local government, is essential to avoid inevitable conflicts arising from the development of leisure and tourism facilities, particularly in sensitive areas such as heritage coasts, conservation areas or AONBs. Planning authorities have been successful in the UK in preventing the worst excesses that have been witnessed in some other parts of the world. Examples of good practice include:

- *The re-use of existing buildings* – This practice is often applied at National Trust properties to house cafés, restaurants, reception areas and toilets, thereby reducing the impact of the development on the character of the building.

- *Sensitive design* – Modern shopfronts today are often designed in traditional materials or shapes to blend and integrate into their surroundings. Screens of trees and bushes can be planted to hide the less artistic aspects of a building which conflicts with the landscape. Center Parcs, for example, is well hidden in Sherwood Forest.

- *Improving derelict land* – Many leisure and tourism developments can be used as a focus for major restoration schemes. The West Stow Country Park in Suffolk is located on old gravel workings, while the Garden Festival at Stoke-on-Trent was held on 164 acres of derelict industrial land that used to belong to British Steel.

Task 1.21

Chartwell in Kent is a historic house owned by the National Trust. Although not large, it attracts around 180 000 visitors each year. Unfortunately, most visitors arrive in the peak summer months, which has led to some damage and long queues as the house has become unpleasantly overcrowded.

1 In groups of three, decide how the above problem could be tackled.
2 What action would you recommend the National Trust to take in order to spread demand at Chartwell over the year?

▪ Assignment 1.4 ▪

Completing this assignment leads to coverage of PCs 1, 2, 3 and 4 and Core Skill coverage of communication 3.1 PCs 1, 2, 3, 4 and 5, 3.2 PCs 1, 2, 3, 4 and 5 and 3.4 PCs 1, 2, 3 and 4 and IT 3.1 PCs 1, 2, 3, 4, 3.2 PCs 1, 2, 3, 4, 5 and 3.3 PCs 1, 2, 3, 4, 5 and 6.

This is a group assignment made up of three parts.

Part 1
– A description of leisure and tourism facilities chosen from a local area, using the context headings of leisure, recreation, travel and tourism.

Part 2
– An investigation into the impact the facilities are having on the selected industry.

Part 3
– An evaluation of the impact each facility is having on its locality.

Notes:

1 You are required to investigate two facilities from each of the contexts in order to provide breadth to your assignment.
2 Coverage of all three parts will be best conducted by a series of tasks, which are listed in sequence in order to help you. These tasks are further detected within the Tutor Resource pack.

Task 1

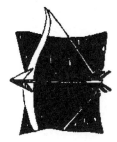

Form groups of four or six members. After initial research, possibly at your local TIC, decide on two leisure and tourism facilities and provide a description of both. Split the group into two sub-groups and decide which facility each will investigate.

Task 2

Find out the names and addresses of each facility and identify any contact names (e.g. attractions manager, publicity manager, etc.) and log the details.

Task 3

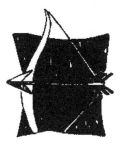

Visit the facility and plan, through observations and asking questions, to obtain data on:

● *The facilities market, in terms of types and numbers of visitors, when they come, how they arrive, how much they spend and what they spend their money on*
● *The organization of the facility, in terms of the amount of money invested in the facility, the revenue it generates, numbers of people it employs (full- and part-time) as well as its impact on local suppliers*
● *Whether or not the design of the facility is in keeping with its environment.*

Task 4

As a group, design a questionnaire which each sub-group member can use at their chosen facility to observe and ask questions in order to obtain the information required in Task 3.

● *Remember to look at the types of people who use the facility, e.g. old, young, male, female, organized party or independent visitors*

- *Is there any provision for customers with special needs?*
- *How well does the facility blend into its environment?*
- *Is there information for overseas visitors available by means of good signage (possibly multi-lingual)?*

Task 5

Both groups to meet and share their information on each facility. An analysis of the data on each facility to be compared and described.

Task 6

Each student to prepare an individual report on the impact the facilities are having on their selected locality. Each should conclude their report by evaluating both the positive and negative aspects of the economic, social and environmental impacts.

The report should be no more than 1500 words, preferably word-processed, and supported by relevant statistics, tables and charts.

Task 7

The group is to prepare a presentation which evaluates the key economic, social and environmental issues involved and how well they are being tackled at each facility.

HUMAN RESOURCES IN LEISURE AND TOURISM

Note: Throughout this Unit, people are referred to generally as male. This does not mean that the role of the female is undervalued, but male is simply used as a convenient term and should be taken as referring to both men and women.

Introduction

Human resources, as the name suggests, is about people and how they function within an organization. It is about individuals and teams working within an organization towards pre-set goals. Some of those goals are negotiated and others are not.

This means that there is a wide variety of situations that can arise – after all, we are all different. As a result, human resources tries to understand people, to find out why people act the way they do and to encourage them to work effectively in whatever aspect of employment they are asked to carry out.

Obviously the study can be very wide, but we are going to look at some very specific areas.

Therefore, within this Unit we are going to review:

- Organizational structures within leisure and tourism
- How teams operate in leisure and tourism
- How to recruit and select staff in leisure and tourism
- Work standards and performance in the leisure and tourism industries.

Element 2.1 Investigate and compare organizational structures in leisure and tourism

In this Element we aim to:

- Describe types of organizational structures in leisure and tourism
- Explain factors which influence organizational structures
- Explain how organizational structures affect the operation of facilities
- Explain key job roles within organizations
- Compare organizational structures.

Organizational structures

The term 'organization' is one that we use frequently in relation to the workplace, but what do we mean by it? We use it to cover a wide range of industries, from industrial and commercial operations to service industries and public service activities.

Task 2.1

By completing this task it will lead to coverage of Element 2.1 PC 1, and Core Elements may include Communication Element 3.1; 3.2

How many different types of organization can you think of? I expect that your list will be fairly long and include many different examples.

We tend to understand **organization** as a collective label for any group of people who interact together in order to enable the achievement of pre-set goals.

From any list of companies, we can then further classify them into private and public sector organizations.

Private companies, such as banks, private health clubs, travel agents, leisure clubs associated with hotels, etc. which operate in the sector of this country's economy which aims to buy and sell at profit, are called **private sector organizations**.

Those that are funded by local or central government, such as public swimming pools, tourist information centres, schools, colleges and local authority leisure centres are known as **public sector organizations**.

The aim of the public sector is to improve the quality of life for people in a cost-effective manner because they are using taxpayers' money. The aim of private sector provision is to give a service, but also to make a profit while doing so.

Organizational structures evolve as a result of the company and the product it makes. Structures are constantly changing, but any organization is the total of what it was or what it is at present and also what it wants to be in the future.

We are constantly hearing about changes taking place within companies – yet another reorganization of staff and job responsibilities. All this takes time and money, but hopefully also allows the company to move forward and develop rather than remain static.

With that information in mind, we can now review 'standard' organizational structures, always remembering that there will be variations and differences as the structures have to reflect the requirements of the organization.

We also have to remember that the customer is very influential in the process. Due to our industry being something related to 'fun' and not 'essential for life', people will have varying amounts of money to spend (or disposable income) at different times, depending on their commitments. The purchasing behaviour of customers can have far-reaching influences on the industry. Partly as a result of this and partly due to the product on offer, different organizational structures have evolved.

The **simple structure** relates to companies that carry out the entire process of producing goods – from the idea through to selling the product. This can be seen in the example of a private health club. The owner/manager has an idea about the type of provision that he wants to give. He decides on the facilities he wants to provide for the clients – whether to include a multi-gym as well as free weights, perhaps a sauna or sunbeds. He then decides on the staffing levels and expertise necessary for clients' safety. All aspects of setting up and running this operation are the responsibility of one or more people on a joint basis. The structure is very simple, with possibly only two or three levels of responsibility. Many small organizations are run in this way.

Within any formal structure of an organization the work usually has to be divided among the employees, and different jobs have to be related logically to each other. The way in which activities can be divided or linked together can be varied and give rise to the different organizational structures.

Functional structures are based on the grouping of organizational activities according to a specialization, the use of the same resources or the shared expertise or skills of members of staff. The organization decides how the split into sections, departments or functions takes place, but a typical example can be seen in Figure 2.1.

Apart from organizational structures which are determined by either the organizations' general activities or by whether they are public or private sector, it is likely that there will be an internal structure built up within the company itself.

Few groups of people operate well without leaders or followers. Whether the group is formal or informal, eventually an order will establish itself.

Organizations also follow this pattern. When they are composed of 'layers' or 'gradings' of employees they are called **hierarchies**. Sometimes this idea is known as **the organizational pyramid**. An example is shown in Figure 2.2. The larger the organization, the more layers there are in the structure.

As with the functional structure discussed earlier, a further example of the pyramid effect in organizations is the split of the workforce into specialist (or functional) areas which are responsible to a more senior co-ordinator or manager. Each area or department will have its own **pyramid structure** with a head of section or department, senior, middle and junior staff. The possibility of promotion or advancement is likely to encourage staff to attempt to 'climb' the pyramid and gain promotion.

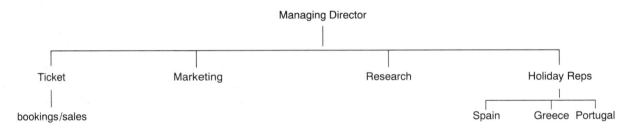

Figure 2.1 Functional organization structure (e.g. a holiday company)

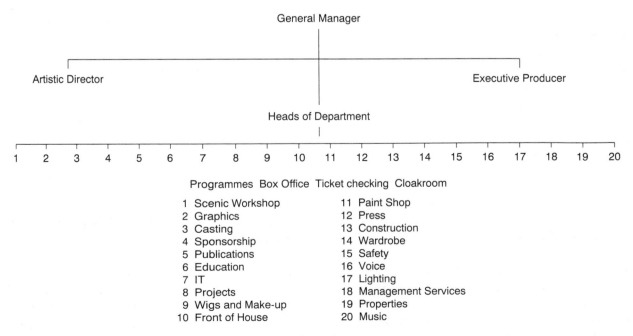

Figure 2.2 Hierarchical structure (e.g. a large national theatre)

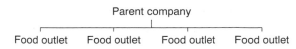

```
                    Parent company
                         |
  |----------|----------|----------|----------|
Food outlet  Food outlet  Food outlet  Food outlet
```

Figure 2.3 Flat organizational franchising structure

Sometimes a company is described as having a **'flat' organizational structure**. A good example of such an organization is one that operates franchised systems. This means that the company provides the services and sometimes the premises, while the franchise holder operates semi-independently within an allocated area. This means that although a standard product may be offered, its style of service may vary. Figure 2.3 shows an example of how some fast-food outlets operate on this principle.

The final aspect within this section is that of **centralization** versus **decentralization**. Many large organizations have to allow for decentralization where different units are run independently, because of problems with the size of the organization, the location of the different units or the need to provide a product or service in a remote area.

There are arguments both for centralization and for decentralization which the organization has to take into account. They include the following:

Centralization

- It is easier to introduce and maintain a standard policy that applies to everyone
- It prevents units from inventing their own strategy
- Co-ordination of work and management control is easier
- There may be a reduction in costs because everything is standardized.

Decentralization

- Means decisions are made closer to the work which they affect; therefore they are more relevant
- Departments which give support to other areas, such as administration, are more likely to be

effective because they know the people they are working with
- It provides opportunities for management training
- It usually motivates and encourages staff.

Generally, decentralization is easier to introduce in the private sector than in the public sector because the public sector has a greater level of accountability, as organizations are using public money for their operations and they have to give uniform treatment in all sectors.

Whatever structure the organization adopts, no matter which sector it is functioning in, it is important that the structure is right for the company – as long as it works, there are no rights or wrongs!

Task 2.2

By completing this task it will contribute to the coverage of Element 2.1 PC 1, and Core Elements may include Communication Elements 3.1; 3.2; 3.3; and 3.4.

Find out the organizational structure of your school or college. Start with the Head/Principal and show the hierarchy.

Do you have departments or sections? Also show the structure of these.

Having collected this information, which of the structures we have discussed does your school/college fit into?

Factors which influence organizational structures

There are many factors which influence organizational structures, and each of these will have some effect on the final type of structure the organization has. We are now going to review some of those factors.

Figure 2.4 Local tourism centre

The important features can be split into two areas – those that are affected by the organization itself (internal factors) and those that are affected by the market in which the organization is operating (external factors).

Internal factors

These factors will be influenced by the organization itself.

1 **Size** As successful companies manage to establish themselves, they tend to become larger and so employ more people. This means that the company probably then has to sub-divide, and there may be problems of co-ordinating the processes that have to be overcome.

   Many large organizations have allowed some responsibility to be given to smaller, readily accountable units, which may be carried out on a geographic basis. For example, tourist information centres only have information about the immediate area around them. If a customer wants any further information about another area, either the centre rings ahead and charges the customer, or the customer does it himself.

2 **Location** We have already mentioned how the geographical situation can influence the way in which the organization operates. The location is important in other respects as well. For example, if an outward bound centre was located in the city centre, either the number of outdoor activities would be limited, or else transporting people to another location would be expensive and time-consuming, so reducing the amount of time people had to experience the events. The other extreme would be a cinema complex in the middle of nowhere, without a transportation link (no buses or trains), which would only serve a small number of people who have their own transport.

   Aspects such as location and transport links do have to be remembered when planning the location of a venue. An example is Glyndebourne Opera House, which sells itself as an evening out in the country as much as an opera house.

3 **Nature of the product** Again very important. Depending on what service is being given, staff will require certain skills. An aerobics teacher will need technical, social and organizational skills as well as first aid qualifications, while the driver of a tour bus will obviously still need technical and social skills, but in this example the driving skills he develops are possibly the most important. Therefore, the type of product will place different demands on employees.

Figure 2.5 Glyndebourne Opera House

4 Management styles The way in which senior management see their workforce will also influence the organization process. From this the different styles of management will develop. Autocratic-style managers tend to make most of the decisions themselves, while democratic-style managers will be prepared to share decision making.

Public sector organizations make their decisions partly as a result of government policy. Again because of public accountability, they tend to require committee-type decisions that are influenced by legislation and bureaucracy (excessive office routine, especially because there are too many offices or departments).

Private sector organizations have far fewer legislative or bureaucratic demands placed on them, and decisions can be made quickly and need fewer people involved.

These four areas are influenced by the organization itself. We now move on to external factors.

External factors

1 **Ownership** We have already reviewed the influences of ownership in some detail. However, this public or private sector influence will mean that the company has to follow certain procedures. Even if a company is operating in the private sector, there will be important factors. Many private sector companies are 'Limited'. This means that people have bought shares in the company and they will have the right to have some say in the way in which the company is run as well as taking a share of the profits the company has made. This means that, even though the processes involved in decision making are not as involved as in the public sector, there are still important accountable considerations to be made.

2 **Competition** This will be covered in great detail in Unit 3. Knowing who your competitors are and their style of product is very important. Many organizations try to develop their own 'gimmicks' to attract customers. If there is the time and money, this can be very successful.

However, knowing your own product and its strengths and weaknesses helps deal with the competition.

3 **The market**   Probably the most important factor is the market you are catering for. Obviously the customers' demands will influence the type of staff required, but aspects such as seasonal fluctuation are also important. A bingo hall with a fairly steady level of usage will have very different demands from those of a holiday tour company, whose business is seasonal and who will not need as many staff through the winter as through the summer. The bingo hall will have a fairly stable level of workforce while, although the tour company will have a nucleus of permanent key staff, it will be boosted by seasonal labour as demand increases.

4 **Technology**   The technology of a particular sector is also important. Advances are being made all the time. This will affect the product being offered to the customer. Museums are a good example. Traditionally, everything was displayed in large cases, with lots of examples of the same type of product, and people were not allowed to touch them. This is now changing, and many museums are becoming interactive, with videos, computer games and things to try becoming very important to the product itself, so encouraging repeat visits.

5 **Government policy**   Whatever business we work in, we are all subject to the law and legal requirements. Ignorance of the law is no defence in court, so it is our duty to be aware of legal implications. Many of these (but by no means all) will be dealt with later on in this Unit.

Task 2.4

By completing this task it will lead to coverage of Element 2.1 PC 2, and Core Elements may include Communication Elements 3.1; 3.2; 3.3; and 3.4

In a small group, review the internal and external factors that influence organizations.

Decide on a local company with either a leisure or tourism product.
Make an appointment with the manager and find out about the environment within which the company operates.
Present your findings to the rest of your group.

How organizational structures affect the operation of facilities

Again, we are going to review this in terms of factors within the company and those external to the company. Many of the points will be explored in greater depth later on in the Unit.

Internal factors

1 **Working relationships**   This is sometimes called a 'staff relationship' and covers the way in which people interact in the workplace. In the formal structure of the organization there is likely to exist a clear line of authority, from a director to a sales assistant, as shown in Figure 2.6.

However, communications in particular, do not always follow these lines. A regional manager may want to communicate directly with a sales assistant who has performed well. As a matter of courtesy, he should inform the branch manager, but this does not always happen.

2 **Job opportunities**   Once the formal structure of the organization has been identified, there are usually clear paths for people to follow in order to gain promotion. Defined roles and responsibilities will exist that give layers or a

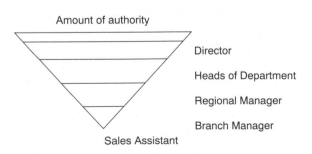

Figure 2.6   Line authority in a national travel agency

hierarchy to the organization, so that people are able to identify clear progression routes.

3 **Decision making** This tends to follow the same route as the line of authority within the organization. Decision-making authority is associated with the level of authority within the organization and the two are linked. Although someone at a lower grade will have a certain level of decision-making power, it will be fairly limited.

4 **Change** Nothing is ever static. Changes constantly occur in all aspects of life, and the organization is no exception. Information technology and products are constantly improving. As a result, industry constantly updates its staffing requirements and levels. As a result, change is something that certainly larger organizations integrate into their functioning relatively easily. Smaller companies may choose to structure themselves to minimize the effects of change.

External factors

Many of these aspects have already been mentioned earlier in this section. They include the use of technology, competition, the market and the influence of government policy.

Key job roles within organizational structures

There are many roles that people play within organizations – far too many to review here. However, we are going to look at some of the main jobs and their responsibilities.

1 **The chairman (or woman)** In private sector organizations the chairman is found at the head of the organizational pyramid. He or she will be elected by the board of directors and chairs the meetings of the board of directors. He may also have executive status, which means that he has the authority to make decisions which affect the running of the company, or he may leave the day-to-day business of running the company to the Managing Director.

In public sector organizations the chairman of a public corporation is responsible and accountable to a central government department for the administration of a public corporation.

In turn, the central government department will be headed by a Permanent Secretary (a senior civil servant). Apart from the chain of responsibility above this type of chairman, the duties resemble those of a company chairman.

2 **The executive director** In the private sector, the executive director has overall responsibility for the running of the organization and has authority over all staff. The Executive Director is also a member of the board of directors.

Generally the directors decide important matters and policies at board meetings. They have legal obligations under the Companies Act 1985 and they may be able to influence the activities of the company because of the number of shares they hold within the company. The board of directors has to present an annual report to the shareholders at the end of each trading year.

In the public sector, decisions about spending the taxpayer's money are made by the district or county council. Members (councillors) are elected by people who are registered to vote in each area. Normally a councillor is a member of a political party, but not always. Councillors make decisions either in full council meetings or in committees and they, along with their colleagues, are responsible for setting budgets and carrying out legally imposed duties.

3 **The non-executive director** In private sector organizations, this individual will sit on a board of directors in an advisory role. He will have some skills or expertise that the organization can benefit from, or will be able to put an alternative point of view. Non-executive directors do not have any voting powers on the Board and so cannot influence policy directly.

4 **The departmental manager** Within the private sector, the departmental manager is responsible to the managing director for the work carried out in one department within the organization. This individual directs the work carried out by staff within the department and ensures that targets are met.

In the public sector office, the counterpart of the departmental manager is the local government officer. He or she is a full-time officer who carries out the policies of the chief executive. Again, these officials are divided into departments and sections covering specific areas of work.

Task 2.5

By completing this task it will lead to coverage of Elements 2.1 PC 4, and Core Elements may include Communication Elements 3.1; 3.2; 3.3; and 3.4.

Large companies that have shareholders have to produce an annual report. These reports contain lots of information.

Obtain an annual report from a large leisure organization, e.g. Mecca, Rank (keynote reports), or from a hotel group and show a hierarchical breakdown identifying the main roles that we have discussed above.

Where do people fit in and what responsibilities do they have?

Organizational charts

Up until this stage we have looked at the structure of an organization as an organizational chart. This shows how the work is divided and how activities may be grouped together, the levels of authority and formal lines of communication. We have explored quite thoroughly these different aspects. They are useful in explaining the outline structure of the organization. They may also be used to indicate where problems may occur, e.g. an overlap in areas of authority or functions necessary to the organization which have no staff at present. These are the advantages.

There are also disadvantages. They can only give a view of how the organization *should* work, rather than how it *does* work and what the structure should be. They also do not show how much responsibility an individual may have by

comparison to someone else or how much authority is delegated to subordinates.

Despite the drawbacks, the organizational chart is very important. However, there are some features that will help to improve its reliability. For example:

- It should be dated when it is drawn up, so people know how current the information is
- Whether it is an existing or proposed structure should be indicated
- The name of the organization should be shown, along with the branch or department that it refers to
- The name of the person who drew it up, should be given as a future point of reference.

Bearing all this information in mind, we now move on to the assignment associated with this Element.

Portfolio builder

If you have completed these tasks, you should have:

- A comprehensive list of different types of organizations
- An organizational structure of your school/college
- An inventory of skills needed by people in different occupations in leisure and tourism
- A presentation, detailing internal and external factors that influence organizations
- An organizational chart developed from an annual report showing people's responsibilities.

These can go into your portfolio as evidence towards your qualification.

▪ Assignment 2.1 ▪

By completing this assignment, it will lead to coverage of Element 2.1 PCs 1, 2, 3, 4, 5 and 6, and Core Elements may include Communication Elements 3.1, 3.2, 3.3, 3.4,. and I.T. Elements 3.1, 3.2, 3.3, 3.4.

Scenario

In order for an organization to achieve its goals and targets, the work has to be divided among the employees. This requires that some sort of structure has to be developed in order to allow for important activities and not to overlook any areas.

Details

1 You are going to be comparing the organizational structures of two facilities – one in the private sector, the other in the public sector. They can relate either to leisure or to tourism, but obviously they must provide a broadly similar service in order for a reasonable comparison to take place.
2 Give general information about leisure and/or tourism facilities within your area.
3 Select two organizations – one from the public sector, the other from the private sector.
4 Show an organizational structure as a diagram for each sector and indicate how it 'fits in' with the rest of the organization.
5 What emphasis does it have within the organization? e.g. how important is this aspect of the company? What sort of profile does it have?
6 Compare and contrast the facilities provided by each. Do they fulfil the needs of the area? If not, what improvements could be made?

Note: If you have completed a work placement that is relevant, or you are about to do so, collect any information that may be relevant and use that.

Element 2.2 Investigate how leisure and tourism teams operate

This area looks at how teams operate within leisure and tourism. We are going to be reviewing specific areas, which include:

● The structure and purposes of teams in leisure and tourism

● Factors that influence the effectiveness of teams
● Roles and responsibilities and how they affect team objectives
● The lines of authority within teams.

Note: This Element deals with the theory of teams and their operation. Unit 8, Event Management, also deals with teams and how they function in a practical situation. Remember that Units are supposed to have relevance to each other and that the information in this Unit will apply to Unit 8 and vice versa.

The structure and purpose of teams

Teams are made up of people, and people are individuals. Before we can review how teams operate, it may be useful to find out a little about individuals. We pride ourselves on being 'different'; most of us think we are unique. Having established that, it is important to be able to accept some basic differences.

Whenever we look at someone, we take in information about them without perhaps even realizing that we are doing so. We notice things like height, weight, colour of hair, as well as sex and ethnicity. Have you ever had to describe someone to another person? We actually use their physical characteristics to help us.

Apart from how we appear physically, there are other differences between us as well.

Task 2.6

By completing this task, it will lead to coverage of Element 2.2 PC 2, and Core Elements may include Communication Elements 3.1; 3.2; 3.3; and 3.4.

Look at the following symbols for three minutes.

Memorize the symbols below
Detail is important – absolute accuracy is essential

1  POWER

2 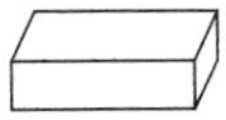 BUILDING

3 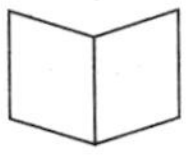 BOOK

4  DREAM

5  FEAR

6 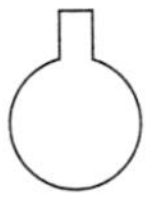 BOTTLE

7  GRAPES

8 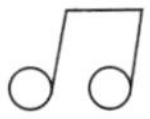 MUSIC

9 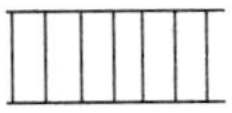 CAGE

10  MONEY

6  ELECTRICIAN

7 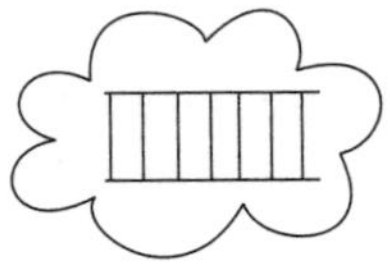 FOREST

8 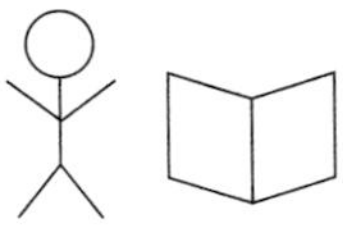 PLAINS

9  CITY

10  PRISON

Reproduce the following symbols without referring to the book.

1 Bottle
2 Book
3 Cage
4 Fear
5 Money

Check your answers with the book/handout.

How did you do? Probably very well.
Try a similar exercise.
Again, look at the symbols for three minutes.

Reproduce the symbols listed again without looking!

1 Musician
2 Philosopher
3 City
4 Prison
5 Teacher

How did you do that time? Was this exercise as easy? If not, why not?

Memorize the symbols below
Again – accuracy is very important

1 OLD WOMAN

2 GIRL

3 MUSICIAN

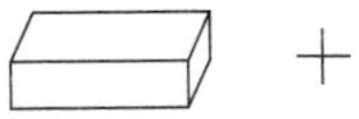

4 PHILOSOPHER

5 TEACHER

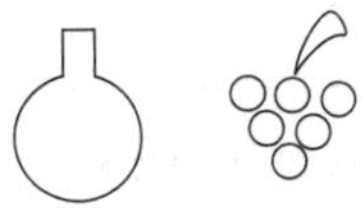

The exercise you have just completed is useful in helping to identify different aspects of individuals. Was that testing intelligence or memory? If you answered them all correctly, does this show that you are brilliant?

The task was actually a memory test. Some people have very good memories, others do not but have different skills.

Memory tends not to be reliable and will be easily influenced by other things that are going on. Depending on the time of day you do this exercise, lots of situations may influence your results. Perhaps you had a bad journey into school/college, perhaps you have had an argument with someone, perhaps you are not interested in this exercise. All of these will influence how you perform.

Let's try something else.

Task 2.7

By completing this task, it will lead to coverage of Element 2.2 PC 2, and Core Elements may include Communication Elements 3.1; 3.2; 3.4.

Answer these questions.

1 What does frozen mean?
 a) Glued   b) Liquid
 c) Solid   d) Water

2 Which is the penultimate letter in the word HELP?
 a) H   b) E   c) L   d) P

3 Which is the odd one out?
 a) Foam   b) Mush   c) Bubbles   d) Surf

4 Who is the third in alphabetical order?
 a) Skipworth   b) Smith
 c) Sinclair   d) Skinner

5 What does debate mean?
 a) Comment   b) Talk
 c) Argue   d) Create

How did you get on this time? Has this been easier or more difficult than the last Task?

Tests like this are called intelligence tests, but do they really test intelligence?

They test very specialized skills and do not allow for a person's creative ability, business or organizational skills. People can be 'trained' or 'coached' to see the correct response, so the answer is no. They do not indicate intelligence, they simply illustrate that an individual thinks in a logical and 'linear' (straight) manner. These people who produce one solution to a problem are called **convergent thinkers**.

Divergent thinkers, on the other hand, have lots of solutions to problems and are able to select the best for the situation in hand. They tend to have very good creative abilities and vivid imaginations.

Neither type of thinker is superior, but this does show how diverse people are.

As can be seen from these limited examples, the possibilities for individuals are almost limitless. There are obviously many other factors which allow us to be individuals.

However, when we are hoping to produce a team, we have to acknowledge people's individuality, but work with it to advantage.

A **team** is a group of two or more people who are working towards a goal. This could either be a social or an organizational goal; nevertheless, when people start sharing ideas and solutions, they are effectively working as a team.

We have already mentioned that we may be part of a social group or team. Here people are in the group because they have similar interests or aims – fan clubs or supporters' clubs are formed because people gather together to show their support, share information and the success (or otherwise!) of the team. These are **informal teams**.

Even within organizations, people will have friends whom they meet for lunch or socialize with outside work.

We mention these 'teams' because they can be useful to the organization. Friendships can mean that people are more prepared to give and take, and that teams can work effectively together. It is far more pleasant to work in an atmosphere of support than in one where there are feelings of ill will.

Formal groups take longer to establish themselves. Here someone else (probably in a management position) has decided that certain people will work together. People leave or move on to other jobs and replacements have to be introduced.

Whenever a new formal group is put together, there are certain recognized stages that the team has to go through. These are known as:

- Forming
- Storming
- Norming
- Performing.

An example would be the box office team at a new cinema complex.

Forming

At this stage, team members will be trying to find out what their responsibilities are, which systems they should use and the information they need. It is at this stage that they would look for an acceptable leader from within the group. So in our example, this stage would need people to become familiar with booking procedures, issuing tickets, taking money and keeping records. It is likely that the organization will already have made certain decisions, so training will also be needed.

Storming

Once people know each other better, the team may go through a time of conflict (particularly if new people join an existing team), as new ideas are brought in. This usually arises because there is a difference between what people are expecting from the work (their expectations) and what is actually happening. If the team is able to move beyond this stage, the team members will have a strong bond developing between them, giving a strong foundation on which to build.

Norming

Having managed to arrive at this stage, the team then starts to function as a unit. The group considers itself to be established and then develops standards, and individual roles are identified. There is an exchange of ideas, and other views are accepted.

Performing

This is when a team reaches its highest level of performance. There will be constructive ideas and solutions put forward to solve any problems which may arise, and productivity will be high.

The structure of teams

Just as there are many different types of organization structures, so there are a wide variety of team structures. However, we are going to review two types that are common in all work situations – organized teams and ad hoc teams.

Organized teams

We have already distinguished between the importance of formal and informal groups. Another important aspect to remember is that we have an element of choice in informal groups, whereas we do not have the same degree of choice in the formal situation.

As you will remember, informal groups form out of situations such as common interest and friendship, whereas formal groups are put together by someone in authority to work towards a common goal.

In organized groups, pre-set goals and work targets are important. They are the reason why the group is together in the first place. Therefore, individuals have relatively little choice about the membership of such a work team other than applying for the job initially. Someone else has made a decision about an individual's suitability and skills for a position, and although friendships are likely to grow out of the situation they are not the primary reason for joining.

Examples of such work teams include reception area staff, enquiry teams in information centres or pool attendant teams in a leisure centre or football teams.

Ad hoc teams

The term 'ad hoc' means 'for the purpose of'. These teams are specially put together to achieve a specific purpose. They will include specialists and experts with specific skills needed to carry out a certain project.

Although membership is still not voluntary, people are selected for their skills and, once the project has been achieved, the team will be disbanded. They are together for a limited time.

Examples would include a team working towards a special event, such as an open day or a sports day. You will be experiencing such a team when planning your event in Unit 8. You will have different roles and responsibilities to fulfil.

Whichever team style is adopted will depend on the reason why the group has been formed. There are many purposes that groups are brought together to achieve. They may be long-term projects, such as the development of a

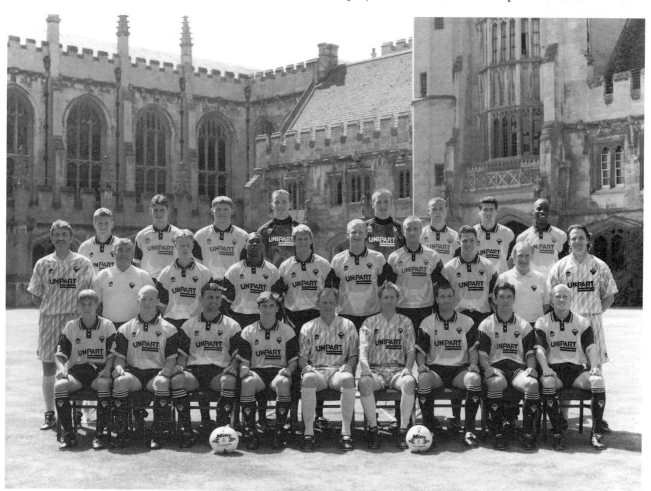

Figure 2.7 Oxford United

multi-services project which would include the development of a computerized system to assist the running of a leisure centre. It would cover aspects such as lighting, heating, ventilation, air conditioning, pool temperature, court temperatures, admissions and bookings. This is obviously a very complex and long-term project which would require specialist skills. The people in this team would work together for years rather than weeks to achieve this goal. A specialist firm may even be brought in. This is obviously the opposite of the 'ad hoc' or short-term project team we have already mentioned.

Task 2.8

By completing this task, it will lead to coverage of Element 2.2 PC 1, and Core Elements may include Communication Elements 3.1; and 3.2.

Look at the structure of your school/college.

Apart from formal and informal groups, what sort of working groups or teams does it have?

Find out if there are any long- and short-term teams within that structure.

Who is in those teams? Are people in more than one team? Are students included in any of those teams? Do students have any of their own groups/teams? If so, what are they? Are staff invited to join?

Influences on the effectiveness of teams

Having reviewed the theory of how groups operate, we now need to look at some of the influences outside the group's control that can affect how successful the group is in its operation.

One of the major considerations is that of **communication**. This will be explored in greater

detail in Unit 6, but we need to be aware of its importance here.

We all consider ourselves to be good communicators. After all, it is something we have been doing from an early age, and we have all managed to make others understand what we want. So what is communication?

When asked this question, many people answer, 'talking' or 'using words'. This is, of course, correct. We communicate in a number of ways, one of which is verbally. However, communication is more than simply using verbal techniques. If I said 'Penblwydd hapus' to you, I am still communicating verbally, but there may be a problem. Unless you are familiar with Welsh, you would not necessarily understand me.

This is a very important part of the communication process – understanding is the ultimate test of communication. By the way, I wished you 'Happy Birthday'.

In addition to giving information in a language that is understood by the person receiving the communication, the person receiving also has a responsibility within the process. You could shout as loud as you liked, or you could write as much as you liked, but if no-one is listening or reading, then the communication process is not taking place. I may have discovered something very important, such as how to win the Lottery, but if you do not pay attention you will not know the answer!

So, in addition to having something to say and then choosing the most appropriate means through which to say it (writing, speaking, drawing pictures, etc.), the responsibility for the communication process then falls on the person receiving to actively participate by listening and reacting accordingly.

If I said 'Go and close the windows' and you did that, this would be an example of effective communication in action.

In real-life situations, unfortunately, things are not that clear-cut. Usually there is a lot of noise going on around us. Just think of the noise in a swimming pool area – people laughing and shouting and generally having fun. If you had to communicate with a colleague about a possible dangerous situation in the pool, how would you do it? Would you whisper? Would you shout? How would you gain their attention?

Usually whistles are used – because they can be heard and a code may be developed to signal different types of problems so that the staff can react.

In a real situation there are lots of examples of where we may need to communicate effectively and quickly but where there may be distractions. It is important to be aware of these so that dangerous or costly problems may be avoided. This consideration is going to influence how effectively a team works together and the problems it may have to overcome.

There are other aspects to consider as well, and we are going to review each in turn.

*The dictionary definition of **dynamics** is 'a branch of physics that deals with matter in motion'. Due to nothing being static, everything continually changes, and group dynamics deals with how groups change and move forward and how they relate and communicate with each member.*

One of the most interesting areas in group dynamics is the structure of the team because of the interlocking roles and relationships that it has – in other words, because of its structure. When we refer to the team structure we are talking about an established pattern of interaction and operation, and there are going to be factors that influence the structure. These will include:

- *The age of the team* – We have already studied the formation of teams and the stages that they go through. The longer a group is together, the more rigid it is likely to become because it does not have to change. When members leave or new people join, there may be some resistance to change from the remaining team members.
- *Previous contact* – If any of the members of the team have had contact before a new team's

formation, this will form the basis of the new structure, particularly if that contact has been friendly. This will form what is called the **nucleus** around which interaction between team members will take place.
- *The task itself* – The way that the task has to be undertaken will affect the structure of the team. For instance, the tourism service of currency exchange means that people have specific procedures to follow, while a team working within a tourist information centre will have to be far more flexible in its approach to dealing with the different areas of enquiry. Although they may have specialist areas of knowledge, they also require a good general knowledge of the area.
- *Communication skills* – We have already reviewed this in some detail. However, each team will develop its own lines of communication as they arise, to form a structural link.
- *Status of team members* – The way in which people can influence teams through high status – either informally through the force of their personality or formally within the structure of the organization – can result in a team structure being created that is centred around themselves.
- *Infra-group feelings* – Strong antagonism or strong attraction between team members can affect the development of the team.
- *Management styles* – These will also influence how the group functions. We have already mentioned two extremes of management styles in Element 1.1. These were the democratic and autocratic styles.

Within a team that has an autocratic, authoritarian management style, the team will be very dependent on that manager. Here people are encouraged to ask before carrying out processes and check rather than using their individual abilities to solve problems. This team operates on strict and rigid lines.

The democratic manager listens to ideas from team members and encourages them to develop those ideas. Individuals are encouraged to take on responsibilities within the team and to solve any minor problems that may arise themselves. Here the manager is available to advise where necessary and there is far more flexibility within the team.

*A dictionary definition of **resources** is given as 'available assets'. Depending on where the team is operating and the functions of that team, the resources it needs will be very important. For instance, a gymnasium would not be able to operate without any equipment for people to use, or a tourist guide service would not function if they did not show people around an area.*

The level of resourcing has to be appropriate for the team to use. Unfortunately, this costs money. It is an investment, but not all companies have the levels of money available to them that they might like. This means that a constant compromise must be achieved between what is necessary to function and what would be desirable.

This aspect in turn will affect the **working environment** in which the team functions. The amount of equipment and comfort in one case may not affect a team who only uses that as a base and works away from that area, whereas a team which operates in a small area with limited equipment may be deeply affected by the work area. Again, compromise is the important key to the situation.

Task 2.9

By completing this task it will lead to coverage of Element 2.2 PC 2, and Core Elements may include Communication Elements 3.1 and 3.2.

From the last task you were able to identify certain teams that are in existence. Now we are going to review the influence on their effectiveness.

What influences are going to affect how the team operates?

What is its structure? Who is the leader? What style is adopted? What environment does the team function in and what resources are available to it?

Taking all these aspects into consideration, how well does the team do in achieving its aims?

Roles, responsibilities and relationships

We have already looked at the general responsibilities of people within an organization in Element 2.1. We now need to look at job responsibilities at team level.

A theorist called Peter Drucker has identified five basic operations in the work of **managers**. These are:

1 Setting objectives and deciding what needs to be done in order to achieve those objectives. This information then needs to be communicated to the people who are going to achieve the objectives. For example, if a manager decides that people need telling that once a ticket is a confirmed booking a refund cannot be given against it, then he needs to communicate this effectively to the staff. He also needs to establish how the information is going to be communicated to the customers, and whether it is going to be necessary to keep records.
2 Managers organize their teams by dividing the work into manageable jobs.
3 Managers communicate and motivate, so creating a team out of the people who are responsible for the various jobs.
4 Here some assessment of the team and its members takes place – analysing, appraising and interpreting the performance of the team and possibly making adjustments accordingly.
5 Managers, according to Drucker, develop people. They direct them or misdirect them. They bring out what is in them, or they stifle them.

Managers are in place to help the team work towards the aims of the organization, while helping individuals to attain their potential.

First-level **supervisors** may encounter particular problems. These may include some of the following:

- Supervisors' level of training and age may be closer to that of the team they supervise than that of the group they are supposed to identify with – management.
- Supervisors depend on the co-operation of the team to work towards the goals. However, they are separate from the workforce.
- Even though supervisors are the first level of management, they have very little authority.
- Supervisors need to maintain a high level of morale within the team, but may spend most of their time checking standards of work performance or carrying out administrative tasks.
- Supervisors do not contribute towards policy-making decisions, but they are expected to work towards the goals and to defend the system.

Operatives are concerned with actually carrying out the task or service that the organization offers. They may have a general background that requires some specialist knowledge of the organization, but they do not necessarily possess any specialist skills.

A **technical ability** means that team members do possess technical skills that the organization requires. For instance, to be a tour guide someone may need to be conversant in two languages and be able to answer questions and queries that may arise. This technical expertise will be a prerequisite for the job applicant, and is a method of selecting the right person for the right job.

When dealing with the public, everyone has certain **responsibilities** in addition to their roles. We are in a service industry which means that we provide a service for the public to use or not, as the case may be.

Therefore, there are certain responsibilities that we all have. We have to ensure that we use **customer care skills** (these will be dealt with in Unit 6) to help the customer and avoid unnecessary problems arising. We also have to ensure that the

products and services we deliver to the customer are the best available at the time, to ensure that they come back and use the facilities again.

We also have **legal** responsibilities for the health and safety and security of our customers, and again we will be looking at these in greater detail in Element 2.4.

Whatever functions we may have within organizations, we will all have certain responsibilities – to ourselves, our colleagues and our customers as well as the organization.

When someone applies for a job it will already have been decided what sort of responsibilities they will have – this goes to form the **job description**, which we will look at in greater detail in the next Element. Within the job description, responsibilities will be defined and they will then be used to identify a role for the individual within the organization. Also, the objectives of the team will help to define the roles individuals take. If a team wants to provide a good service, it will work together to help individuals in order to achieve that objective. For example, if members of a reception team are working together, they all deal with the customers and their enquiries rather than leaving the tasks to one individual while everyone else stands around chatting!

Therefore, the team objective should be working towards the targets that have been agreed with the organization, supporting team members to do that, remembering that we all have times when we need support from colleagues, and, finally, encouraging individuals to develop skills and abilities they may not realize they possess.

Lines of authority

When we were looking at the structures of organizations in Element 2.1, we established lines of authority. These follow the organizational structure and can be used to identify who has responsibility for different areas.

The traditional view of authority was that subordinates carry out the manager's requests

Figure 2.8 Making an impression

because of the authority that the organization has given the manager. A more recent view is that employees only accept orders and instructions given to them within 'well defined limits' such as in a contract of employment or job description, and unless the employee is prepared to accept the manager's additional requests the manager can do little about it.

In addition to the recognized authority that goes with the position that the manager holds, there are other sources of authority as well. These include:

- *Reward and punishment* – Many managers have the power to offer pay rises or promotion to employees or, alternatively, to reprimand or ultimately dismiss the employee.

- *Making the job easier* – The flow of information is often controlled by the manager, and this might either help or hinder the employee in his work. Examples include the control over the way the work is organized and the physical and social environment that the employees work in or control on the employee's status by serving on committees, etc.

- *Expertise* – People generally work well with those whom they regard as experts in the particular field. This does not necessarily mean academic qualifications but also includes experience within the industry. For example, in a museum, the curator of a certain department with expertise in the area may command more respect and authority than the head curator.

- *Personal power* – We all know individuals who command respect and authority because of their characteristics. This is often known as 'charisma'. It is not necessarily something that people are born with – it can be learned, and hopefully this shows that, through effective communication, motivation and interpersonal skills, individuals can become respected managers in their own right, not just because of the jobs they hold.

The purpose of these lines of authority is to allow the organization to function and prosper. It is to allow teams to be controlled and directed correctly so that accountability to taxpayers or shareholders can be demonstrated. It is to allow

for good communications to develop so that people are prepared to take responsibility, and, finally, it is to allow for the reporting procedures to take place so that senior management knows what is happening within the organization.

Portfolio builder

If you have completed the tasks in this Element, you should have:

- Examples of memory tests
- Examples of intelligence tests
- Identified groups and teams within your school/college
- Identified influences on the effectiveness of teams.

These can go into your portfolio as evidence towards your qualification.

▪ Assignment 2.2 ▪

By completing this assignment it will lead to coverage of Element 2.2 PCs 1, 2, 3, 4 & 5, and Core Skills may include Communication Elements 3.1; 3.2; 3.3; 3.4; and I.T. Elements 3.1; 3.2; 3.3; and 3.4.

Scenario

Teams function within all organizations, and leisure and tourism facilities are no exception. This assignment is about the structure and purpose of teams, which then develops into an analysis of two specific teams from different areas of leisure and tourism.

Details

1 Explain why teams may be necessary within leisure and tourism facilities.
2 Describe the structure of the teams within the facilities and discuss the factors which influence their effectiveness.

3 Carry out an in-depth investigation into the operation of two work teams in two different leisure and tourism facilities. This should:
- Identify roles and responsibilities within teams and how they relate to each other
- Explain the relationship between the roles, responsibilities and team objectives
- Identify the lines of authority and their purpose.

You should include charts to illustrate lines of authority within the selected teams.

Note: If you have completed a work placement that is relevant, or you are about to do so, collect any information that may be relevant and use that.

Element 2.3 Investigate and prepare for recruitment and selection in leisure and tourism

In this Element we are going to be reviewing the recruitment and selection of staff and we will establish the importance of appointing the correct person to the correct vacancy. Areas we will be covering include:

- Recruitment and selection procedures
- Legal implications
- Job descriptions and person specifications
- Letters of application and CVs
- Interview techniques and evaluation of those techniques demonstrated.

Recruitment and selection

When trying to fill any position within an organization, it is very important to recruit and select the correct person for that position. If this does not happen, it can be very expensive for the organization, either because the person may leave the company quickly or because the dynamics of the team become upset. Both of these will be costly in terms of money and time. Therefore, it is important that any recruitment policy aims to attract the applicant with the necessary qualities through the advertisement of the vacancies.

Advertisements can appear in many places, and when looking for employment it is important to know where those places are. They may appear in the national press or the trade press. Radio stations advertise vacancies and so do recruitment agencies and job centres.

Task 2.10

By completing this task it will lead to coverage of Element 2.3 PC 1, and Core Elements may include Communication Elements 3.1; 3.2; and 3.4

Research, in the press and through recruitment agencies, to find out a range of vacancies which are available nationally or in your local area.

What information do the advertisements give?

What would catch your interest and encourage you to send for further information?

From an organization's viewpoint, having generated interest, it then needs to start the selection process.

Once candidates have completed the necessary application forms, a decision has to be taken about who to call for interview. This process is called 'short-listing'.

In an ideal world, everyone would be interviewed for the position. However, due to the number of applicants for positions nowadays and the cost incurred, it is easier and cheaper to set up a short-list of the most suitable candidates for the position. Here the qualities necessary for the position are matched to the skills people have through information given on the application form or through a CV (curriculum vitae, which we will discuss in greater detail later).

Information can also be given by means of the references the candidates have chosen to include.

Referees are people who usually have either knowledge of the candidate in a work situation or knowledge of the candidate as a person. Someone who has experience of you in each situation should be chosen, for example, a head of year or course tutor. However, a relative should not be used, as their opinions tend not to be objective enough.

Having cleared the first hurdles, the interview comes next. Depending on the organization's policy, the job being filled and the level of that job, various different interviews evolve.

An **interview** is basically a conversation with a purpose which can be interpreted in many ways. It may be very formal with a panel approach, meaning that a number of interviewers are present, with different areas of expertise. All will ask relevant questions about their own field. There will be a chairman, who has a casting vote and ultimately the final say in the decision.

Less formal approaches may also be adopted, with only two people involved. Whichever one is decided on, you are likely to meet very different styles and approaches. Some interviewers may be friendly and supportive, others will not. Some may appear very direct and others will not. Some will try to put you at ease and others will not. Just as we are all individuals, so are interviewers and the panels on which they appear.

You may be asked to take your Record of Achievement (ROA) along to the interview with you. Again, it is a way of the panel trying to assess you without knowing you as an individual. As you are aware, a ROA is a positive statement about you in different situations, as well as you identifying what you are good at, or what you are working towards. This document can be very useful when trying to match people to vacancies.

Throughout the interview, the panel will be assessing your performance. You may see them making notes throughout the interview – these will only be to help them make a decision on the best candidate, because they will be asking everyone the same questions and it is difficult to remember everything that is said!

Once all the interviews have taken place, the panel then needs to make a decision. During the interview, they will have indicated how and when the successful candidate will be informed. Obviously time-scales will vary, depending on the number of candidates and workloads that the individuals have.

When a decision has been made, it will then be the responsibility of the chairman of the panel to confirm the success of the candidate. This could be done verbally; however, it is necessary for this to be confirmed in writing so that both the organization and the successful candidate have a written record.

After the candidate has accepted the position, the unsuccessful candidates need to be informed that the position has been offered to someone else.

Legal and ethical obligations

Although we will be reviewing legal requirements in much greater detail later on, it is important to recognize some of the obligations at this stage.

There is a lot of legislation in this country that determines the way in which organizations can operate. This is to protect both the individual and the company.

Whenever an advertisement appears, it has to comply with certain legal requirements. The equal opportunities legislation requires that there is no discrimination against people on the basis of their sex or ethnicity. This could be further extended to include opportunities for disabled people, and there have recently been 'test' cases in the courts against companies who have a young image and only employ young people. It has been argued that this is 'ageist' and therefore a form of discrimination.

Contracts of employment are also very important and legally binding, and again we will explore this in greater detail later on. However, we need to be aware that a contract is a legally enforceable agreement between an employer and an employee, and it provides certain rights on both sides. Anyone who is employed for more than eight hours a week is entitled to a contract after three months' service.

Ethical obligations are also important. They are very difficult to prove, as they are to do with the integrity of the individual. Again, there are ethical obligations for both the employer and the employee.

Here we are talking about honesty and objectivity. If an employee falsifies parts of his application form, which is then found out after he has been employed, the situation could result in dismissal. If an employer requires an employee to carry out a dishonest act, he, too, can be taken to court.

Objectivity is even more difficult to prove. This is where someone should make a decision based on the facts of the situation, without any emotions being involved or favouritism being shown. Again, this is very difficult to fulfil in some situations.

Task 2.11

By completing this task it will lead to coverage of Element 2.3 PC 2, and may also include Core Communication Elements 3.1; 3.2; 3.3; and 3.4.

If you have a part-time job, try to find out the equal opportunities policy that the company uses. In some situations it may only be verbal, in which case make notes.

If you do not have a part-time job, try to obtain an equal opportunities policy from school or college.

Compare the two documents. What areas are common to both? Where do they differ? Is it a useful document or is it restrictive? Could improvements be made? Is the language easy to understand?

Job descriptions and person specifications

Before details of a job description or specification can be drawn up, there are some basic questions that need answering, such as does the job exist?

By establishing that it does, we have actually started to carry out a **job analysis**. Perhaps this analysis will prove that a job does require filling. On the other hand, it may also show that change is needed. A job may be split and carried out in a different way, or it may be added to the duties of someone on a different grade. No one likes a 'non job', and a variation in duties can enhance an existing role.

Having established that there is a post to be filled, we now need to produce a written description of the roles and responsibilities. This is called a **job description**. The aim of job descriptions is to detail areas of responsibility, so that people are appointed on the basis of information rather than relying on a 'hunch' or intuition.

There are many different formats that can be used and are used within the industry, but the following is a useful general guideline for a job description.

1 Title of the post.
2 To whom the appointee is accountable.
3 Tasks for which the appointee is directly responsible.
  Tasks for which he or she is indirectly responsible (in other words, tasks carried out by subordinates).
4 Resources controlled:
  – human
  – financial
  – mechanical/physical
5 Liaison links required:
  – internal to the organization.
  – external to the organization.

It may be useful to give an example. I have deliberately chosen a clerical job, as it is not specific to our industry but positions such as this are still necessary.

```
TITLE            Clerical Officer
RESPONSIBLE TO   Support Services Manager
REPORTS TO       Assistant Support Services
                 Manager
PURPOSE OF JOB   To provide clerical and
                 secretarial support to the Staffing
                 Officer and to Heads of Section
1 MAIN AREAS OF RESPONSIBILITY
  1.1  TYPING –  Responsible for producing
                 correspondence for the Staffing
                 Officer. This will include minutes,
                 letters, forms and all general
                 correspondence.
  1.2  WORD-PROCESSING
                 Use of a word processor for general
                 correspondence.
                 Input new personnel records and update as
                 required.
2 GENERAL DUTIES
  2.1  Photocopying.
  2.2  Responsible for dealing with outgoing mail.
  2.3  Maintain records of staff sickness.
       In the absence of the Personal Secretary to the
       Services Manager, required to carry out the
       following duties:
       2.3.1  Maintain good telephone relationships.
       2.3.2  Deal with all telephone enquiries, internal
              and external.
       2.3.3  Create and update staff personnel files.
       2.3.4  Issue and maintain relevant records.
3 MISCELLANEOUS
  Required to undertake other duties as determined
  and agreed with the Services Manager.
```

Figure 2.9 A job description

In this example, the resources controlled and the liaison links were integrated into the other points and were not detailed separately.

Task 2.12

By completing this task it will lead to coverage of Element 2.3 PC 3, and Core Elements may include Communication Elements 3.2; 3.3; 3.4; and I.T. Elements 3.1; 3.2; and 3.3.

Either find an advertisement for a job within leisure and

tourism, or if you already hold a part-time job within the industry, use that as a basis.

From your research material, produce a job description under the headings we have already discussed.

Having produced a job description which will be sent out to applicants along with an application form, it is then necessary to produce a **person specification** which will be used during the interview.

The person specification is used to give a 'pen portrait' of the ideal person for the job showing the ideal characteristics. The interview process is about matching the candidates to the image of the ideal person.

Taking the example we have already used, we can now produce a 'person specification'.

This, again, is only an example; many other areas may also be included. There may be more specific areas of competence or qualification necessary for the job that the organization is trying to fill. This

```
POST              Clerical Officer

QUALIFICATIONS
MINIMUM           Relevant typing and word
                  processing qualifications
                  recognized in the area

IDEALLY           Advanced qualifications, both
                  vocational and academic NVQs
                  and GNVQs in Business
                  Administration

EXPERIENCE        Minimum of five years' relevant
                  clerical experience, with some
                  responsibilities demonstrated in
                  positions already held

PERSONAL CHARACTERISTICS
                  Must be motivated and able to
                  work with minimum supervision.
                  Flexible in approach and style,
                  able to adapt to a wide range of
                  people, calm temperament and
                  able to deal with pressure
```

Figure 2.10 A person specification

is by no means rigid, and each organization adapts the format to its own needs.

Task 2.13

By completing this task it will lead to coverage of Element 2.3 PC 3, and Core Elements may include Communication Elements 3.1; 3.2; 3.4 and I.T. Elements 3.1; 3.2; and 3.3.

Using the job description you have already produced, now create a person specification. Note: It may also include information such as an ideal age range and the salary on which the company would like to appoint the successful applicant.

This process is one of constant evaluation and matching. An appraisal of the candidates has to take place to match their skills and expertise to the job requirements, as mistakes at this stage can be very expensive for the organization. Appoint the wrong person and he may leave as the position is not in line with his expectations, so resulting in a re-appointment, going through the process again, or it may result in the team being disrupted and so underperforming.

Simply appointing the best person for the job on the day does not mean that is the end of staff development. Training and development are very important to the individual and the company. Changes are constantly being made within the workplace, and staff should be encouraged to keep up with these.

Letters of application and curriculum vitae (CV)

Whether you have found a job for which you would like to apply or you are sending a speculative letter (a letter asking if an organization has any vacancies), there are certain conventions that should be followed.

The letters themselves may fall into one of three categories. The first is a short 'please find enclosed' type of letter. This sort would accompany an application form for a specific job.

You may also want to send a letter along with a CV to an organization to inform them of your qualifications in case they have any relevant vacancies.

Finally, you may write to someone within the organization whose name you may have been given.

Whatever the reason for writing, it should draw the attention of the person to particular information which makes you a suitable candidate for consideration. The layout, style and content follow the same basic rules.

1 Ideally the paper should be A4, white, unruled and of good quality – in other words, not a page torn out of an exercise book!
2 Use good, legible handwriting. Most companies actually expect this letter to be handwritten, not typed.
3 Keep it brief and to the point and also keep a copy for your records.
4 Put your address at the top right-hand corner and, slightly below it on the left-hand side, the name (if you know it) and the position of the recruiter, the department and the company with its address.
5 Unless you know the name of the person to whom you are writing, always start 'Dear Sir/Madam' and end 'Yours faithfully'. If you do know the name, start 'Dear Mr/Mrs or Miss' etc. and end 'Yours sincerely'.
6 The first paragraph should mention the position applied for, where and when the position appeared and any reference number.
7 The second paragraph should contain any special selling points you have which are relevant to the job.
8 The final paragraph is a polite closing off.
9 Having signed the letter, print your name underneath.

A **curriculum vitae** is information about you and your achievements. It gives positive and relevant information about what you have done and achieved so far. Again, a standard format is recognized.

Remember, it is important that the information is correct and has been read through. It should be word-processed so that photocopies can be produced.

Task 2.14

By completing this task it will lead to coverage of Element 2.3 PC 4, and Core Skills may include Communication Elements 3.1; 3.2; 3.3; 3.4; and I.T. Elements 3.1; 3.2; 3.3; and 3.4.

Produce your own CV.

Remember that if this is produced properly it can be used when you apply for jobs.

There are also some points to remember when completing **application forms**.

- Before filling anything in on the form, take a photocopy in case you make any mistakes.
- Read the application form through properly and decide what information you are going to include in each section.
- Notice where there are instructions such as 'USE BLOCK CAPITALS' – this may be for your name. Also, there may be directions to complete the form in **black** ink as this photocopies more easily than blue ink.
- Try to avoid using liquid paper on mistakes – be sure what you are answering.
- Answer every question. If some do not apply to you, write 'Not applicable' or N/A.
- Usually application forms ask why you would be good at the job. Think this through carefully and perhaps ask a tutor for help. Generally keep this section short, modest and simple, stressing relevant details.

PERSONAL DETAILS

Full name   Date of birth
Address and telephone number
Marital status
Nationality
Driving licence

EDUCATION

Secondary school
College or university (with dates)

QUALIFICATIONS

GCSEs
NVQs
GNVQs

EMPLOYMENT EXPERIENCE

> Usually starting from the most recent and working backwards.
> You need to include the name of the organization, location, the job you held, range of duties, responsibilities and reasons for leaving.

INTERESTS

> Leisure activities, hobbies, showing responsibilities where they are appropriate. Do not make this section too long

---

Figure 2.11   A CV

- You will usually be asked for two referees. Always ask people before using their names, titles and addresses. Where possible, select someone who can:
  - comment on your academic or work abilities, such as a course tutor or a present supervisor
  - comment on your personal attributes and qualities. This should be someone outside your family.
- Finally, use the correct-sized envelope, so that you only have to fold the application form once.

Interview techniques

These fall under two headings, both of which may be relevant to you at some stage. Certainly you will be an interviewee, but there may also be occasions when you will be involved in the interviewing process.

Types of interview

Individual ('one to one')

In this situation there is only one interviewer, which means that this style is more personal and relaxed, so making it easier for the candidate. It takes less time to set up because the interviewer sorts out the questions and paperwork so no-one else is involved and, as a result, it is cheaper. The disadvantage is that only one person's view is involved and any opinions may be biased.

Structured

This follows a rigid or set format. The interviewer will ask the same questions of each candidate, so making it easier to compare interviewees and draw conclusions. This does not allow for candidate individuality or for questioning of certain answers given on the application form.

Semi-structured

This means that a wide range of topics can be covered and that questions can be tailored to candidate requirements. It also allows for follow-up questions in certain areas and allows candidates to demonstrate their individuality. However, a clear focus has to be maintained, otherwise the emphasis may wander away from the subject.

Unstructured

This is really a conversation, as there are no specific topics or areas. The candidate has the opportunity to reveal a lot about himself, but this may also mean that the candidate can control which elements of his personality he does reveal – something that may be important to the organization.

As well as the candidate being well prepared, the interviewer also needs a good level of preparation. Apart from questions being decided

upon, the environment also needs to be checked. An appropriate-sized room should be booked and there should be no interruptions such as telephone calls. Before the interview, the interviewer should have read all the applications and prepared appropriate questions. In addition, he or she should also have a list of things to tell the candidate about the job and the company.

Task 2.15

By completing this task, it will lead to coverage of Element 2.3 PC 5, and Core Skills Communication Elements 3.1; 3.2; 3.3; and 3.4.

You are going to carry out a role-play for an interview process.

In small groups, decide who is going to be on the panel and who is going to be interviewed.

Decide on the format you are going to use and who is going to ask which questions.

What is the job they are applying for? What information will they need?

Present the exercise in front of the rest of your group/class.

Find out what they thought and where improvements could be made.

Evaluation techniques

The last part of the above task was about finding out from others how they felt your group performed. As both a candidate and an interviewer, there are various techniques that can be assessed and that will help in the situation.

The interviewer

Believe it or not, this is also a stressful role. We want to make the best decisions for the company and the individual and we do not want to look stupid in our choices. Many interviewers are just as nervous as the candidates.

We have already looked at the format of interviews, and it is important that, whichever is chosen, the style adopted is objective – in other words, the same for everyone.

Listening is a very important technique – how many people do you know who simply want to talk without really hearing what is being said?

So as well as phrasing questions so that people will understand what we are asking, we have to listen to the answers they give.

The interviewee

Job interviews can be extremely traumatic, especially if you really want the job. There are many different ways an interview could go, so you could help your confidence by being sure of the following:

- That you want the position
- That you understand the main details and conditions of the job
- That you are able to do the job
- That you will be an asset to the employer.

It may also help to try to remember the importance of the following:

- Keenness and enthusiasm
- Effort and responsibility
- Initiative and knowledge
- Reliability and discipline
- Listening and answering techniques.

We have mentioned non-verbal communication quite a lot, and this will be explored in greater detail in Unit 6, but remember, we tell people a lot about ourselves in the way we react non-verbally to situations.

Whichever job interviews you go for–GOOD LUCK–and, even if you are unsuccessful, remember that interview experience is never wasted. You may learn from the situation and decide to do something different next time.

Portfolio builder

If you have completed the tasks in this Element, you should have:

- Research, showing the range of vacancies in your area
- An equal opportunities policy
- A job description
- A person specification
- A CV
- Role-play evidence of interview processes.

These can go into your portfolio as evidence towards your qualification.

▪ Assignment 2.3 ▪

By completing this assignment, it will lead to coverage of Element 2.3 PCs 1, 2, 3, 4, 5, and 6, and Core Skills may include Communication Elements 3.1; 3.2; 3.3; and 3.4. and I.T. Elements 3.1; 3.2; 3.3; and 3.4.

Scenario

Recruitment is a very important process for any organization. If it is done incorrectly, the organization may have to live with the consequences for a long time. When it is correct, the organization can move from strength to strength, with the right people in the right jobs.

Details

1 Give a brief outline, in report form, of how recruitment and selection takes place within leisure and tourism. Explain the procedures involved and include relevant examples of advertisements, application forms, job descriptions, etc.
2 Describe the ethical and legal obligations that are included in recruitment and selection for the leisure and tourism industry.
3 When giving relevant examples, include one from a leisure aspect of the industry and one

from tourism. Compare and contrast the differences between the two areas.

4 In groups, devise an interview panel for a job within the industry. Produce an advertisement, application form, job description and specification.

5 Ask three people from another group to complete the application form.

6 Decide on interview panel roles, responsibilities and questions and interview your three candidates. Hopefully, this can be recorded in some way as evidence for your portfolios.

7 As a panel, decide who you would appoint and why.

8 Produce a report of your interview panel processes and justifications.

Note: EVERYONE in the group should be on a panel and should undergo the interview process. Remember, this experience may help when you are trying to obtain a job, so treat it seriously.

Element 2.4 Investigate workplace standards and performance in the leisure and tourism industries

Note: The work covered in this area relates closely to the information included in Unit 1 investigating health, safety and security in leisure and tourism.

In this Element we are going to be looking at working standards and how they are maintained in the industry. We are going to review specifically the following areas:

- The purpose of legislation in relation to work standards and conditions
- Standards of performance and behaviour
- Occupational standards
- Sources of information and advice.

The purpose of legislation

In this country the legal system falls into two separate categories:

- Criminal law
- Civil law.

Criminal law is handed down by elected officials to regulate individual behaviour. There are set punishments, depending on the amount or degree of injury, which include prison, probation, community service or fines. Prosecution, as a result of an offence, is carried out by an official body – that is, the police or Customs and Excise – and the prosecution is undertaken at the public expense.

Civil law deals with a collection of rules and principles which have developed since the Norman Conquest to regulate the relationships between individuals, public bodies and institutions.

There are various different categories. For example, law of contract regulates business dealings, while law of tort protects the individual against negligence and **defamation** (a slanderous statement). Here there are no set punishments but damages or **injunctions** (a writ of prohibition) depending on the seriousness of the offence.

Under civil law, any court cases are at the individual's expense – to sue someone, if the person bringing the case loses, they may have to pay the defendant's costs as well as their own.

Generally it will be civil law that governs the workplace. However, whichever aspect of the law is involved, the law is there to try to cover all eventualities, so preventing any problems arising.

Task 2.16

By completing the following task it will contribute to coverage of Element 2.4 PC 1, and Core Communication Skills 3.1; 3.2; 3.3; and 3.4.

Read the following statement, then answer the questions.

Extract from the Wages Council Act 1959, Licensed Residential and Licensed Restaurant Wages Council

Licensed restaurant does not include any place which forms part of a licensed residential establishment or which constitutes or forms part of a railway refreshment establishment or any place at which intoxicating liquor can legally be sold or supplied for consumption on the premises by reason only of the fact that in relation to that place an occasional licence is for the time being in force, being a licence granted to some person other than the person carrying on, or a person in the employment of the person carrying on the activities (other than the supply of intoxicating liquor) of a catering undertaking at that place.

1 What is a licensed restaurant?
2 List the examples that are not licensed restaurants.

Confused? I'm not really surprised if you are. This extract is written in such a general way as to try to cover all eventualities. We have all heard of 'loopholes' in the law and, as a result, a statement such as the example above is produced. No wonder we need legal experts!

Legislation is also necessary to protect people in the case of leisure and tourism this would be the employer, the employee and the customer. All these categories have rights and expectations under the law, which have to be complied with legally.

There is specific legislation that applies to the workplace, but we are going to concentrate on:

● Health and safety
● Employment.

Health and Safety at Work Act 1974 (HASAWA)

Everyone at work, except domestic servants in private households, is covered by this Act. It imposes a general duty of care on most people associated with work activities.

Its main aims are:

● Securing the health, safety and welfare of persons at work

● Protecting other people against the risk of harm from activities carried out at work
● Controlling the acquisition, storage, handling, transport and use of explosive and other dangerous articles and substances
● Controlling the emission into the atmosphere of noxious or offensive substances from any prescribed type of premises.

Responsibilities of employers to employees

All employers must ensure, so far as is reasonably practicable, the health, safety and welfare of employees. Employers are required to provide and maintain:

● Safe systems of work and plant
● Arrangements for the safe systems of use, handling, storage and transport of articles and substances
● Information, instruction, training and supervision as necessary to ensure the health and safety of employees
● A safe and healthy place of work and necessary means of access and exit
● Safe and healthy working conditions.

Responsibilities of employees

Every employee while at work must:

● Take reasonable care of the health and safety of himself and of other persons who may be affected by his acts or omissions at work
● Co-operate with his employer or anyone else who may have legal responsibilities, so far as is necessary, to enable them to comply with any duty or requirement imposed on them by this Act.

In other words, the employee also has to pay due care when at work. For example, if he is cleaning an area, it is his responsibility to use the hazard notices associated with the task because if an accident occurs, if someone slips on a wet floor and there is no hazard sign, the employee and the employer will then be liable.

Responsibilities to the consumer

Every employer must ensure, so far as is reasonably practicable, that persons not in his employment are not exposed to risk to their health and safety as a result of the work that he or his firm is doing.

An example from a leisure centre may be appropriate here. If a swimming pool does not have the correct levels of chlorine in it, it can cause problems. Chlorine gas is poisonous, so it is a hazardous substance. If the levels are too low, the chlorine will not inactivate micro-organisms, which is one of the reasons why it is put in to the water. If the levels are too high, chlorine can cause eye and mouth problems, so under the HASAWA the levels have to be closely monitored for both staff and consumers.

Fire Precautions Act 1971

If a fire occurs in a place where there are a lot of people, such as a nightclub, pub or busy leisure centre, then there could be tragic consequences. The Fire Precautions Act 1971 was passed to improve fire safety standards in premises that are used by the general public. Generally a Fire Certificate is required by most premises; however, there are a few exceptions. These include factory, office, shop and railway premises in which either no more than twenty people are employed to work at any one time, or where no more than ten people are employed to work other than on the ground floor.

Fire Certificate

An application for a Fire Certificate is made on the appropriate form to the local Fire Authority. The application will detail the type of business that the building is going to house and will also include information about the specification and structure of the building.

An inspection of the building will then be carried out and a Fire Certificate issued, provided that:

- There is a means of escape from the building if a fire breaks out
- The escape can be secured, but it can still be used safely and effectively at all necessary times
- Relevant fire-fighting equipment is provided and is functional

- Some sort of alarm system is provided should the need arise.

In other words, the premises must be reasonably equipped with fire-fighting facilities, it must have a means of escape and there must be an alarm system. If this is not provided, a criminal prosecution could result of 'persons failing to comply with the provisions of the Act'. It is also important that comprehensive fire insurance is obtained for the premises and its contents.

Employment legislation

Although we have to be aware of legislation relating to recruitment and selection of employees, such as racial discrimination, sex discrimination and equal opportunities, it is important that employers are familiar with the Trade Union Reform and Employment Rights Act 1993, which brought together all the legislation on employees, rather than with the previous separate Acts.

Terms of employment

This is generally called a contract of employment. Under the legislation above, from 30 November 1993 all new employees whose employment continues for a month or more are entitled to a contract. This must be provided within two months of the employee starting work.

Sometimes employers may issue a written statement, and legally this is different from a contract. A contract, whether verbal or in writing, is legally binding, whereas a written statement of particulars is just a statement 'for information only'.

The statement can be provided in instalments over a three-month period, rather than all at once. However, whichever method is decided upon, there are various items necessary to form a contract.

The main aspect or the **principal statement** contains the following information.

1 The names of the employer and the employee.
2 The date when employment began.
3 The date at which the employee's period of continuous employment began. (This would be

Fire action
Any person discovering a fire
1. Sound the alarm.
2. [   ] to call fire brigade.
3. Attack the fire if possible using the appliances provided.

On hearing the fire alarm
4. Leave building by [   ] route.
5. Close all doors behind you.
6. Report to assembly point.

[   ]

Do not take risks.
Do not return to the building for any reason until authorised to do so.

Do not use lifts.

Figure 2.12   Fire instructions

important if someone had gained promotion within the company.)

4 The scale or rate of pay, or the way it is worked out.

5 Pay intervals (hourly, weekly, monthly).

6 Terms and conditions relating to hours of work, including normal working hours.

7 Terms and conditions relating to holiday entitlements, including public holidays and holiday pay. (This should also include rules on the entitlement to accrued holiday pay on the termination of the employment.) These rules must be clear enough to allow the entitlement to be calculated.

8 Job title or brief job description.

9 Place of work, or, if the employee is required to work at various places, an indication of this and the employer's address.

The extra information required within two months includes:

1 Any terms and conditions relating to sickness/injury, including sick pay.

2 Rules on pensions and pension schemes additional to the statutory scheme.

3 Length of notice required to be given by the employer and the employee.

4 If the contract is temporary, an indication must be given of the expected duration or the end date of a fixed-term contract.

5 Particulars of any collective agreements which directly affect the terms and conditions of employment.

6 If an employee is expected to work outside the UK for a period of more than one month, details of the length of posting, the currency in which payment will be made, details of additional benefits arising from the posting and any terms and conditions relating to the employee's return to the UK.

7 Disciplinary rules and the disciplinary appeals procedure.

In addition to civil law requirements, there are also **common law** obligations. So, having signed your contract, it is important to be aware of other aspects such as:

- Obeying lawful orders
- Giving careful service

- Being loyal to the employer
- Accounting to the employer for any loss or damage caused through negligence.

Just as the employee has responsibilities, so, too, does the employer. These include:

- Payment of the agreed remuneration (wages or salary)
- Provision of safe working conditions for the employee
- Observation of all laws relating to the maintenance of welfare and safety conditions (statutory sick pay, Health and Safety at Work Act, etc.).

Hopefully, many years of happy and productive service will follow.

Maternity rights

Female employees who satisfy particular qualifying conditions, such as a minimum of two years' continuous service with the organization, may be entitled to receive certain statutory payments during a period of absence due to pregnancy or confinement and have the right to return to work after the pregnancy. However, although the terms and conditions that the woman returns to must be 'no less favourable', she does not necessarily have to return to the job she vacated. A position must be available to her, but not necessarily her 'old' job.

Paternity rights

Many organizations are now introducing these rights for fathers; however, they are an individual concession, not a right. Usually the company allows an extra week in addition to normal holidays when the baby arrives.

Standards of performance and behaviour

Wherever we finally gain employment, there will always be workplace rules and standards with which we are expected to comply. These are present to ensure that certain levels of performance are maintained by everyone and that everyone is treated fairly.

Individual companies will vary in what they expect their personnel to do and the way they expect them to do it; however, there will be basic similarities between all organizations.

Many of the standards of behaviour expected from employees will be fairly obvious, but the following list may give some insight.

- *Attendance* – This will be very closely monitored. Again, there exist many ways of indicating that you are present at work – you may be expected to 'sign in', or you may be on some type of flexible working that allows you to accrue hours for time off. This will also register your presence or otherwise. A security card to gain entry to a building or reserved area may also be linked into a registration area. However, whichever method is used, if you are off work for any reason, such as sickness, that has not been agreed before the day, you will be expected to notify someone in the organization. This is usually your supervisor, who will then notify the personnel department. Attendance and sickness will always be monitored, and if they prove to be a problem further steps may be taken.
- *Timekeeping* – Again, records of this will be kept in different ways – either manually, such as signing in or out, or computerized, such as a flexi-time scheme. This is useful for both the organization and the individual to keep a check on the hours worked and to monitor any overtime payments claimed and made.
- *Dress* – Dress codes will exist and will be in line with the job you hold. Some organizations will provide a uniform, others will not. If you have contact with customers, you will be expected to have a smart, clean appearance, as well as a helpful attitude, whether the company provides uniforms or not.
- *Attitude* – This falls under two headings – attitude towards customers and attitude towards other staff. We are in a service industry, giving service to other people. The business we generate is more than the product

offered and can mean the difference between people returning to use the facilities or not. Therefore, although the customer is not always right, there are ways of dealing with people which are appropriate to the situation. Other staff may also become customers at different times and would expect to be treated accordingly. Also, it is likely to be stated in your contract that certain actions towards other staff, such as hitting them, are not allowed and could result in disciplinary action.
Attitude will be dealt with in greater detail in Unit 6, Customer Service.
- *Responsibilities to the work environment* – We have already looked at the Health and Safety at Work legislation and noted that we all have certain responsibilities under this legislation to ensure everyone's safety, including our own. However, this can also be extended to include a pleasant working environment in which we feel happy. There is nothing worse than graffiti everywhere and broken furniture. Although an extreme case, it can be scaled down – for example, if you are working in an area that is used by a lot of staff, and you are sharing documents, paperwork, phones, etc., such as in a reception area. We all have responsibilities to work as efficiently as possible, and and this may prove difficult in an untidy area.
Organizations also need to keep **records** – not only for their own purposes, but also for legal requirements. For example, they need to keep records of staff wages for themselves and also legally, so that eventually the Tax Office can check how much income tax has been deducted directly from wages.

Other records are also kept on employees, and this is one of the main functions of the personnel department. In small companies, apart from basic details and the necessary wage records, the employer will probably rely on memory and personal contact for information concerning the employee. In larger establishments, the information is likely to be held on computerized databases, which can speed up processes and prove more efficient.
- *Attendance records* – We have already reviewed attendance. These records will be necessary for

a variety of purposes, including sick pay, holidays, etc.

- *Performance records and appraisal* – It is important that any workforce is able to meet the demands and expectations of the organization, and that employees achieve the performance or productivity levels that the company has agreed with the workforce. Therefore, it is important that people know what the organization is aiming for, but this needs to be broken down into achievable segments which are delegated to the appropriate teams. Records need to be updated regularly to show whether this is being achieved or not.

Feedback and assessment of individual's work is also very important. Here individuals are made aware of the clearly defined aims that the organization has for them. By carrying out an appraisal of the work performance these aims can be recognized. Here standards will be defined and targets set for individuals and teams to work towards, and the appraisal system is the monitor of how effectively the targets have been met. This also gives a basis for the modification of the individual's performance if standards are not being maintained, and so it may be used as a system of control. This also provides an avenue for supervisors feedback to the individual.

- *Disciplinary matters and grievances* – Legally there is a wide range of responsibilities placed on the employer to provide employees with fair and just conditions of employment and safeguards against unfair dismissal and discrimination. It is important that this procedure is only taken after the case has been thoroughly investigated and grounds for action established, and that employees are not simply dismissed for a minor breach of discipline, except in the case of gross misconduct such as theft, etc.

The system should allow for employees to know that a complaint has been made against them and to respond to this with their case before a decision to proceed is made. The employee has the right to be accompanied by a 'friend', who is either a trade union representative or a fellow employee, when stating their case. Employees should also know the penalties that can be imposed and be told about the appeals procedure.

Grievance procedures have been developed to maintain satisfactory working relationships between employees. Therefore, if a problem arises with the terms and conditions of employment, working conditions, methods of work or any other aspect of employment, employees know that they can discuss these issues. There should be recognized stages in the procedure, although it is important to try to resolve the problem as near to the point of origin as possible. People dealing with grievances obviously need training in this area.

Task 2.17

By completing this task, it will lead to coverage of Element 2.4 PC 2, and Core Communication Skills 3.1; 3.2; 3.3; and 3.4.

Find out how the industry deals with disciplinary issues and grievances.

From your research, draw up a comprehensive disciplinary procedure that allows for different levels of grievance.

Then draw up a grievance procedure that is fair and allows problems to be resolved.

These procedures can be placed in your portfolio of evidence to be presented in your claim for your qualification.

- *Employee Charters and Customer Charters* – In these documents information is given about the customer's entitlement to the highest standards of service which will be fulfilled by the vendor or service, etc. There are many examples of customer charter available which state information and indicate compensation available if the service is not up to standard. There may even be a Students' Charter at your school or college. If so, what information does it include?

Occupational standards

Occupational standards, as the term suggests, indicate the levels to which employees should be working. They have generally been agreed with the workforce through the unions and give clearly defined levels of expertise.

On a larger scale, the industry will also have developed standards that employees should work towards, so that someone giving a product or service in one part of the country will be providing a largely similar product or service in another. In other words, we are talking about standardizing levels of provision on a voluntary basis, which is what many organizations are attempting to do.

In addition, the way in which the qualification system is developing in this country allows for the standardization of skills levels, particularly in the area of National Vocational Qualifications (NVQs). These are skills-based qualifications that can be taken as levels of competence in certain areas.

Task 2.18

By completing this task it will lead to coverage of Element 2.4 PC 3. and Core Elements may include Communication Elements 3.1; 3.2; and 3.4.

Why do you think we need to have occupational standards?

What benefits are there for the organization and the individual?

We are now going to review some of the points that you have raised.

For the individual, qualifications can be used as an indication of levels of knowledge or competence within that industry. However, these are a means to an end, and can be useful in ensuring that you obtain an interview, but how you perform in that situation and at work if you get the job indicate the real standards. The qualifications are simply a key to open up opportunities for you. You will also learn a tremendous amount once you do start work.

Qualifications, along with experience, may also allow access to promotion, so again, if standards are defined, this can be used to advantage by the individual. These standards can also be used by individuals to give them confidence in themselves and in the service they are giving to customers and the organization, which hopefully, if all factors work together, will allow for recognition of the individual.

Skills gained in an employment situation will also be transferable to other situations, and those skills can lead to individual enrichment.

Quality is something which is very important in all aspects of service and, again, is something that industry is aiming to standardize. This can be done in various ways, and recognized awards, such as Investors in People, are something that many organizations are working towards. Under such schemes, organizations have to carry out certain processes to allow individuals to develop, to acknowledge good practice and to overcome aspects of bad practice that may exist.

We have already discussed appraisal schemes and their function, but they are evidence that occupational standards are being applied to the workforce.

Training needs of individuals are another area of concern, and the assessment of training needs of individuals, carried out on a regular basis, is important. In some organizations this has been extended into a skills audit or a training needs analysis to highlight any areas that require development. Moreover, if this is carried out by job function on a regular basis, it can be used to develop on-going job descriptions for later use.

Sources of information and advice

There are many different sources of information available to help you in different situations, whether you are an employer or an employee.

At a national level in industry, employers are represented by the Confederation of British Industry (CBI) and employees by the Trades Union Congress (TUC). We are now going to review some of the organizations available to offer help.

Trade associations

These are voluntary bodies of independent organizations formed to protect and advance the interests of their members. Trade associations are based both locally and nationally and are non-profit-making.

As well as having a protective role, trade associations have developed a range of services available to their members, such as product and service information. They will also negotiate with other official bodies.

Publications

Although not linked to trade associations, trade publications often take up issues on behalf of the industry and provide a role for their readership, whichever association they may belong to. Examples include *Leisure Management, Leisure Opportunities* and the *Leisure Manager*.

Professional bodies

A professional body is an organization of individuals who are employed within a particular occupation, and who have gained qualifications or experience within that occupation. The professional body will lay down standards by which members have to qualify for membership and these standards will be based on knowledge, expertise and competence to carry out the occupation. It will also set a code of conduct for its members to abide by in order to retain their membership.

Membership of a trade association is related to the business which is the qualification for membership, while a professional body represents an individual who will carry membership from one position to another. Some professional bodies require academic qualifications to a certain level, either from a recognized examination body or through their own qualifications; others may require experience to gain entry. In most professional bodies there are different levels of membership, ranging from Student or Associate to Fellowship, and it is possible to progress from one level to another, subject to certain requirements.

The principal association for the leisure and tourism industry is the Institute for Leisure and Amenity Management (ILAM). Another example is the Institute for Entertainment and Arts Management (IEAM).

Trade unions

As the leisure industry is relatively young, the involvement of trade unions is fairly limited. The union's main function is to represent its members, the employees, in all kinds of matters. Its expertise is called upon when problems or disputes arise, to help resolve them.

The Advisory Conciliation and Arbitration Service (ACAS) also exists to help resolve disputes between employers and employees. It is totally independent and neutral, and tries to help both parties to find common ground on which to build. However, it has no legal authority and is only called into a dispute if both sides agree.

Legal advice

There may be some situations that require legal advice. If you are not in a trade union, and therefore not eligible for its assistance, there are still other options available. The Citizens' Advice Bureau is a voluntary organization that will give advice on situations regarding rights and obligations as well as financial information.

Portfolio builder

If you have completed the tasks in this Element, you should have:

- A knowledge of disciplinary and grievance procedures
- A knowledge of occupational standards.

These can go into your portfolio as evidence towards your qualification.

▪ Assignment 2.4 ▪

By completing this assignment, it will lead to coverage of Element 2.4 PCs 1, 2, 3, 4, and 5, and Core Skills may include Communication Elements 3.1; 3.2; 3.3; and 3.4., and I.T. Elements 3.1; 3.2; 3.3; and 3.4.

Scenario

There has been a good deal of research carried out into staff turnover which has revealed that the highest turnover occurs during the first two months of employment in a new company/job. This possibly indicates that proper induction procedures are beneficial to the organization and the job.

Details

Once new staff have been appointed to a job, they need to be given a short training period aimed at familiarizing them with certain things.

A Research within the industry and produce an induction booklet for new staff. The booklet needs to include:

1 Company policies.
2 Rules, procedures and workplace standards.
3 An overview of the company's activities.
4 The range of products and services.
5 The structure and organization systems.
6 Introductions to the employee's section of work.

B Write a brief report, explaining in general terms the following:

1 The purpose of legislation relating to workplace standards and conditions in leisure and tourism.
2 Procedures for maintaining standards of performance and behaviour.
3 The benefits of occupational standards.
4 Sources of information and advice available in the industry.

MARKETING IN LEISURE AND TOURISM

Element 3.1 Marketing principles, activities and objectives in leisure and tourism

In this Element we are going to:

- Explain the principles of marketing
- Explain the marketing activities carried out in leisure & tourism organizations
- Describe key marketing objectives
- Explain the elements of marketing strategy
- Explain how organizations grow through the development of products and markets
- Account for factors influencing pricing decisions.

What is marketing?

There are many misconceptions as to what marketing is. Most people not involved professionally in marketing tend to think of the subject as being something to do with research, selling and promotion. This is not really surprising, since each day we are bombarded with TV commercials, posters, news ads, mail shots and people trying to sell us something. Although very important aspects of marketing in leisure and tourism, they are nevertheless simply parts of a much wider marketing mix of activities that work together to affect the market place.

Marketing has been defined as

A social and management process by which individuals and groups obtain what they want through creating and exchanging products and values with markets to everyone's satisfaction.

In its basic form, marketing is a philosophy of business which puts the customer and potential customer at the center of the organization's decision making. It works on the premise that companies without customers have no business. The function of marketing is, therefore, everything to do with business which attracts and keeps customers. This supports the core concept of marketing, which is concerned with getting the right product to the right customer at the right price at the right place and time.

There are several principles that need to be explained in supporting this concept which are illustrated in Figure 3.1 opposite.

The key marketing principles

Needs and wants

All people have needs, which can come in many forms, such as *physical needs* for food or water, warmth and security; *individual needs* for status and self-fulfilment; and *social needs* for love and affection. Maslow put forward the theory of a Hierarchy of Needs, which stated that a person's needs must be satisfied in some hierarchical order starting first with physical needs and then followed by social and psychological needs, as shown in Figure 3.2 opposite:

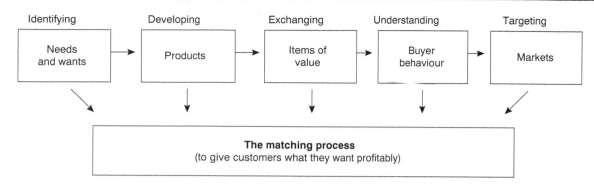

Figure 3.1

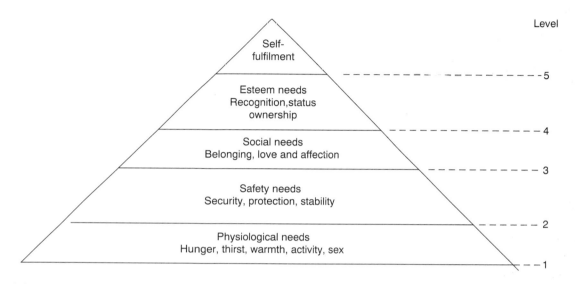

Figure 3.2

Maslow believed the order of the levels of need to be important. As needs at level 1 are satisfied, so those on the next level become more dominant, and so on.

When someone has a need they seek some object to satisfy that need. However, where a person has a choice of objects to satisfy a need, then they express their needs as wants. A thirsty person may need a drink, but wants a beer, a coke, possibly a cup of tea to satisfy the need.

Most people have lots of wants, but unfortunately cannot always afford what they want for lack of money. However, when you have the money to back up your desires, then wants become demands. Demand in the leisure and tourism industry can be expressed in many ways, such as the number of nights spent in different accommodation, the number of visits to the UK by overseas visitors, the amount spent on tourist attractions in a year.

- *Family holiday insurance for travelling abroad*
- *Wearing a well known expensive perfume/aftershave*
- *Buying a suntan lotion.*

1 *List your requirements as to what you expect from the product before you buy or take part in the activity.*
2 *State your needs and wants in relation to Maslow's Hierarchy of Needs.*

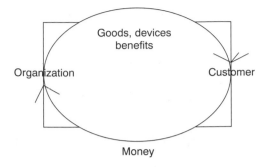

Figure 3.3 Exchanging things of value

Products

People seek products and services in order to satisfy their needs and wants. This being the case, companies have to develop products that people want in order to stay in business. Of course, not all products or services are equally desirable. Different products offer different benefits, either real or perceived, which make them stand apart from other products. For example, some people choose to travel by train for speed, others for comfort, reliability or safety.

Anything that can satisfy a need can be called a product. So, in addition to goods and services, we can also include people, places, activities and ideas. The customer basically decides, for example, which holiday destinations to travel to, which bands to listen to on the radio, or whether to buy a lottery ticket or spend his money on an hour's swimming. If the item on offer is of value to the customer, then it is a product.

Exchange

Marketing has been said to occur when people decide to satisfy their needs and wants through exchange. Exchange is the social act of obtaining a product from someone by offering something of value in return (i.e. money). Normally, in addition to actual money spent it is necessary to invest time in studying holiday brochures or visiting a travel agent or other outlets. This two-way exchange process is illustrated in Figure 3.3 below.

People choose to buy products which they perceive will provide the greatest value satisfaction for what they can afford. Organizations must, therefore, know what

customers want, what they judge to be of value, in order to create the products that will satisfy their wants. The Camping and Caravanning Club, for example, follows up all its holiday bookings by sending out a questionnaire to its customers which seeks to obtain information as to what they liked or disliked about their holiday and what improvements could be made. By carrying out this research the company can hopefully identify those aspects of the offering that its customers deemed of value to them.

In seeking exchange, all leisure and tourism organizations are trying to elicit some behavioural response from their markets, namely by buying their products.

Buyer behaviour

There are two fundamental questions we need to ask in understanding what makes people buy:

- How does the market buy?
- Who buys?

How does the market buy?

The process by which buying decisions are made is illustrated in Figure 3.4.

The model shows the buyer passing through a series of stages in order to reach a purchase decision. It also highlights the fact that the buying process starts long before actual purchase and continues after purchase in affecting future purchase decisions.

The process begins with a recognition of a problem or a need being felt for a particular product or service. This is usually stimulated by

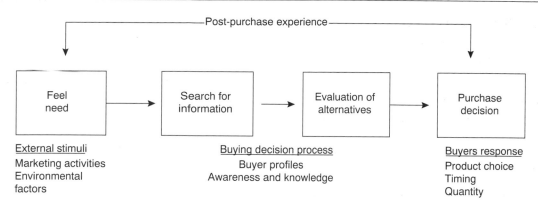

Figure 3.4

some external stimuli. For example, having recently taken the children paddling at a local seaside resort, a leaflet arrives next day through the mail offering swimming lessons for beginners. The parent feels a need for the children to be safe in water and believes it is his or her responsibility to ensure that they learn to swim.

Having identified the problem, the next step is information search, which is where the buyer (parent) seeks further details of what type or form of swimming lessons are being offered or are available elsewhere. Having identified the alternatives, the buyer must decide which type of swimming lessons to book for the children. The decision, of course, may be not to book the lessons at all or put off the decision to a later date. However, having chosen to book the lessons, the time and place, etc., the buyer, in consultation with the children, will reflect on the decision as to whether they are satisfied or dissatisfied with the experience.

What determines buyer satisfaction is the customer's expectations of the product's performance. These expectations are based on messages received from the organization, such as via the leaflet received, other commercials, from friends and relatives or other stimuli. It is very important that customers are at the very least satisfied, at best delighted with their purchase, for the reason that company sales come from two basic groups:

- New customers
- Repeat customers.

By giving customers the satisfaction they seek, they not only repeat their purchases but tell others about the product and so encourage new customers to try it.

Task 3.2

As customers, we are sometimes more or less satisfied with our leisure experiences. From the list below, state whether you were satisfied or not with your last visit to these leisure providers:

	Satis-fied	Dis-satisfied	Action
1. Bowling alley			
2. Cinema			
3. Air travel abroad			
4. Leisure centre			
5. Library			
6. Museum			

Give your reasons and state what actions, if any, the leisure provider could take to improve the leisure experience.

Who buys?

It is interesting to note that in the example above of the parent booking swimming lessons, the child is the user while the parent is the customer or buyer of the product. In families as in business, different members can play different roles in the purchase of a product or service. These roles can be identified on five levels, as shown in Figure 3.5.

Consider the decision to book a family holiday in the USA. The idea may come from the family members or it could come from some marketing stimuli such as a leaflet, brochure or holiday commercial. The influencer could be a holiday programme on America or possibly a neighbour, friend or relative who has been on holiday there themselves, or even the local travel agent. The final decision to buy may be that of the husband or wife or both equally, as might the actual act of buying. The final user is likely to be the whole family. Given the number of possibilities, it is important that holiday companies determine who plays what roles in the purchase decision because it can affect product design as well as advertising messages. If the holiday company finds that the wife makes the key decision as to which holiday to book, it will design and direct most of its messages towards women. Of course, husbands, children and others who might influence the decision will also be included, particularly when it comes to designing the holiday product with features which will attract these participants.

Market

The words 'customer' and 'market' are often interchanged to mean the same thing. The word 'customer' in this text is used to describe any individual or organization buying or using a product or service.

The word 'market', although it can be used to describe a place where buyers and sellers meet to exchange goods and services, also represents a set of potential and actual buyers and users of a product.

In the private sector, customers are those who purchase leisure goods and services, such as

Buying Roles	Description
Initiator	– Person who first suggests or thinks of an idea to purchase a specific leisure product
Influencer	– Person whose opinions carry some weight in the final decision
Decider	– Person who ultimately decides what and how to buy
Purchaser	– Person who buys
User	– Person who consumes or uses the product

Figure 3.5 Buying roles

tennis racquets, a holiday abroad, a drink in the pub. In the public and voluntary sectors, however, a customer could be a purchaser or simply a user of the product.

Offering a product or service to everyone presupposes that all customers are the same and will receive the same benefit or satisfaction from it. Not everyone wants to go on holiday abroad, to the cinema or to a theme park. The characteristics of customers in terms of their age, sex, home address, social class, will vary, depending on the leisure and tourism experiences and facilities on offer. Customer expectations regarding a particular tourist destination or leisure facilities will also be different, depending on the customer's social and cultural background, education and religion.

Libraries, museums, galleries and theatres are often frequented by people of higher education levels. People with large incomes often seek higher grade hotels and restaurants and more expensive tours because they expect a better level of service and interest.

Building up profiles of customers helps organizations to divide up their markets and so better understand what it is their customers want. For example, buyers of various models of cars, records, fashion products, often tell us something about the types of people they are. Think of products or services you use which reflect on your personality. They may include your clothes, hairstyle the holidays you take.

Marketing organizations have long recognized that there are few products or services that can attract everyone successfully.

Task 3.3

Imagine you are the manager of a local multiplex cinema involved in programming the films to be screened. Popular as they may be, would you wish to screen only action films, or would there be other types of films you would wish to show?

1 Identify any other types of films and draw up a profile of the customers who you think would want to see them.

2 How might the needs and the profiles of these customers differ from those watching the action films?

As can be seen from the task above, there are very often sub-groups to your market who have different needs. Why not offer these sub-groups different products and services? Dividing up markets into sub-groups or segments is an activity called market segmentation.

The great advantage of this marketing activity is that it focuses the organization into identifying exactly which market and what needs it intends to serve. It helps organizations to refine their offer; for example, a leisure pool facility may consider whether it is more profitable or efficient to offer swimming facilities for mums and toddlers (segment) during certain times of the day rather than have the baths open to the general public, or it could choose to operate special events (swimming gala) in order to attract clubs (segment). In effect, the organization uses segmentation to target its customers.

Matching customer needs

Of course, there will be times when the organizations capabilities in terms of resources and skills are not sufficient for it to best supply the customers needs, and so it will have to look elsewhere for its business.

The most successful leisure and tourism organizations are marketing-orientated, in that they look at what they are doing from the customer's point of view rather than their own. The reason for their success is really straightforward:

- The more organizations find out about potential customer needs, wants, perceptions, buying roles and anything else relevant to their buying decisions, the easier it is for them to promote their products
- Actually finding out what customers want first and then giving them what they want is inevitably more profitable than merely producing what you think they may want and then trying to convince them to buy when they do not immediately respond.

These activities are called the marketing process, which, if successful, should result in both satisfied customers and organizational objectives being met.

Consider Blackpool Pleasure Beach, which in terms of numbers of visits is the UK's biggest and most famous leisure park. Traditional it may be, but in terms of meeting customers' needs for exciting thrills it constantly assesses its market in order to find out how well it is matching its offer to what the customer wants. The latest of its white knuckle rides 'Pepsi Max', which opened in 1994, is an example of its commitment to stay No. 1 in the minds of its market for spectacular thrills.

Task 3.4

From the list of leisure and tourism organizations below, decide which target markets are a good match for what the organizations are offering:

*Leisure and tourism
    organizations*

*Saga Holidays
Mecca Social Clubs
Alton Towers
Butlins Sun Worlds
Camping and
    caravanning clubs
Fred Olsen Cruises
Give reasons for the
    markets chosen.*

Target markets

The matching or marketing process is at the heart of the marketing concept, and how it is achieved is illustrated below in Figure 3.6.

The start of the marketing process is identification, via market research, of who the customers or potential customers are, their needs and wants. These will be assessed against the company's own objectives and resources and skills available in determining whether the company is in the business of serving such customers. Successful matching depends upon how well customer needs are assessed and analysed and then how capable the company is of developing an acceptable offering to meet those needs. The process relies not simply on developing the right product, but also ensuring that the customer is aware that the product is on offer at an acceptable price and is available at a location and time to meet his or her requirements. These particular aspects of the marketing process are called the four Ps, which stand for:

- Product
- Price
- Place
- Promotion.

Together they form the main elements of the marketing mix.

Marketing mix

The marketing mix refers to the tools of marketing – the activities which the organization

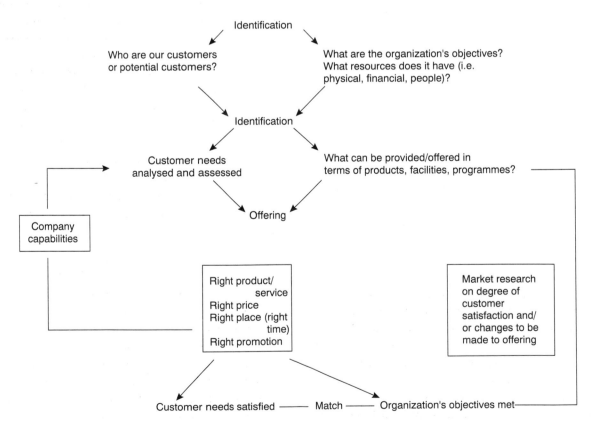

Figure 3.6 The matching process

uses to influence customer demand for its products and services. Together with the four Ps they are like the ingredients of a cake mix, each dependent on the others for its contribution. Think of a baker, who needs the right balance of ingredients mixed in the right way to satisfy different customers' tastes. The skill lies not just in the baking, but in anticipating what your customers want or prefer in satisfying their needs.

Product

The term 'product' covers a wide range of goods and services. Below are a few examples of leisure and tourism products:

Goods	Services
Cricket bat	Concert
Rugby shirt	Rugby match
Beach mat	Film
Leisure centre	5-a-side football
Night club	Show
Hotel	Package holiday
Swimming pool	Coaching
Theme park	Rollercoaster ride

Most products are physical or tangible, such as trainers, a beach ball, a hotel or leisure centre, but services such as being served at a bar, a concert or a 5-a-side session are also products (sometimes called service products).

The service product in effect consists of a set of satisfactions which the organization delivers to the customer. These satisfactions or characteristics can include quality of service, the standard of facilities, atmosphere, friendliness of staff, even image.

Many leisure and tourism services are intangible. You can't, for example, touch or see a package holiday, a session on the 5-a-side pitch – you can, however, experience it. These services are also perishable. Unlike a tin of beans, you cannot store a session on a 5-a-side pitch, a cinema seat or a bowling alley lane. An unsold train ticket cannot be resold the next day. Services also involve people, which means that it is difficult to ensure the quality of service, time and time again.

Customers who do not receive the service they expect will often go elsewhere. Training in customer care is a necessary requirement in successful product/service management.

Task 3.5

In small groups, identify and list the product/service characteristics you expect to find at:-

- *a theme park*
- *a nightclub*
- *on a Channel ferry.*

Price

Of all the ingredients of the marketing mix, price is the one which creates sales revenue – all the others create costs. It is only through the prices an organization charges that it is able to cover its costs by generating revenue, thereby satisfying its own aims for profit. However, organizations have to be aware of the value which customers place on their products and services, i.e. what they are willing to pay for them. The prices charged in the leisure and tourism industry often varies for the same product at different times of the year, week, even day. Train fares can cost up to four times as much at peak hour travelling time at, say, 7.00 a.m.–9.00 a.m. and 4.00 p.m.–7.00 p.m. than at some other times of the day. Channel ferries will cut their prices by up to 75 percent in the off-peak months of January to March, compared with July and August.

Promotion

Promotion is a term given to a collection of techniques which an organization uses to communicate either directly or indirectly with its markets. In its most basic form, promotion is concerned with telling customers about our products and services in the hope of influencing their perceptions and behaviour. In simple terms, people are unlikely to buy your products or services if they have never heard of them.

Needless to say, we cannot promote our services until the product, price and place have been determined. When they are, it is important to use promotion to attract our customers by creating favourable images of what our organization and its products can do for them.

The aims of promotion include, for example:

- To maintain and expand sales of an existing product or brand, e.g. increase numbers of visitors to ride on Nemesis
- To maintain or expand the organization's share of a particular market, e.g. Channel ferry operator seeking to maintain or increase its share of the number of holiday makers crossing the Channel each year
- To create a favourable image of the organization and its products, e.g. 'British Airways, the world's favourite airline'.

Figure 3.7 highlights some of the main promotional methods or techniques used.

Place

Place is concerned with getting the right product to your customers at the right time. The leisure product or service will not be of much use to the customer if it isn't located where people expect to find it or made available when they want it.

Most services, such as a game of squash, a football match, a concert, are sold at the place where they are produced. However, most products are made some distance away from the

place where customers want to buy them. The principal objective of place is, therefore, to do with distributing the product to a place where the customer wants to buy it.

In achieving this objective, distribution of leisure and tourism products is concerned with:

- *Transportation* – ensuring that the product is delivered to the right place at the right time
- *Packaging and display* – trying to make the product more manageable in terms of the space it takes up in the shop, how it can be stored or displayed
- *Stock holding* – ensuring that there is sufficient stock of hotel beds, airline seats, tennis racquets, football boots available in readiness for when customers want to buy them
- *Communication* – providing advice on availability of tickets for a large event, delays on arrival times and for handling complaints.

Not all leisure and tourism organizations have the finance or resources to provide all the above functions. An airline wanting to sell flights direct to the public would have to provide a network of shops in all the major cities in the UK and abroad in order to sell its flight tickets. It could sell direct by accepting bookings over the phone or through the mail, but is this the place where the customer wants to do business? Imagine if each airline had its own distribution system – the cost of providing the tickets would be extremely high and would duplicate the retailing effort. Some products are sold direct; the majority pass through a chain of intermediary organizations who deliver the product to the customer. Figure 3.8 highlights the key distribution channels involved.

If we use the example of an airline once again, the airline is the producer of a transport product or seat. The airline can sell its seats in a number of ways:

- *Direct to the customer* – possibly at the airport or by direct booking
- *Through a retailer* – 70–80 per cent of airline seats are sold at travel agents
- *Via a wholesaler* – large numbers of airline seats are sold to tour operators, who in turn use these seats to create package tours

Indirect (mass selling approach)	Direct (personal approach)
Advertising – TV, radio, newspapers etc.	Personal selling
Publicity	Telephone selling
Point of sale – displays, posters	Direct mail
Merchandizing	Sales promotion – exhibitions
Packaging	Press conferences,
Competitions	visits
Free gifts	
Sponsorship	

Figure 3.7

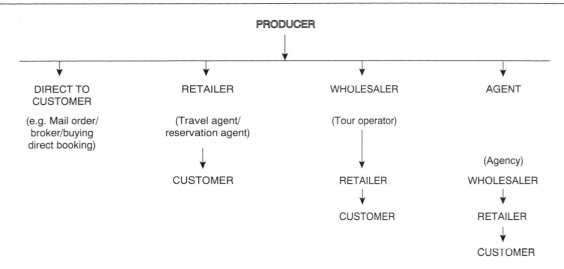

PRODUCER

DIRECT TO CUSTOMER	RETAILER	WHOLESALER	AGENT
(e.g. Mail order/ broker/buying direct booking)	(Travel agent/ reservation agent)	(Tour operator)	
			(Agency)
	CUSTOMER	RETAILER	WHOLESALER
		CUSTOMER	RETAILER
			CUSTOMER

Figure 3.8 Channels of distribution

- *Via an agent* – Agents or airbrokers often purchase large numbers of seats at bulk prices on behalf of several smaller tour operators so as to share the risk of not selling all the seats.

Task 3.6

In groups, consider what distribution channels could be chosen by leisure and tourism producers to sell the following:

- *Hotels in seaside towns with empty rooms available for letting*
- *Unbooked theatre seats*
- *Packaged holidays abroad*
- *Cruises on the Norfolk Broads.*

Individually, consider the role played by the following in the distribution of leisure and tourism services:

- *Reservations agency*
- *Travel agent*
- *Tour operator.*

Location plays a major part in the success of leisure and tourism. Consider how many more people would be able to use the National Gallery in London if it could be transported around the country at dates and times to suit all. Leisure and tourism providers very often rely on customers visiting their locations. However, where there is a large range of leisure products or activities available in a location, such as a town centre, leisure complex, shopping area, people/customers will be prepared to travel several miles to it.

Task 3.7

In small groups, examine the following leisure organizations and decide where best to locate them, giving reasons why:

1 *Tour operator*
2 *Further education college*
3 *International hotel*
4 *Travel agent specializing in exotic holidays/business trips*
5 *Theme park.*

Some possible choices of location are given (town/city centre; edge of town; countryside; suburb; near major motorways/airports; location not important).

Choosing the wrong location can be a serious error for many tourism and leisure organizations.

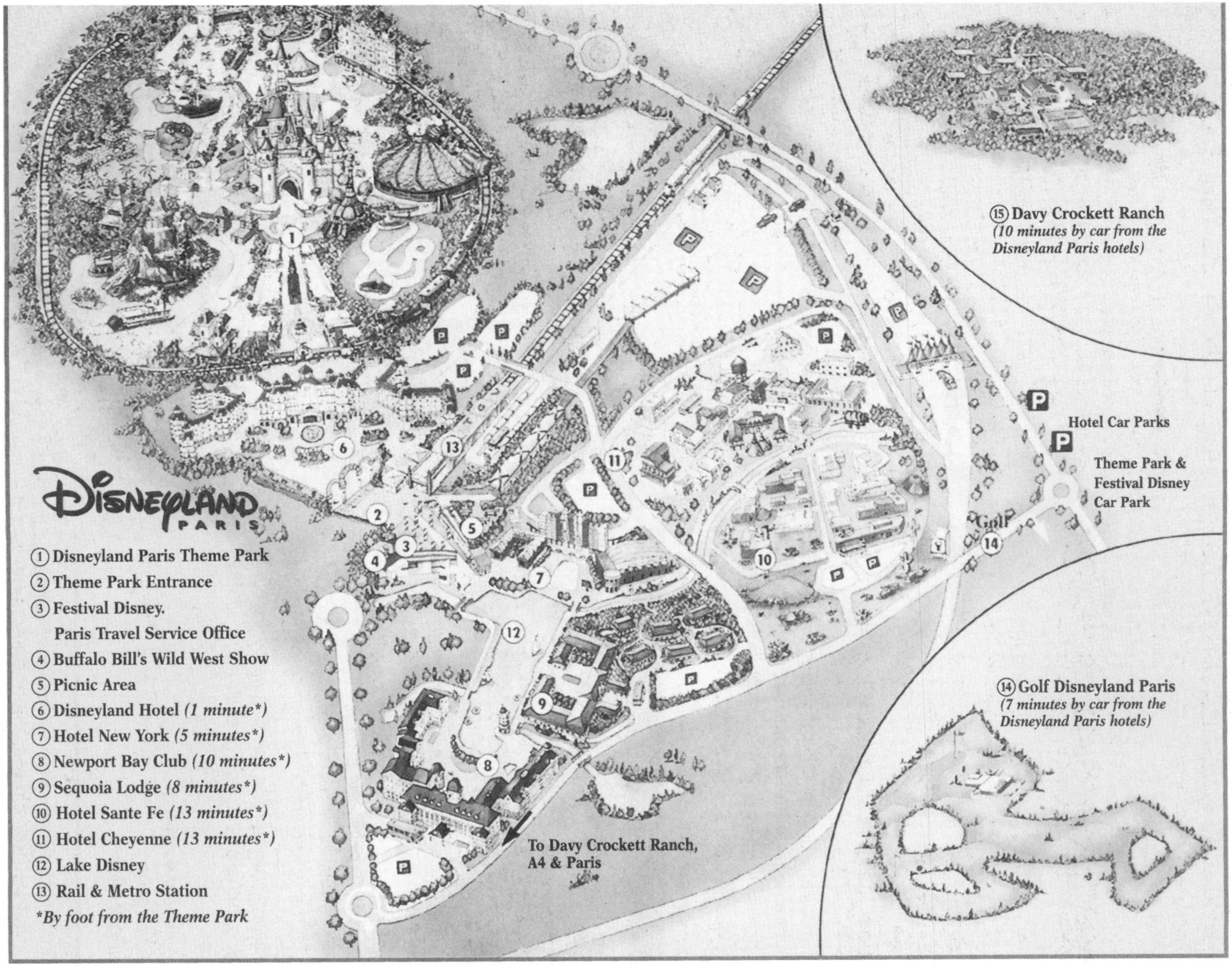

Disneyland Paris

1. Disneyland Paris Theme Park
2. Theme Park Entrance
3. Festival Disney,
   Paris Travel Service Office
4. Buffalo Bill's Wild West Show
5. Picnic Area
6. Disneyland Hotel (1 minute*)
7. Hotel New York (5 minutes*)
8. Newport Bay Club (10 minutes*)
9. Sequoia Lodge (8 minutes*)
10. Hotel Sante Fe (13 minutes*)
11. Hotel Cheyenne (13 minutes*)
12. Lake Disney
13. Rail & Metro Station

*By foot from the Theme Park

15. **Davy Crockett Ranch**
    (10 minutes by car from the Disneyland Paris hotels)

Hotel Car Parks

Theme Park & Festival Disney Car Park

14. **Golf Disneyland Paris**
    (7 minutes by car from the Disneyland Paris hotels)

To Davy Crockett Ranch, A4 & Paris

Figure 3.9 Eurodisney

Think of the cost of building a new hotel, a swimming pool or a football stadium. These facilities cost many millions of pounds. We need to attract lots of customers over many years if we are to make any profits.

Depending on the benefits that the target market seeks, the company may focus its attention more on the product, in providing a wider choice of leisure activities, coaching and training sessions, rather than on price. This is particularly true of a luxury cruise, for example, on the QE2, where the quality of the service, the stately surroundings, the people you mix with, are more important than the price charged.

On other occasions, it may emphasize lower prices, but offer restricted access to the product at certain times of the day. Basically, marketing seeks to ensure that each element of the marketing mix is effectively managed and that the interaction of the four Ps is such that the final offering actually does provide the benefits to satisfy customer needs.

Marketing activities in leisure and tourism

The marketing environment

A key activity in marketing management involves understanding the changing business environment in which all leisure and tourism organizations operate and planning the company's resources and skills in order to deliver the goods and services to meet its customers' wants.

No organization operates in a vacuum. All businesses, including leisure and tourism organizations, are surrounded by the environment and are affected by and have influence over their environment. The marketing environment consists of a set of forces which affect the organization's ability to seek out exchanges in managing demands for its products. These forces are best viewed as demand determinants, and because of them demand for leisure and tourism products is constantly changing. What is popular today as a leisure product is often neglected tomorrow. One has only to look at the disused cycle ramps in local parks to see how people's tastes, fashion and hobbies change over time.

Some of these forces are beyond the control of the organization and are termed **uncontrollable variables**. These can be contrasted against the so-called **controllable variables** which, for marketing purposes, include such activities as marketing plans, pricing, product development and promotion, as shown in Figure 3.10.

In the Figure the controllable variables can be seen to be surrounded and thereby influenced directly or indirectly by the uncontrollable variables of the marketing environment. The importance of understanding the company's marketing environment is that it helps companies to plan for change. If you view the environment as a jungle

Micro environment	Macro environment (external uncontrollable variables)
Company Customers Suppliers Channels Competitors	Political Economic Social Technological
Internal (controllable variables) Marketing plans and marketing mix	

Figure 3.10 The marketing environment

where all inhabitants or forces feed off each other, then understanding a company's environment will define its future threats and opportunities. To succeed, it must constantly adapt its operations in terms of its marketing plans and activities to take account of environmental changes, or it will fail.

Task 3.9

Think about the uncontrollable variables that can affect your choice of holiday – possibly a holiday in the sun, but instead of being sunny it rained most of the time. Climate in this context is an uncontrollable variable, something which neither you nor the travel agent could have control over.

In pairs, begin to plan a holiday for next year.

1 Identify and list the uncontrollable variables that could affect your plans and therefore your enjoyment of your holiday.

Imagine you are both managing a tour operating company promoting holidays to the place you have chosen in 1 above.

2 Identify and list the controllable variables that the company can use to offset the uncontrollable variables identified above.

The marketing environment is made up of the micro environment and the macro environment.

The micro environment

The micro environment consists of forces close to the organization and over which it has a degree of control or can strongly influence in its ability to serve its customers. These forces include the company itself, customers, suppliers and the competition.

- *Company* – In an industry where service is such a vital aspect in delivering customer

satisfaction, the marketing concept must permeate the whole organization. Everyone must consider the customer in everything they do, because all activities have customer implications. This, of course, should be the easiest part of the micro environment to control, whether it be a company, local authority or voluntary organization. When all is said and done, if a company cannot control itself it is hardly likely to be able to control anything else.

- *Customers* – All marketing activities are geared towards influencing buyer behaviour. It is important to build up good relations with customers to ensure that they continue to get what they want. Good training, supportive management and customer care practices are vital here in ensuring that quality standards are maintained. Failure to provide this service will often mean that buyers will not repeat their business.

- *Suppliers* – All companies rely on their suppliers for a variety of products and services. A hotel relies on supplies of fresh food for its restaurants, flowers to decorate the rooms and clean laundry for the beds. If suppliers let you down, you may unavoidably let your customers down. However, by maintaining good relations with suppliers as with customers, the company can ensure that its own products and services are delivered in good time, and are available as and when required.

- *Channel environment* – Many leisure and tourism products have to pass through several hands in order to reach the final consumer or user. The channel or distribution system for an airline is made up of middlemen who range from agents, brokers and wholesalers to travel agents and reservations agencies. If British Airways did not use such a distribution system it would probably have to set up its own booking offices in all the major cities throughout the UK and around the world. The same is true of theatres and clubs, who rely on reservations agencies and corporate client service companies to sell on large numbers of their seats.

Marketing needs to be aware of changes in the channel design. The future of retailing is moving significantly away from small shops towards shopping malls. More people buy their food and drink for the month, not the week. Shoppers seek the benefit of 'one stop' shopping, together with more leisure time.

- *Competition* – The competitive environment in which leisure and tourism companies operate is extremely hostile. The extent of direct competition in leisure and tourism can be quickly realized if you look down the brochure rack of travel agents or view the leisure pages of your local paper. However, it is often areas like branding, programming, sales promotion and advertising that help the company to take control over the competition since it is these activities that often determine the customer's final choice rather than the composition of the product itself. Of course, competition may come from less direct sources – for example, holiday companies may compete with car manufacturers for the same customer's disposable income, a theatre may compete with a restaurant, a National Trust property with a visit to the cinema.

The macro environment

The macro environment consists of four broad forces termed PEST. They are Political, Economic, Social and Technological forces which shape opportunities and pose threats to the company.

- *Political* – Government ideology towards business can create a more favourable environment for it. The 'open door' approach to trade internationally has seen a tremendous growth in foreign imports into the UK, particularly in such leisure products as hi-fis, TVs, cameras, cars and computer games. The changes in Sunday trading and licensing laws have meant that many more retailers are open longer hours for business through the week.

  Political groups such as Greenpeace and Friends of the Earth have aroused concern for the natural environment, which has become a powerful influencer on consumer behaviour and needs to be taken into account. For example, the demonstrations, particularly in Germany, against Shell Oil's decision to sink a redundant oil rig in the North Sea resulted in a huge fall-off in sales for Shell products.

- *Economic* – If the economy of the country is doing well, generally people have more disposable income to spend. In times of recession, there is less disposable income and people will change their purchasing behaviour – for example, they are less likely to take more than one holiday a year, they will eat in rather than eat out in restaurants, they will visit friends and relatives rather than stay in hotels or buy drinks from the supermarket rather than frequent the pub.

- *Social* – The social environment can be split into two categories: demographics and behaviour.

  - Demographics – Although the UK population continues to rise, it is getting older, with a slow-down in birth rates as well as death rates. The dominant market group in the 1990s is the 'middle agers', who seek very different products from people in their teens or twenties. Also, the typical family is no more – Mr and Mrs Average, in their first marriage with two children, where the husband works and the wife is at home, represents just 4 per cent of all UK families.

Task 3.10

In groups of four, discuss the effect that these demographic changes are likely to have on the leisure and tourism industry.

  - Behaviour – Society is changing. Aspects of this include such social changes as the emancipation of women and the resulting rise in the number of working mothers. Women are becoming ever more dominant as both the decider and the purchaser of goods and services. There is also a growing interest in health and fitness, short-term working and anti-smoking campaigns. All these forces affect our recreational pastimes and, as such, are important to the marketing of leisure and tourism products.

- *Technology* – Technology is a driving force for change everywhere. Customers today often expect things to change for the better – improved facilities, better availability of services and instant communications regarding reservations and bookings. Some commentators believe that as much as 80 per cent of all products today will not be around in ten years' time. The computer games industry certainly supports this claim. It is less than ten years ago that computer games used cassette tapes. These gave way to floppy disks, which in turn are under pressure from digitalized disks. If this is the case, the life cycles of leisure and tourism products are going to become much shorter, and new product and service development will be a necessary requirement for all leisure and tourism businesses.

SWOT analysis

The analysis of the marketing environment is a necessary first step in establishing where a company stands in its market place. A common marketing technique for assessing the company's particular situation is to carry out a SWOT analysis (Strengths, Weaknesses, Opportunities, Threats). This activity involves listing all the key internal factors, strengths and weaknesses over which the organization has some control and the external opportunities and threats which are really beyond its control.

Strengths can include any advantage, whether by design or historic good fortune, in the company's market or product make-up. For example, increasing sales of a product, the company's image and reputation, the professional skills of staff in providing customer service, distribution systems and product range can all be used to enhance the offering to the customer, and so this constitutes a strength. For example, one of British

Airways' strengths is often seen to be its sheer size in being the world's largest airline. However, one of Virgin Airlines, strengths is its public image of offering the highest quality customer service.

Weaknesses range from ageing products in declining markets to bad-tempered or inexperienced staff. A customer's view of a company's weaknesses may, of course, be a matter of perception rather than fact. A local authority leisure centre may be perceived as being badly managed, offering limited activities and poor facilities, whereas the reality may be completely different. In this circumstance, the authority may be able to emphasize its strengths by repositioning its leisure centre to stress the wealth of activities it can offer, the specialist coaching staff and its new refurbishment programme.

An important point about the strengths and weaknesses of an organization is that they must be stated in terms that show that they are recognized by customers and not by the organization undertaking the study.

Opportunities come from some change in the external environment or some development of the product or service which gives the organization a competitive advantage. The advancement in aircraft design in the 1960s, providing for fast, low-cost travel, opened up the Mediterranean countries for mass tourism on a scale never before seen. More recently, the development of digital computer games has enabled companies like Sega and Nintendo to come from nowhere to become two of the top twenty companies in the world.

Threats can come about from internal factors or from external events, such as a change in government policy. For example, the introduction of compulsory competitive tendering (CCT) has meant that many leisure services such as sports centres, swimming baths, libraries, museums, etc., normally operated by local authorities, have been put out for tender so that private companies can compete for providing the service. Other factors, such as changes in the exchange rate, can radically increase (or decrease) the cost of leisure products or services. How much did you get for your pound when you went abroad this year? Was it more or less than last year? Changes in oil prices have a major impact on travel, but so, too, can changes in the law, how much you earn and, not least, what the competition is doing.

A threat to one company often means an opportunity to another. The example of the expansion of low-cost air travel was and still is a major threat to the traditional UK seaside resort, but for the Mediterranean countries it is an opportunity.

Planning the business

Ultimately, an organization will have to decide what business it is really in, what it can produce and for whom it is producing. The answers to these questions are often complex, but, provided the company is true to the marketing concept, the answers will be given with a consumer perspective, not an organizational or production perspective. An example is provided in Figure 3.11.

A bowling alley, for instance, is not just in the business of providing a game of bowls. Other services offered to the public based around the activity could include everything from a sweet shop to a vending machine offering cans of Coke, to a licensed bar or even full restaurant facilities.

Marketing requires an organization to make the most of its relationship with its customers and to think of its total offering in providing for customer needs. For example, the bowling alley manager should consider whether there is anything else that could be offered to the customer. Could the bowling alley start selling bowling balls, shoes and other accessories? Could customers be offered party-time slots for families only, expert tuition for the more enthusiastic players, possibly a supervized toddler softball play area, so that mum and dad can enjoy a game of bowls with the rest of the family? Clearly, different groups of people will have different needs, but it is only by having an understanding of the strengths as well as the weaknesses of the business that a company can fully develop to satisfy many needs and so reach its full potential.

Marketing research

For marketing to be effective, it must have information on all aspects that are likely to affect the organization and what it is offering. It is, therefore, necessary to be able to collect and analyse data on both the micro and macro environments within which the organization operates.

With an ever changing environment, the data must be collected on a regular basis and circulated to the appropriate persons who may have need of it. Most information can be obtained from within

Organization	Production-orientated answer	Marketing-orientated answer
Football League Club	We run a football club	We are in the entertainment business
Passenger railway	We run a transport facility	We offer fast, comfortable, traffic-free travel
Tour operator	We package together the services operations of places, accommodation, etc. to provide holidays	We offer dreams, a chance to put away, your inhibitions and share excitement and fun with others
Sport centre	We operate a swimming pool and squash court	We promote healthy, competitive exercise and a venue for people to meet and enjoy the occasion

Figure 3.11 What business are we in?

the organization – from the finance department, from operations and, of course, from the sales department. In addition, there are many outside sources of information, both public and private, that can provide a host of data – so much so that the organization will have to be selective about what is collected and analyzed. This invariably means setting up some form of Marketing Intelligence System (MIS) to monitor the organization's environment on an on-going basis.

An MIS system has been defined as follows:

A marketing information system consists of people, equipment, and procedures to gather, sort, analyse, evaluate and distribute needed, timely and accurate information to marketing decision makers.

P. Kotler,
*Marketing Management Analysis
Planning and Control*,
Prentice Hall, 1992

The objective of the MIS is to provide the most relevant, up-to-date data on the key forces that impinge on and affect the organization's marketing performance. Its aim is to reduce the level of risk when making decisions regarding which markets to serve with which products and services.

Positioning

Once a company has decided which market segments to enter, it now has to decide what position it wants to occupy in those segments relative to the competition. All products and services must have a distinctive and desirable position in the consumer's mind relative to competing products for them to have any reason for wanting to buy it. For example, Airtours may wish to position themselves in the packaged holiday market on low price, Thomsons Holidays based on wide choice and Club Mediterranean on high quality.

Positioning requires the company to offer something different from the competition in providing the target market with a product that offers greater value satisfaction. A company can do this by offering lower prices than the competition or by offering more benefits to justify the higher prices.

To differentiate its product, companies provide more product features, better services, improved booking facilities, have better trained staff. To differentiate its offering effectively, however, companies must choose differences that have been identified as important to the customer.

Task 3.11

Think about different clubs, leisure centres, museums and theatres, for example in your area. What types of people do they appeal to?

In groups of three or four, choose one or more leisure or tourism products in your area and:

- *Identify and describe the target groups they seek to serve.*
- *Identify the product features that appeal to the target group.*
- *Determine how the product is positioned in relation to its competitors.*

Many leisure and tourism companies produce product positioning maps, revealing the customer's image of existing competitors in the same markets. Travel companies do this by conducting a random sample of holidaymakers who are asked a series of questions to find out what particular features of their holiday are very important to them when they decide to book and how competing travel products 'fare' in relation to each of these features. Their answers are plotted along a two-dimensional matrix, as illustrated in Figure 3.12.

Marketing objectives

Having scanned the environment and analysed and assessed the opportunities and threats facing

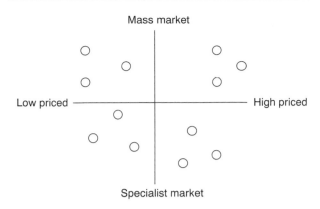

Figure 3.12 Product positioning map for overseas holidays

the organization, the next stage is setting the marketing objectives. This stage is very important in determining where the organization wants to go. Imagine a cruise liner being tossed around on a turbulent sea (environment). The captain needs to know where the ship is headed and how to get there. Marketing objectives in a leisure and tourism environment act like a navigator in providing the answers to help the captain to make decisions to co-ordinate the various activities on board in order to achieve its destination. Without the answers to these questions, a leisure and tourism organization is like a ship without a rudder – it can move, but it lacks a clear sense of direction.

Most organizations do not simply have one key objective, but several. Among the most frequently encountered objectives in companies are the following:

- To survive
- To maximize profits
- To increase sales and market share
- To dominate one region or country and so become a market leader
- To become the technical leader in a product field
- To expand the business
- To have social responsibility (i.e. putting the environment and the community first).

In the leisure and tourism industry an organization's objectives often differ, depending on which sector of the industry (private, public or voluntary) the organization operates in.

Private sector

The marketing objectives of a leisure organization such as Ladbrokes may be to maximize profits by increasing the sales revenue of its nightclubs by 15 per cent per annum. Alternatively, a successful holiday company like Airtours may seek to increase its market share by expanding the range of holidays on offer.

Public sector

The public sector relates to either central or local government, as well as to organizations such as the Arts Council and the Sports Council which operate on behalf of government. Here the objective of the organization may be to provide a benefit to the community through the provision of leisure services such as libraries, theatres, museums, art galleries, schools, events and shows. Many of these facilities may not be provided privately because of cost constraints, with little opportunity to make profits. Swimming pools, for example, are very costly to build and run and are therefore invariably subsidized by local authorities. Many theatres, libraries and schools would not be provided if they were not financially supported by the public sector. The primary objective here is to ensure that financial and other constraints are not a barrier to participation.

Voluntary sector

An overall aim of the voluntary sector is to provide the facilities and activities not provided by the other two sectors. This takes many forms, and includes all types of organizations such as clubs, societies and charities which are neither controlled by the state nor operated solely for profit. Most of these organizations are concerned with the general welfare of society, in such forms as conservation or environmental protection, or simply as a means of encouraging constructive use of leisure, such as swimming and athletics clubs, Scouts and Guides.

A major objective of voluntary groups may be to recruit a certain number of members each year to raise a sum of money for a specific purpose or to bring a problem to the public's attention by influencing their perception of the product or service under review.

Characteristics of objectives

Among the most important characteristics of objectives there are five basic components. These have been summarized by the acronym SMART, which requires objectives to be:

- Specific – objectives should relate to specific products and markets
- Measurable – objectives should be quantified, such as to increase sales by $x\%$ over the same period last year
- Achievable – those tasked with attaining the objectives must believe them to be realistic, otherwise they will never be acted upon
- Relevant – marketing objectives should relate to the organization's overall goals
- Time (constrained) – all objectives should state when the objective is to be achieved by.

Where objectives are not clearly defined as above, confusion rules. The more precise the objectives are, the clearer targets to be achieved, the easier it is to assess how well the organization is progressing towards achieving them.

Case study

British Airways is not only the world's largest international airline, but is also one of the most profitable of the UK's leisure and tourism organizations. However, not so many years ago British Airways was a much maligned, publicly run state airline. Its difficulties then stemmed from having confused organizational objectives.

British Airways' marketing objectives have always been to increase profits and to gain a greater share of its market from its competitors. However, the organization's past public

or corporate goals were to provide a readily available schedule of services for regional, national, as well as international flights at affordable, if not profitable, prices. Often the two sets of objectives were incompatible, which led to confusion as to what British Airways wanted its business to achieve. Losses, not profits were incurred, and its services also suffered.

After privatization, the organization immediately sought to rectify this problem by aligning its corporate goals with those of its marketing objectives. Its corporate objectives are now to maintain growth and to take advantage of anticipated global expansion of the travel industry. To achieve this objective, British Airways has decided to expand its activities in regional British cities as well as those abroad.

As air travel becomes more common and more frequent for many people, their expectations as to what to expect from airlines grow. As a means of maintaining a world leading position, the marketing objective for British Airways is to provide better quality goods and services and good value for money in every market segment in which it operates. This often involves maintaining quality, adding new service features, developing its product offer, whilst constantly responding to the requirements, preferences and aspirations of its customers.

Task 3.12

Consider carefully the objectives mentioned in the case study. Describe how achieving the marketing objectives will enable British Airways to reach its corporate goals.

Marketing strategy

Having decided what the organization's objectives are, the next stage is to decide on the means of achieving them. This is termed marketing strategy. Marketing strategy has been described as consisting of two distinct marketing activities:

1 Identification and selection of target markets – a process called market segmentation
2 The marketing mix – the determination of a mixture of product, price, place and promotion combined to satisfy the target market which has already been covered.

Selecting the target market

This involves finding a group of people whose characteristics suggest that they will be interested in the product or service being offered. Each group or market segment will have a different perception of the benefits the product offers. Market research and analysis will help to identify individual markets fairly accurately, but selection of the appropriate market segments requires an understanding of buyer behaviour in answering three key questions:

● Who buys?
● Why do they buy?
● How are their needs being satisfied?

There are a number of segmentation techniques for helping companies to classify and profile different customer groups. Two of the best known are:

● Geographic segmentation
● Demographic segmentation.

Geographic segmentation divides up a market into different geographical areas, either by country, region, town or city. A travel company may operate internationally but pay attention to geographical differences in different countries' needs and wants.

Regional Tourist Boards often use geographic segmentation as a means of analysing the visitors attracted to their regions. The broad segments given below, although not comprehensive, do illustrate the range of possibilities they cover.

Demographic segmentation involves classifying customers by:

● Age (under 10, 15–24, 25–34, 35–44, 45–54, 55–64, 65+)
● Sex (male or female)
● Occupation (professional, technical, clerical, housewife, student, etc.)
● Family size (1–2, 3–4, 5+)
● Social class
● Family life cycle.

Most of these classifications are used by consumer research agencies as a means of analysing markets. Clearly, age is an important classifier of purchase behaviour. The young adult market, with its emphasis on ghetto blasters, bowling alleys and games machines, is light years away from the retired market sector, with its emphasis on the home, DIY, gardening and healthcare products.

Social class, which is usually based upon occupation of the head of the household, tells us something about the level of disposable income which each group may have available and thereby provides guidelines as to what may be bought by each class.

Life cycle

The life cycle classification method recognizes that needs, disposable income and consequent expenditure for a family will vary over a period of time. The following changes in the concept of the family life cycle and their likely impact for leisure and tourism products are given below:

● *Bachelor stage* – Young single person, male or female, living at home, with few demands and a reasonable level of income. These people are likely to attend football matches, buy CDs and computer games, frequent pubs, clubs and the cinema.
● *Newly married couples* – Both work, have no children and are setting up home. Disposable income is generally higher, with leisure pursuits focused in part on the home, for such items as

TV and hi-fi purchases, but also on eating out, going to the theatre and holidays abroad.

- *Full nest I* – Young married couple, with youngest child under six. Generally lower disposable income, as one of the partners looks after the child. Focus here is on the home, and leisure pursuits are centred around the family, with trips to parks, tourist attractions, etc. Holidays become more organized and are often taken at home.
- *Full nest II* – Youngest child over six, but pressure still on disposable income. Children dominate leisure pursuits of the family, with a lot of activities involving voluntary groups, such as Cubs and Brownies, swimming and football, PTA and charity fairs. Camping holidays do well with this group.
- *Full nest III* – Older couples with dependent children. Incomes may start to improve. Leisure focuses back on the home in terms of replacing TV, video, furniture. Emphasis on visiting friends and relatives.
- *Empty nest I* – Older couples, no dependent children. Disposable income at a high level, and time to enjoy those overseas holidays but in better accommodation. Also demand for short breaks and day trips, often of an educational nature, to learn and experience different surroundings.
- *Empty nest II* – as above, but head of household possibly retired, with a resulting drop in income. Where this is the case, leisure pursuits involve walking, reading and watching TV, also day trips out with the grandchildren.
- *Solitary survivor* – Single/widowed person, possibly in work, but more likely retired. Pressure on disposable income. Leisure interests once again around the home and garden.

How organizations in leisure and tourism grow

The planning gap

No company in a competitive environment can afford to stand still in the long term. Therefore, inherent in all strategic thinking is the element of growth. In this context, objectives are about helping to direct decisions to allow the organization to arrive at some improved point in the future. Where companies' projections differ from their objectives (i.e. what they want to achieve compared with what they expect to achieve), there is a 'planning gap'. The planning gap as illustrated in Figure 3.13 shows the difference between desired sales or profit objectives and a forecast of projected sales and profits based on past performance.

For the gap to be closed, the company must expand its business somehow. This will often involve modifying existing products or developing new products and may involve developing new markets.

Strategic options

If objectives relate to the where and when of planning, strategy formulation is concerned with the how. Igor Ansoff developed a matrix for helping organizations to decide which growth options to adopt. As shown in Figure 3.14, the

Figure 3.13 The planning gap

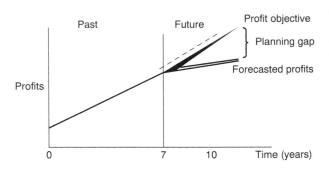

PRODUCT		
	Existing	New
MARKET Existing	Modify existing product to attract increased sales from existing market (i.e. Market penetration)	Introduce new product to existing market (i.e. product development)
New	Reposition on existing product to attract a new market	Develop new product for new market (i.e. diversify)

Figure 3.14 Ansoff's growth matrix

matrix identifies four possible courses of action for leisure and tourism organizations.

Market penetration

This is a strategy for expanding sales based on existing products serving existing markets. For example, where a tour operator serving the summer sun holiday market sector as its principal market decides to expand in this sector by modifying its existing products, any rise in sales above the natural market growth would represent an increase in market share, since the additional sales would have had to be gained from its competitors.

Market development

This is a strategy of expansion based on entering a new market not previously served by the company with existing products. Center Parcs is a holiday village concept that was originally developed by an international operator based in the Netherlands. The company has developed its market by bringing the concept to Britain.

Product development

This strategy entails developing and launching new products for sale in existing markets. A theatre may decide to screen films as well as offer shows to its market segments. A restaurant could decide to include a range of vegetarian dishes alongside its usual cuisine. These decisions represent an addition to the product range or portfolio – this is known as product development.

Diversification

This is the riskiest of all strategies, since it entails a company expanding on the basis of offering new products to new markets. Diversification can take a number of forms. A travel agent, such as Pickfords, might choose to diversify into new travel products by moving through the channel of distribution into operating an airline or running tour operations. Alternatively, diversification may be totally unrelated, such as a tobacco company like BAT moving into the production of children's toys.

Factors influencing pricing in leisure and tourism

Pricing is a major reason why people do not participate in leisure and tourism experiences. Leisure and tourism organizations are well aware that some people are willing to pay more for a product or service, while others will only buy if the product costs much less. As such, it is customary in the industry to charge different amounts for the same product or service at different times of the year, even different times of the day. These differences reflect the variation in geographical demand, seasonal demand, peak and off-peak demand of customers.

Before looking at some of the pricing strategies used to price leisure and tourism products, it is necessary to understand some of the factors that influence price.

Cost

All organizations must be aware of the costs of producing products and services when deciding on a price. The price change must, in the long term, at least allow the organization to cover all its costs. While private organizations will be motivated by profit, this is not the case in the public or voluntary sectors. However, even these organizations cannot ignore the actual cost associated with a particular leisure and tourism activity. In the public sector, any shortfall in revenue has to be made up by local taxpayers, while in the voluntary sector, it has to be met by the members of the club or society concerned.

Demand

It has been shown that the same product can command a higher price at different times according to customer demand. British Rail will charge higher prices overall for long-distance, travel to reflect the higher transport costs, but in many locations, particularly in the south-east of the country, the prices charged for journeys into London are disproportionately higher, which simply reflects on the higher demand for rail services in that area. People will willingly pay higher prices for ice creams, ferry and plane fares in the summer or higher prices for toys at Christmas, reflecting the seasonal fluctuations of demand. They will also pay higher prices for perceived quality, image or exclusivity, such as a cruise on the QE2 or a flight on Concorde.

Competition

Where customers have choice, they will choose a product that offers them the greatest value. In a highly competitive environment such as leisure and tourism, all organizations, whether private, public or voluntary, need to be sensitive to what is or offer elsewhere to ensure that their prices are seen to be offering good value.

Market forces

The population of the UK is increasing but growing older, and, as such, the type and amount of leisure and tourism provision available for the older sectors is set to increase. Of course, changes in the state of the economy nationally and internationally, such as the current recession, have a downward pull on prices, reflecting the demise of people's incomes. Fluctuations in currency values have seriously affected how much the pound is worth and in turn restricted the number of overseas trips to certain holiday destinations. However, the long-term trend in disposable income per household (despite the recession) is set to continue to rise. Both these factors will have a bearing on price. Where demand for certain leisure and tourism products increases, so price is likely to follow.

Product life cycle

This concept proposes that products and services, like humans, have a life cycle of their own, in that they are born (launched), they grow, mature and eventually, because of lack of demand, die. We are all familiar with the rise and fall of Mutant Ninja Turtles, Cabbage Patch Dolls and the chopper bike. Although the exact duration of a product's life cycle cannot be forecast, all products exhibit characteristic life cycles as illustrated in Figure 3.15.

If all products eventually decline and die, there must always be a case for introducing new products to ensure survival and growth in the future. Company policy here will be an important factor in setting prices.

The prices charged can be different for each stage of the life cycle. At the launch, the company may seek to set a high price in order to recover some of the heavy costs of development. However, in the growth stage, more opportunities for growth will attract greater competition, which will generally lead to lower prices to maintain growth impetus. The mature stage indicates a flattening of sales as more and more competitors' products enter the market. To maintain market share many

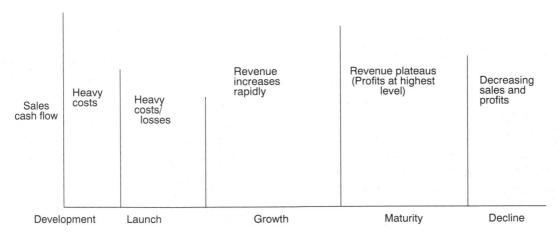

Figure 3.15 The product life cycle

companies will begin to cut prices. As the product enters the decline stage and sales and profits begin to fall, so the company will generally cut prices further as a means of stimulating demand or will raise prices to get what profit they can from the product before people stop buying. Kodak adopted this approach when pricing its cine-sound films in response to the fall-off in sales because of the competition from video cameras.

▪ Assignment 3.1 ▪

Students are to investigate the marketing operations of two leisure and tourism organizations. One should be from the commercial (private) sector and the other from the non-commercial (public or voluntary) sector. A description of the organizations' objectives and marketing activities is required, together with an explanation as to how the development of products and services helps them grow and the factors that influence their pricing decisions.

Coverage

- Element 3.1
- Performance Criteria 1,2,3,4,5
- Core skills opportunities
  Communication
  IT
  Managing Self and Others

Task 1

In small groups, decide on two leisure and tourism organizations that you wish to investigate – one from the commercial sector and one from the non-commercial sector.

Task 2

Describe the marketing objectives of each organization.

Task 3

Identify and explain the range of marketing activities and its marketing principles with reference to the marketing mix.

Task 4

Explain how the organization implements its marketing principles with reference to the marketing mix.

Task 5

Explain how the organization has grown through the development of products and services.

Task 6

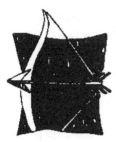

Identify and describe the factors that influence their pricing decisions.

Task 7

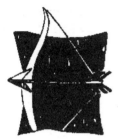

Produce a group report which provides details on both organizations. The report should not exceed 2000 words, preferably be word-processed and include tables, charts and diagrams.

Task 8

The group is to provide a presentation which highlights and contrasts the findings on each organization.

Element 3.2 Analyse and undertake marketing research on leisure and tourism organizations

Performance criteria

This element will cover the following performance criteria:

1 Explain the objectives of marketing research in leisure and tourism organizations.

2 Investigate sources of secondary marketing research data used by leisure and tourism organizations.

3 Explain primary marketing research methods, including content methods.

4 Explain how marketing research information contributes to marketing decisions.

5 Undertake marketing research in order to identify opportunities for product development in selected leisure and tourism organizations.

6 Summarize and present marketing research findings.

3.2 Marketing research

The role of marketing research

British Airways developed a sales campaign for their own workforce entitled 'Put the Customer First' – if we don't, someone else will! To put customers first requires you to know who they are and have information about them sufficient to be able to anticipate and quickly respond to what they need and want. In effect, marketing research helps to keep those who provide goods and services in touch with those who want to buy goods and services.

The AMA (American Marketing Association) has defined marketing research as:

the function which links the consumer, customer and public to the marketer through information – information which is used to identify and define marketing opportunities and problems

An alternative working definition states: 'marketing research is the systematic gathering, recording and analysing of data about problems relating to the marketing of goods and services'.

Marketing research objectives

The key purpose or objective of any marketing research programme of study is, therefore, to provide answers to questions. Having obtained the answers, it is hoped that it will be sufficient to help the company to plan ahead with greater certainty rather than rely on hunches or guesswork.

Let's look at this definition in the context of the organization. If we refer back to Element 3.1, you will recall that marketing puts the customer at the centre of its decision making because customers are the focus of the company's activities. Their satisfaction is achieved by making adjustments to the marketing mix, but the results of these adjustments are uncertain because the marketing activity takes place within an uncontrollable environment, as depicted in Figure 3.16.

Marketing research is basically used for planning, problem solving and control. When used for planning, it is concerned with studying the macro environment in order to determine those opportunities that are viable. Problem solving marketing research focuses on the short- and long-term decisions of the marketing mix, while control research helps management to keep

abreast of current operations and to check on its own performance.

There are five steps in setting up a marketing research programme. These are illustrated in Figure 3.17.

Before undertaking marketing research, a leisure and tourism organization must try to identify exactly what information it requires. There is an old adage: 'A problem well defined is a problem half solved'.

Marketing research is not a cheap exercise, so it is important to ensure that the information sought is relevant to what is required to solve the problem. Essentially, marketing research objectives seek to provide answers to five basic questions: who?, what?, when?, where? and how? (and sometimes why?).

In practice, the objectives concentrate on a limited number of recurrent problems, often on a continuous basis, which might include:

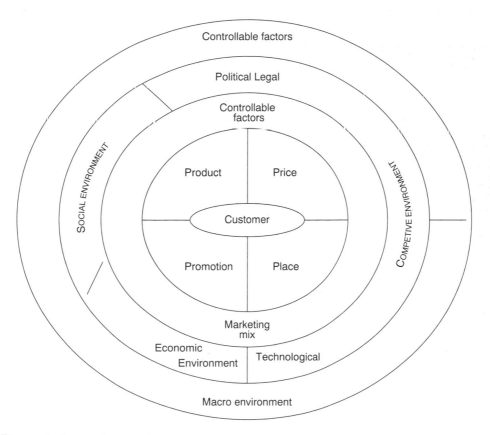

Figure 3.16 The marketing environment

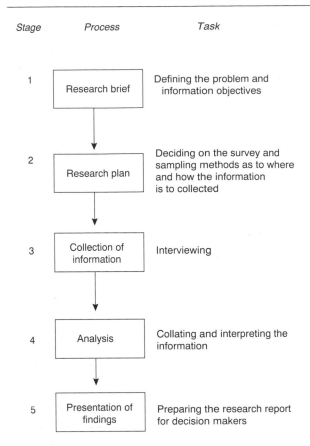

Stage	Process	Task
1	Research brief	Defining the problem and information objectives
2	Research plan	Deciding on the survey and sampling methods as to where and how the information is to collected
3	Collection of information	Interviewing
4	Analysis	Collating and interpreting the information
5	Presentation of findings	Preparing the research report for decision makers

Figure 3.17 The marketing research process

- Identifying new markets
  (where they are located, size or potential size of market)
- Determining the characteristics of existing and new markets
  (identifying changes in customer needs or preferences by monitoring the sales performance of different products)
- Understanding changes in the market place
  (sales trends, competitor actions in order to identify opportunities, threats)
- Testing new products and modifying existing products.

Case study

Alan Thompson and Fred Weedon have been making home-brew beer as a hobby for many years. Over this period they have developed several unique beer products which have proved very popular with their friends and relatives. For months they have talked about turning their hobby into a business, and early in 1995 developed the first in a line of several possible beers which they called St Antony's.

The beer is a light bitter with a unique nutty flavour which has proved popular with their male and female friends. Operating from a cellar in one of their houses has meant that production is limited to five barrels a week, but with some investment this could easily be increased ten-fold. Both are willing to find the necessary finance, provided they can be assured of increased distribution for their beer in a number of pubs or clubs.

From initial research, Alan and Fred have discovered that the brewery industry is vast, with an estimated turnover of approximately £11 billion but the distribution of beers, even guest beers, appears to be tied to several major manufacturers. They realize that they have limited brewery experience and limited knowledge of marketing. However, from the reaction of their friends when sampling the beer, they believe they have brewed a winner. Before they invest in much larger production they believe that a lot of research data is required.

Task 3.13

Agree the objectives in terms of the sort of information you believe Alan and Fred should attempt to obtain before investing money in the business.

Qualitative and quantitative data

By data we mean raw facts about the object being researched which, once collated and interpreted, becomes information. In effect, data is the raw material and information is the finished product, but without data there is no information.

Before proceeding with a research project, it is important to determine the type of data required. There are two types of data, qualitative data and quantitative data, the difference between them being:

- *Qualitative data* – provides information about opinions, and is unrepresentative of the target market
- *Quantitative data* – provides factual information, which is representative of the target market being researched.

Qualitative data is data which is based on descriptions and conveys impressions or attitudes rather than precise information. The way people see Eurodisney (perception), why they visit (motivation), and how they feel about its location, service and attractions (attitudes) are of interest to the marketing people at Eurodisney. These ideas, and how the data is collected, are explored further when we look at in-depth interviews and group discussions.

Any information that can be expressed using numerical procedures is considered to be quantitative data. In effect, quantitative data records what people do, which in the case of Eurodisney could include the rides they decide to go on, how many times, etc. Table 3.1 provides an example of how quantitative data is normally set out.

Quantitative data includes not only numerical data which can be obtained from the company's own accounts or sales records, but also ratings or numerical values which can be attached to opinion polls or buying intentions.

Clearly, there is a place for both kinds of data in building up a picture of markets and the people in them.

There are two broad sources from which information (i.e. data) can be obtained:

- Secondary sources
- Primary sources.

Secondary sources of information

Secondary information is data which has been produced for another purpose but may be relevant to our understanding of customer needs.

There are two types of secondary data available: internal data, which is information available within the company, and external data, which is published material that the company can buy or subscribe to (see Figure 3.18).

Internal sources

Often much of the information in a leisure or tourism organization is held within the company itself. For example, in any organization there are sales returns on what is bought, by whom, in what quantity, when. The accounts department keeps records on prices charged and revenues

Table 3.1 Quantitative data

Trend in number of visits to attractions in England from 1976–1990

	Historical %	Gardens %	Museums %	Wildlife %	Others (incl. theme parks) %	All %
1976	100	100	100	100	100	100
1981	94	103	96	84	105	99
1986	101	123	100	94	119	106
1990	118	154	111	112	144	124

*Indices (1976 = 100%)

Source: *Insights*, ETB, 1991

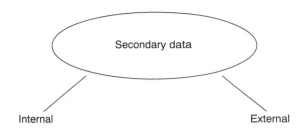

Figure 3.18   Secondary sources of information

Figure 3.19   Internal sources of information

obtained. The secret is knowing what is available, where to find it and then how to retrieve it. Figure 3.19 provides some of the clues as to what to look for in different organizational departments.

Today a lot of internal data is held on computer files. Computer databases have changed the way information is stored, retrieved and analysed, making the task of dealing with internal information much easier and quicker. Think of a travel agent booking airline seats with a major airline via one of the reservation booking systems, such as Sabre or Galileo. The database system automatically advises on what seats are available on what flights, at what airports, and up-dates its files each time a reservation booking is made. It provides control information to the airline as to what is available at any given time so that it can take action over any unsold seats. It also provides a wealth of data on which travel agents have booked seats, how many, on what flights, type of seats sold and when.

External sources

There is an enormous amount of data available from a variety of external sources, such as:

- National and international organizations
- Commercial organizations
- Professional and trade associations
- Publications and journals.

National and international organizations

Many national private, public and voluntary organizations produce publications and reports which contain valuable statistical information to the leisure and tourism industry. Several of the largest organizations are listed below in Figure 3.20.

Britain's national tourist boards commission an annual UK Tourism Survey (UKTS), which is an in-depth research into holiday travel of British people over the past year.

One unexpected source of information is the Department of Employment, which publishes the International Passenger Survey which includes information on UK residents travelling abroad and the purpose of the visit defined by destination area.

There are many international organizations who provide useful data and publications. For example, the United Nations publishes a directory

Public	Private	Voluntary
Sports Council	Water companies	National Trust
Arts Council	Ladbroke Group	YMCA
Independent	Mecca Leisure	Outward Bound
Broadcasting	Granada Leisure	The Pony Club
Authority	The Pearson Group	Friends of the
National Tourist	Thomson Holidays	Earth
Boards	Airtours	Royal Society
England	Eurodisney	for the
Scotland	Carlton	Protection of
Wales	Communications	Birds
Northern Ireland		
British Tourist		
Association		
Area/Regional		
Tourist Boards		
Local Authorities		
Department of		
Environment		
Department of		
Employment		

Figure 3.20   External sources of information

of international statistics and a demographic yearbook. The Organization for Economic Co-operation and Development (OECD) publishes various surveys and forecasts, including the main economic indicators. However, the major international source of information on tourism is the World Tourism Organization (WTO), which is based in Madrid, Spain. This organization liaises with national tourist organizations and agencies across the world and produces most of the international data on tourism, via such publications as:

- *World Travel and Tourism Statistics* (annual)
- *Economic Reviews of World Tourism* (biennial)
- *Current Travel and Tourism Indicators* (quarterly).

In addition, the BTA provides overseas country reports.

Commercial organizations

There are a number of commercial research organizations which gather together information from various industries, including leisure and tourism, and process data into market reports which they then sell to prospective clients. Some of these organizations include:

- Euromonitor
- Mintel
- A. C. Neilson
- Retail Audits.

In addition, companies can subscribe to on-going syndicated consumer research studies, which will provide information about the amount of leisure time people have available and where and how they spend it.

The Home Audit Survey produced by Audits of Great Britain (AGB) is a syndicated research study of 11000 households which provides data on UK leisure and travel habits.

Professional and trade associations

Specific leisure and tourism data can be obtained direct from a variety of professional and trade associations, such as:

- ABTA (Association of British Travel Agents)
- TOSG (Tour Operators Study Group)

- BCC (Bus and Coach Council)
- HCIMA (Hotel and Catering Institution of Management Associations)
- BHHPA (British Holiday Home Park Association)
- ILAM (Institute of Leisure and Recreation Managers)
- IBRM (Institute of Baths and Recreation Managers)
- ITT (Institute of Travel and Tourism).

Although only a few are listed, these professional and trade associations relate to specific parts of the leisure and tourism industry, such as catering, hotels, attractions, bus and coach holiday companies, each of which can be contacted by referring to the *Directory of British Associations*, available in most major libraries.

Periodicals and trade journals

There are a number of government publications available from HMSO. It is recommended that you familiarize yourself with the following:

- *Business Monitors MQ6* and *MA6*. (Department of Trade) – these provide quarterly and annual sales figures on individual leisure and tourism products and services
- *Census of Population* – Published every ten years, this is an analysis of the UK population which includes data on origin of birth, sex, age, socio-economic groups
- *Regional Trends* – This is an annual publication which provides details of UK regional trends, including details of current and projected population shifts by area
- *Family Expenditure Survey* – This annual publication provides an analysis of total household income and expenditure, and is particularly useful in determining how much and on what the family is spending overall on leisure and tourism
- *General Household Survey* – Published annually, this publication provides details on UK residents travelling abroad
- *International Passenger Survey* – Published annually, this publication provides details on UK residents abroad.

Task 3.14

Population Statistics in the UK

Study the projected population figures for the UK.

1 *Discuss in pairs what information can be extracted from the data.*

2 *Prepare a short essay (250 words) explaining how these figures may be of use to a leisure organization looking to redevelop and expand its pub and club operations in the long term.*

UK population

	1980		1985		1991	
	(000)	(%)	(000)	(%)	(000)	(%)
England	46787	83.1	47112	83.2	48248	83.4
Wales	2816	5.0	2812	5.0	2852	5.0
Scotland	5194	9.2	5137	9.1	5107	8.8
N. Ireland	1533	2.7	1558	2.7	1594	2.8
Total overall	56330	100.0	56619	100.0	57801	100.0

Projected UK population

	1995	2000	2010	2020
Resident population	58.5	59.5	60.9	61.7
Male %	48.9	49.1	49.3	49.5
Female %	51.1	50.9	50.7	50.5

Age distribution %

	1995	2000	2010	2020
0–4	6.7	6.5	5.9	5.8
5–14	12.8	13.1	12.4	11.5
15–29	20.5	18.8	19.2	18.7
30–44	21.5	22.4	19.9	18.2
45–64	22.7	23.4	26.1	26.6
65+	15.8	15.8	16.5	19.2

In addition to government sources, there are a number of other publications to do with leisure and tourism that you should be aware of. Below are some of the more popular ones:

Sport and Leisure
Leisure Studies
Leisure and Recreation and Tourism Abstract

Travel Trade Gazette
Travel News
Travel Weekly

Catering and Hotelkeeper
Coach and Bus Week

Leisure Week
Conference and Incentive Travel
Executive Travel

Tourism in Action
Annals of Tourism Research
Tourism Management International
Tourism Reports
Overseas Jobs Express
International Tourism

Primary marketing research methods

Sometimes secondary data sources may not provide the information to all the questions that need to be answered. The data may not be available in the form required and, more often than not, will be out of date. If secondary data does not provide sufficient information to satisfy research objectives, primary data must be collected. There are four widely used methods for collecting primary marketing research data:

- Observation – looking
- Experimentation – testing
- Depth interviews – searching
- Surveys – asking.

Observation

Here data is collected by observing people. No questions are asked. Qualitative data gained by observation can include viewing and listening to travel agents handling customer enquiries. Observation is used when it is impossible or too expensive to obtain data through a survey. Examples could include:

- Monitoring the traffic flow of people who use an airport terminal to check on any possible bottle-neck
- Viewing and recording details of competitors' products on display in a shop or at an exhibition
- Studying purchasing patterns or usage of a particular attraction.

A company will often use electronic counters to record the number of people passing through its doors. Turnstiles are used at sports stadiums to provide a constant check on the number of people entering the ground.

Case study

The regional tourist boards use observation methods to check on the quality standards of accommodation which carry the Crown Classification Scheme of the English Tourist Board. Inspectors are employed to book into different accommodation, such as a hotel or guest house, to observe the facilities and services available and to assess how customers are treated. The inspectors will compare what they have seen and heard against the ETB's criteria for the classification and grading of the accommodation. The next day the inspector will make his or her presence known to the manager and will advise on his or her findings. If the accommodation does not meet the criteria specified, the classification and/or grading can be changed.

Task 3.15

1 In groups of three, decide whether observation is an appropriate method for researching accommodation. Give your reasons why.
2 Carry out one or more of the following observations, record and tabulate your results.

(a) Visit a local leisure centre on successive days. Count the total number of cars and empty spaces at hourly and half-hourly intervals
(b) Observe lunchtime refectory queues at your school or college over different days of the week. Identify the female/male split, speed of service (how long it takes to get served), types of meal produced and which are the most popular.

Experimentation

This method involves trying to obtain data on how a product, change in price or promotion might fare under certain controlled conditions. Research experiments can be conducted in a 'laboratory' situation or in the 'field'. Field experimentation is known as **test marketing**.

Shopkeepers who switch their merchandise around on the shelves to see how this affects customer selection and sales are conducting controlled experiments. Travel agents often do this with their travel brochures and poster displays.

Case study

Having developed a new, technically superior surfboard, Surfers Limited is not sure of what price to charge. It could decide to charge a premium price and hope for the best. On the other hand, it could invite the public to come and view the new board alongside a selection of competing boards in a controlled setting. This would then enable the company to assess reaction to the higher price.

A second possibility that occurred to Surfers was to launch the product in a test market area. The product would be launched in the normal way (e.g. using advertising and sales promotion to support it) and the price sensitivity of the market would be assessed against the anticipated sales figures. Even if customer response to the price of the new board was good, changes in price may still be required as a result of test findings, such as to charge different prices at different times of the year.

Task 3.16

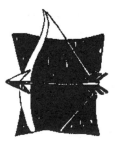

Which experimental method would you adopt?

Give reasons for your choice of method.

Depth interviews

This method involves face-to-face interviews with either an individual or a group of individuals (between five and twenty). In individual depth interviews the interviewer has a list of subjects of interest to discuss as opposed to a set of questions. He or she is free to create questions and probe for responses as the interview progresses. This is seen to be a particularly good approach when seeking answers to questions of a confidential or embarrassing nature, such as asking people about their smoking habits, or where a highly detailed understanding of human behaviour is required, for example, planning a family holiday. This approach is normally used when conducting business-to-business interviews.

Group discussion, on the other hand, is often used for generating new ideas or product concepts, in answering questions such as how to improve the service at a hotel establishment or what new destinations would consumers like to experience. It is also used to check a consumer response to new promotional or packaging ideas. Group discussions are usually recorded or videoed to aid recall of individual responses and to assist in preparing a summary of the group's responses.

Both techniques are excellent qualitative tools for preliminary research in helping researchers to identify the real problem areas and to focus on the questions to ask in a more structured, quantitative study.

Surveys

Surveys are about asking structured questions of a large number of people to see how they would react to a range of issues contained in a questionnaire. There are two types of survey:

Census   this involves asking questions of everyone in a particular market (or universe, as the statisticians call it) for example. It could also include the whole population of a country, all the shops in a given area or town or it could include, for example,

surveying all the professional football clubs in the Football League.

Sample   often a company cannot reach everyone in the target market, or the cost in terms of time and money would prohibit a census being taken. In this case, a sample of the target market is selected for questioning.

Sampling

The most important thing about sampling is that the sample is fully representative of the target market. If the selection is fair and accurate, then the information will be statistically reliable. If the sample is incomplete and does not accurately represent a group of customers, then data obtained could be misleading and the sample is said to be biased.

Careful rules need to be drawn up to avoid bias in a sample. Suppose a sample of British football supporters were to be surveyed and interviews were all held in London with male supporters only. The sample would be unbalanced and biased towards males from the south-east of the country.

Selecting a sample

Sample falls into two categories, as shown below. **Probability** samples or **simple random** samples are chosen on the bases that every individual in the target market has an equal chance of being selected.

A simple random sample of adult people in the UK could mean getting lists of every adult from the electoral registers and choosing one person in every 25 000 to interview. Of course, there are difficulties with this, in that the respondents

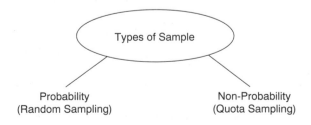

Figure 3.21

chosen could be scattered all over the country and be difficult to find, entailing lots of travelling time.

One solution is to use 'cluster' sampling, where you divide up the country into areas or regions and randomly select two or three regions, then towns within those regions and, finally, streets within those towns. The sample could then be chosen, for example, by selecting every fourth house in each street. The resultant sample would be less representative than a purely random sample, but would still be acceptable for marketing research.

Although random sampling, if properly conducted, produces the most accurate results, it can be very expensive and time-consuming and in some areas it may not be possible to identify a purely random sample. In this case, non-probability sampling is more commonly used.

Non-probability sampling, generally known as **quoted** sampling, is based on specifying in advance the types of customers, people or organizations that need to be interviewed. Here interviewers are given specific instructions as to the number of people to interview within certain characteristics of the target market. This is required to ensure both representativeness and also to reflect the importance of certain groups whose views may be deemed more important than others. These characteristics may relate to age, sex, socio-economic group, frequency of visit or usage of the product. For example, a survey of pub usage may place more weight on the views of heavy users, such as, say, middle-aged males rather than on light users, such as middle-aged females, and so may include more heavy users in its sample.

Another approach is to select a sample based on the socio-economic groups as a percentage of the population. This social classification, used universally in marketing research, is based on job or occupation of the head of the household (i.e. the occupation of the highest paid wage or salary earner in the household). A classification of the social grades by occupation type as a percentage of UK population is provided in Figure 3.22.

Using this method, from a sample of 100 persons the interviewer would be required to identify and then survey the following numbers that fell within each classification.

Social classification	Sample size
A	3
B	12
C1	22
C2	33
D	20
E	10
	100

Questionnaire design

A questionnaire is used in surveys to collect data on a respondent's behaviour (past, present or intended). At the same time, it is used to obtain classification data on the individual, such as age, sex, occupation, where they live, etc., so as to identify which market segment they belong to and what it is they want or need.

Before a questionnaire can be designed, answers are required to the following questions:

- What information is required?
- From where is it required?
- Which method of collecting the information will be used?
- Are the questions asked sufficient to generate the required information?

A good questionnaire will:

- Ask questions that relate to information needs
- Not ask too many questions
- Only ask positive questions (i.e. 'Which is your favourite pub?')
- Not use leading questions, such as, 'Do you prefer the friendly coaching skills of the leisure centre?' Such questions invariably lead to high Yes responses, because people read into the question that this is the response the interviewer wants
- Not ask questions that the respondent can't or is unwilling to answer truthfully

GRADE	DESCRIPTION		Percentage of UK population (approximate)
	General	Services	
A	'Upper-middle class' Higher managerial, administrative or professional – has demand for 'quality' and luxury products as well as 'normal' requirements – may be trend-setter too.	Good demand for banking, investment; better grade hotel and restaurant; more expensive tours and independent travel probably with 'special' interests (music, art, archaeology, etc.).	3
B	'Middle class' Middle to senior management and administration; up and coming professional – often likes to be trend-setter. Requires most products	Usually has need for investment and banking; probably strong interest in insurance as means of saving as well as protection; good middle grade hotels etc.; more adventurous tours and group travel.	12
C1	'Lower-middle class' Junior management, supervisory and clerical grades. Tends to ape the trend-setters even if finances overstretched.	Minimal use of banking and investment services; insurance for protection and some 'compulsory' saving; probably 3-star hotel and restaurants; packaged tours but could also have special interests (music, art, etc.).	22
C2	'Skilled working class' Usually a manual trade. Requires the less costly products usually.	Limited banking (current account)' some protective insurance; 2- and if possible 3-star hotels, etc.; packaged tours (could also have special hobbies/interests).	33
D	'Working class' Semi- and unskilled worker. Mainly interested in the least expensive products.	Very limited use of banking and insurance; probably 2- and 1-star hotels etc.; one holiday a year, if abroad the cheaper package and probably Spain. Could still have special interests.	20
E	Pensioners and widows.	Minimal demand, if any, for all services.	10

Figure 3.22 A classification of consumers by social class

- Not use ambiguous questions, such as, 'Do you go on holiday a lot?' – this will mean different things to different people
- Put questions in a logical sequence
- Have been piloted (or tested) with trial interviews and, where necessary, alterations made before being administered.

Types of questions

There are basically two types of questions that are asked in a questionnaire: closed and open questions. Closed questions usually require an answer to be selected from a range of options, including simply Yes or No. Most quantitative research surveys use closed questions, so that they can be answered quickly, often with a simple tick

in a box, and because of the ease with which answers can be coded for later analysis. Open questions, on the other hand, allow the respondent to give an opinion. Figure 3.23 provides some examples of the main types of questions that can be asked under the headings 'Closed questions' and 'Open questions.'

Case study

Sunset Travel is a successful chain of city centre travel agents which has built its success on offering a wide selection of upmarket travel and holiday products for the family. In order to continue to grow, it is considering branching

Closed questions		
Type	Description	Example
Dichotomous	Answer is usually Yes/No/Don't know	'In booking a hotel room, do you' Book direct? Yes ☐ No ☐
Multiple choice	Choice of one of several listed possible answers	Is there anyone else staying with you? No-one ☐ Organized tour ☐ Spouse ☐ Business colleague ☐ Spouse and children ☐
Attitude scale	A statement that is designed to gauge strength of feeling towards a product or service	'Small hotels give better service than large hotels'. Please indicate the extent to which you agree or disagree with this statement. Strongly agree ☐ 5 Agree ☐ 4 Undecided ☐ 3 Disagree ☐ 2 Strongly disagree ☐ 1
Open questions		
Unstructure	Respondent is asked to expand on his or her choice, to give reasons and opinions	'What is your view about the service of this hotel?'
Sentence completion	Incomplete sentences are shown to the respondent for him or her to complete	'When I choose a hotel the most important thing that determines my choice is...'
Picture completion	A picture of two people is shown, with one making a comment. The respondent is asked to reply as if he or she were the other person	

Figure 3.23 Types of questions

out into the suburbs. A number of locations have been identified, using secondary research data, which appear to offer good business potential in terms of the number and social economic grading of the local population being served.

The investment required to open the new branches will be costly and will need to be partly funded by a loan from the company's bank. The bank in turn seeks further reassurance that the investment will be a profitable venture and so has asked the company to conduct further research. Primary research data is required to determine the level of demand for a travel agency in each location and also to decide where best to locate each branch. A research agency has been recruited by Sunset Travel to survey the local areas and has produced a draft questionnaire (Figure 3.24 below).

Leisure and tourism questionnaire

Interviewer code _____

Location _____   Date _____

Introduction

Good morning/afternoon, I am conducting a tourism survey for a commercial organization which is considering locating in the area. The survey findings will not be divulged to any other individuals or organizations. Would you mind answering a few questions in complete confidence?

Q1 Did you go on holiday last year?

    Yes   ____

    No   ____

Q2 How often in a year do you go on holiday?

    Once   ____

    Twice   ____

    More (please specify)   ____

Q3 Where did you decide to go?

    UK   ____

    Western Europe   ____

    USA   ____

    Elsewhere   ____   _____

    (please give country and destination)

Q4 Do you normally make:

    Your own arrangements   ____

    Use travel agents   ____

    Go direct to tour operator   ____ _____

    (please state with whom you booked)

Q5 Please explain your reasons for the answer given in Question 4.

_____

Q6 Who goes on holiday with you?

    Friend   ____ _____

    Spouse   ____ _____

    Spouse and children   ____ _____

    (please state number of friends and children and ages)

Q7 Please indicate by ticking the box the extent to which you agree or disagree with the following statement:

I think it would be a good idea for a new travel agency to:

	totally agree	agree	un-decided	dis-agree	totally disagree
Open in the evenings	___	___	___	___	___
Open on a Sunday	___	___	___	___	___
Offer a wide choice of upmarket family holidays	___	___	___	___	___
	5	4	3	2	1

Q8 If there were to be a new travel agency, where do you think it should be located?

    In the village   ____

    Shopping centre   ____

    Side street   ____

    Other   ____ _____

    (Please state where)

Q9 What opening times would attract you to visit the travel agency?

Monday–Friday	Weekends
9–12 p.m. ___	9–12 p.m. ___
1–5 p.m. ___	1–5 p.m. ___
5 p.m. onwards ___	5 p.m. onwards ___

(Please state when)

Q10 What type of holidays and travel arrangements would you like to see on offer?

_____

_____

Classification Data

Where do you live? (show map)

Local   ____
5-mile radius   ____
Elsewhere   ____   _____
                       (Please say where)

Which age group are you in? (show card)

16–24   ____
25–39   ____
40–59   ____
60+   ____

What is the occupation of the head of the household?
(i.e. on the highest income)

_____

Observation

What is the sex of the respondent? Male ____   Female ____

Figure 3.24   Leisure and tourism questionnaire

Task 3.17

1 Individually review the questionnaire and identify the different types of questions being asked.
2 What other information could Sunset Travel be interested in?
3 Design questions to obtain the information identified in 2 above and show where you would place the questions in the present questionnaire.

How marketing research contributes to decision making

Decisions are about taking decisions today that will affect customers' responses tomorrow or in the near future. Predicting the future brings with it uncertainty, which in turn can be interpreted as risk. For example, when Sunset Travel makes decisions on which holiday products to develop and offer, who to promote the product to, at what price, in which location, it involves them risking

the resources of the company to achieve its own objectives for growth. Nobody in business like risk and so will actively seek to reduce it by acquiring more information through marketing research.

The resources referred to here relate to the marketing mix of the company, including product, price, place and promotion. Marketing research will seek to aid decision making in each of the following areas:

Product research

This can involve a number of activities generating new product ideas. Sources of new product ideas can come from monitoring secondary sources (such as journals, competitors' literature), group discussions with consumers or businesses.

Concept testing

In-depth interviews can be held with target customers to describe a product idea, its application and benefits. This approach provides a cost-effective way of assessing the demand potential for the product before developing a prototype.

Product modification

Most product changes are modifications to existing products in terms of volume, service levels, choice of programmes, even packaging. Sources for new ideas are similar to those above.

Test marketing

This involves testing new products in a limited geographical area.

Pricing research

This involves making decisions on the pricing of new and existing products.

Estimating costs

The costs of modifying an existing product or developing a new product have to be determined in order to help decide the price to charge.

Demand analysis

This can involve experimentation to check on the sensitivity of the target price to different price levels or to check on the intention of people to buy at a given price.

Studying competitors' prices

Sources of competitors prices will come from monitoring secondary sources, such as competitors' own literature, but also from observation.

Place research

Location studies

Secondary data sources on the distribution of population and businesses can help plan the location of retail outlets and attractions by providing data on the volume of traffic, level of competition and socio-economic characteristics of the people in the area chosen.

Assessing merchandise and display effectiveness

Experimentation methods are useful here in assessing the effects of, say, a change in a display on customer sales.

Promotion research

Advertising effectiveness

Primary research is used here to assess the effectiveness of advertising in terms of measuring awareness, attitudes or intention to buy before and after a campaign.

Sales preference

This is desk research, analysing the effectiveness of a sales campaign by looking at a company's sales compared with the same period last year.

Media selection

This involves using secondary data to assess the cost-effectiveness of the various media in reaching the company's target market.

In addition to the marketing mix, marketing research will also seek to provide information, and thereby better decision making, regarding the company's markets and consumers. Figure 3.25 highlights the scope of the decision-making areas that marketing research provides.

Direct mail is the most popular method of collecting survey data. Since it does not involve interviewing, the method is cheap, with few bias

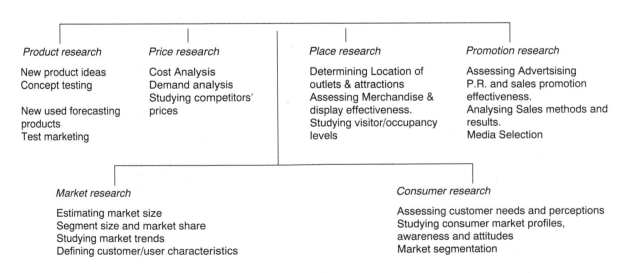

This is by no means comprehensive, but serves as an ouline as to the possible decision making areas of marketing research

Figure 3.25 Marketing research decision-making areas

Table 3.2 Methods of collecting data

	Method	Uses	Advantages	Disadvantages	Comment
1	Personal	Good for in-depth structured studies about participation in leisure activities such as holiday taking patterns and buying habits (Self-completion questionnaires can also be left at a person's home)	Greater flexibility and more opportunity for interviewer to restructure questions and obtain more answers Can show products and advertisements. Obtains the highest response levels. Personal data more easily obtained	Relatively expensive if large and widely scattered sample is taken. Possibility of respondent bias either to please interviewer or create false image Difficult to go back and revisit people who were not at home	Used by most leisure and tourism organizations because of its adaptability in the field to aid recall, obtain greater accuracy and improve responses
2	Telephone	To contact large numbers of people at the same time and when respondents are some distance from the interviewers	Takes a lot less time than face-to-face interviews and is a lot cheaper to conduct. Can be times to coincide with events (i.e. have you seen the TV advertisement for the new concert/show)	Little time given to respondents to consider the questions. Personal approach can inhibit replies. The number of questions asked is usually limited. 15% of the population still do not have telephones	Increasing use of the telephone. Good for conference, exhibition and general business travel surveys
3	Direct mail	When respondents are difficult or inconvenient to contact or where there are very large numbers of respondents to the survey	Low cost – no interviewer bias. Mailing lists are readily available for wide number of markets	Difficult to obtain totally reliable mailing lists. No guarantee that replies are truthful. Limitation of information. Possible ambiguity of replies. Low response levels	People replying may not be representative of the whole population or target markets. However, it is often found to be a useful method for evaluative research such as customer satisfaction surveys

problems. It is particularly suited to surveys where the respondents are scattered across the country, making it the most cost-effective survey method.

Today there is a wide selection of mailing lists which can easily be bought. However, the lists quickly become out of date and the rate of response can be below 5 per cent, despite the incentives that often accompany the questionnaire, including a personalized letter, free prize draw and reply-paid envelope.

Presenting marketing research findings

Interpretation of data

Having collected the research data, the next task is to make sense of the data obtained, to analyse and present it in an acceptable format for management to consider. This usually means presenting the information as a formal marketing research report.

The collated data needs to be interpreted for the eventual reader, drawing conclusions and offering recommendations that may be appropriate. Layout is very important, since lots of lists and tables tend both to confuse and bore the reader. It is essential that the information is organized and summarized into a form that is easily read and understood. Simple tables are useful, but it is better to use pie charts, line graphs and bar charts to emphasize specific points, as shown below in Figures 3.26, 3.27 and 3.28.

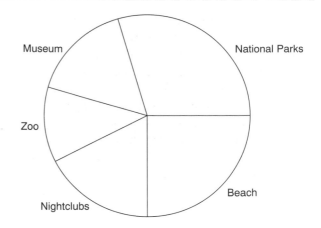

Figure 3.26 Pie chart of leisure activities

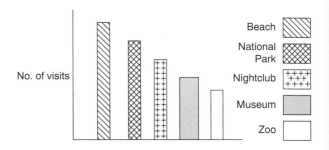

Figure 3.27 Bar chart of leisure activities

Getting going

Marketing research reports are not written for experts in marketing but for general managers. Therefore, care needs to be taken to submit a report which is readable, concise and easy to understand.

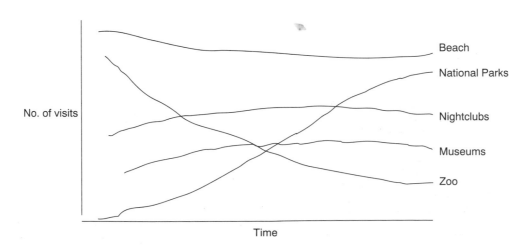

Figure 3.28 Line graph of leisure activities

There is often a tendency to put off report writing because it is seen to be difficult and it is often felt that a little more analysis of the data will make the process of writing much easier. This is rarely the case – report writing is always difficult, so don't delay. Another regrettable practice is to leave all the writing until the last minute. Very often, large parts of the report can be written much earlier in the process. These can include the introduction, statement of objectives, outline of the report framework, description of the research methodology, arranging for maps and illustrations to be included.

Although you may have had previous experience in report writing, there are certain features of a marketing research report that you should note. These are illustrated in Figure 3.29.

The report layout

Title page

Besides the formal title of the report, the names of the author, client or institution should appear on the title page, together with the date of publication

Marketing Research Report		
Title page	–	Title of report, client (or sponsor) author
Contents page	–	Includes all aspects of the report
Preface/Foreword	–	Explanation of the origin of the report leading to its purpose
Terms of reference	–	Defines the problems and outlines the research objectives, methodology and limitation of the report
Executive summary	–	Summary of the research report, including: introduction/background/data sources, synopsis of main findings, conclusions and recommendations
Main body	–	All data revealed by the research considered to be relevant to the survey
Appendices	–	Detailed analysis of statistics and tables; competitors' literature, maps, etc. Copies of questionnaires used

Figure 3.29 Marketing research report layout

Contents page

All reports should have a contents page which refers to the parts of the report highlighted below

Contents	Page(s)
Preface/Foreword	x
Terms of reference	x
Executive summary	x
Main body or findings	xx
1 Section I	xx
2 Section II	xxx
3 Section III	xxx
Conclusions	xxx
Recommendations	xxx
Appendices	xxx

Preface/Foreword

This is generally seen as the introduction to the report. It explains to the reader the origins of the study, detailing the problems on which it is hoped the research will shed some light. For example, before altering the schedule of ferry sailing times it was agreed to determine which parts of the timetable customers wanted left unchanged, were unconcerned about or which extra sailings they wanted.

The preface can also be used to explain any unfamiliar terms and to acknowledge any assistance received during the research project.

Terms of reference

No marketing research report should be without a terms of reference. The terms of reference, in effect, state in a numbered format exactly what the research seeks to achieve, for example:

1 To define the problem presented
2 To agree the research objectives
3 To explain the methods and techniques used to obtain the data.

Executive summary

The summary is the most important part of the report and, as such, should be written last but situated before the main body findings. Many managers will only read the summary; others will read more but even they will use the summary as a guide to finding the information necessary for them to take action. In this respect, the summary should stand on its own, separate from the main body of the report. It should encompass all the necessary background information as well as all the important results and conclusions. This is to enable a busy executive to understand what conclusions have been drawn from the research without having to plough through a lot of detail first.

Main body findings

Details of the research are contained in the body of the report. It is usual to number not only the main sections or chapters of the main body but also to number the subsections within chapters, an example of which is shown below:

    1 Major section/Chapter
        1.1 Sub-section
            1.1.1 Sub-sub-section
        1.2 Sub-section
            1.2.1 Sub-sub-section, etc.
    2 Major section/Chapter.

In some reports, paragraphs may also be numbered, which can be useful for reference purposes. Paragraphs are usually numbered in a single series for the whole report or chapter by chapter (e.g. 1-1, 1-2, 1-3, etc. in Chapter 1 and 2-1, 2-2, 2-3 in Chapter 2).

The structure of the report should follow that of the contents page, with target word or page lengths. The findings need to address the specific problems identified and should be supported with tables, graphs and pie charts.

Reports should be structured in a logical order, which in most cases does not mean following the sequence of questions in the questionnaire. This is not a good way to proceed. Questions structured to conduct interviews generally do not provide a suitable structure for a report.

Conclusions and recommendations

Conclusions are the creative interpretation of the facts and should follow logically from the

findings. Recommendations should follow logically from the conclusions. Although not all research surveys ask for recommendations, where they do these should be kept short, numbered and be action statements, for example:

1 'The new attraction should be priced at £x in the summer season'.
2 'The ride should operate for 4 minutes only to avoid unacceptable queuing.'

Appendices

All technical data can be included in the appendices, together with copies of questionnaires used and analysis of respondent replies, competitors' literature, diagrams, tables and lists.

▪ Assignment 3.2 ▪

A local cinema in the area has requested the support of your school/college in researching the current viewing habits of the cinema-going market. With better information it hopes to develop its product offering in terms of the films it shows, the prices charged, even the facilities it offers, such as providing another screen, café or bar area.

Coverage

- Element 3.2
- Performance Criteria 1, 2, 3, 5, 6,
- Core Skill opportunities
    – Communication 3.1, 3.2, 3.2
    – IT 3.1, 3.2, 3.5
    – Application of number 3.1, 3.2, 3.3

Information requirements

The manager of the cinema is interested to know what level of demand there is for different types of films. Moreover, information is required on the numbers of people who currently visit the cinema, how often they go, the types of people (i.e. age, sex, social background) and the sorts of films they like to watch. By assessing the level of demand, the type and frequency of visitors, and the types of films which attract the biggest audiences, the manager believes that he will be in a better position to decide as to how to develop the cinema product offer.

Task 1

In pairs, decide on the objectives of your marketing research (i.e. your information requirements in relation to the marketing decisions that the manager will have to make in developing the cinema product offering).

Task 2

Identify the secondary sources of information available in respect of Task 1.

Task 3

Determine what primary sources of information are required and explain the method(s) most appropriate for collecting the data.

Task 4

Design a questionnaire for obtaining the data.

Task 5

Carry out the survey, collate and interpret the results of the research.

Task 6

Produce a formal report for the manager which details the research survey findings and provides conclusions and recommendations. The report should not exceed 1500 words in length, preferably be word-processed and should include all relevant statistics, tables and diagrams.

Element 3.3 Investigate and evaluate marketing communications in leisure and tourism organizations

This element will cover the following performance criteria.

1 Explain with examples how advertising is used to promote products and organizations.
2 Explain with examples how public relations are used to promote products and organizations.
3 Explain with examples how sales promotions are used to promote products and organizations.
4 Explain with examples how direct marketing communications are used to promote products and organizations.
5 Explain with examples how personal selling is used to promote products and organizations.
6 Evaluate and compare the effectiveness of marketing communications in selected leisure and tourism organizations.

The Role of promotion

However good a product is, it will seldom sell itself. Knowledge about the product has to be communicated and promoted. Product, price and distribution cannot create sufficient sales on their own. Potential visitors to a holiday destination, a museum, or spectators at a major event may never become aware of the organization or its products unless they receive information about them.

Promotion in leisure and tourism is concerned with communicating messages to inform and persuade people to buy or use specific products and services. If a leisure and tourism organization wants to manage customer demand for its products it must be willing to develop effective programmes of communications and promotion.

The principal role of promotion is, therefore, to:

- *Inform* customers and create awareness for a product

- *Remind* and reassure customers about the existence or use of a product
- *Alter* perceptions and project favourable images about a company and its products
- *Stimulate* demand for products
- *Provide* incentives and give *reasons* to buy a product.

The communication process

Promotional campaigns are about sending messages to potential customers through various channels or media in order to create awareness and understanding as to why they may wish to buy a particular product or service. In this context, leisure and tourism organizations are the senders of the message and the target market customers are the receivers of the message.

Figure 3.30 shows the stages in the process by which an organization communicates with its target market.

The process of communication starts with the source of information, i.e. the leisure and tourism organization with a message to deliver. The organization must determine what message to deliver to its target market in order to create awareness and understanding. For example, Eurotunnel may want to send different messages to the different target markets it serves. To the business market segment, the purpose of the message may be to communicate details of its high-speed links with European cities or to inform them of its unique roll-up-and-run train schedules. The leisure market segment may be more interested to hear about new low prices in the main holiday periods.

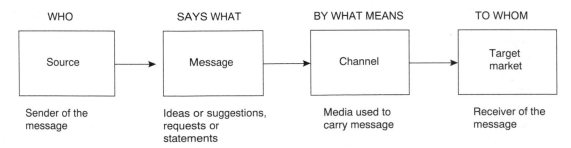

Figure 3.30 The communication process

The purpose of promotion is to generate movement of customers towards some action. The type of action it seeks should ultimately lead to increased sales, greater use of a facility or, in the case of cinemas, more 'bums on seats'. The organization's promotional objectives must, therefore, relate to the promotional techniques most likely to achieve them.

The promotion mix

The leisure and tourism industry uses a number of promotional tools or techniques to communicate a message to its target markets. Often referred to as the promotion mix, these include:

● Advertising
● Public relations
● Sales promotion
● Direct marketing
● Personal selling.

Whichever technique is chosen, it is likely to adopt the principle known as AIDA, which sees the customer passing through successive stages of attention, interest, desire and action. These stages are as follows:

Attention – A new swimming pool captures a customer's attention, possibly through the use of colour or big headlines in the local press so that she/he is made aware of the product

Interest – Having created awareness, interest is created by an invitation to receive information especially prepared for the target market (such as swimming clubs, early learners)

Desire – The customer is persuaded that he or she will be missing out if he or she does not use the facility, possibly by highlighting those currently taking advantage of free junior swimming lessons or a special limited membership offer.

Action – This ultimately involves the purchase of a ticket for the pool or paying a membership fee. Action is inspired by sending out application forms to targeted customers or publishing them in the local newspaper. It may be further encouraged through advertisements reminding the consumer of the closing date of the membership offer.

The point to remember is that the AIDA model assumes that with each succeeding stage there is a higher probability that the customer will buy or use the product.

The type of promotional techniques we choose to use will depend on the target market and the message to be delivered to it. In this respect, marketing communications can be divided into two categories of communication:

● *Non-personal* – This is one-way communication, where messages are sent to large numbers of people
● *Personal* – This is two-way communication, where messages are addressed to individuals or small groups.

Figure 3.31 illustrates the promotional techniques under each of these categories.

Task 3.18

In groups of three, consider whether non-personal or personal methods would be better for communicating with potential customers about the following:

● Specially designed conference facilities for travel businesspeople
● A Christmas pantomime
● A luxury cruise
● A GNVQ Leisure and Tourism course
● A reduction in price on theatre tickets.

Whatever your answers were, you should now realize that promotion is dependent on what the organization wants to achieve. Personal

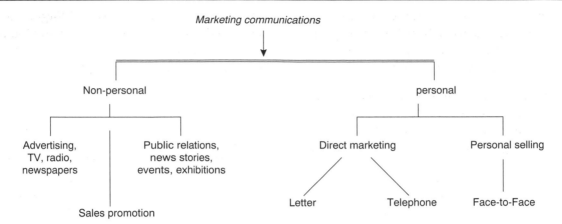

Figure 3.31   Marketing communication mix

communication, such as direct marketing and selling, is generally viewed as most suitable for situations where there are many risks for the customer making the decisions, such as choosing the right conference venue, education course, or booking a luxury cruise. The opposite is true for cheaper, possibly more readily available leisure and tourism products or services, such as going to the pantomime or the theatre. Here mass, non-personal methods are more appropriate.

Hopefully, you will have also come to the decision that both methods have a part to play in communicating with the market. The luxury cruise can be advertised in a newspaper or in a brochure (non-personal), but will eventually be sold by a personal visit to the travel agent or the cruise reservation office. The GNVQ course will be advertised in the local press and in the college students' handbook, but it is better explained to employers and students by appropriate college personnel.

Non-personal communications

Advertising – Advertising has been defined by the American Marketing Association as 'any paid form of non-personal presentation of ideas, goods or services by an identified sponsor'.

Every year, many leisure and tourism organizations, such as British Airways, First Leisure and Coca Cola, promote their products and services using advertising. Advertisements

are messages sent through the media which are intended to inform or influence the target market which receives them. The adverts are often targeted at consumers (i.e. the general public), but they can also be targeted at the trade (i.e. tour operators, reservations agencies, pubs or clubs, etc.).

Advertising objectives

Advertising in the leisure and tourism industry is no different to advertising in any other industry in that it seeks to influence customer behaviour in managing demand for the organization's products. The objectives for advertisers are many, but the principal ones are listed below:

- To create awareness
- To project favourable images or positions
- To reassure or remind customers of a product resource
- To stimulate desires and build demand for a product or service
- To promote favourable attitudes
- To generate action/response (i.e. increase sales or enquiries).

Media selection

The term 'media' refers to the various channels of communication used in advertising. Media selection will depend on the target market audience in respect of:

- *Coverage* – the number of potential customers the advertiser wishes to reach

- *Frequency* – the numbers of times the advertiser wishes the message to be heard or seen by the audience to have any effect. (This is often termed 'opportunity to see' (OTS)).

Remember, most advertisements are never seen or heard. Therefore, for advertising to be effective it must have good coverage and sufficient frequency to deliver the right impact on its target audience.

The most common advertising media used by the leisure and tourism industry include TV, radio, cinemas, newspapers, magazines, outdoor posters, point of sale and brochures.

Broadcast media

Broadcast media includes commercial television and commercial radio.

Television as a medium is outside the range of all but the largest leisure and tourism organizations, because of cost. However, it is seen as the most powerful media channel available because of its coverage in reaching some 98 per cent of all households, with viewing figures exceeding 20 million. TV commercials are of a high quality. Messages can be dynamic as they convey images, movement, sound and colour, with the ability to repeat the message over and over again. The main disadvantage is that it is very costly to produce and broadcast a TV commercial to a specific group of customers without incurring a lot of wastage.

Advertising is offered on independent television such as ITV, Sky Television, and, in selected regions, on cable television. ITV covers thirteen regions in the UK and offers advertisers the choice of regional or national advertising. Sky Television, together with Good Morning Television (GMTV) and Channel 4, offer national advertising. TV advertisements can be as short as a few seconds, or rather longer. ITV rates for advertising vary from region to region and from hour to hour. Prime viewing time is normally from 6.00 p.m. to 10.00 p.m. each evening.

Commercial radio is represented by approximately 120 independent local radio (ILR) stations as well as several independent national radio (INR)

stations, such as Classic FM and Virgin. Local radio stations can be geared to different audiences at different times of the day. The attraction to listeners is a constant stream of music, open chat shows and news about local events.

Overall, radio audiences are young people, housewives, and people driving to and from work. Although profiles differ by region, females outnumber male listeners. The great advantage of advertising on radio is that it gives a sense of urgency or action when communicating with consumers, such as, 'sale starts tomorrow' or 'book your seats today'. The cost of advertising on radio is also far less than on TV, but, like TV, rates vary by region and from hour to hour. Most large leisure and tourism organizations which advertise nationally continue to use TV, so most advertising on radio comes from local leisure providers.

Printed media

This is by far the largest sector of the media, with around 9000 regular publications in the UK which can be used by the advertiser. The sector includes all newspapers and magazines, both national and local, including trade press, periodicals and professional journals.

The major circulation of newspapers is in the tabloid press. Circulation and readership often determine the rates that are charged. However, in addition to the national press there is a much larger number of regional and local newspapers, the majority of local papers being free papers (i.e. you don't pay for them).

Basically, there are two types of advertisements that are placed in newspapers:

- *Display ads* – these advertisements are generally bigger and much more expensive. They are placed among news stories so that they stand out and get noticed
- *Classified ads* – these advertisements are normally only a few lines of copy listed under category heading. They are also the lifeblood of local newspapers.

TAUNTON DEANE LEISURE

Leisure Staff c. £8,485

We are looking for two enthusiastic, achievement orientated staff to continue the success of Taunton Deane Leisure (one post must be female).

You must be:-
- Flexible in approach to shift work.
- Dedicated to customer service.
- Able to achieve RLSS pool lifeguard.

We offer:-
- excellent working environment.
- Fast track career path.
- Varied and quality facilities.

Facilities Include:-
Dance studio, main halls, squash courts, indoor and outdoor tennis, fitness studios, health suites, climbing wall, dry slope skiing, indoor pools, golf course and licensed bars.

For an application form contact Wellington Sports Centre, Corams Lane, Wellington, Somerset TA21 8LL or telephone 01823 663010.

For an informal discussion contact Gary Fletcher on the above number.

Closing Date: Monday, 5th August 1996

Equal Opportunities Employer

Figure 3.32 An advertisement

There are many types of magazines, which differ considerably in terms of size, appearance and target readership. The most common types are:

- *General* – These are produced mainly on a monthly basis. The magazines are aimed at mass markets, although they generally cater for women (e.g. *Nova, Cosmopolitan, Woman, Prima, She*)

- *Specialist* – There has been a tremendous growth in the development and sales of these magazines, particularly in the hobby and leisure areas such as photography, home computers, DIY, gardening, holidays and sports

- *Retail* – These magazines are provided for business, and include the *Travel Trade Gazette, Hotel & Catering* and *Leisure*. Advertisers tend to be producers who wish to inform retailers of their new products and services

- *Professional* – Most professional associations have their own monthly or quarterly publications. The majority are circulated by post to their members rather than sold in shops.

The great advantage of the printed media is that it allows for accurate targeting. Customer types can be identified by analysing readership profiles. Long and complex messages can be sent, as the message is durable and can be read repeatedly. They can carry coupons, and many publishers are willing to support ad campaigns with news stories called advertorials about new products or changes in holiday destinations. Of course, there are disadvantages, the most notable being the amount of competing messages in any publication. Printed advertisements have static rather than dynamic qualities and, as such, are sometimes criticized for having poor impact.

Cinema

Cinema offers advertisers all the sound and colour of television plus a larger screen. However, gone are the days of the 2000-plus seated cinemas. Most cinemas today are multiplex cinemas, providing seats for a few hundred people. Advertising is usually concentrated at the start of the showing of a film. Audiences tend to be in the 16 – 24 age group, people on dates or young married couples. These people generally have money to spend, so advertising tends to concentrate on items such as cosmetics, cars, confectionery, car hire, soft drinks, holidays and fashion wear.

Unfortunately, audiences can fluctuate widely, depending on the popularity of the films being shown. Commercials tend to be shown only once during a programme and so are not reinforced unless the receiver is a regular cinema-goer.

Outdoor media

Outdoor media includes posters, hoardings, flashing signs, advertising on buses, trains or taxis, etc., even hot air balloons. This last is a particularly useful medium for attracting attention so as to remind people of a product or to reinforce a more detailed TV or newspaper message.

If situated in a well frequented site, the outdoor medium can have a considerable impact. Unfortunately, all the best sites are pre-booked several years in advance.

Point of sale

Point of sale includes a variety of media, including shelf takers, mobiles, illuminated displays, banners, stickers, flags, all of which are designed to attract our attention and direct the customer's eye to a particular message. The medium is very often placed directly above the product it is referring to and positioned where most people decide to look, try or buy.

Brochures

Whatever the product being promoted in the leisure and tourism industry, it is likely that a brochure of some kind will be produced. A college will need a prospectus, a resort area a guide or directory, an airline a timetable, a restaurant a menu. There are many types of brochures, including accommodation directories, specific product brochures (e.g. farm holidays, theatre weekends, car rental, train and bus timetables). There are also attraction leaflets (e.g. theme parks, museums, art galleries and amusement parks), tourist board brochures, not forgetting tour operator holiday brochures.

In the case of tour operators, the brochure represents the holiday product in a tangible form. It spells out in print and through colour what the tour operator's products and services consist of. The brochure allows the company's product to be displayed on shelves and to be taken home.

One of the questions often faced in leisure and tourism is whether to produce one or several brochures (or leaflets) for different market segments. It is for this reason that you can obtain travel brochures on trains, ferries and bus services and separate brochures on short- or long-break holidays using the same travel services, but offering accommodation and services, possibly under different holiday destination headings.

The great advantage of the brochure is that it not only lends a tangible form to a leisure or tourism experience, it can also convey a great deal of information and interest to selected targeted groups of customers, through a variety of channels. Most travel brochures are provided via travel agents. However, advertisements on TV, radio or via the press are also effective in getting customers to make enquiries about brochures. However, where companies have built up customer databases, direct marketing techniques can be used to target the brochures direct to known interested markets. In addition to the brochure, several organizations, including theme parks, hotels and regional and national tourist boards, have introduced videos to provide movement and greater use of pictures.

Public relations (PR)

This form of promotion is to do with marketing an organization's image. Unlike advertising, which is a primary source of communication under the control of the organization which you pay for it, PR is not under your direct control and is 'free'. It includes such sources as word of mouth, editorial comment and promotional activities. In turn, because of the impartial nature of these sources they tend to carry a lot of weight with customers, making PR a very persuasive form of communication.

Public relations or PR can be divided into press and corporate relations. Figure 3.33 illustrates the key PR activities under each of these headings.

Press relations

Media contact – A key task in PR is to maintain contact with the key journalists in the media. Through such contact, the PR representative of the organization learns about and can contribute to features which will be appearing in the media (possibly a holiday feature on camping and caravanning in the UK). On the other hand, journalists become more receptive to news stories from the organization about its products and services.

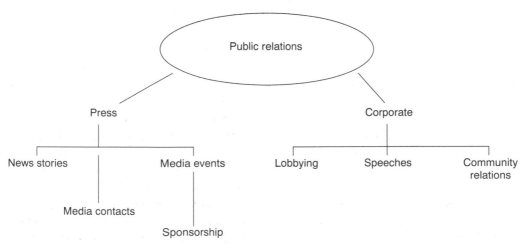

Figure 3.33 PR activities

News stories – Providing interesting and entertaining news items about the company and its products, whether genuine or manufactured, is at the heart of good PR. Editorial news coverage can be carried in all forms of media, such as newspapers, magazines, on the radio and even TV. Think of the number of times in a TV news bulletin or chat show that pop and sports stars, company products, even politicians get a mention. To be successful, the stories must be well written and directed for the consumption of specific target audiences.

Media events – When opening a new leisure centre, library or college, putting on a new train service or launching a new leisure product, the media event is a good, tried and tested PR activity for getting your message across. It involves inviting journalists for a free lunch or dinner and exposure to the product being launched. To be successful, this PR activity needs to be very well planned. Not only has the event got to be newsworthy, the accompanying product message must be very well presented in a form that readily lends itself to be carried in subsequent editorial stories (*Note*: remember always to include interesting black and white photographs).

Sponsorship – Sponsorship is about giving money to support an organization or event in exchange for which the sponsor usually gains some free publicity. This is a growing area of promotional activity in which the leisure and tourism industry, particularly sports, does extremely well.

Some examples of sponsorship include:

Sponsorship	*Sponsor*
Round the World Yacht Race	Whitbread
Football League	Endsleigh Insurance
British Library	Digital Equipment Co.
Rugby World Cup Series	Famous Grouse Whisky
London Marathon	Nutra-Sweet
Young Athletics League	McDonalds
Professional Tour of Britain Cycle Race	Kelloggs
European Football Championship	Sega

Sponsorship is often seen by companies as a very effective means of building a positive corporate image with its target markets. For some companies who, because of the law, have limited access to the media, such as gaming organizations or tobacco companies, this is a very productive channel for getting their product name across. The activities they sponsor are invariably well supported and followed with interest by their markets and, by association, it is believed that their markets will become interested in the sponsor and its products, or simply gain a favourable awareness of the name.

Corporate relations – Corporate relations generally involves promoting the organization to specific groups of people who have a stake or say in the running of it, such as shareholders, employees, local authorities, trusts, financial institutions, even government. Corporate PR enables the organization to build strong relationships and favourable images of the company through:

Community relations – This activity involves publishing and issuing company newsletters, annual reports and prospectuses, company magazines, sponsored journals and so on. Other activities can include open days, exhibitions, charity events, providing prizes for sports days, etc. The Sellafield Visitor Centre, for example, is seen as providing a PR window on the nuclear world, and has itself become a top tourist attraction in the North of England.

Preparing speeches – Senior management in leisure and tourism organizations are often requested to give talks to interested groups. Often the job of the corporate PR is to 'ghost write' the speeches and prepare the presentation, including press kits.

Lobbying – This PR activity is to do with influencing those with political power. Political consultants are employed by the very largest of leisure and tourism organizations, such as British Airways, British Rail and the water companies. Whether the political issue is airline mergers, the takeover of water companies or home audio-taping, lobbying goes on. MPs, civil servants, even government ministers can be lobbied. The Northwest Regional Tourist Board has in the past lobbied its local MPs on environmental issues in the area by presenting its arguments by mail and in person and by organizing a politicians' tea party at the Houses of Parliament. The main effort was in identifying its target market of MPs who were likely to be favourably inclined towards what the organization had to say, wanted to achieve or wanted to see happen. These MPs were then briefed on the issue, in the hope that they would influence others, preferably in government, to take some action. It is generally agreed that such lobbying was very effective in changing the Sunday trading laws, in getting the political backing for the Channel Tunnel to be built and, more recently, in changing the gaming laws of the UK in order to set up and run the National Lottery in its present form.

Case study

The travel workshop

The Travel Workshop is a special type of exhibition which restricts its public to include only the buyers and sellers of the travel trade who are invited for the purpose of negotiating travel business. British travel workshops are often organized under the supervision of the national tourist boards (NTBs) or even regional tourist boards (RTBs) with venues in the UK and overseas.

Typical overseas sites for the British Tourist Authority (BTA) include New York, Chicago, Los Angeles, Sydney, Frankfurt, Dublin and Paris. Some workshops have particular themes, such as coaching holidays, canal cruises, golfing breaks, whereas others have a regional or destination emphasis, such as tourism in England's North Country (Cumbria, Northumberland and Carlisle). Suppliers with an interest in incoming tourists, such as hoteliers, coach companies, attractions, ground handling agents, etc., will arrange to rent desk space at the workshop, which normally runs for up to three to four days.

Airlines, ferry operators, tour operators and others from the tourism-generating countries can use the workshop as a convenient way of meeting UK suppliers of tourism products under one roof. Such companies can negotiate next season's tour programme requirements – such as bedspace, transfer services, excursions, catering, etc. – without having to travel far from home.

Task 3.19

1 Imagine you are the Marketing Manager for the regional tourist board seeking to arrange a travel workshop in Japan in order to promote your region of the UK to the Japanese travel trade. Decide on an appropriate theme which would help you to promote the workshop, giving your reasons why.

2 Decide which tourist suppliers from your region you would invite to rent space at the workshop.

Sales promotion

Sales promotion is to do with encouraging people to make a purchase, and although for some this would simply mean in-store merchandising (that is, the way goods or services are presented for sale), most would agree that it covers a wide variety of non-personal forms of communication.

The Institute of Sales Promotion defines sales promotion as:

the function of marketing which seeks to achieve a given objective by the adding of intrinsic, tangible values to a product or service

Sales promotion objectives might, for example, include:

- Selling excess products, such as seats on a plane

- Promoting new restaurant to help gain awareness
- Achieving brochure display in travel agent's
- Securing dealer support for stocking a new line of leisure wear
- Increasing usage of leisure centre at off-peak times of the day.

The essential feature of sales promotion activity is that it involves short-term inducements which add value to the product by encouraging customers to buy now rather than later – for example, buy four cinema tickets and get 20 per cent off', or 'visit our restaurant and receive a week-end break accommodation voucher.'

Sales promotions come in many forms, but they can be divided into two broad categories: trade and consumer.

- *Trade* – those activities designed to enhance the sales of the product to the trade
- *Consumer* – those activities which assist the trade in promoting and selling products to the final consumer.

Figure 3.34 below lists the sales promotion techniques under each of the categories.

Some examples of these techniques are explained below:

Trade promotion

Discounts and allowances – Also referred to as dealer loaders, these are generally schemes which allow the trade a reduction in the price of the product provided they sell or stock a certain quantity of goods. For example, airlines and

TRADE	CONSUMER
Discounts	Samples
Allowances	Coupons
Free products	Competitions
Free gifts	Special offers
Exhibitions	Gifts
Shows	Loyalty incentives
Educational visits	

Figure 3.34 Sales promotion techniques

hotels will discount their seats or provide preferential terms to tour operators for advance block bookings. Manufacturers of sportswear will discount the price of a new sports strip for shops who will stock a given number of outfits or who achieve pre-established sales targets over a given time period.

Free products – are often provided as a means of getting the product accepted and put on the retailer's shelf for sale. For example, a free football kit may be provided with every twenty purchased.

Free gifts – such as bottles of spirits, clocks, watches or diaries, sometimes influence the choice of goods stocked by the trade

Exhibitions and shows – provide a venue for allowing the trade to sample or test the products on offer.

Point of sale – materials such as displays, posters, brochure racks, even brochures and leaflets can be offered to the trade free of charge or on loan in support of volume orders for a company's, products. Record companies will often provide special racking for shops selling their CDs, records and tapes, together with posters and supporting top 40 album chart lists.

Educational visits – are used by a number of organizations in leisure and tourism to promote their services to key target groups. When a new leisure facility such as a leisure centre, museum, school or swimming pool is being opened, selected groups of people who might want to use these facilities are often encouraged to come and view and try the facilities free of charge. Travel organizers, in conjunction with the national tourist boards, will often arrange what are called familiarization visits to the UK to educate overseas travel trade customers as to what is available.

Consumer promotions

Samples or trial packs – are either given or sold to consumers at low prices to encourage them to try the product, in the hope that this will stimulate further purchases.

Coupons – these are often given in the form of money-off vouchers which are distributed door-to-door or appear as part of an advertisement or offered on a pack (for example, 50 per cent off the price of entry into a theme park when submitting the money-off voucher).

Special offers – are numerous in the leisure and travel industry, and can include such offers as 'buy two meals, get one free', 'half price for children for every full paying adult', etc.

Competitions – these often interest people, particularly if there is an attractive prize, such as a holiday for two abroad. Scratchcards, free draws and bingo cards are popular.

Loyalty incentives – these often come in the form of discount vouchers or points such as Air Miles, which are very popular in getting customers to repeat their visits or purchases again and again.

Personal communications

Direct marketing – Direct marketing, like selling, is another means of talking directly to your customers. Unlike selling, which is face-to-face, direct marketing uses the mail or the phone to communicate with much larger numbers of people. Direct marketing in this context can be defined as the use of non-personal media to personally introduce products to consumers and encourage their purchase direct from the company concerned.

With the growth of computerization, many companies, large and small, have found this method of promotion to be very cost-effective in communicating with its markets. Companies build up lists of customer names from a variety of sources which they believe will have some interest in their products, for example from:

- Sales receipts bearing the names and addresses of past customers
- Responses to advertisements for their products
- Membership lists, annuals or directories
- Hiring or buying other organizational lists (from list brokers).

The most common direct marketing techniques in use are:

- Mail order
- Direct response advertising
- Direct mail
- Door-to-door distribution.

Mail order – this communication technique generally makes use of catalogues from which consumers can order products direct, either through the mail or direct from company outlets. Direct marketing holiday organizations such as Portland or Owners Abroad use this method of communicating with their target markets, using their holiday brochures to sell their holidays in the same way as Grattans or Next catalogues would sell their leisure goods.

Direct response advertising – this involves placing advertisements in the media which encourage consumers to reply direct to the supplier, often using a coupon in a newspaper or magazine. Other media used to sell direct can include radio and television, where the target audience is advised to contact a given telephone number or address to order the goods or, as so often is the case, to receive further information in the form of a brochure.

Direct mail – is a technique whereby companies communicate directly with their potential customers by mail, in order to try to persuade them to buy. With the sophistication of computer techniques, companies such as Readers Digest can send letters to its customers which to all intents and purposes, look as if they have been written just for you. The great advantages of this technique are that:

- Messages can be personalized and even graphics added, such as a map showing the location of the nearest retailer stocking the product
- Customers who have a interest in your product can be more accurately targeted, thereby increasing the effectiveness of the technique in terms of customer response and lower-costs.

A direct mail campaign can be carried out very quickly, for example in leisure and tourism:

- A leisure pool can mail all the local schools, clubs and societies in the area about a new gala event it is running
- A hotel mails to all its previous guests a sales promotional offer inviting them to return in the autumn
- A theme park mails details of its educational or group rates to coach operators, group organizations and schools.

Door-to-door distribution – this method of communication is to do with dropping printed material through people's letterboxes using private organizations rather than the Post Office. It is much less expensive than direct mail in that it does not seek to target particular individuals or groups of customers; rather, it focuses on covering all households within a given area. This can be done on a national basis (a method favoured by the football pools companies) or it can be done locally. Local restaurants, sports centres, theatres and clubs, etc. often find this to be a very effective way of communicating with a large number of people direct within a given distance of their premises.

Personal selling – Face-to-face selling is about talking to individuals or small groups of people. It includes face-to-face selling between, for example, tour operators and travel agents or between travel agents and the public. It is an extremely powerful way of communicating and persuading people to buy, but very costly for this reason. Where personal contact is involved, the target market is often very small. Each customer in the market can be made to feel that he or she is being approached as an individual.

For the leisure and tourism industry, personal selling is a vital component of the communication mix. When all is said and done, the leisure and tourism industry is a people business – that is to say, the people who attend to the needs of the visitors or customers form an essential ingredient of the product itself. Personal selling in this context can involve sales staff behind a shop counter, a receptionist at the leisure pool, a resort representative at a holiday destination or, for that matter, any of the hundreds of staff with whom

customers have contact (e.g. coaches, bar stewards, coach drivers, porters, waitresses, etc.). All play a role in providing the product or service satisfaction.

A point to remember is that selling is about helping people to buy rather than selling them something they do not need or want.

Telesales – somewhere between direct mail and the face-to-face sales call lies 'telesales', also called 'telemarketing'. This is a personal form of promotion, as communication with the customer can be two-way. It is a medium that is used most often in the business or trade side of the leisure and tourism industry. Its advantage over face-to-face selling is the rate at which calls can be made. Up to fifty telephone sales calls can be made in one day, compared with as few as twenty-five face-to-face calls a week. With the advances in telecommunications, telephone selling is expected to become even more prevalent in the leisure and tourism industry.

Telesales are often linked to national advertising campaigns in various media, with telephone numbers to ring when ordering. This is called **inbound marketing**. British Telecom offers telemarketing organizations both the Freephone service (via the operator the average call cost is about £1.75) and Linkline 0800. This latter method allows the customer to contact the advertiser direct free of charge. The opening up of ISDN (integrated services digital network) lines and the creation of multimedia packages may, in the future, mean that more selling will be done 'down the lines', with visual packages being presented PC to PC.

The advertising agency

Small businesses such as guest houses, restaurants or local attractions may seek to undertake their own advertising, PR or design and arrange to print their own leaflets or brochures. However, if the services or products for sale require you to communicate with a very large target audience, it may mean having to produce a major holiday brochure, a TV or radio commercial or a colour advertisement in a national magazine. In this case, professional help may be required in the form of an advertising agency, who will provide or acquire all the necessary skills and expertise to handle all aspects of a promotional campaign.

Once a promotional campaign is agreed, the agency may be responsible for undertaking not only the advertising but also PR, sales promotion, direct mail and print. Most advertising agencies will provide:

- Creative services, providing original concepts and ideas in developing the message via copy writing, designing all visual material, including brochures
- Media selection, scheduling and purchasing of the space in both the broadcast and printed media, even direct mail, and the evaluation of the campaign
- Artwork and general production and supply of the finished items, including brochures, display and point-of-sale material.

With all creative work, a general rule which should always be observed is KISS – Keep It Short – Keep It Simple. Never try to promote more than one or two key messages at the same time. Promoting too many messages confuses people as to what you are trying to say and dilutes the effectiveness of the main message.

Agencies are paid on commission (15 per cent) which they receive from media owners when they buy advertising space for their client. In addition, fees will be charged for work which is not covered by the commission, such as for PR, sales promotion or direct marketing activities. Most agencies would be pleased to do business with leisure and tourism organizations who had up to £20,000 to spend, but even with budgets of smaller sums, smaller local agencies will often be happy to offer their professional services.

Evaluating the effectiveness of marketing communications

Pre- and post-testing of the market

The most common method of evaluating the success of a promotional campaign is to test the views of a representative sample of your target market both before and after the campaign. Pre-testing will determine what proportion of the market are already aware of the organization's product and their perceptions of the product or the organization before the campaign begins. Post-testing will involve asking the same questions of another sample of the market so as to gauge what movement in awareness, attitudes or possibly sales has been achieved by the campaign.

Assessment criteria

Because of the problems of isolating the effects of the various promotional techniques on sales, the best way of assessing different promotional expenditure is to review the promotional objectives set for each. All promotional objectives are basically concerned with some form of movement in persuading the target market to behave in some way. The persuasion pendulum, as shown in Figure 3.35, reflects the likely impact of the key promotional techniques in getting the market to move towards action over time.

Some of the key criteria often used in terms of customer response relate to:

1 Increased sales (i.e. greater usage of the leisure pool, more beds occupied in a hotel or more 'bums on seats' at a theatre)
2 Increased market share (reviewing sales performance as a proportion of the overall sales for the market as a whole)
3 Repeat business (checking to see how many of the sales are coming from past customers)

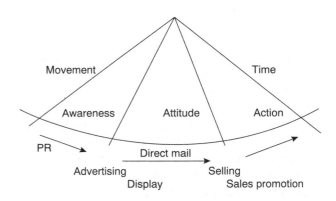

Figure 3.35 The persuasion pendulum

4 New business (checking to see how many of the sales are coming from new customers).

Measuring the effectiveness of the promotional techniques

● The effectiveness of press or magazine advertising can be relatively easy to measure, provided the advertisement includes a pre-coded response coupon. The code on the coupon identifies the magazine or newspaper from which an enquiry was received. Have a look at advertisements which carry coupons, and it is likely that you will see a code in the corner of the coupon, such as DE25/5-1. The code often identifies the paper and the date of insertion of the advertisement – in this case, *Daily Express*, 25 May, first insertion.

● Television and radio advertising are more difficult to measure, unless they are seeking a response by getting viewers to call a certain telephone number or write to a given address. This form of media advertising is often used to create or improve the perception and image for a leisure product or service. Organizations will judge the effectiveness of their advertising over time by monitoring the effect on ultimate sales, but in the interim pre- and post-testing of the market will provide a measure of the success or failure of their promotional advertising techniques in improving awareness or altering the behaviour of their markets in some way.

● Public relations, like television and radio, is also hard to measure because it, too, is often involved with building awareness and improving the image of the organization and its products. Again, pre- and post-testing is an effective measure. However, organizations can measure the amount of free editorial coverage obtained in the press or on TV, etc. The number of articles, features and pictures of its products covered in the press can be measured in what is called 'column inches', or those carried on TV or radio can be measured by the amount of 'air time' obtained. The value of the free coverage can be calculated against the advertising rates the media would normally charge, which can then be compared with the costs incurred in putting the PR package together.

● Point-of-sale and display are, again, very much involved with gaining attention and building on the perceptions and image of the product or organization, and so can only be effectively measured over time, using pre- and post-testing techniques. Interestingly, because of the cost, some of the larger retail stores try to isolate this promotional technique in order to measure customer reaction. How they do this is by inviting local customers to view and make comment on changes in design of their stores. The sales of the store are then monitored over an agreed time-span and compared with sales previously obtained.

● Sales promotion requires a quick response from our market: for example to take up an offer of a free gift. The emphasis is on action, which generally makes it easier for the leisure and tourism organizations to monitor its effectiveness.

● Direct marketing, including selling and direct mail, are relatively easier to measure because of the targeted nature of the promotional techniques. Mailings to households can include coded coupons or tickets similar to the advertisements so that responses can be accurately recorded. Selling, on the other hand, can be monitored against set budgets or targets to see how each salesperson is performing.

▪ Assignment 3.3 ▪

Students are to investigate the marketing communications of two leisure and tourism organizations. One should be from the leisure and recreation industry and one from the travel and tourism industry. A report is required which compares and evaluates the effectiveness of the marketing communications of each organization. The findings of the report should cover the organization's marketing communications objectives and promotional activities.

Coverage

- Element 3.3
- Performance Criteria 1,2,3,4,5
- Core Skill Opportunities
  - Communication
  - IT

Task 1

In small groups, decide on the two leisure and tourism organizations you wish to investigate – one from the leisure and recreation industry and one from the travel and tourism industry.

Task 2

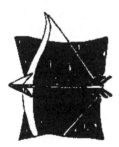

After investigation, describe the marketing communications objectives of each organization.

Task 3

Identify the likely target markets to whom the communications will be addressed.

Task 4

Explain how the organization achieves its communications objectives in terms of the promotional techniques it applies, using the headings:

- *Advertising*
- *Public relations*
- *Sales promotion*
- *Direct marketing*
- *Personal selling.*

Task 5

Evaluate and compare the effectiveness of each organization's communications using the following criteria:

- *Increased sales*
- *New business*
- *Repeat business*
- *Brand/customer loyalty*
- *Public awareness*
- *Increased market share*
- *Keeping within budget.*

Task 6

Share information and produce an individual report, preferably word-processed, of not more than 2000 words and supported by market analysis data, advertisements, leaflets, posters or other promotional material.

Element 3.4 Develop a marketing plan for a selected leisure and tourism organization

Performance criteria

This Element will cover the following performance criteria:

1 Identify the organizational objectives of selected leisure and tourism organizations.
2 Analyse the marketing environment in selected leisure and tourism organizations.
3 Explain the key marketing objectives of the marketing plan for a selected leisure and tourism organization.
4 Propose marketing research methods to be used.
5 Propose marketing communication methods to be used.
6 Explain how the plan can be implemented.
7 Describe evaluation techniques and criteria for effectiveness to be applied.
8 Present a marketing plan for a selected leisure and tourism product/service.

What is marketing planning?

All leisure and tourism organizations, however big or small, are engaged in marketing activity. For example, the local cinema has to make decisions about which films to show, what times to screen the films, the prices to be charged and how to advertise and preview the films. Some organizations will operate from what is termed the 'seat of their pants', by reacting to situations as they occur. Marketing decisions will be taken on the spur of the moment, with little or no regard for the future. Others will spend a great deal of time and effort in charting a future course of action, by scheduling and costing out what has to be done to achieve their objectives. This process can be defined as marketing planning, which is the application of the organizational goals and resources to achieve marketing objectives.

Why plan at all?

The importance of planning stems from a changing and often hostile environment in which all leisure and tourism organizations operate, together with internal factors which interact to affect the organization's ability to achieve profitable sales. Planning is needed in the short term to simply identify where the company is at now, where it will be next week, month, even year. Companies need to know where their current sales are coming from in order to arrange to pay their own bills, such as salaries and overheads. Of course, beyond this companies need to plan to achieve longer-term objectives, to develop new products or markets. A cinema company may need to obtain funding to help build a new cinema or buy a chain of existing cinemas. The company will need to have these planning details in place if it is to persuade a bank or prospective investor to lend them the finance required.

The marketing planning process

Marketing planning should be seen as a sequence of stages or activities leading to the setting of marketing objectives and the formulation of plans for achieving them. A good marketing plan will seek to provide answers to several key planning questions. The marketing stages or activities required to address these questions provide a structure for preparing a marketing plan, as shown in Figure 3.36.

To start the process requires the organization to review its goals and resources as well as the

Questions	Planning stage
What business are we in?	Organization's goals or mission
Where are we now?	
Where do we want to go?	Situation reviewed. SWOT analysis
How should we get there?	Marketing objectives
(i.e. how should we organize our resources?)	Marketing strategy, including marketing programmes
How will we know when we have arrived?	Evaluation and control

Figure 3.36 The marketing planning process

marketing opportunities it wishes to exploit. To do this effectively, the marketing plan must begin by:

- Defining its business purpose – This is often presented as a statement which describes the nature of the business, the products to be offered and the markets served. In effect, it provides direction and purpose for all parts of the organization

- Setting the marketing objectives that relate to the overall aims and mission of the organization

- Formulating strategies to achieve the objectives, including both a marketing budget and implementation programmes, which detail what will be done, by whom and when

- Evaluating, controlling, monitoring and reviewing the implementation of the strategy to ensure that the marketing objectives are being achieved

- Reviewing the current situation in the market place by analysing its marketing environment (using PEST and SWOT, as indicated in Element 3.1). Although this is the start of any plan, it naturally positions itself at the end as the process begins all over again (see Figure 3.37).

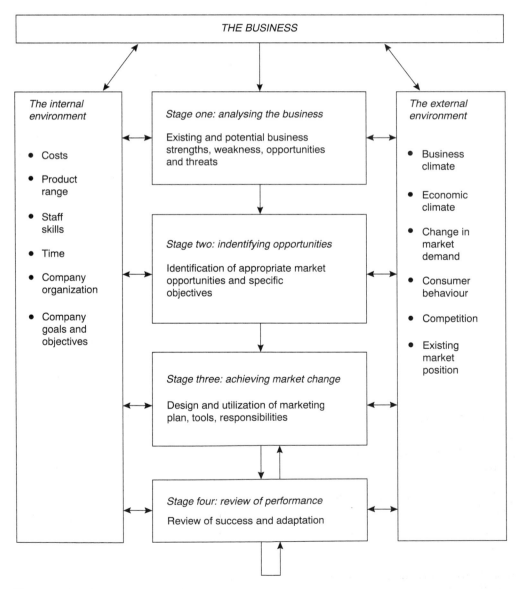

Figure 3.37 The planning cycle

Organizational objectives (What business are we in or should we be in?)

Defining the business

All business start with some resources which they want to use to achieve something. In deciding what it wants to achieve, a leisure and tourism organization must ask itself two questions:

1 What business are we in?
2 What business do we want to be in?

For many, this will mean continuing within the boundaries of their existing business. In other words, a restaurant may decide that it wants to continue to be a restaurant, possibly offering different meals to an older market, but wants more profits. However, it may wish to alter the whole nature of its business by turning it into a sweetshop (i.e. diversifying) or simply by selling the business.

The role of mission statements

Having defined the business, the company needs to set out its organizational goals or mission. Many companies start this process by developing a mission statement, which seeks to encapsulate what the business wants to achieve, the product and markets it seeks to serve – in effect, the general direction the company should follow. Most mission statements are broad and short, but overall they set out the purpose and values of the organization. Extracts of mission statements that leisure and tourism organizations might adopt are provided below:

To become the market leader in telecommunications
Source: Cable & Wireless, Report and Accounts, 1990

To be the best and most successful company in the airline business
Source: British Airways, Report and Accounts, 1991

To become the market leader in Theme Parks
Source: Thorpe Park, UK

Task 3.20

Whose mission do you believe the above statement best refers to?

These broad aims, however, are often refined by those who have a stake in the business, such as those listed below:

Stakeholder	Concerns
Owner	To set realistic goals and receive sufficient reward for their efforts
Staff	To provide job security and future prospects
Visitors	To provide satisfying experiences
Central and local government	To ensure that public facilities and funds are being used efficiently to help provide jobs
Investors	To get the maximum return on their investment
Suppliers	To receive prompt payment on their loans and ensure that their investment is safe
General public	To ensure that greater access to leisure and tourism facilities does not lead to unacceptable levels of safety, congestion, pollution and changes in lifestyle, etc.

To this end, the British Airways mission statement goes on to explain its goals in fuller detail:

Mission
To be the best or most successful company in the airline industry.

Goals
'Safe and Secure'
To be a safe and secure airline.

Financially strong
To deliver a strong and consistent financial performance.

Global leader
To secure a leading share of air travel business worldwide, with a significant presence in all major geographical markets.

Service and value
To provide overall superior service and good value for money in every market segment in which we compete.

Customer-driven
To excel in anticipating and quickly responding to customer needs and competitor activity.

Good employer
To be a good neighbour, concerned with the community and the environment.

Task 3.21

1 *Identify likely stakeholders (i.e. those with an interest) of British Airways and link the appropriate parts of the mission statement that would have a bearing on them.*
2 *How does British Airways' mission statement provide direction for the organization?*

Analysing the marketing environment (Where are we now?)

Anyone who has been involved in marketing will advise you to keep an eye on the marketing environment in which you operate. Although an organization has within its power the ability to change aspects of its internal environment and operations, it nevertheless operates within an external environment over which it has little or no control, as shown in Figure 3.38.

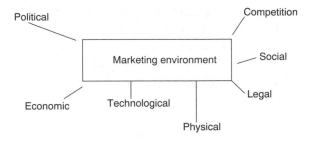

Figure 3.38   External marketing environment

This represents the **diagnostic** stage of the planning process in assessing the impact of forces such as politics, competition, economy, technology, etc., on the marketing performance of the company. For example, boom and slump in the economy can both harm and improve the chances of a new product becoming successful. One important factor of the environment that greatly affects tourism is the weather. A poor summer in Britain will often lead to an increase in late demand for holidays abroad. Of course, economic factors play a part here. A sudden late demand for foreign holidays will have the effect of pushing up prices as operators try to buy extra hotel beds and airline seats. In turn, the British operator will be in competition with the German, French, Dutch and Scandinavian countries, who may be prepared to pay higher prices and so force the prices up further.

The diagnostic stage is based on marketing research in drawing together available published and unpublished data for analysis of trends under four basic headings. These are summarized below as:

1 **Sales trends** All organizations should attempt to monitor up to five yearly movements of company sales as well as total market sales. This will identify whether the market is growing and will provide information on market shares. For example, a hotel group could compare its sales data with government or tourist authority accommodation data.
2 **Consumer trends** Details of who buys what, when and in what quantities, including details on demographics, lifestyle, attitudes and behaviour, need to be compared with competitor or customer profiles. Some of the

data will be available from company records, the rest through market surveys.

3 **Product trends** Plotting the sales movement of the product and its competitor products over time will identify the product life cycle movements and, in particular highlight those products that are growing and those that are declining. Trade associations will often provide market data on product/service types which can be compared against internal business records as well as articles written in the trade press.

4 **Environmental trends** Changes or trends in the external environment, such as technology, politics, exchange rate movements, the economy, can all affect a company's performance. Imagine the impact that the recent change in the licensing law had on drinking habits. With pubs now being open all day, there is no longer the urge to rush out for a drink at set times. Possible changes in health and safety or the law, such as seatbelts being fitted to all coaches or bulkheads being required on all roll-on-roll-off ferries, possible motorway taxes, etc., will impact on the company's cost of operation and so affect price.

These changes are many and can be obtained by constant scanning of the news and trade press. However, it may be necessary to carry out some marketing research studies to assess the consumer response to any such changes occurring.

The next stage in the planning process, called the **prognosis** stage, is also research-based, but it is to do with forecasting the likely outcome if certain changes occur. Leisure and tourism organizations must use the information from the diagnostic stage to judge or forecast the likely changes under each of the four headings.

Having collected all the relevant data through the process of diagnosis and prognosis, which in effect tells us the situation the company is currently in and where it is likely to be headed, the next stage is to decide where the company *should* be headed. A useful framework for this assessment is called SWOT.

Case study

The video age

Philips is an international manufacturer of leisure equipment, including TVs, computers, radios, hi-fis, CDs and video recorders. In the late 1970s Philips launched its state-of-the-art Video 2000 system in competition with several other video systems, such as Sony's Betamax and Matsushita VHS system. Despite several decades of research, culminating in what was seen by the trade as the most technologically advanced video recording system of its day, the Video 2000 system failed.

Internationally, it was quickly realized that consumers wanted only one system that was compatible with all. Despite teething repair problems, the major reason for the system failing was believed to be its late entry into the video market, coupled with the mistaken belief at the time that users would have little interest in hiring or buying commercially produced videos. At the same time, several national companies within the Philips group of companies were designing their own products and communication packages for their own markets. The North American Philips Corporation, for example, did not even attempt to sell the Video 2000 system, preferring instead to concentrate on promoting the VHS system only. After a short life span, Philips had to withdraw its video system for lack of sales, and instead was forced to adopt the VHS system using Japanese technology. This meant that costs were higher and it would not gain the market share it had anticipated from a growing leisure market product, and, in turn, lost millions of pounds in the process.

Things are different at Philips today. The corporate headquarters in Holland co-ordinates all product launches and campaigns around the world, leaving the separate national companies to develop their sales nationally.

Task 3.22

1 *How many of the problems that Philips encountered can you identify as being of an:*
   (a) internal weakness
   (b) external influence?
2 *How can Philips plan for change in its external environment?*

3 *How might a corporate mission statement help Philips co-ordinate its activities worldwide?*

SWOT analysis

SWOT, as identified in Element 3.1, stands for strengths, weaknesses, opportunities and threats. An example of such an analysis, identifying the potential strengths and weaknesses, opportunities and threats of a travel agent planning to open a new outlet in a city centre, is given in Figure 3.39 below:-

Strengths	Weaknesses
(These factors are internal to the organization)	
The new outlet is very conveniently situated in the centre of town	Difficult to attract the right calibre of staff on affordable wage
The outlet has good open access for displaying the holiday products	Much higher costs operating in town centre
	There are no car parks in the immediate area
Opportunities	Threats
(These factors are external to the organization)	
The business community is within a 5-minute walk, providing another large potential market	The shopping area is poorly served by public transport
A new department store is planned to open in the near future which should attract even more potential customers	A major competitor is looking to lease space in the new department store

Figure 3.39 SWOT Analysis

Task 3.23

Individually or in groups, carry out a SWOT analysis of a leisure or tourism organization known to you.

Examples could include:

- *The school or college you attend*
- *A club of which you are a member*
- *A youth club, church or charity you may be involved with*
- *A museum or gallery*
- *A cinema or theatre*
- *A local bus or train company.*

Marketing objectives (Where do we want to go?)

The difference between organizational goals and marketing objectives is the difference between general and specific aims. Organizational goals relate to general objectives, such as:

- To enlarge the market
- To increase market share
- To increase profit.

Following an analysis and review of the business environment, these should then be turned into much tighter, more specific marketing targets as to where the company wants to go, such as:

- To increase the company's share of the cinema market by 10 per cent within three years
- To incorporate new cinematographic technology to attract custom away from the competition
- To attract 20 000 extra visitors to a cinema over the next twelve months
- To reduce the seasonality of demand by attracting 15 per cent more visitors in the winter months of November through to March
- To increase profits by 5 per cent over the next twelve months

- To introduce a new product in a growing market (i.e. a bistro to be attached to the cinema).

The marketing plan will be designed to achieve one or more of these objectives by the use of selected choice of strategies.

Marketing strategies (How should we get there?)

Marketing strategies form the answer to the question, How are we going to achieve our objectives?

Marketing strategies are usually based on manipulating the marketing mix to help the leisure and tourism organization to implement its strategy. As discussed earlier in this Unit, the marketing mix is made up of the four Ps – product, price, place and promotion. However, in a predominantly service-based industry such as leisure and tourism it may be more appropriate to include three extra Ps – people, physical surroundings and process. In deciding on the most appropriate mix of these seven components, a leisure and tourism organization will need to consider:

Product – features, benefits, service, quality, image

Price – pricing, costs, fares, subscriptions, surcharges, discounts, demand, competitor pricing

Promotion – advertising, PR, sales promotion, direct marketing, personal selling

Place – distribution, location, accessibility, opening times

People – staff, training, appearance, behaviour

Physical (surroundings) – layout, design, furnishings, noise

Process – policies and procedures, returns policies, booking procedures, reservations, queuing, customer care.

Examples of strategic options for achieving the organization's objectives in a variety of leisure and tourism organizations are given in Figure 3.40.

Choosing a strategy

A leisure and tourism organization can basically choose one of three strategies:

- Undifferentiated marketing
- Differentiated marketing
- Concentrated marketing.

Undifferentiated marketing is where a single marketing mix is offered to the total market (see Figure 3.41). Very few companies follow this strategy successfully because most markets are made up of different types of customers with many differing needs and wants.

Coca Cola did follow the approach for many years, offering only one standard product and marketing mix for all markets. However, today it offers a variety of colas and soft drinks aimed at many market segments.

Differentiated marketing is an attempt by a company to tailor individual products and marketing mix strategies to different segments of the market (see Figure 3.42). For example, the airline market may be divided up into an economy class segment, first or luxury class segment, even business or executive club class segments.

Concentrated marketing is when a company selects one segment of the market and concentrates on customizing its product with the most effective marketing mix in getting these customers to buy from it (see Figure 3.43). It is often the best strategy for a small company to adopt. Many small voluntary organizations adopt this approach, as do some commercial organizations such as Porsche Cars, Fred Olsen Cruises and the Caravan Club.

Most companies will try to identify and then dominate market segments. Where competitive reaction means that similar products or services are offered, they will attempt to create differences in their products or services which customers will perceive as offering them greater value. These differences from the company's positioning strategy in creating a differential advantage over its competitors.

Objective	To Enlarge the Market	Increase Market Share	Increase Profits
Strategies	(a) *By improving existing salesproducts such as adding new features so more people have reason to buy.* For example providing better shops and catering facilities at a museum or new types of shows at a theatre. (b) *By providing new users for an existing product.* For example sportswear was made into a fashion product worn by non-sporting people. Alternatively it could involve industrial heritage attractions such as Iron Bridge or Wigan Pier trying to attract overseas visitors to visit them while on holiday in the UK (c) *By changing the scale of its operations.* A successful touring circus may decide to run extra tours in a season	(a) *By emphasizing product development* To show how good your new product or service is. A recently refurbished leisure centre may seek to attract users from other centres by emphasizing its new facilities or variety of programmes. (b) *By changing its distribution.* A hotel may decide to expand its sales by offering its accommodation through travel and reservation agencies rather than simply by direct bookings (c) *By altering its advertising and sales promotion.* A restaurant which has always advertised in local press may decide to use promotional vouchers delivered door to door (d) *By reducing its price.* A major tour operator such as Airtours may decide to maintain lower price level, to its major competitors as a way of attracting extra sales	(a) *By expanding its sales and distribution* For example a hi fi manufacturer will seek to strengthen its sales and distribution by selling to as many different outlets. (b) *By restricting its range of products.* A theatre for example may discontinue its afternoon matinee for lack of attendance (c) *By changing its opening time,* A branch library may be closed or its opening times reduced as a means of cutting costs. (d) *By charging a premium price* Blackpools Pepsi Max is a unique white knuckle ride experience and as such the price charged reflects this.

Figure 3.40 Marketing strategies for leisure and tourism organizations

Figure 3.41 Undifferentiated marketing

Implementing the plan

Determining the marketing mix programme

Determining the right marketing mix involves the combination of techniques, resources and tactics which form the basis of the marketing plan. This generally involves a mix of promotion and distribution programmes and other activities which are undertaken to influence the buyer to choose our products.

Combining the individual programmes creates what is known as a marketing campaign. A campaign has been described as a

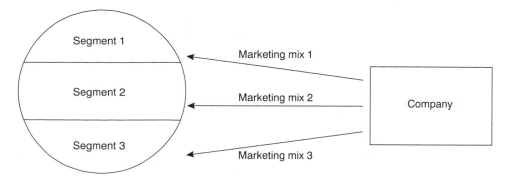

Figure 3.42 Differentiated marketing

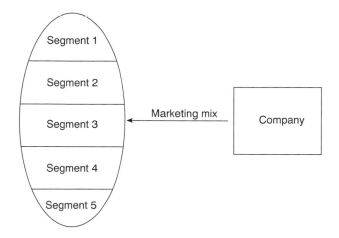

Figure 3.43 Concentrated marketing

co-ordinated series of promotional effort built around a single theme or idea and designed to reach a predetermined goal

W.J. Stanton,
Fundamentals of Marketing, McGraw Hill,
6th Edition

A list of the major marketing techniques used by leisure and tourism organizations is provided, as a menu, in Figure 3.44.

The menu, which for the most part is promotional, represents the choices from which the marketing manager will select in supporting each leisure and tourism product in each market. Choosing the correct mix is important in getting the market to respond. For example, offering 50 per cent off a skiing holiday may be an effective means of promoting a ski resort to tourists, but only if the message is directed at people who can and want to ski and can afford the time and

Advertising	TV, radio, cinema, press
PR	Stories, editorials, events
Sales promotion	Short-term incentives
Direct marketing	Delivering printed material
Sponsorship	A means of building an image; getting known
Exhibitions/shows	A way of meeting the trade and distributing literature
Brochures/sales literature	A means of making the service product tangible
Personal selling	Meetings, telephone, face-to-face, workshops aimed at the trade
Price discounting	Bonuses, allowances, commissions
Distribution	Channels for delivering goods and services, booking and reservation services, opening and closing times
Familiarization trips Educational visits	A way of motivating customers, including the trade, to visit, view and sample what's on offer

Figure 3.44 Menu of marketing mix techniques

money to pay for it. How many of you would be tempted to go to sunny Spain in the winter, despite a 50 per cent reduction on summer prices?

There are many factors which can affect the successful implementation of a campaign. These include:

- Costs
- Budgets
- Timing
- Professional/design skills.

Costs

Television as an effective medium is obvious, but equally understood is the fact that it is extremely expensive. The costs of advertising nationally or even on regional television can be prohibitive except for the very largest of leisure and tourism organizations. Besides the screening costs there is also the cost of producing the advertisement. Not surprisingly, having produced a TV commercial, many organizations want to screen it frequently.

Most leisure and tourism organizations need to produce some form of brochure or sales leaflet so as to explain or show what they have to offer. Some will use advertising and PR in the local press or on radio or at the cinema. However, inevitably it all comes down to what an organization can afford, i.e. what budget is available.

Budget

The marketing budget can be defined as:

the sum of the cost of the company's marketing mix programme judged necessary to achieve specified objectives and targets set in the marketing plan.

The amount of money budgeted for a marketing campaign can restrict the techniques to those that can be afforded. It can also restrict the length, frequency and coverage of the campaign, which in turn can extend the timescale within which the company's objectives can be met.

However, all too often the budget set is based on what can be afforded rather than what is required to achieve the company's objectives. Setting budgets as a percentage of estimated target sales revenue is one method that is often used. For example, with sales revenue from a product expected to achieve £1 million, the budget would be set at 5 per cent or £50,000.

All organizations have a limited amount of money to spend on a marketing campaign, most of which operates on an annual budget. The sum agreed must be split between the products and the markets included in the campaign. For example, an airline budget of £500,000 may be split as shown in Figure 3.45.

The following sums would then be required to be split between the chosen promotional techniques to achieve the company's objectives or target for that particular product or market. For example, the budget of £100,000 allocated to the North American market would now need to be divided between the various marketing mix techniques or programmes which have been chosen and designed to achieve the target sales objective of £2 million.

Timescale

This involves not only setting the timescale for achieving the company's objectives, but also the timing and scheduling of activities to meet them. What constitutes an appropriate timescale for marketing activities, and therefore, the distinction between long- and short-term plans, will vary from company to company. Changing buyer

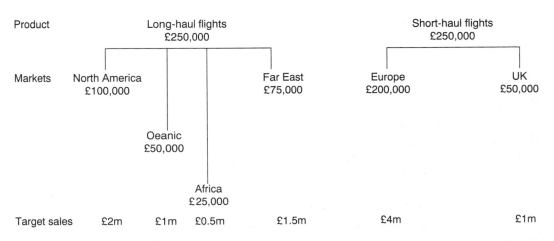

Figure 3.45 Marketing budget allocation

behaviour, for example, in getting holidaymakers to spend more of their leisure time in Britain rather than travel abroad, may be seen to take several years, whereas getting increased numbers of people to visit a new white knuckle attraction such as Alton Towers' Nemesis may be planned to take place in one year.

The many promotional activities used to achieve these objectives, such as brochure production, distribution, advertising and sponsorship to name a few, also have different timescales, and so there is considerable planning required in scheduling programmes and implementing the work. Most media, for example, can carry messages within a very short space of time. Local papers and commercial radio will accept prepared advertising copy only 24 hours before publication. However, in the case of national magazines, bookings sometimes have to be placed several weeks in advance, and, in the case of television, often many months in advance.

Professional/design skills

Most promotional activities require lots of specialized skills, in planning and preparing campaigns (e.g. from carrying out marketing research, generating ideas, preparing copylines, visuals and logos to preparing press releases and buying media space). Most leisure and tourism organizations do not have all those skills in-house, and so are restricted to what they can do themselves and what they can afford for others to do for them.

Writing the marketing plan

There are many ways of writing a marketing plan – there is no right or wrong way. The point to remember is that the plan should include a statement of the company's resources (expressed in financial, human and physical terms) that will be required for implementation. It should also state with whom the responsibility lies and the deadlines for carrying out the tasks.

Figure 3.46 provides an example of a marketing plan that has been written for a hypothetical community theatre in Devon.

Evaluation techniques and criteria for effectiveness (How will we know when we have arrived?)

Evaluating the marketing environment has been put at the end of the plan, since it involves assessing and measuring the results achieved by the action programmes or plans against the planned objectives and targets. The intention behind this part of the planning process is to assess where the company is now. Moreover, it is used to determine how well the company is doing compared with the targets set so that it can:

- Quickly respond to any changes in sales or profit performance
- Learn from current experience
- Adjust marketing objectives
- Make changes to its action plans to get the company back on course.

A variety of evaluation techniques for measuring the performance of a marketing campaign were discussed in Element 3.3. However, some of the more commonly used criteria for monitoring the effectiveness of a campaign are given below:

- Sales analysis based on occupancy levels (e.g. hotels), load factors (e.g. airlines), usage (e.g. libraries, museums, sports centres, etc.)
- Market analysis
- Customer satisfaction analysis (based on brand or customer loyalty).

Sales analysis

The more specific the marketing objectives made in terms of sales volume or value, by product and market, the easier it becomes to measure results. Hotels, for example, forecast their occupancy by type of rooms (single, double, suite), whereas airlines forecast passenger volume by first, economy and business class.

Actual sales achieved when compared against targets set provide plus or minus variances in volume or value terms, which indicates to the company which products and markets are achieving the sales they require and which are falling short of the targets.

Goals

- To secure a major share of theatrical business in the South West
- To be viewed as offering a quality product by its many market segments.

Objectives

- To attract 10 percent more first time visitors from the adjacent regions of Somerset, Dorset and Cornwall
- To establish and improve relations and partnerships with at least five local community contacts from a range of colleges, schools, youth or community businesses, etc.
- To attract 15 percent more educational visits, and group visits at off-peak times
- To increase awareness levels for the theatre by 10 percent among the local population.

Action Plan	*When*	*Who*	*Cost*
Advertising			
Prepare programme schedule of theatre showings for the year	July/Aug 96	Theatre Manager	No cost
Pre-book programme ads in the Leisure Guide section of the local and regional press	Aug 96	Ad agency	£12,500
Design and produce three radio commercials for summer season	Feb/Mar 96	Ad agency	£1,000
Book radio slots for summer	May 96	Ad agency	£4,000
Printed material			
Produce 3 × 100, 000 leaflets to promote theatre's shows in autumn/winter, spring, summer	June/autumn Winter 96/97 Oct/Nov Spring 97 May/April Summer 97	Design section of a local printer	£20,000
Produce posters for school and college notice-boards	July	Local printer	£2,000
Public relations			
Design press releases to local press and radio to raise awareness	All year	Theatre Manager and local PR agency	£5,000
Extend school and theatre group shows to other regions. Publicize event and organize chat show with local radio	Autumn 96	Theatre Manager and PR agency	£2,500
Offer competition to the local press in exchange for free editorial regarding future shows. The winners of the competition would receive free tickets to a show of their choice	Off-peak	Theatre Manager and PR agency	No cost for tickets
Sales promotion			
Special offers to increase off-peak sales to be offered via press advertisements. Offers to include free ticket with every two adult tickets purchased	Autumn/ Winter/ spring	Theatre Manager	No cost for tickets. £4,500 to cover costs of ads
Group discounts for businesses, schools and colleges who purchase 10 or more tickets	All year	Theatre Manager	£7,500
Holiday specials for families, 50% off return visit to the theatre promoted via 100,000 promotional leaflets/vouchers			No cost for tickets £10,000 for print of leaflets/ vouchers and advertisements

Figure 3.46 Marketing Plan – South West Community Theatre 1996/97

Invite schools, voluntary groups, colleges to view rehearsals and so build up image and raise the theatre profile.	All year	Theatre Manager	No cost

Selling

Use of casual staff at peak times to promote shows via telesales	Oct/Nov/ Dec 96 Mar/Apr 97 Jul/Aug 97	Theatre Manager	£10,000 (over year)
Use of students on unpaid placements or nominal wages	Jul/Aug 97		£2,000 (allowance)
Customer care training course for all new staff to be run by local college	All year	Theatre manager and local college	£1,000

Evaluation and control

All adverts and leaflets/vouchers to be coded so that customer response levels can be monitored to check the effectiveness of each promotional activity	All year	Theatre Manager	No real cost

Pricing

Monitoring of all competitors' prices to maintain price relationship	All year	Theatre Manager	No real cost
Promotional pricing for off-peak educational groups		Theatre Manager	Part of promotional spend
Review viability of selling unsold seats 72 hours before a performance via reservation agency at 75% discount to bring in managerial revenue		Theatre Manager	No cast

Distribution

Membership of the Regional Tourist Board Distribution of theatre leaflets to libraries, halls, leisure centres, clubs, schools,	August 96	Theatre Manager	£250
colleges. Tourist information centres, hotels, etc. Distribution to be via the service offered by the Regional Tourist Board to all members	All year	Regional Tourist Board	£250 (distribution fee)
Opening times to be extended to allow for school visits to view rehearsals throughout the day.	Off-Peak	Theatre Manager	No cost
Door to door distribution of theatre leaflets to selected postcode areas in the local regions, which have been identified as heavy theatre going public.	Sept/Oct 96 Jan/Feb 97 May/June 97	Theatre Manager Research Distribution Co.	£3,000

Marketing Research

Analyse on-going research information from customer comment forms	April 97	Theatre Manager	No real cost
Purchase of leisure studies report produced bi-annually by the South West Regional Tourist Board	Nov 96	Theatre Manager	£500
Mail questionnaire to all schools and colleges in the region to check their level of awareness for the theatre, its shows and their opinions	Feb 97	Theatre Manager Local College	£1,500

Contingency

Reserve £13,500	All year	Theatre Manager	

Figure 3.46 *Continued*

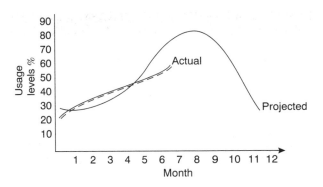

Figure 3.47 Usage variance against targets for a swimming pool

In Figure 3.47 projected usage of a swimming pool represents monthly planning targets based partly on previous years' usage figures and partly on the diagnosis of the marketing environment. In months 5 and 6, as usage drops significantly, the manager of the pool must decide whether to take any further action to generate a greater usage of the pool.

Further analysis of the usage figures may be able to provide a clearer picture of what is going wrong. For example, further investigation may show the major reason for the shortfall to be a drop-off in existing customers returning to the pool. As soon as the drop in repeat sales is identified, the marketing manager must establish the cause for the drop and consider what action to take. This could mean, for example, targeting schools or clubs whose attendance has fallen with a direct mail package, highlighting the new refurbishment work just completed or offering loyalty discounts or special inducements to book extra swimming lessons over the remainder of the year. Often the contingency fund is used to cover the cost of these activities.

Market share analysis

Market share analysis is calculated by dividing the company sales by the total sales for the industry. Although highly desirable, industry sales information is not always available, or easy to get hold of. Many trade associations will endeavour to compile sales data on behalf of their members to provide such information. However,

all too often general marketing intelligence on competitors' sales can prove to be misleading. The point to note is that market share analysis, like sales analysis, increases in value when the data available can be broken down into market segments.

Customer satisfaction analysis

This evaluation technique is based on measuring customer satisfaction levels against the key attributes of the product or service provided. The measure is often based on a scale from, say, 1 to 6 as follows:

| 1 | 2 | 3 | 4 | 5 | 6 |

(very dissatisfied)   (very satisfied)

For example, the service attributes for a hotel group might include:

- Reception
- Standard of accommodation
- Room charges
- Bar services
- Restaurant
- Housekeeping.

By averaging the customer scores for each attribute across a number of hotels, a group rating can be obtained for each attribute. Each hotel can now be assessed individually against each attribute, indicating the level of customer satisfaction. If the restaurant score for a hotel falls significantly, then management can take action to rectify the problem before it starts to affect future business.

▪ Assignment 3.4 ▪

Assume the role of a marketing executive in the planning department of a major marketing consultancy with special responsibility for the leisure and tourism industry. Your agency has been approached by a leisure and tourism organization to help them develop a new product or service in advance of the year 2000 and beyond.

You are required to prepare a detailed marketing plan on the development of a new product or service at a leisure and tourism facility of your choice.

Coverage

- Element 3.4
- Performance Criteria, 1,2,3,4,5,6,7,8
- Core Skills Opportunities
  - Communication
  - IT
  - Application of Number

Task 1

In small groups, identify a leisure and tourism facility, either a locally or nationally, and identify the organizations' goals/objectives.

Task 2

Assess the marketing environment and carry out a SWOT analysis on the organization.

Task 3

Identify what new product or service (i.e. planning development) may help the organization to maximize its strengths, minimize its weaknesses and so make the most of its opportunities while meeting the threats in the market place.

Task 4

Propose marketing research methods to be used.

Task 5

Propose marketing communication methods (i.e. promotional techniques to be used).

Task 6

Explain how the plan can be implemented.

Task 7

Describe evaluation techniques and criteria to be applied.

Task 8

Produce a group report of no more than 3000 words, preferably word-processed and including relevant statistics, tables and diagrams.

FINANCE IN LEISURE AND TOURISM

Introduction

In this Unit we are going to take an in-depth look at the thing which, it is claimed, makes the world go round – money!

We will look at three main areas of finance in leisure and tourism organizations:

- Financial performance
- Financial accounts
- Budgets.

You will learn a lot about the **jargon** (specialized language) of finance and realize that much of the mystique which has evolved around finance and accountancy exists because of the jargon and when it is translated into everyday language the concepts are, in fact, familiar and not at all strange.

You will probably be surprised to realize that you already operate financial control and budgeting in your own life. With only a little effort you will be able to read a balance sheet, profit and loss account and cash flow forecast (all of which will be explained in depth in this Unit). They may sound a little daunting, but you will be surprised how easily you learn to understand them.

The difference between any leisure and tourism organization and your own experiences with money is one of scale: organizations, whether in the public, private or voluntary sector, will have a lot more people involved in their ventures than are involved in your activities and they will have a great deal more cash to handle than you do.

They are also accountable to a number of people (shareholders of corporate companies, trustees of registered charities, customers of a business). These will vary according to the type of organization which is being operated, and are considered in greater depth as we progress through the Unit.

If you have a paid job and earn above a certain amount, you will have to pay income tax. This will usually be collected from you by your employer, who is accountable to the Inland Revenue and has a legal obligation to ensure that its employees' income tax is collected and paid under the PAYE (pay as you earn) system. This is a tax on earnings which is payable by employees. It is withheld from their wages and paid directly to the Inland Revenue. Every time an employee earns some money he also pays income tax (there are some exceptions when this does not happen, usually in the case of people on a very low wage).

Many organizations in the leisure and tourism industry pay company tax on the profits they make, and each organization has a legal responsibility to ensure that it pays the correct amount of company tax to the Inland Revenue. Some organizations are accountable to Customs and Excise, who collect VAT (more about this later). All companies must keep their financial records up to date and in such a way that they can be understood by any official who has a right to view them.

What does finance involve?

The answer may appear to be obvious, 'It's all about handling money'. This is true, but money is handled in many different ways and stages and each stage has its own name.

Accounting is the process by which financial data is collected, summarized and then presented in one of many standard formats.

The purposes of keeping accounts are:

- To satisfy legal requirements
- To provide managers who are not necessarily specialists in dealing with money with information that can easily be understood and used by them for a number of purposes. They may need to know:
  - How much money is coming into and going out of the organization
  - How much is in the bank at a given moment
  - Whether maximum profits are being achieved on every venture
  - Whether the organization is going to be able to pay its debts as they become due
  - What the anticipated profit is for the next financial year.

Auditing is the process of checking accounts which have been prepared by accountants. An audit may be undertaken by accountants from within the organization just to ensure that the accounts do present a true picture of the financial state of the organization, or perhaps when the whereabouts of some cash cannot be accounted for, or even as a preventative measure, so that staff who handle money are aware that if any does go missing, it will be noticed very quickly.

Some leisure and tourism organizations (for example, those which have limited liability, which will be explained in detail later in this Element)

have a legal obligation to have their accounts audited by external auditors. These are accountants who are not employees of the organization but who are brought in just to check the accounts. When there is a legal obligation involved, the auditors must be accountants who have qualifications in accountancy.

Book-keeping is the basic function of recording details of all the money which is received and paid out. The advent of information technology (which is looked at in depth in Unit 5) has meant that ledgers – the accounts books which were once used by virtually all organizations – have now been replaced in many organizations by software packages such as Sage, which allow accounts to be kept on computer.

Financial accounting is the term applied to the process of preparing and providing financial information in a highly summarized format. This is usually for the most senior people within an organization so that they can get to and use the financial information they need for decision making without having to wade through lots of figures which are not relevant to their needs.

Financial management is a concept which has only been around for about twenty years. Before that, it was an integral part of the general senior management function. It may seem rather simplistic, but it is a fact that 'financial managers manage finance'. A financial manager will ensure that an organization which has cash to spare invests it sensibly and gets a good return on investment. He or she will be involved in setting financial objectives for the organization and planning how the objectives can be met.

Management accounting is similar to financial accounting, except that management accounting provides information for management of any level, for any purpose.

The above explanations should have given you an idea about the process of finance and accounting, but there are other words you will come across which may also need explanation.

Some financial jargon

Some words will be explained as we progress through the Unit, but here are some important ones to get you started. Most of these will be explored in greater depth as we continue to investigate finance.

- **Expenditure** is money which the organization spends.
- **Profit** is made when the money earned by the organization is greater than the expenditure.
- **Revenue** is money which the organization earns.
- **Turnover** is the amount that comes into an organization within a specified period of time. An average weekly turnover of £10,000 means that the organization has an annual turnover of £520,000.
- **Solvency** – an organization which is solvent is able to pay all its bills as they become due for payment.

The first two Elements of this Unit are very closely related to each other, and we will look at them together. Element 4.1 introduces the concept of investigating financial performance; this is done by examining financial accounts, which is what we have to do in Element 4.2. This means we can combine the two elements when we are studying them, although to undertake the tasks and assignments you will have to analyse the content of Element 4 and extract the relevant information to enable you to complete the exercises.

Element 4.3 allows you to explore the concept of budgeting and to prepare a budget for an event. We will look at Element 4.3 after you have learned about the concepts in Elements 4.1 and 4.2 and had a chance to gather evidence for your portfolio.

Element 4.1 Investigate financial performance of leisure and tourism organizations

Element 4.2 Examine financial accounts in leisure and tourism organizations

In these elements of the Unit we will consider the various ways in which we can look at an organization's finances to ascertain how the company is performing financially. You will learn how it is possible to monitor financial performance (take a close and regular look at how the organization is handling its finances) and discover how the monitoring can be accomplished.

At the same time, we will look at a number of criteria which can be used to make judgements on whether the organization is doing well financially, or whether there is room for improvement (there often is, even when an organization is making good profits).

We will look at factors both within and outside the organization which may have an effect on how the organization performs financially. We will also consider some of the ways in which financial information can be displayed so that management can use it to form opinions and make decisions.

Finally, you will have the opportunity to prepare a financial statement and extract information from it that would help you to make decisions if you were managing a leisure or tourism organization.

Leisure and tourism organizations exist in all sectors of the business community and financial control is equally important in each of them, although the emphasis may be different depending on the reason for the existence of each, specific organization.

The public sector

A large number of leisure centres, country parks, art galleries and museums belong in this sector. They are owned and operated by local or central government. A number of people can be regarded as stakeholders in these publicly owned organizations (stakeholders are people who can rightfully claim to have an interest in the organization and its financial performance).

- The board of trustees, which oversees the financial requirements and performance of the facility
- The director or curator of the facility, who is responsible for its day-to-day operation

- Members of the public, who contribute financially to the facility via their council tax or income tax
- Visitors to the facility.

The main objective of council-owned leisure centres is usually to provide a service to the public – a place where any member of the public can go to undertake sporting and health awareness activities. The councils certainly do not want them to operate at a loss, but making huge profits is not a primary concern. Many councils will be quite happy if their leisure centre can break even (cover their own overheads – wage bill, rent, repairs, etc.) and very happy if the centre makes a profit and can pay for its own investment programme (a programme of improvements, perhaps re-fitting a shower room or installing lifts for clients who have difficulty climbing stairs).

Country parks are also not usually expected to make a profit. They are often very heavily subsidized (money which has not been earned by the efforts of the people who run them may be allocated to them by local or central government). Few parks charge people to walk around them; they may have a centre where food, drinks, maps, etc. are sold, but this is intended to reduce their losses (the difference between the amount it costs to run the park and the amount they make) rather than to make a profit.

A country park may have three primary objectives:

- To preserve the environment so that animal and plant life can flourish
- To educate young people by showing them the variety of wildlife represented within the park
- To provide areas for members of the public to walk and relax in the countryside.

Public sector organizations may not have profit making as their primary objective, but their financial performance is still very important. The director of a park which has been allocated an annual budget (the amount of money allocated to it) of £650,000 by central or local government will have enormous problems if he spends all the money in the first quarter of the year, perhaps on wages and new machinery. How will he pay its staff for the rest of the year? How will he be able to afford to pay the electricity bills for the café and gift shop?

Although financial gain is not the main objective of the park director and his wardens, they must control the money they handle just as carefully as any organization which operates primarily for the purpose of making money. They must ensure that budgets are set (money is allocated for specific purposes and not spent too quickly, or on things for which it was not allocated) and that staff and management work within the budget (we will look more deeply into budgets in Element 4.3).

The voluntary sector

Voluntary sector organizations are those which are supported by voluntary contributions. Many have charitable status, which gives them some advantages over public and private sector companies. For example, registered charities can, with the permission of the local authority, hold 'flag days', when supporters go onto the streets and ask the public to donate money. Registered charities also have special consideration in the area of taxation.

Many people make a bequest (leave money in their wills) to voluntary sector organizations; others donate some of their income on a regular basis. Not all the money has to be donated in order for an organization to be regarded as voluntary; some voluntary sector organizations earn a part of their income from entrance fees and sales in gift shops and cafés. Some of the larger charities have mail order operations which provide them with profits to boost their funds.

Some organizations in the voluntary sector are given subsidies by local or central government or charitable trusts (money may have been invested by a wealthy person and, either during their lifetime or after their death, the profits from the money are given each year to a worthy cause. The decision on which cause will receive the money is made by the trustees (the people who look after the money)). Subsidies cannot be guaranteed each year, so voluntary sector companies must try to ensure that their finances are sufficiently well handled to cover all their expenses, even without subsidy.

Stakeholders in charitable organizations include:

- The board of trustees or governors
- The director or curator of the facility
- People who donate money to the facility
- Volunteers who donate their time to assist in various ways at the facility
- Visitors to the facility.

There are some similarities between the voluntary and the public sector: they often exist for the preservation of our heritage or the country's wildlife; and making large profits is not their primary function. However, monitoring and controlling their finances is just as essential as it is for organizations for whom profit is their primary reason for existing.

Some voluntary organizations have an obligation to people far more than to profits and these organizations may choose not to modernize their administration by using computers, electronic cash registers or other, up-to-the-minute equipment. An example of one such organization within the leisure and tourism industry would be a café and craft centre run by a charity, where the food and goods for sale are made and sold by people who are disabled and find it difficult to cope with modern, high-tech equipment. Higher profits could be achieved by introducing more modern equipment, but high profits are not the reason for this organization's existence.

A financial expert who is used to examining the records of organizations which exist to make a profit may well be surprised by the charity which exists to provide a rewarding place in society for handicapped people rather than to make profits. Even a charity, however, must take care of its finances, as it must operate within its budgets.

The private sector

There are many leisure and tourism organizations in the private sector. They exist primarily to make money for the people who own, or own shares in, the organization. A private sector company may be:

- A sole trader
- A partnership
- A limited company
- A co-operative
- A public limited company.

Sole trader

A person who wishes to work on his own or to be the only owner of a company employing other people can set up as a sole trader.

A sole trader may have to use his house or other assets (items or property which belong to him) as collateral (security against a loan taken from a bank or other finance house). If he runs into financial problems, and is unable to pay his monthly instalments on the loan, his home or other assets may be taken by the company which made the loan available to him, in place of the money which he cannot repay.

Partnership

When two or more people decide to go into business together they can form a partnership. This, just as with a sole trader, means that private possessions (house, car, furniture, etc.) may be forfeited if the partnership falls into debt.

In some respects it is even worse than the situation faced by a sole trader who loses his home because his business fails, as partners are responsible for each others' debts. So, if one partner disappears and takes all the company's cash with him, the other partner(s) in the business may find themselves losing their homes because of the partner who disappeared.

Limited company

A person working on his own or owning a business with others could decide that, rather than risk becoming a sole trader or entering into a partnership, with all the financial drawbacks that these two types of businesses entail, he will make his business into a limited company.

This option is one which attracts many companies, because homes and other personal possessions are not at risk as they are in the previous two options. Each person's liability (the amount they must pay if the business fails and becomes bankrupt) is limited to the amount of the shares they bought in the company. It is quite feasible that the owner or partners in the business will only have paid or pledged £100 each in shares, so if the business becomes bankrupt they only have to find £100 each towards the company's debts and their personal possessions are safe.

Public limited company (PLC)

Many, but not all, companies in this category are described as having been floated on the stock exchange or stock market. This is the place where shares in many public limited companies are bought and sold to the general public.

The word 'public' may appear in the description of the company, but it is not public in the sense that it is owned by local or central government. Members of the public are usually able to purchase shares in the company through a dealer. It is also possible, but unusual, that the PLC is owned by a minimum of two partners who own the shares between them and who do not wish to make any of them available to the general public.

Companies which are entitled to use the descriptor PLC must have a share capital of at least £50,000 and will have been subjected to intense financial scrutiny. They must have been able to show that their financial performance is good before they can be granted PLC status.

The main reason for the existence of a public limited company is exactly the same as in the case of a sole trader, partnership or limited company – to make money. Once the overheads have been covered and any money needed for reinvestment has been put back into the company, the profit is shared out among the shareholders (people who have invested in the company by buying shares in it. This could be as few as two people, but could be thousands of people if the company is a very large one). Each shareholder receives a dividend. Dividends are funded by sharing the profits (after tax has been paid and any money needed for reinvestment has been taken out) between the shareholders.

PLCs are large organizations with an annual turnover (the amount of money which goes through the organization's accounts in a year through selling goods or providing a service, after the deduction of VAT but before paying suppliers) of millions of pounds. Many airlines, shipping companies, large hotel chains, tour operators, tourist attractions, football clubs and privately owned health club chains are PLCs.

Many people can be stakeholders in privately owned companies; they include:

- Owners and partners
- Members of the board
- Management and employees of the company
- Customers
- Shareholders
- Providers of finance (banks, government, etc.).

Co-operative

This is a less common type of organization than those previously discussed and frequently exists for political, ethical or social reasons. A co-operative does not have 'bosses' and 'workers', it is run by the workers, each of whom has voting rights. In a true co-operative all the assets of the company belong to the workforce and the profits are shared among them.

Task 4.1

This will provide you with evidence towards Element 4.1, PC 1 and Core Skill Communication Element 3.2, all PCs.

Write a list of at least fifteen leisure and tourism organizations in your local area and specify whether they are in the private, public or voluntary sector. Keep the list in your portfolio.

Write a brief explanation of the terms 'public', 'voluntary' and 'private' sectors. Your report should be neatly set out and it should be possible for a person who has no knowledge of the subject to understand it.

Financial requirements of the three sectors

As we have seen, some of the requirements may vary between the three sectors, but all have a legal obligation to keep accurate accounts and a business need to monitor and evaluate their financial performance by regularly checking the accounts and considering ways in which their financial performance could be improved. Every organization, no matter which sector it falls into, needs to constantly look out for ways of improving performance.

Why do leisure and tourism organizations monitor their financial performance, and how do they know if they are doing well?

All organizations need to take a regular look at how they are performing, otherwise they will not know:

● Whether they are solvent
● Whether they are achieving maximum profitability (you must remember, of course, that some voluntary and public sector organizations may not aim to be profitable, only to earn or collect sufficient money to enable them to carry out their primary function, which could be caring for a property or looking after animals or ensuring that a natural attraction is not spoiled)
● Whether money is coming into and going out of the business as it should
● Whether they are meeting their financial targets
● Whether they are working within their budgets.

Let's take a look at each of these reasons for monitoring financial performance in more detail.

Solvency has already been explained briefly. A company which is solvent is able to pay its debts as they become due. These debts not only include sums which are owed to suppliers for goods provided, but also staff wages, rent, telephone and electricity bills and any other bill which is due. A company which cannot pay its debts at the due time is insolvent and may face proceedings instigated by its creditors (people to whom it owes money), which will eventually mean that the company must cease trading.

It is obviously of great importance to ensure that any organization's solvency is monitored, as any oversight could mean that a bill is not paid, which could, if the company to whom the money was owed took the matter to court, lead to the dissolution of the organization.

Solvency can also be used as a measure of whether or not an organization is doing well. An organization which is not solvent, or is constantly teetering on the brink of insolvency, is an unstable organization and needs to review its financial performance, making changes where necessary.

Profit is the financial advantage which is gained when the difference between income and expenditure is assessed and income is greater than expenditure (or costs). To put it a little more simply, take the amount it costs to make or provide something (the expenditure) away from the amount for which it can be sold (the income) and you have the profit.

Income	=	50.00
Minus expenditure	=	45.00
Profit	=	5.00

Profitability is closely related to profit. It is a comparison between the expenditure and the level of profit. Take a look at the following figures:

Venture A		Venture B	
Income	100.00	Income	100.00
Minus costs	98.00	Minus costs	80.00
Profit	2.00		20.00

You will see that both these ventures are profitable – they both make money – but Venture B has a much higher profitability level than Venture A. Ensuring that every venture or project has as high a profitability level as possible is extremely important in every leisure and tourism organization.

Assessing profitability can be a much more complex exercise in the leisure and tourism industries than in industries where there is a tangible end product (you will have met tangibility in the marketing Unit). A company which makes boxes of chocolates knows exactly how much each finished box has cost. It will know the cost of

● The chocolates
● The inner wrappings
● The labour costs and other overheads
● The outer wrappings.

However, the tourism industry and many sectors of the leisure industry are predominantly service industries, so costs can vary even when the end product is the same.

Two people book a holiday with a travel agent. The size of their families is identical, they book for the same hotel, on the same meal plan, leaving from the same airport on the same day and for the same duration. The amount they pay to the travel agent is identical, and yet the cost of providing the service by the travel agent was not the same.

Try to work out why this could be the case before you read any further.

One person insisted that the manager of the travel agency did the booking and took nearly two hours of her time; the other saw a junior clerk and the booking took five minutes. The cost to the travel agency of providing the service is quite different – the manager is paid higher wages and a far greater length of time was taken. The profitability of the two bookings is different, although the invoiced amount and the commission (the amount paid by the tour operator to the travel agent for handling the booking) will be identical.

Task 4.2

This will provide you with evidence towards Element 4.1, PC 2.

Following the reasoning in the above example, think of five examples of how profitability could be affected in other leisure and tourism organizations, three examples taken from leisure and two from tourism. Write down these examples and keep them for your portfolio.

The example of profitability which you were given above is a very simple one. Establishing profitability and comparing the profitability between two projects can be very complex indeed. When an organization is faced with more work than it can handle, the decision in respect of which work to accept may have to be taken on the basis of profitability. The piece of work which makes the most profit is usually the one which is accepted, although a great deal of information may sometimes have to be studied and evaluated before the most profitable piece of work can be ascertained.

Case study

Barlick Manor, an Elizabethan manor house, was approached by a company which organized craft fairs. It wanted to use the grounds of the house for a craft fair throughout the August Bank Holiday weekend. The company was willing to pay for the use of the grounds, and it could guarantee that there would be at least twice as many visitors paying to come into the house and gardens as usually did on that weekend.

The owner of the manor house was also approached by a re-enactment society. (Re-enactors are people who are interested in a specific era of history, often a particular battle, and they act out something which happened during that era or the battle which interests them.) The re-enactors only wanted to use the grounds on the Bank Holiday Sunday, they were willing to pay for the use of the grounds for one day, and they could guarantee that at least four times as many visitors as usual would be prepared to pay the entrance fees so that they could visit the house and gardens and watch the re-enactment.

Only one of the organizations could be accommodated, so the manor house owner had to work out which event would have the highest profitability ratio, that is, which would bring in the most money. There were considerations apart from a straightforward comparison of the money which would be taken at the weekend: the craft fair organizer only wanted a one-off event, whereas if the re-enactment went well in August the re-enactors wanted to return the following year at Easter and Spring Bank Holiday as well as August.

There were also other considerations:

- Which event would get the most free publicity for the manor house?
- Which event would be the most suitable and would enhance the atmosphere at the manor house?
- Which event might lead charitable trusts which dealt with historic properties to view the manor house in a favourable light if it ever needed a grant to renovate a room or plant a new garden?

The decision which had to be taken was based on a great deal of complex data, and making a comparison of the profitability of the craft fair as opposed to the re-enactment was difficult to achieve, unlike a comparison between two boxes of chocolates, where the exact costs would be known and the comparison would be simple.

Leisure and tourism organizations must constantly monitor the profitability of their operations so that decisions can be taken and adjustments made when necessary.

The travel agent we looked at earlier may decide on a change of seating or decor if too many clients begin to take a long time when they are making a booking. Uncomfortable seats could deter clients from wanting to spend unreasonable lengths of time in the agency, and certain colour combinations are known to make people feel they want to move on as quickly as possible. Investing in new, less comfortable chairs and wallpaper could increase the agency's profitability and thus improve the company's financial performance.

Profitability can also be used as a criterion for evaluating the financial performance of leisure and tourism organizations. If an organization is spending a lot and only making a little, its profitability is low and its financial performance is poor. Conversely, if a high profit is returned for a low spend, the profitability is good so financial performance is good.

Some organizations – those in the voluntary and public sectors – may not make a profit, so are unable to calculate the profitability of their organization. They could, however, calculate the profitability of some of their attractions, perhaps a gift and souvenir shop at a stately home or a café in a leisure centre.

Cash flow is the term used to describe money as it comes into and goes out of an organization. All organizations must ensure that money comes in when it is needed so that it can flow out again when bills have to be paid. Leisure and tourism organizations which are seasonal in nature (they do most of their business in one season or another, like a football club in winter or a seaside hotel in summer) face particular problems to ensure that their cash flow is healthy throughout the year.

Organizations which constantly monitor their financial performance will be able to predict when a cash flow problem is likely to arise and they will be able to take steps to prevent any problems, such as insolvency, occurring.

Cash flow is monitored by producing both a cash flow forecast, which looks into the future and predicts when cash will come into and go out of the company, and a cash flow chart, which shows the actual position regarding cash coming into and going out of the business. A comparison of the two is an excellent way to monitor financial performance. A financial manager who predicted that £2,500 would come into the organization in March and intended, therefore, to pay some major bills in April would know immediately that he had problems if only £800 was received. He would look into the reasons why the inflow of cash was so much lower than predicted and would also take steps to ensure that the April bills could be paid.

Financial targets are another good reason why monitoring financial performance is so essential to any leisure and tourism organization. Targets may be set by many different organizations:

- A tour operator's sales representative is given a financial target to achieve. If he fails to reach the target over a period of three months he will become too expensive a member of staff, and other methods of getting bookings from travel agents will be considered
- The café in a country park must reach a financial target each day of the week. If it fails to meet the target on more than ten Mondays, Tuesdays, Wednesdays, etc., it will stop opening on that day

- A golf club sets a financial target for the professional's shop. If it does not take the expected amount, it will be closed and used for catering instead.

However, there would be no point in setting these targets if somebody is not going to monitor the situation by regularly checking to ensure that the targets have been reached.

The same targets can also be used as criteria to evaluate the financial performance of the sales representative or the café or the professional's shop.

- The sales representative may easily reach his target each month, thus proving that he is doing a good job as far as generating income for his company is concerned
- On Monday and Thursday each week the café does not quite reach the target which it has been set. However, on other days it does very well indeed. The management of the organization would have to make a decision about opening on Monday and Thursday after considering a number of factors. Not reaching the financial target is very important, but there are other considerations:
  - Customers who eat there on Mondays and Tuesdays or Thursdays and Fridays may decide not to eat there at all if the café closes on one of the days they patronize it, so business would be lost and a currently profitable day may become unprofitable
  - Staff may look for new jobs, which means that new staff would have to be trained, and training costs money.
- The golf professional uses a building which could have many other uses. If he is seen not to be reaching his financial target (because his accounts are closely monitored) steps could be taken by the golf club committee to ensure that a more profitable venture is allowed to take over the building, thus improving the club's financial performance.

Budgets – we will look at budgets in depth when we cover Element 4.3, but we also need to consider them now. They are used by all leisure and tourism organizations to ensure that they do not spend all their money on one area of the business, or too quickly.

You probably operate budgets for your spending, possibly without thinking about it. Perhaps you have been saving up to go on holiday. You know that the holiday cost is going to be around £200, you want to have the same amount for spending when you arrive in the resort, and would like to buy some new clothes before you go. You have worked hard and have managed to save £550. You allocate the money to three cost areas (areas in which you will spend money), each of which has its own budget.

You know that if you go out a couple of weeks before the start of the holiday to buy some new clothes, you must carefully monitor the amount of cash you spend. If you spend too much on clothes, you will have to reduce your holiday spending budget. When you arrive on holiday you will carefully monitor your spending to ensure that you do not spend all your money on the first day. If you do, you will not be able to eat or have fun for the rest of the holiday!

There are some people, of course, who are not very good at handling budgets. They are the ones who never have any money, they spend it as soon as they get it and then, when they need cash to pay a bill, it is not there. Some companies are not much better: they allow their finances to go without monitoring – they are the companies which do not last very long!

Companies do not budget just for one event, they plan their budgets for a longer period of time, usually twelve months, but broken down into portions so that they know, month by month, how much is going to go out of the budgeted amount.

Companies which do monitor their budgets will also use them as a means of evaluating how they are performing financially. An accountant may notice that the staff budget has been overspent. He will investigate this, and it may lead him to draw any one of a number of conclusions. He might ascertain that business has been so brisk that it has been necessary to take on additional staff. On the other hand, it could show that there

has been a lot of staff absenteeism, so temporary staff have been brought in. In either event, he must find out whether the organization's profits have been adversely affected and take steps to put matters right if there are problems.

Factors which affect the financial performance of leisure and tourism organizations

All organizations are affected by both internal and external factors and all need to be able to recognize what these factors are in order to deal with them to avoid problems or to use them to their advantage.

External factors

External factors are those which occur outside the organization. They may cause enormous problems for the organization, but they may also be beneficial. The important thing is that the management of any leisure and tourism organization should be able to recognize that these factors are present and take suitable action to either limit the amount of damage or turn them to an advantage.

Some external factors which affect the economic performance of an organization may, in themselves, be economic, but there are other factors which can affect any company. Managers concerned with financial performance (and all managers should be interested in the organization's financial situation) need to keep up to date with local, national and international news so that they understand the external factors which may be affecting their organizations.

Most, but not all, external factors which may affect an organization's finances fall into one of four categories. If there is an unexpected 'blip' when the financial situation is reviewed, a PEST analysis, which looks at these four factors, can be undertaken.

- P political
- E economic

- S social
- T technological.

A PEST analysis can also be used as a means of forecasting possible problems or benefits. There are other factors which may affect the financial performance of leisure and tourism organizations, but we will look at the four aspects of the PEST analysis before going on to consider these other factors.

Political factors

These can have a great effect on organizations in the travel and tourism sector:

- A tour operator who specializes in tours to one area, perhaps a single island in the Pacific or Caribbean, will suffer a loss of bookings, and consequently financial losses, if there is a war in the area to which it operates. Future bookings are also jeopardized.
- An airline which flies over two countries which declare war on each other may decide to take a safer but much longer route in future, avoiding the volatile airspace. This means spending more on fuel. The crew are legally only allowed to work for a set number of hours, and the longer route may mean that a stopover or additional crew are needed. This also increases operating costs.

Political events may also have an effect on the leisure industry:

- A government or local council which was committed to caring for the environment, the arts and the heritage of the country loses an election. The newly elected body withdraws all subsidies from countryside projects, museums, art galleries and historic houses and monuments. If the organizations are to survive, they must find new ways of earning the money which would previously have come from public coffers.

Economic factors

Some economic factors may only affect conditions in a local area:

- A factory opens up, providing employment for hundreds of local people. This has a beneficial effect on local businesses, as people living and spending their money in the area have more to spend.
- The opposite happens. A company closes and many people are made redundant. There is less cash to be spent and this has an effect on other companies, who have to make cutbacks, make staff redundant or even close.

Some economic factors may be generated by government. These are likely to have a nationwide effect, although some areas may be affected more than others. The results of government-led economic changes may be difficult to distinguish from political factors:

- An unpopular government tries to avoid losing power at the next election by reducing taxes. Working people throughout the country have more spending power, and sales increase. A politically motivated act has had an economic effect.

When changes to the taxation system are made early in the period of a government's term of office, these can be viewed as less politically motivated. The economic effects of tax changes are quite clear:

- Taxes are increased, which reduces the amount of money people have to spend on travel and leisure. Organizations within the leisure and tourism sector suffer loss of business.
- Taxes are introduced where they did not exist before. This increases the price of the service and it no longer appears to be an attractive proposition. Patronage is reduced; this obviously affects income and financial performance.

Other government decisions may have an effect on a local economy:

- A run-down area is designated as an area of special need, and central government offers incentives (special deals, with a financial advantage) to companies to move into that area. This has an effect on all businesses in the area as local spending power increases.

Some economic factors which affect the financial performance of leisure and tourism organizations have extremely complex explanations. They often appear to happen spontaneously, and no matter how much governments attempt to control them they are unable to do so. They can apply to a whole nation, or even the world:

- A recession (a time when companies find it difficult to sell their goods, which results in high unemployment and people having little money to spend) bites into the spending power of an organization's customers. Business and income are lost through no fault of the organization. Financial managers must react to the losses by reducing budgets, making staff redundant or diversifying (going into new areas of business).

- An economic boom is experienced. In this situation, which is the opposite of a recession, unemployed people find work, new companies open up, trade is better for everybody and most people have more money in their pockets than previously and are working harder. They want to make good use of their leisure time and they can afford to. Organizations within the leisure and tourism industry experience a boom which reflects the boom in other areas, and the financial performance of the leisure and tourism organizations experiences a welcome boost.

Social factors

These can be local or nationwide and may affect leisure sectors and tourism sectors equally.

- Demographic changes (changes in the structure of the population) can alter the way people spend their leisure time and the amount of leisure time they have. Most demographic changes are gradual – for example, the average number of children in a family has slowly decreased throughout this century. Financial managers would be able to foresee these changes and make provision for them in their strategic planning (plans for a number of years into the future).
  Some demographic changes happen much more quickly and may affect financial performance in the short term. For example, the population in a local area can be altered

completely by residential developments which change the nature of an area:

- An exclusive golf club in a semi-rural area may suddenly lose members and income from membership, green fees and its restaurant if a developer is given permission to build low-cost housing around the perimeter of the golf course. The financial performance of the golf club could be very adversely affected by such a demographic change in the area, and managers would have to work out ways to reduce the club's losses.

- A travel agent in a run-down residential area may make a healthy profit from selling low-cost holidays. This may be affected by the local council's decision to upgrade the area by investing money in it. They may allow developers to knock down some of the older properties and replace them with high-grade, expensive, office developments or residential apartments. The travel agent's financial performance will suffer unless he reacts to the changes. His product must reflect the fact that there are now fewer low-income families and that high-income single people and families have moved into the area.

- Social trends can alter the financial performance of any leisure and tourism organization.
  - People are now much more environmentally aware than they were even ten years ago. Any holiday company which, just a few years ago, offered excursions to shoot wild animals will have seen a decrease in income, as killing animals just for fun has become an almost universally unacceptable pastime. This trend has evolved over a number of years, but a well publicized environmental issue could affect the income of many tourism organizations in a very short space of time.
    Leisure sector companies have also been affected by changing attitudes to the environment and animals. Many old-fashioned zoos have been forced to close, as public opinion about the way in

which the animals were kept in small cages and enclosures has persuaded the public to stay away from many traditional zoos.

Technological factors

Technology is changing rapidly, and a company which was once at the cutting edge of the technology revolution may, within a short space of time, find that it has fallen behind and lost the advantage it previously had.

Ensuring that an organization stays at the forefront of technological innovation can be a costly exercise – too costly for many organizations. The alternative is that another organization, with the resources to invest in the most up to date technology, gains the competitive edge over its rivals. The finances of the organization which invests in technology are affected positively while rivals' finances are affected adversely:

- A coach operator loses customers to a rival who constantly upgrades his fleet to offer the most modern facilities available on coaches. They are also more economic on fuel, so there are hidden advantages as well as the obvious advantage of wooing customers away from a competitor.
- A leisure centre instals state-of-the-art exercise equipment and upgrades it constantly. Other leisure centres in the locality must think of ways of ensuring that their takings do not drop to such an extent that they become insolvent.
- A stately home invests in audio-visual equipment and pays a professional film-maker to produce an interesting and professional presentation. It receives a great deal of publicity, which attracts visitors who would, without the attraction of the modern technology, have visited other homes.

Other external factors which affect financial performance

Some factors can be foreseen, and plans can be made to counteract the possible effects of adverse external factors before they become a problem.

Seasonality

Many leisure and tourism organizations are affected by the seasons.

- Most holiday companies and all the organizations which work with them – ferry companies, airlines, hotels, etc. – carry the majority of their passengers during the summer months and their peak loads at school holiday times.

They know that this will happen each year so they are able to plan ahead to try to maximize their income during the off-peak times. They may offer a different type of product in the winter: long-stay holidays for retired people or special prices for people travelling together who are interested in the same thing (these are known as special interest groups and may have interests as diverse as ballroom dancing, birdwatching, hill walking or opera). They may offer special prices for educational trips during term-time, when fewer family holidays are taken, or may try to persuade businesses to let them arrange conferences and all the attendant travel arrangements.

Many attractions – outdoor pursuits centres, country parks, leisure centres, etc. – experience a similar peak of bookings, although their peaks may be linked to the time of week, or even the time of day, rather than the season of the year.

A leisure centre which is inundated with swimmers between 4.00 p.m. and 6.00 p.m. may offer reduced price entry after 6.00 p.m. or during the morning. Schools are almost certain to be approached with a view to them filling the pool at otherwise quiet times.

A stately home which is packed at weekends may introduce a special rate for visitors who call during the week, or it may try to attract visitors on quiet days by offering additional facilities: talks on the paintings in the house; guided walks around the garden, etc.

A hotel with a large, outdoor swimming pool could have a special cover for it in the winter and erect a pitch and putt course on the cover to provide a winter attraction for visitors. An income may be earned by charging non-residents for playing pitch and putt instead of swimming.

Competition

Few organizations have a monopoly (they are the only organization undertaking their business) and those who know they are in competition must take steps to ensure that they can hold their own against their rivals. Some organizations may know all about the competition which they face, and they are therefore able to tailor their own product to offer something a little different from the competition.

Sometimes an organization may be doing quite well, but then a new company starts up which is in direct competition. In this situation, the anticipated financial performance may be affected, and the organization will have to take steps to ensure that it does not lose too much money.

The weather

This is an important factor for leisure and tourism organizations:

- A long, hot summer in the UK can persuade many people not to travel abroad. Airlines, hotels, tour operators and travel agents all suffer loss of income. Late bookings – a good source of income for all the organizations mentioned – are particularly badly affected.

  The same conditions will be welcomed by many UK-based organizations: accommodation providers, swimming pools, leisure centres, parks, garden centres, attractions, etc.
- Bad weather, on the other hand, produces a boom for companies who take people to sunnier climes for their holidays and is a problem for many UK companies who need good weather to make them attractive.

News items

These can have an immediate effect on many organizations – frequently an adverse effect.

- The leisure and tourism organizations in a seaside town which receives bad publicity for

the state of its beaches may all suffer financially through no fault of their own. They will find it very difficult to fight the adverse publicity, which may even have been screened on national television.

  Managers in these organizations must work very closely with local council and tourist board officials to try to ensure that the area does something about its problems in the future. The immediate task, limiting the financial damage which has been done to their organizations by the bad publicity, is a very difficult one indeed. They may have to rely more on making staff redundant and cutting back their activities rather than finding ways of encouraging customers, who will not be persuaded to visit the area until the beach problem, which is outside the control of the individual manager and may take some time to put right, has been rectified.
- Health items in the news may have a financial effect on some organizations. The current worries about the increase in the number of people suffering from skin cancer has had a detrimental effect on many health studios which have invested heavily in sunbeds. Even though the use of the sun beds has declined, they still have to be paid for, but payment is difficult when they are not making money through rentals.

Task 4.3

This will provide you with evidence towards Element 4.1, PC 3 and Core Skill Communication Element 3.2, all PCs.

Think of an example of how each of the following factors could have a beneficial or adverse effect on the financial performance of a specific leisure or tourism organization.

- *Recession*
- *Boom*
- *Local conditions*

- *Seasonality*
- *Competitor activity.*

Write an explanation of how the factor could affect the financial performance of the organization of your choice.

The explanation should be worded in such a way that it can be understood by an intelligent reader who has no knowledge of the subject.

The financial performance of leisure and tourism organizations is not only affected by external factors, over which the management of the organization has little or no control. There are many internal factors which can make a great deal of difference to the organization's financial health. Management usually has a great deal of control over these factors.

Internal factors

Overheads

This term applies to a wide range of costs which are incurred by every organization. These are costs which no organization can avoid. Overheads include rent, rates, stationery, telephone calls, postage, interest on loans, wages, bills such as heating, lighting, water rates, and the cost of buying and maintaining equipment, furniture, company cars, etc.

Overheads are unavoidable, but it is possible to ensure that they are not too high. Organizations which spend more than they need on overheads find that the high cost of operating the organization affects profitability, whereas sensibly managed overheads ensure that profits are maximized.

Fixed overheads

These are overheads which do not fluctuate with the season and are not dependent on the level of business which is being undertaken. Here are just a few examples of fixed cost overheads:

- **Rent** is usually fixed, at least for a set period of time. Managers should always make sure that any property they rent is suitable for its purpose. There is no point in having far too much space, all of which has to be paid for, or renting expensive, high street property for a seat sale operation which does 99 per cent of its business over the telephone.
- **Insurance** is needed by all companies. Insurance on the building and contents will be paid once a year, and the company will be aware at the beginning of the year of the amount it must pay. Most organizations ask a number of insurance companies to give them quotations for their insurance needs and accept the quotation which offers them the most advantageous terms.
- **Wages** for permanent staff are a fixed cost. Key staff who are needed even when business is rather poor must be paid. This cost could be altered if business is very bad indeed and it becomes necessary to make some staff redundant. In this case, consideration must be given to the fact that they will be needed again when business picks up and they may not be available when they are needed. It can be very costly to train new people to take over the jobs of staff who have been made redundant, and many organizations take the view that they would rather dispense with other services (a company vehicle, the floral displays) than trained staff who are good at their jobs.
- **Telephone equipment and line rental** are fixed costs. Sensible managers ensure that the telephone system and number of lines rented are adequate for their business needs. They do not purchase equipment that is too sophisticated and therefore more expensive than is necessary, or equipment that cannot keep pace with the requirements of the business, in which case business could be lost. No organization should have too few telephone lines, causing them to lose business, nor so many that money is being spent needlessly.

Variable overheads

These are costs incurred in running the business which vary, often depending on the level of business being taken.

- **Telephone calls and postage** vary from season to season and depending on the amount of business being taken. A travel agent who experiences a dramatic reduction in bookings will not have to pay as much on postage as an agent who is experiencing a boom, simply because he does not have to send out invoices and then travel tickets to clients who have made bookings. (The agent who has had to find money for postage is, of course, in a better position as he will also have received payment for the booking, some of which will have been his profit.)
- **Wages for temporary staff and overtime payments for permanent staff** are also variable overheads. They are only paid when the workload warrants the expense.
- **Decoration** – A theatre, leisure centre, stately home or art gallery may wish to have floral arrangements to make it look more attractive. The decorations are not essential and, if business is bad and costs need to be cut, they can be dispensed with so that no further cost is incurred.

Task 4.4

This will provide you with evidence towards Element 4.1, PC 3.

Arrange to interview somebody at a local leisure or tourism organization who can help you to identify five more costs which are fixed costs and five which are variable costs. Write a brief explanation as to why each is fixed or variable.

Sales

It is essential for most organizations in the leisure and tourism industries to meet their sales targets. Some organizations, for example those which exist to protect the countryside and in so doing provide recreational facilities for leisure purposes, may not have any targets to meet.

In commercial organizations in the private sector where there are no subsidies or 'helping hands' for those which do not achieve their targets, companies must meet their targets in order to generate the revenue they need to keep the company running.

Extra sales are usually welcome, although there are some situations when this may not be the case. Holiday companies are inundated with bookings for just a few weeks during July and August, when it is difficult to find accommodation for all the people who wish to go on holiday. It would be much better for the companies if these bookings could be spread over a longer period so that they could increase the volume of their sales in mid or low season. This, of course, is difficult. The reason for the summer peak is that schools take their long breaks during July and August, so holiday companies must think of other ways of increasing sales outside high season.

Higher sales than anticipated may cause companies a headache when they are trying to locate accommodation for their clients, but failing to meet sales targets causes an even greater headache. Without the targeted volume of sales, the revenue which the company needs to finance itself will not be forthcoming. This may lead to redundancies for some staff or even the closure of the company if sales are so far below the predicted level that the company simply cannot find the cash needed to pay its debts.

Levels of credit and debt

Both these affect the financial performance of any organization. They go hand in hand and it is impossible to have debt without credit.

Many organizations do not like to grant credit – that is, they do not like to give people or other companies time to pay for goods or services they have received. At the same time, they may be more than happy to accept credit terms from somebody who supplies them.

A restaurant may purchase its stock from a supplier which only sends out invoices at the end of the month and then allows its customers two weeks to pay their bills. The restaurant has received credit from its supplier and, until it pays its bill, it is in the supplier's debt.

The same restaurant will probably demand that its own customers pay their bills before they leave the premises. It does not grant credit facilities to anybody.

Granting and accepting credit terms are standard practice in most companies (a few organizations will not participate in credit agreements for religious reasons), and credit does not cause a problem if it is handled well and not allowed to get out of hand. An organization which does not ensure that it collects debts as they become due will find its financial performance badly affected and may not have sufficient funds to settle its own debts.

Stock control

There are two types of stock, and mishandling of either can result in expensive losses for any organization:

1 Consumables are items which are used by the organization so that it can function. Items like notepads, photocopy paper, paper clips and pens are all consumable items. Consumables which are not subjected to strict stock control can lead to unnecessary costs being incurred by an organization.
   - A leisure centre which orders enough letterheads (notepaper with its name, address and logo, the symbol which customers associate with the organization) to last two years, because there is a special offer on printing one week, may find that there is a telephone number change before all the stationery is used, so the 'bargain' becomes a disaster which can only be used for scrap paper.
   - A tour operator buys all the stationery from a large organization which has ceased trading. There is so much stationery that he has to rent premises just to store it. The rent for the premises outweighs the savings which have been made and, because the stationery is off-site (not on the operator's premises), the

stationery controller keeps forgetting about it and ordering from a local stationer. By the time the ballpoint pens are collected from the store, they have all dried out and have to be thrown away.

2 Non-consumables are items which form part of the goods or services which are sold on to the customer. They must also be subjected to strict monitoring and control.
   - A café within a stately home must ensure that all stock is rotated so that the oldest food is sold first and nothing is kept past its 'sell by date'.
   - The shop in an art gallery must not order too many postcards which refer to a visiting exhibition, as it will be difficult to sell the cards once the exhibition is over.
   - A coach tour operator must ensure that his stock (the seats on the coach, the beds in the hotel) is sold by its 'sell by date' (the date the coach departs) as he cannot make money out of a holiday once it is over.

Where is all the financial information recorded and kept?

The information can be recorded in a number of places, from a simple receipt book to a complex balance sheet. The people who do the actual recording are called book-keepers because they enter data into books (which are usually called ledgers in accounts offices), although more and more companies now record their financial transactions electronically, using a computer and an accounting software package (you will learn a lot more about computers and software in Unit 5). In these companies, the people who do the recording may be known by a number of names: perhaps accounts clerk or input clerk. The titles vary between companies, but the people all do the same job – they make a record of financial transactions and information, which is essential if the organization is going to keep track of its cash.

There are three very important financial records which give an overview of the finances of the entire organization. We will look at these in much greater depth later in the Unit. They are the cash flow forecast/statement, the profit and loss forecast/statement and the balance sheet forecast/statement.

There is, however, a great deal of other financial information which needs to be recorded, some of it obviously important, but some may appear quite trivial. This is not the case. All the seemingly trivial transactions contribute to the overall picture of the organization's financial health. Two examples of recording financial information are:

- Petty cash slips are issued when a small purchase is made, for example a jar of coffee, a few stamps, urgently needed supplies for the first aid box. The slips are then filed (the details are often first entered into a petty cash book), along with the receipts issued by the grocery shop, the post office or the chemist, and produced when the annual audit takes place. They also provide useful management information, as a manager who takes a look at the petty cash book can easily see if too much is being spent on non-essential purchases. Financial performance is not only governed by sales but also by controlling spending.
- Electronic tills in a leisure centre's cafe or a museum's gift shop will record each cash receipt from sales. The till rolls can be kept and will serve as a useful check during an audit. They can also be used to provide management with information about sales figures.

▪ Assignment 4.1 ▪

This will provide evidence towards Element 4.1, all PCs and Core Skill Communication 3.2.

Scenario

You are the treasurer of a youth club which is a registered charity. The club is self-funding: this means that it does not receive any subsidies or grants, so it must make enough money to pay its

bills or it will have to close. The money required to run the club is raised in a number of ways:

- It levies a small membership fee on members (this is waived in certain circumstances)
- There is an entrance fee at some events
- A number of fund-raising events are held throughout the year.

The money is then spent on:

- Maintaining the clubhouse (a wooden building on a small plot of land)
- Purchasing new equipment and repairing or renovating old equipment
- Paying its regular bills (heating, lighting, etc.)
- Financing more fund-raising events and some social events.

It is your job to ensure that:

- The club stays solvent
- Its income is used as wisely and effectively as possible
- All financial records are correct and up to date.

You have given the committee notice that you will only be able to carry on as treasurer for another year, and they have asked you to explain the nature of your duties to your successor. You have decided that the new treasurer will need some background information. The easiest way to provide this is to write a report on the factors which you must consider when you are handling the club's finances. You start with a brief introduction to the organization, explain what having charitable status means and continue to:

1 Explain the reasons why you monitor the club's finances.
2 Explain what criteria you use for evaluating the club's financial performance.
3 Explain the factors which affect the club's financial performance.
4 Describe the financial accounts which provide you with the information you need in respect of financial performance.

In your conclusion you explain how the things that you do in your small organization are also relevant in larger organizations in all three sectors.

Who are the people who use financial information and accounts?

The planning and operating stages of any organization's finances are usually kept highly confidential, and access to their accounts is only given to people who need or have a right to see them. Commercial organizations (those which operate primarily to make a profit) are particularly sensitive about other companies discovering their plans or viewing their accounts. It would give competitors quite an advantage if they were able to plan retaliatory action because they knew the confidential plans of a rival.

However, even very confidential information has to be made available to a number of people. The titles given to the positions they hold may vary between organizations, but they have similar functions:

- **The executive management** of any organization – the people who make important decisions, such as those on policy and strategic planning – must be able to gain access to information which will tell them about the financial state of the organization at any time. If the organization is a sole trader or partnership they will be the owners of the company. A corporate company (one with limited liability or a PLC) will have a board of directors, while an organization in the public domain or voluntary sector will have a board of governors or trustees.

  This level of management will have a right to view any financial information contained within the company's accounts at any time.
- **The senior management** are the level of managers who do not actually sit on the board but who are very important in terms of decision making and control. Many decisions cannot be made without reference to financial information, and senior managers will have a right to view the accounts which appertain to their own area of responsibility at any time. In some organizations they may be given access to financial information in respect of the entire operation.
- **Middle and junior management** are usually responsible for a fairly narrow function within

the operation and need to have access to financial information which concerns their department or function.
- **Employees** who are not on the management team may need to be able to view financial information. For example, a clerk responsible for ordering stationery may suspect that there is a sudden increase in the quantity required. This may be attributed to pilfering, so the clerk may need access to historical records for checking purposes, or simply to compare current and historical costs. The wages clerk must have access to financial information which concerns salaries.

You will see that the more junior a member of staff is, the more limited the access to financial information is. Members of the management and staff of an organization may be provided with information in any form which they and the accountants choose. The information may even be in the form of raw data (lists of figures which have not been summarized or put into an easily understood format).

There are other people who have a right to view financial information, and they will be provided with it in one of a number of standard formats which have been used to summarize the raw data (we will consider these in depth later in this Element).

- **Shareholders** of corporate companies are provided with an annual report which gives details of the company's accounts.
- **Stakeholders** may have a right to view the accounts of an organization; it will depend on the situation. A customer of a sole trader may ask to view the sole trader's accounts. He does not have a right to see them, but if access is denied it may give the impression that the accounts are not healthy, and the customer would be well advised to take his business elsewhere. There could be another explanation for the trader's reluctance to show his accounts – perhaps the 'customer' is suspected of being a rival who was just trying to get access to his books.
- **The Inland Revenue**, who collect income tax and company tax, have a right to view the

accounts of virtually any organization on demand. They will make an appointment if they wish to inspect the accounts.

- **Customs and Excise,** who collect value added tax (VAT), have greater power than the Inland Revenue. In the event that they wish to inspect the accounts of a company which is registered with them, they may make an appointment, but they have right of access to the organization's premises at any time – they do not have to make an appointment. Not all goods and services are subject to VAT and not all organizations register with the VAT authorities.
- **Providers of finance,** such as banks, trustees, local and central government, may make it a condition of the loan or subsidy that they have access to the organization's accounts.

Task 4.5

This will provide you with evidence towards Element 4.2, PC 2 and Core Skills Communication 3.2 and Information Technology 3.3.

Make up a group with three other people. Each of you investigates the users of financial accounts in one sector of the leisure and tourism industry. You may each study one organization if you wish and write about the specific people in that organization. Write a joint report, explaining who uses financial reports in each sector. Word-process the report in a 'house style' (consistent format) and illustrate it with appropriate graphics.

You have seen that a number of people and authorities have a right to view an organization's accounts, but what would they be shown if they asked to see them? The management and staff of the organization may be given access to the ledgers or information which is held on computer, but external users of the accounts will probably be shown one of the three primary accounting summaries.

Financial statements

We have described the people who have a right to view the organization's accounts and considered the need to monitor financial performance and the criteria which can be used to measure performance, but how can we actually do the viewing, monitoring and measuring? It is often done by looking at various projections, or forecasts, of how the organization is expected to perform and then comparing the forecasts with what happens in reality and is reported in the actual accounts.

There are three very important documents which can be used both for projections and for reporting actual figures. Any organization which has a legal responsibility to produce accounts (corporate companies, registered charities and others) must produce them to a specified format. The sub-headings can vary from one organization to another, but the basic structure is the same.

Organizations which do not have this legal obligation (sole traders, leisure clubs, etc.) may use any format they choose. Most choose to use the standard formats, as they are so well recognized. The documents which look into the future and predict what will happen are called **forecasts** and the documents which report on what really did happen are called **statements** or **actuals**.

Task 4.6

This will provide you with evidence towards Element 4.1, PC 4, Element 4.2, PC 1 and Core Skill Communication Element 3.4.

All the information which you need to complete this task is contained in the sections on financial statements which follow.

Read the task, make a note of any words which are new to you, and as you go through the details about the financial statements define the words

---

and gather together the information which you need to complete the task.

When you are able to answer the questions, go to the library and look through some books on finance. Write your answers neatly for your portfolio and illustrate them with quotations from the books you consult. Make a note of the name and author of the book and the page number on which you found the information and quote from the book(s) in your answer.

Which documents would you consult if you needed to know the following information?

1 When your company may be short of cash and may need to arrange a loan.

2 How large the loan would need to be.

3 The amount of gross profit you made in a specific month.

4 The value of your organization's assets at a fixed moment in time.

Write a report, giving details of your answer and explain the purposes behind keeping financial accounts.

The cash flow statement (forecast or actual)

This is either a forecast of when you think cash will come into and go out of your business or a record of when it actually happened.

A cash flow forecast helps an organization to be aware of the times when cash will be required to pay bills. This is particularly important in organizations with seasonal peaks and troughs, as large sums of cash may need to be paid out when little or no money is coming in. Some organizations in the leisure and tourism industry show far greater seasonal variations than others:

- A tour operator which specializes in winter skiing holidays in Europe will show a far greater revenue in autumn (when deposits for holidays are being taken) and in winter (when balances fall due) than in the spring and summer, when very few bookings are being taken and nobody is travelling on European skiing holidays.

The cash flow forecast will provide information which is needed by management so that they can ascertain just how much they need to keep in reserve from the profits they made in high season to see them through the low season. They will be able to identify the times when they may need to ensure that the company 'tightens its belt'. They may even realize that they must arrange for loans, an overdraft or capital investment (money to be put into the business).

- A leisure centre in a town which does not attract tourists will show very little seasonal variation in cash received. The money may come in from varying sources: during term-time schools pay to use the facilities, during school holidays children go independently or with their parents and pay direct to the centre rather than through the school, but cash still comes in.

It is sensible to forecast at least one year ahead, to break down the forecast into monthly, or even weekly, sections and to compare an actual cash flow statement with the forecast on a regular basis. Warning bells will ring when forecast revenue does not match up to actual revenue – management will know that they are facing problems and will take action to get the cash flow back on track.

Figure 4.1 shows the format for a cash flow forecast or statement. This is a standard format, but there is a little room for manoeuvre to allow businesses with greatly differing emphasis to show their cash flows in a way which will be of most use to them. The following explanations of the terms on the forecast will help you to understand what has to be recorded:

The **opening bank balance** is either the amount of money you have in the bank or the amount of money you owe to the bank. If it is the latter, the figure will be shown in brackets.

RECEIPTS, all revenue is shown under this heading.

Fit and Bronze Health Club							
Monthly cash flow forecast (for the period 1 April 199x to 31 March 199x)							
		April	May	June	–	–	February	March
Opening bank								
Balance (A)								
Receipts								
Cash from sales								
Cash from dbtors								
VAT receipts								
Receipts								
Sale of assets								
Capital								
Total receipts (B)								
Payments								
Payment to suppliers								
Cash purchases								
Wages								
PAYE								
NIC								
VAT payments								
Tax payments								
Rent								
Rates								
Water rates								
Heating								
Lighting								
Telephone								
Accountants fees								
General expenses								
Capltal payments								
Interest payments								
Other payments								
Total payments (C)								
Closing bank								
Balance								
(A) + (B) – (C)								

Figure 4.1 Cash flow forecast

Cash from sales is money which is paid at the time a product is purchased. A family of four who visit a stately home may pay the admission fee in cash whereas a coach courier who takes fifty people to visit at the same time may pay by cheque. They are both treated as cash sales. The amount which is entered is the amount including VAT. However, not all sales will include a VAT amount.

Cash from debtors is also money which is due to the organization as a result of the sale of a product or service, but is paid on receipt of an invoice. A coach tour operator who takes large numbers of people to a stately home every week may not pay for each person on arrival but be invoiced each month. The amount entered in this section is, again, the amount inclusive of VAT if this is applicable.

VAT (net receipts) – not all organizations are registered for VAT, so this entry may not appear on all cash flow forecasts. An organization which is registered for VAT and which sells a product or service that is zero rated may claim back VAT from its own purchases, say of stationery or furniture, while not charging VAT on its own sales.

Other receipts may come from sources which are not your main business: a travel agency may take rent from the flat above the shop; a wildlife park may receive donations as a result of an article in a newspaper; an art gallery may receive a bequest from a regular customer.

Sales of assets may produce an income which must be recorded separately from sales made in the regular line of business: a museum with a number of virtually identical objects may decide to sell one of them to raise much needed cash; a gym may decide to upgrade its equipment and sell the items which have been replaced; a tour operator may up-date from a manual system to an electronic one and wish to dispose of the numerous filing cabinets which are now surplus to requirements.

Capital is money which is invested in a business. Sometimes the capital is all made available as soon as the business starts to operate; at other times capital is invested as it is needed or at regular intervals.

Total receipts are added up each month and then finally at the end of the accounting period. In the case of the example you have been given, this would be at the end of March.

Payments are recorded after all the receipts have been accounted for.

Payments to suppliers – in this section you enter payments you will make on receipt of an invoice. The type of supplies will change, depending on the business which is being operated, although there will be some supplies which will be needed by all sectors of the leisure and tourism industry. One thing used by all organizations is stationery

(purchases of equipment, such as desks and computers, go into a separate section). A tour operator may have separate sections for payments to airlines and payments in respect of accommodation, as these are such large and important cost areas. A leisure centre's accounts may display payments in respect of supplies of food for the café separately from cleaning materials as, again, these are both likely to be high. Differentiating them could be of use to managers who are looking for areas where costs can be managed more efficiently.

The amount which is entered is the amount including VAT and it is entered when you intend to pay the bill (if it is a forecast) or when you did pay the bill (on a statement of what actually happened), not on the date the bill became due. Most organizations will not pay a bill as soon as they receive it, as it is advantageous to keep the money in the organization's own bank account as long as possible.

Cash purchases are sometimes made by all organizations. The supplies for a staff canteen may be purchased from a cash and carry warehouse, which means that they are paid for when purchased and not on invoice, although a cheque rather than cash may be used.

Wages/drawings – this section will contain details of wages which are paid to staff and 'drawings', which are taken by the owners or directors of a company as their share of the profits. The amount entered is the amount remaining after income tax and National Insurance contributions have been deducted.

PAYE/National insurance contributions are entered together. PAYE, which was explained earlier in the Unit, must be sent to the tax collector within two weeks of the end of the month. This means that the tax on wages which were paid in April, and which will show in your April entry on the cash flow statement, will be sent to the Inland Revenue in May and will appear on your cash flow statement in May.

The exception to this rule is that a sole trader or partner pays tax and National Insurance contributions only twice a year, on 1 January and 1 July. These are not entered in this section of the cash flow statement, but in the section headed 'Tax payments'.

National Insurance Contributions are payments in respect of pensions, unemployment benefits and the National Health Service which are deducted directly from employees' wages in much the same way as PAYE.

VAT (net payments) are only paid by organizations which are registered for VAT. In this case, the estimated amount of VAT which will be paid each month is entered on a cash flow forecast, or the amount actually paid will appear on a statement of actual cash flows.

Tax payments contains details of tax which will be paid in respect of company profits (for limited and public limited companies) and tax payable by sole traders and partners in non-corporate companies.

Rent – the amount of rent due is entered here, or it could contain the amount of mortgage payable each month if the organization is actually purchasing the property from which it runs its operation.

Rates are payable by most organizations. The terms can vary; they can be paid monthly, quarterly or annually.

Heating/lighting bills are normally paid four times a year. These would usually be payments to an electricity or gas board. Organizations which rely on electricity to run their machinery, perhaps a very heavily computerized tour operator or an electronic amusement arcade, could have a separate system for heating and lighting electricity and operational electricity, in which case there would be separate entries in its accounts statements.

Telephone bills are paid quarterly, in arrears. Payment can be delayed for a short time, about a month, so the payment would be shown the month after the bill was received.

Professional fees are paid to people like auditors, solicitors and business consultants who will be employed for their expertise from time to time. There are unlikely to be any regular payments in this section.

General expenses will include very small cash purchases which are dealt with together under the name 'petty cash' – perhaps a jar of coffee and a bottle of milk each day, plus some cream cakes on special occasions. A theatre may buy newspapers for the reviews after an opening night. The manager of a leisure centre will purchase a roll of film to record a visit by a celebrity.

Postage may also be listed under general expenses, but an organization with high postage charges, such as a travel agent or tour operator, will probably list postage charges separately, under its own heading.

Capital expenditure is incurred when a large piece of equipment is purchased: a new rowing machine or sunbed by a leisure centre; a car for a new sales representative; new office furniture as a company expands, or when the old furniture has deteriorated so much that it needs to be replaced.

When the purchase is made outright, all the cash paid is entered in the month when the equipment is bought. Payments on purchases which are made with the help of a loan will show every month until the loan has been repaid.

Bank interest and charges are payable if you have an overdraft or bank loan and on transactions made on your business account. Bank charges are subject to quite remarkable variations between banks, and a close eye should be kept on exactly what the organization is being charged for the facilities offered by the bank.

Other payments could include details of payments to a trade body, for example, a travel agent or tour operator may be a member of ABTA. It could include details of insurance which has been paid, or any one of a number of other payments.

Closing bank balance is worked out by adding the opening bank balance to the total receipts and then subtracting the sum of all the payments. The closing balance at the end of one month becomes the opening balance at the beginning of the next month.

Task 4.7

This will provide you with evidence towards Element 4.2, PC 1 and PC 3.

Write a cash flow forecast of your own income and expenditure for the next two months and, at the end of each month, write an actual cash flow statement and compare this with the forecast. You will not have as many entries as a company in the public, private or voluntary sector, but you will have money coming in and money going out, so make an entry for each transaction.

The profit and loss account

This, just like the cash flow statement, can be either a forecast of what is likely to happen or an actual account of what did happen. Figure 4.2 shows the format of a profit and loss forecast.

A profit and loss statement shows the total amount of projected or actual sales in a specified period. The amount due from sales will not necessarily have been collected in the period in the figure is entered, but the amount will have been invoiced in that period.

Some organizations prepare a trading account before the profit and loss account. A trading account is used to work out the gross profit which has been made by an organization. It does this by establishing how much revenue has been taken in respect of goods or services sold and how much it has cost to provide the goods and services. The profit and loss account format which we are going to study does not require the completion of a trading account before it is started as these are an integral part of the profit and loss account.

Organizations such as leisure centres, theme parks, stately homes and amusement parks operate on a mainly cash basis, so the sales shown in a month will be similar to the amount shown in 'cash from sales' on the cash flow statement. However, many organizations operate on an invoicing system:

- Tour operators issue invoices for balance payments on receipt of a deposit, which may be many months in advance of the holiday departure date
- Golf club members may be invoiced for their membership fees when they become due, but may be allowed to take a month or so before they pay.

In these situations, a specific month shown on the profit and loss statement will bear little resemblance to the same month in the cash flow statement.

Look at the outline of a profit and loss record (Figure 4.2). You will recognize a lot of the terms which are used, as they appeared on the cash flow statement and have already been explained. However, some terms will appear to be familiar, but they have a different meaning when applied to a profit and loss statement instead of a cash flow statement.

An explanation follows of those terms that are new, or have a different meaning on the profit and loss statements than on the cash flow statements.

Sales – this entry shows the amount of sales which have been made each month – not necessarily the amount which has been paid in return for goods and services. Some of the money that the organization earns from sales may be paid at a later date.

Cost of sales – this is a list of the direct costs that have been incurred by the organization to enable it to provide the goods or service. Direct costs are costs which are only applied to the specific sale and

Fit and Bronze Health Club							
Monthly profit and loss forecast (for the period 1 April 199x to 31 March 199x)							
		April	May	June	_____	_____	February	March
Sales (A)								
Less cost of sales								
Purchases								
Labour								
Other direct costs								
Total (B)								
Gross profit (C)								
Tax (B) from (A)								
Less overheads								
Rent and rates								
Heating								
Lighting								
Telephone								
Accountants fees								
Depreciation								
Employee costs								
Interest								
Expenses								
Total (D)								
plus other income (E)								
Net profit (F) = (C) + (E) − (D)								

Figure 4.2 Profit and loss forecast

would not have been incurred if the sale had not been made. When sales increase, so do direct costs.

Purchases are those which are made in respect of the specific product or service which is being sold. A hotel which hosts a wedding reception buys in additional wines and spirits to sell on to the guests at the reception. If the reception had not been held there, these extra purchases would not have been made.

Labour – the same hotel may need to take on casual staff to handle the food preparation and serving at the reception. These are direct labour costs attributable to the reception. Regular staff

may also work on the reception, but their wages will be featured in the 'overheads', as they would have been payable even if the reception had not been held at the hotel.

Other direct costs – any other cost which is directly attributable to the sales which have been made during the accounting period is entered here. For example, after the reception the tablecloths which were used will have to be sent to the laundry for cleaning.

Gross profit is calculated by subtracting the direct costs incurred by making sales from the amount of revenue due for sales.

The profit and loss statement then continues to list the overheads incurred in the same accounting period. Most of these are already familiar to you, but some explanation is needed of the following:

Depreciation is the amount you deduct for equipment, furniture, etc. wearing out. An organization may pay £18,000 for computers and decide that they will be worn out in three years' time. One way of showing depreciation is to divide the cost by the three years, which equals £6,000 per year, and then further divide it to give a depreciation cost per month. So the amount shown for the computers' depreciation in the profit and loss statement will be £500. This is a simple method, but not the only one.

Interest is the amount of interest which is payable on loans and overdrafts throughout the year entered as a monthly figure.

The cost of overheads should be added together and then subtracted from the gross profit already worked out. There is then just one more item to be considered ...

Miscellaneous income may come from interest on investments or from other sources already suggested when the cash flow statement was being explained.

The monthly net profit is finally arrived at by:

- Adding together all sales made in the month
- Deducting the cost of the sales
- Deducting the overheads for the month
- Adding any miscellaneous income.

A comparison of the profit and loss forecast with the actual profit and loss statement every month will enable managers to see whether their projected figures were realistic. When discrepancies occur, they can take action to alleviate problems as they are seen to appear.

The balance sheet forecast or statement

A balance sheet shows what is called a 'snapshot picture' of the finances of an organization. This is a picture at one particular moment in time. A forecast shows an estimate of how the balance sheet is expected to look at a specific moment.

Therefore, unlike the cash flow and profit and loss statements, a balance sheet will not contain details of a number of months but will have a heading stating the day which is covered by the balance sheet.

The format of a balance sheet is shown at Figure 4.3. It contains some new terminology: you will find an explanation of the following terms useful:

Assets are owned by an organization. They have a value for the organization.

Fixed assets are owned by the organization and intended for long-term use by it. Indeed, some fixed assets may be essential to the existence of the organization and can never be disposed of. It is impossible to have a country park without the land which makes up the park, a football club without its ground, or a hotel without the building and contents.

Other fixed assets may be used for a relatively long term and then disposed of. Company vehicles, sunbeds, gym equipment and office furniture are usually kept for a number of years before they are replaced.

The value of fixed assets may appreciate or depreciate each year. This would be reflected on an organization's balance sheets:

- The value of the buildings and grounds which make up a stately home will probably appreciate (gain value) each year. A house valued at £2,500,000 one year may appear on the balance sheet with a value of £2,650,000 the following year. Of course, if the property market experiences a depression, or if no money is spent on maintaining the property and grounds, it could also depreciate (lose value).
- The paintings housed within an art gallery will probably gain in value each year, so each time

Fit and Bronze Health Club				
Balance sheet forecast (on 31 March 199x)				
ASSETS				
Fixed assets				
Freehold or leasehold property			£	
Office equipment			£	
Vehicles			£	
Machinery			£	
Other equipment			£	
Total fixed assets (A)				£
Current assets				
Cash in hand and at bank			£	
Stock			£	
Debtors			£	
Total current assets (B)				£
Total assets (A) + (B)				
Capital and liabilities				
Capital				
Stakeholders capital			£	
Profit and Loss			£	
Total capital (C)				£
Medium-term liabilities				
Loans			£	
Current liabilities				
Overdraft			£	
Tax payable			£	
Creditors			£	
Total liabilities (D)				£
Total capital and liabilities (C) + (D)				£

Figure 4.3 Balance sheet

a balance sheet is prepared, the value of these particular fixed assets will grow.

- When we looked in depth at a profit and loss account we considered the depreciation of some computer equipment which had cost £18,000. A balance sheet which had been prepared to show a snapshot of the organization's finances the day after the computer equipment had been purchased would show its value at £18,000. A year later, the balance sheet would show the value at £12,000 – the amount the organization would hope to sell it for if it wished to dispose of it. A year later, it would be shown at £6,000, and the following year it would not be shown at all, even if it were still in use. It would have been written off – that is, it would no longer be regarded as having a monetary value to the organization.

Current assets are owned by and have value for the organization, but are of a more transient nature than fixed assets. Current assets are likely to include:

- **Cash** you can arrive at this figure by extracting it from the cash flow statement.
- **Debtors** are the people who owe you money. The total amount owed to the organization is entered here. The amount can be derived from the cash flow statement and the profit and loss statement.

  Certain leisure and tourism organizations – those where goods are ordered for later consumption and invoiced in advance of the consumption (travel agents, tour operators, airlines, ferry companies) – are likely to show very large amounts here. Others – those whose clients buy and consume the product or service at the same time (a theme park, a craft fair, a leisure centre, a football club or a restaurant) – are unlikely to have many debtors.

  Stock the amount entered here will mainly refer to non-consumable stock (the stock which is used to make up a product and not that which the organization uses itself, as part of its daily operation).

  Leisure and tourism organizations are not production companies, so are unlikely to have a great deal of **non-consumable** stock. A company which manufactures sportswear will include here details of fabric waiting to be made into sweatshirts or tracksuits, or T-shirts which have already been made up but not yet sold. A museum or art gallery will include details of the items on the shelves of the shop inside the facility and, if applicable, in the café's storeroom. The cash flow and profit and loss statements will provide you with the information you need here.

  Consumable stock (items which are used by the organization to support its day-to-day operation – paper clips, envelopes, etc.) could

also be included if they were in sufficient quantities to have a resale value.

By adding the total of fixed assets to the total of current assets you will arrive at the figure for the total assets of the organization.

Capital is the amount of money which was invested in the organization.

Profit and loss can either be a plus figure (when the organization has made a profit), or a minus figure (when the organization has made a loss). A minus figure is shown in brackets and is deducted from the capital, whereas a plus figure is added to the capital.

Medium-term liabilities consist of loans which are not due for payment within one year.

Current liabilities consist of:

- **loans** which are due for repayment within twelve months
- Overdrafts (these figures can be derived from the cash flow statement)
- **Tax payable** (this is payable on profits and will need to be estimated)
- **creditors** (people to whom you owe money) (the cash flow and profit and loss statements will be able to provide the figure you need here).

You can then show the total capital and liabilities in the organization at a given moment.

The annual report

Once a year, a balance sheet, a profit and loss statement and, usually, a cash flow statement as well as other documents are prepared for the shareholders of a corporate company as an annual report. The contents of the annual report can vary between organizations, but all must contain the first two financial statements mentioned. Other information which the organization is required by law to make available to shareholders could be in the directors' and auditors' reports.

In addition, there could be a chairman's report and there may be promotional material which describes the organization's products or services. (Shareholders are also consumers, and many organizations believe that no opportunity to make a sale should be overlooked.)

▪ Assignment 4.2 ▪

Scenario

This scenario continues from the previous assignment.

The proposed new treasurer is very enthusiastic about taking over from you when you relinquish your duties, but you are concerned that he may have problems as he does not have a background in finance, as you do.

You decide to write another report for him, this time giving some information about:

1 The purposes of financial accounts.
2 The people who use financial accounts.

```
                Calby-on-Sea Youth Club
                     Balance sheet
                 as at 31 December 1996
                           1996              1995
 Fixed assets
 Club house             11,000            11,000
 Sports equipment        2,000             1,650
 Office equipment          800               900
 Kitchen equipment       1,100             1,350
 Total fixed assets            14,900            14,900
 Current assets
 Cash in hand
   and at bank             825               600
 Stock                     125                35
 Debtors                    20
 Total current assets           970               635
 Total assets                 15,670            15,535
 Current liabilities
 Creditors                  30
 Total current
   liabilities                     30
```

Figure 4.4

You again decide to conclude your report with information which relates to larger organizations in the private and public sectors as well as your own, voluntary sector.

You also think it would be a good idea to illustrate what you have written by showing him the club's balance sheet from the end of the last financial year (which also gives details of the previous financial year) and explaining what some of the items mean. Look at Figure 4.4 and explain the following:

1 What is meant by fixed assets.
2 Why the amount against sports equipment is more in the current year than the previous year.
3 What is meant by the term 'debtors'.
4 What the total fixed assets are on 31 December 1996.
5 What the total value of equipment owned by the club is on 31 December 1996.
6 Why the date 31 December 1996 has been stressed in questions 4 and 5.
7 What is the status of the £30 next to the entry for creditors:
   Does somebody owe it to you?
   Do you owe it to somebody?
8 Explain the term 'creditors'.

Portfolio builder

You have now been given the opportunity to collect evidence for all the performance criteria in both Element 4.1 and Element 4.2. You can have done this either by completing all the tasks or by completing both the assignments.

Look through your portfolio and make sure that all the performance criteria have been covered, and then take another look to ensure that you have covered them in sufficient depth to cover the required range.

Element 4.3 Investigate and carry out simple budgeting in leisure and tourism

Budgets were briefly mentioned in the earlier section on finance. Now we are going to look at them in some depth and undertake a budgeting exercise to give you practical experience of preparing a budget. Before we go any further, it may help you if you recall what you have already learned about budgets in Element 4.1.

We looked at the financial performance of leisure and tourism organizations. We saw how it is necessary to monitor budgets to ensure that there is no overspend and that the money in the budget is spent in the correct timescale. There is little point in having a budget which is to last twelve months and spending it all in the first three weeks.

We also saw that the ability to operate within budgets can be used as a criterion for evaluating financial performance. Organizations which constantly overspend on their budgets are doing something wrong. Underspending may seem, at first glance, to be a good thing, but this, too, has its problems. An organization which has estimated that it needs a budget of £60,000 for a programme of office renovation and only spends £35,000 may have arranged a loan for half the money and may be paying interest it did not need to pay. It will also point to the fact that the people responsible for setting the original budget did not do their homework and find realistic costs in respect of the renovation.

Before we investigate budgets in depth there is one question we need to answer.

What is a budget?

'Budget' is a word which is probably familiar to you, even if you only know it from the annual Budget for the country which the Chancellor of the Exchequer presents to Parliament each year. The word has two meanings:

- *The simpler definition is that it is an amount of money which is allocated to a specific project or purpose. For example, at home you may have a clothes budget or a holiday budget; at work the management may agree a specific amount of money for*

the Christmas party budget or the stationery budget.
- *The more complex definition is the one which is usually applicable within leisure and tourism organizations: it is a financial plan of income and outgoings over a specified period of time.*

The second definition may appear to have quite a lot in common with a cash flow forecast, which anticipates what money will come into and out of the organization over a set period of time, but there are two words which set them apart: *plan* and *forecast*. A plan lays down what it is intended will happen, whereas a forecast anticipates what will probably happen, or what it is hoped will happen.

How are budgets set and who sets them?

Budgets are set by an organization's management to help the organization meet its objectives. Organizations within leisure and tourism may have very different objectives from each other – we have already considered this in the previous Element. Here is a reminder of some objectives which could be set at the broadest level:

- To make as big a short-term profit as possible
- To make a healthy profit which grows every year
- To save a rare bird from extinction
- To renovate a stately home which is near ruin
- To improve the level of fitness in a local population.

Each of the organizations concerned would set budgets which would help it to meet its objectives. The emphasis placed on the budgets would be different, but they would all serve the same purpose and they would all be administered in a similar fashion.

In the remainder of this Element we look into the aspects of budgeting which would be common throughout all organizations in the leisure and tourism industry, no matter what their objectives.

The requirements of budgets within a leisure and tourism facility

Budgets have four major requirements:

- *They enable performance to be monitored* – Budgets provide a framework which says what should happen in respect of the overall finances of the organization and the finances of each department within a specified period
- *They enable performance to be controlled* – The monitoring process will reveal any discrepancies between what should happen and what is happening in respect of the budget. Any deviation from the budget can be addressed by either putting a stop to whatever is causing the deviation or, if the deviation is sensible, or even welcome, the budget can be altered.

Case study

The snack bar at a swimming pool suddenly deviated quite dramatically from its planned budget and overspent on cold drinks. The pool's manager checked the budgets regularly and spotted the deviation of actual spend from budgeted spend. He was quite relaxed about it, as the deviation could be explained by a combination of hot weather and increased number of clients, both of which would lead to increased profits.

However, if the need to increase the stocks of drinks purchased by the snack bar had not been matched by an increase in sales the manager would have had to investigate further – he may have had a case of pilfering on his hands.

- *They help to control cash flow* – The budget will contain details of when cash comes into and goes out of the organization. Organizations which respect their budgets will not be placed in a position where they do not have cash available to meet essential bills because they have spent money on something which has not had anything allocated to it, or because they have spent money before it should have been spent.

Case study

A health and fitness studio planned to replace equipment over a twelve-month period. At the beginning of each quarter – January, April, July and October – a spend of £5,000 was planned.

At the beginning of May a competitor announced that it was closing and offered all its equipment to the studio for just £8,000. The studio's owner was able to look at the budget to find out if the cash could be made available. He had planned to spend £4,000 in May on having central heating fitted; this amount could easily be transferred and used to partially fund the purchase of the equipment.

He had no trouble at all persuading the bank manager to give him a short-term loan for the other £4,000, as he was able to show the well planned budget. The bank manager could see that the loan of £4,000 could be paid back in June, when the studio's owner would have been paying for the next set of equipment. Even after interest and bank charges, some of the planned spend of £5,000 was saved. The central heating could then be funded in October by using most of the £5,000 which had been set aside for the final purchase of equipment. This no longer had to be made, as the major purchase of equipment in May meant that the studio was fully equipped.

Without the budget, the studio owner would not have known how the money could be made available and would probably not have been able to persuade the bank manager to make the short-term loan.

- *They have a forecasting role* – Budgets promote forward thinking by management and by all the staff who are involved in planning and operating them. They can also highlight discrepancies which are likely to occur between departments.

For example, a direct-sell tour operator's sales manager may have agreed an increased budget for April and May, as he wants his staff to make an extra effort at that time to sell holidays for the following winter. When the operations manager sees the sales manager's budget, he knows that he must ensure that he has sufficient capacity to honour the extra sales that may be generated.

Task 4.8

This will provide evidence towards Element 4.3 PC 1 and Core Skill Application of Numbers 3.1.

Think ahead to either your annual holiday or next Christmas and prepare a budget which will forecast the amount of cash that you will need to have available to meet your requirements. It will also help you to control your cash flow (if you stick to it).

Table 4.1 gives you an idea of how to set out a simple budget for an annual holiday. You can adapt this format for the Christmas period if you prefer.

The limitations of budgets within leisure and tourism facilities

All budgets are subject to certain limitations or factors which must be considered when they are set and used. If consideration is not given to these limitations, the budget may be of little use to the organization. It will possibly even give a false impression, which could be harmful.

- *Accuracy* is extremely important when dealing with any financial information. Figures which are inaccurate or calculations which have been worked out incorrectly for the budget can cause major problems. The organization may base its entire operation on a misunderstanding.
- *Reliability* of the information contained within the budget is essential. Figures which managers may be asked to estimate for the budget must be carefully worked out and not simply the result of an informed guess. A travel agency manager who anticipates taking 1000 bookings in April must have a reason for stating this figure. A comparison with historical records

Table 4.1 Expenditure budget for annual holiday departing 26 July

Item	April	May	June	July
	£	£	£	£
Deposit for holiday	50.00			
Balance payment		350.00		
Clothes to take			120.00	
Health club for tanning sessions	20.00	20.00	20.00	20.00
Suitcases			40.00	
Car hire in resort				150.00
Meals in resort (14 days @ £12.00 pd)				168.00
Spending money on holiday (14 days @ £10.00 pd)				140.00
Duty free				30.00
Total budgeted cost		£1098.00		

combined with a knowledge of the current state of the market would enable him to estimate a fairly reliable figure.

- *Consistency* in the way in which budgets are prepared is desirable, otherwise it would be difficult to compare one department with another, one year with another or one company with another.

  The concept of consistency must be applied to individual entries in budgets.

  For example, a stately home may have laminated cards containing details of the paintings and furnishings on display in each room available for visitors' use. Each year a quarter of the cards are replaced. Also each year a sum appears in the budget which has a direct comparison with the amount for the previous year (there will be a change to the sum, as inflation must be considered). One year the curator of the house decides to completely up-date the information cards, and an amount is entered in the budget under the usual heading of 'Information card replacements'.

It would not be possible to make a valid comparison between this new budget and that of last year as there is a level of inconsistency. There should be a completely different heading for the up-dated information cards, or it will appear to the person monitoring the budget that the cost of the cards has suddenly quadrupled instead of rising in line with inflation.

- *Sensitivity* – It should be possible to amend a budget if the need arises through any one of a number of reasons. A hot, dry summer may lead to increased sales for a company which operates a fleet of ice-cream vans. The drivers may work longer hours than usual and cover more ground than they normally would. It must be possible to amend a number of entries in the budget:
  - They will use more fuel than has been estimated
  - They will expect to be paid for overtime they have worked
  - They will need more raw ingredients for the ice cream
  - The vans will need servicing more frequently
  - The company's income will increase.
- *Stability of period* needs to be observed, otherwise it will be difficult to make comparisons on a historical basis. A heritage centre which opens for a season which runs from Easter to the end of October will have difficulty making direct comparisons from one year to the next, as Easter can occur from any time late in March until late in April.

Task 4.9

This will provide you with evidence towards Element 4.3 PC 2.

Work in groups of four and hold a brainstorming session to think up as many examples of inconsistency in budgets as you can. Keep the list in your portfolio.

Types and structures of budgets

Each departmental manager within an organization prepares his own budget, frequently with guidance and advice from a financial manager within the organization. There will often be areas of similarity between departmental (sometimes known as divisional) budgets, but some budgets will contain items which are not in others.

Most departmental budgets have a number of entries in common with other departments:

- Staff salaries
- Telephone rental and calls
- Stationery
- Cleaning.

Not all items will appear on each department's list of expenses, some will have items in common:

- Cars
- Fuel
- Entertaining
- Overnight expenses
- Travel costs.

Some items will usually appear on only one budget, for example:

- *Marketing budget*: research and development costs
- *Sales budget*: advertising.

There may be a budget produced for a specific project, and this would only contain financial details which relate to that project. For example:

- A country park might organize a craft fair for the Easter Bank Holiday
- A leisure centre might organize an outing in the summer
- A stately home may have a programme of evening entertainment during the long, light, summer evenings
- An art gallery could have a special exhibition.

Budgets can also be produced to serve specific functions, such as:

- A labour costs budget
- The capital expenditure budget
- The cash budget.

The divisional budgets, project budgets and budgets for specific functions are all brought together to form the master budget. The master budget incorporates all the divisional and project budgets into:

- A budgeted profit and loss account
- A budgeted balance sheet
- A budgeted cash flow statement.

Once the master budget has been prepared, it will be closely examined by the senior operational management in the organization, assisted by senior financial managers. They will look for any discrepancies. Perhaps one department is anticipating a drop in sales and another, which works closely with the first, is expecting an increase. The master budget will, among other things, show areas which are under financed or where allowances have not been made for seasonality.

Task 4.10

This will provide you with evidence towards Element 4.3 PC 3 and Core Skill Communication 3.2.

Make an appointment to visit a local leisure or tourism organization and interview somebody who is involved with setting budgets.

Prepare a number of questions regarding the types of budget which are prepared and the way in which the budgets are set out in the organization. Write a report on your findings and include examples of formats used for preparing budgets which you have reproduced using either a word-processing package or a spreadsheet.

This Element has given you the opportunity to learn a great deal about preparing budgets in leisure and tourism organizations and you have been given a number of tasks which will help you to gather the evidence you need for your portfolio.

The following assignment gives you the opportunity to add to your evidence and to prove that you have understood the concept of preparing and using budgets.

▪ Assignment 4.3 ▪

This will provide evidence towards Element 4.3 PCs 1, 2, 3 and 4 and Core Skills Communication 3.2, 3.3 and 3.4, Information Technology 3.1, 3.2 and 3.3 and Application of Numbers 3.1, 3.2 and 3.3.

Scenario

You are the new owner of a travel agency. One of the things which concerned you when you inspected the agency's financial records, before you bought the agency, was that the staff did not work within the budgets which had been set and profits were not, therefore, as good as they should have been. You have decided to hold a training session for your staff to explain the facts about budgets.

Prepare a talk to give to your staff on the requirements of and limitations on budgets and the types and structures of budgets. Your proposed talk should be supported by visual aids and handouts which your staff will be able to take away and study.

You want to be certain that your staff have understood what you have told them (particularly in respect of the structure of budgets) and, as you would like them to take more financial responsibility in the future, that they are able to set out a budget from given figures and do some accurate calculations.

You have managed to locate a memo which you received when you were the events organizer at a stately home and think it would be a good idea to give this to your staff as an exercise. You decide that you will do a sample budget before you give the exercise to the staff. This can be given to them, along with the other handouts, at the end of the session.

Plan your presentation, along with all the supporting materials, and do a 'run through' with somebody who is able to provide you with an evaluation of your work and give helpful suggestions about how it could be improved.

Portfolio builder

Check that you have covered the tasks and assignment in Element 4.3 in sufficient depth to prove that you have understood the concept of budgeting and that you have the practical skills which will enable you to prepare a simple budget.

Make sure that all your work is neat and legible and keep it safely in your portfolio.

MEMO

TO: The Curator

FROM: A. Smith, Events Organizer

DATE: 3 January

I have looked into the possibility of holding a 'country fair' on the weekend of 1 and 2 June, and I can now detail the costs which would be involved.

Outgoings

I need to advertise the weekend locally. The combined cost of printing posters and placing adverts in the local papers is £600. This is needed by 1 April.

I need to employ some casual staff, probably eight people at a cost of £30 per person per day for two days. They would be paid on Sunday evening.

The marquees we require will cost £1,500. The company expects a deposit of 10 per cent immediately, 50 per cent of the balance on 1 May and the remaining balance by 30 June.

I have approached a number of local organizations asking them to participate. Most have agreed, but there are some costs involved:

- The display of medieval crafts will cost £50 per day. They want half their money on 1 May, the other half at the end of the fair.
- The display of falconry will cost £50. They are only available on Saturday, and expect payment on the day.
- The magician is £150 for the weekend, to be paid on the final day.

BUSINESS SYSTEMS IN LEISURE AND TOURISM

Introduction

All leisure and tourism organizations need business systems to support the various functions which are an integral part of their operations. Some systems rely on sophisticated, modern, electronic equipment like computers and complex telephones; others can be supported successfully with traditional equipment such as filing cabinets, wall charts and cardboard files filled with information written on paper.

During the course of this Unit we will look at some of these administration systems. These will include the most basic manual as well as modern electronic systems. We will consider when they are appropriate and how they assist the functioning of an organization. We will also look at how they can have quality standards attached to them by organizations which take a pride in supplying a high standard of service to their customers.

The advent of computerized administration systems has brought with it relative ease of access to confidential information on many people. This has made it necessary to pass legislation to prevent misuse of electronic administration systems with regard to use of data of a personal nature. We will study the Data Protection Act to understand how it provides protection in this respect.

How important are administration systems?

Each year millions of people go to a travel agency to book their holidays: perhaps two weeks on a package holiday to one of the sunshine resorts, a short break to a major European city or a winter skiing holiday to the Alps.

It is quite an easy task for the client to collect the brochures, make the choice and then return to the agency to check availability and pay a deposit. In due course, confirmation of the booking will arrive, either accompanied by an invoice or followed by it some time later. Once the client has paid the balance which the invoice requests, he can sit back and wait for the tickets to arrive, usually about ten to fourteen days before departure. After that the days fly by and, almost before he realizes it, he is in the queue at the airport waiting to check in and board the plane which will take him to his holiday destination.

Every day of the year numerous people visit theme parks and leisure centres. They pay their entrance fees and then enjoy the rides or the sports facilities. They may take a picnic or have something to eat in the cafés, they may swim in an indoor or outdoor pool. One or two may hurt themselves and have to seek help from the first aider who is on duty. It's all so simple – you just pay your fee as you enter and then facilities are laid on for you.

EASY! Or is it?

- What has to happen to make the various stages of the process run smoothly for the holidaymaker?
- How does the travel agent get information from the tour operator?

- How does the tour operator liaise with all the hotels which feature in the brochure?
- How does the airline know how many people to expect for each departure?
- How are invoices and tickets generated?
- What goes on 'behind the scenes' to make it possible for the holidaymaker to enjoy a trouble-free holiday?
- How does the theme park ensure that somebody trained in first aid is always available?
- How does the café within the park make sure that it always has enough food – and people to cook and serve it?
- How does the leisure centre know when a squash court will be available for a new booking or an aerobics instructor have a place to spare in a class?

The answer is that all these organizations have essential administration systems in place which are designed to enable them to operate efficiently. All businesses rely on these administration systems, some manual, some electronic, some a mixture of both, all vital.

Element 5.1 Investigate administration systems in leisure and tourism organizations and evaluate their effectiveness

In this Element we will consider:

- How well designed administration systems assist the smooth functioning of any business
- Administration systems which are used in various sectors of the leisure and tourism industries, including accounts, personnel, stock control, reservations and operations.

We will also look at both routine (standard daily/weekly/monthly procedures) and non-routine functions (procedures which are carried out occasionally: reaction to a problem; as a prelude to expansion, etc.). We will look at systems and think about how they can be improved. We will consider the concept of quality and the process by which quality can be proven, thus raising public confidence in an organization.

What is an administration system?

In every organization many people spend their time doing individual tasks which, when put together with other tasks, form an activity which needs a system to support it. Individual systems which support one specific function then interact with other small systems to become part of a larger system, supporting a much wider-ranging function.

Example

Many museums and stately homes which are open to the public offer audio tours to visitors. These consist of a tape recorder and tape (sometimes a number of choices of language are offered) which are hired to a visitor on entry and collected on departure.

When we subject this seemingly simple activity to functional analysis (break down what is done during the course of the entire transaction into little chunks) we realize that even this simple system is, in reality, quite complex and long-winded. The system devised to support this service could be broken down into a number of activities and then further divided into discrete tasks (small, stand-alone chunks).

The first activity in respect of the audio service could be:

Before opening the house each day staff must check that all the equipment needed to operate the service is in place.

Some of the discrete tasks which make up this activity are to check that:

- The advertising sign is in the right place
- The cash box is in the correct place at the entrance
- The cash box contains the correct petty cash
- The tape recorders and tapes are in the right place
- The explanatory leaflets are in the right place and in sufficient quantities for the day ahead.

It is obvious from these tasks that a number of items are needed at the entrance, where the visitors hire the machines: the sign, the cash box, the leaflets, etc.

More discrete tasks and supporting equipment will be involved at the exit, so that visitors do not just walk away with the equipment – perhaps a sign to let visitors know where to leave the recorder and tape and another cash box to hold money to give back deposits (when a deposit has been left at the entrance).

So the first activity within the audio tape hire system is to make the checks. The next activity could be:

Undertake a transaction where audio equipment is hired out.

Again, a number of discrete tasks are involved in this activity:

- Explain to prospective clients how the audio guide works
- Take money for the hire
- Explain where to leave the recorder and tape at the end of the tour
- Record the transaction, particularly the cash which has been taken
- Record the language of the tape which was hired.

There would be other activities within this system and this system will interact with other systems. For example, the accounts department will become involved when it collects the cash and records its receipts each day. The marketing department may request information on the most frequently requested languages or the time of day and day of the week on which the equipment is most frequently hired. This information may assist with future promotional campaign plans.

There will then be an administration system within the accounts department for collecting, recording and banking takings from each activity within the organization: ticket sales, souvenir shop sales, audio equipment hire and café sales. There will also be a system within the marketing

department for keeping records in respect of originating countries of clients.

Each system will have materials to support it: a cash book, a filing system, a wall chart to show sales figures, a receipt book, etc.

Task 5.1

This will provide you with evidence towards Element 5.1, PC 2 and Core Skill Communication 3.2.

Study the example of the audio equipment hire service and design a manual (also known as paper-based) system for recording additional information in respect of:

- *The languages of the tapes*
- *The time of day and date of the hire*
- *Cash which has changed hands.*

Can you think of any other information which it may be useful to record as an aid to future management decision making?

Consider what would happen if two people were allocated to operate the hire service and one of them was dishonest and pocketed some of the money. Can you design a system for taking cash which has measures built into it to ensure that employees are not tempted to become dishonest?

Who needs systems?

Everybody does! They are vital in all areas of any organization and yet, surprisingly, one of the common complaints of many people at all levels in business is that they cannot get on with their real job because of paperwork. Even more surprising is that the same people can often be heard complaining that somebody else has not completed their paperwork – making it impossible for the complainer to get on with important work!

Administration systems and the paperwork which goes with them are unavoidable – what can be avoided are poorly designed systems which add to the workload instead of keeping it to a minimum.

Companies simply cannot function without systems. If they are not designed they simply evolve, and in this situation they are not necessarily efficient. When systems are ignored, mistakes, dissatisfaction and reduction of profits will ensue.

Administration systems are not just for clerks. Everybody needs them: management, sales and marketing, cleaning staff, sports coaches – everybody will need systems to enable them to do their jobs.

Task 5.2

This will provide you with evidence towards Element 5.1, PC 2 and Core Skill Communication 3.2.

Write a brief report or essay on the systems which you encounter in your life as a student. Explain how they work and what goes wrong when people do not observe them. You could consider things which apply to your academic work, such as the system for handing in your assignments, and also social aspects of college life – what happens when trips are arranged to places of interest? If you are involved in sports, how are you notified about sporting events?

What could go wrong if a system is ignored?

The following case studies are all real. All the procedures which should have been followed were routine – that is, they should happen on a regular and frequent basis. The staff who ignored the routine procedures caused problems, some of them quite costly.

Case studies

- A tour operator's representative had to deal with complaints in a resort. He did not bother to follow company procedure and write reports for each complaint. When clients returned home and made claims for damages because their holiday went badly, there was no way that the UK office could check what had happened in the resort. When clients took the operator to court it could not put together a good defence because it just did not know if anything had been done to help the clients when they were on holiday. The representative could sometimes remember what had happened, but without documentary evidence the court never gave a great deal of credence to his story. As a result, his company usually lost the case.

- A golf club had a system whereby anybody wishing to book a session with the professional could ring the clubhouse and make a booking through the steward. A diary was kept in the steward's office for this purpose. The professional bought himself a mobile phone, which he took onto the golf course with him. Whenever anybody rang him direct, he accepted a booking for lessons. Each time he returned to the clubhouse he would tell the steward of the bookings he had made and sometimes discover that the steward had taken bookings for the same time. The steward would then have to telephone people and offer them an alternative time and date. It annoyed the steward, it annoyed the clients and eventually the number of bookings declined as people went to a more efficient professional for lessons.

These are just two examples of what can go wrong when simple procedures are not adhered to.

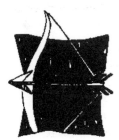

This will provide you with evidence towards Element 5.1, PCs 2, 3 and 4 and Core Skill Communication 3.2.

Consider the following case study.

Whenever a travel agent sent tickets to a client he made two notes: one on the client's file, one in a post book (a book used to keep a record of every piece of mail sent out each evening). The new clerk could not see why entries were necessary in two places and only recorded the information once, in the post book. One day a client did not receive his tickets when promised. The new clerk was on his day off when the client telephoned to complain, and when the clerk on duty checked the client's file he did not find any record of tickets having been sent. He issued new ones and rushed them to the client's house in a taxi. The client received the original tickets in the post the next day.

Analyse the contents of this case study and list the ways in which damage was caused to the travel agent and why. Do not just think about the amount of money it cost to hire a taxi but also about such things as reputation and the strained relations which would have existed between the staff in the agency when it was discovered that the tickets had been sent but the new clerk had not followed the system.

Evaluate the effectiveness of the system which was in place to record the despatch of tickets and suggest ways in which it could be improved.

So we have established that having systems, and following them, is essential, but how do we know which system is the right one for the job?

Planning the administration system

There are often many, many ways of doing the same task – so many that choosing the correct administration system for a specific job can be quite difficult. It is not unknown for companies to choose a system, spend money developing it (sometimes quite a lot of money) and then have to completely re-think it, or even replace it, as soon as it becomes operational. Problems such as this show that not enough thought was given at the planning stage and, as a result, not only is money wasted but a large amount of time can be lost and a serious backlog of work can result.

Companies thinking of installing a computerized system can employ a systems analyst (a person who looks at the overall picture of what needs to be done, analyses it and works out the best way of doing it), but this could be costly and unless it is a large company with a big task to be analysed it is more likely that supervisory staff or management will work out the best way of operating the system.

It is important to plan the system thoroughly. Everything that has to be done, the order in which it needs to be done and what must be achieved must be considered before a system can be designed.

Supporting the administration system

Systems involve processing information (receiving, inputting, accessing, distributing) and this is looked at in greater depth in Element 5.3. However, it is essential to have some understanding of processing needs in order to decide how to support the system, that is, how to operate it, manually or electronically.

In a manual system traditional methods are used, the work is done by people unaided by technology, and information is stored in various ways, perhaps on paper in filing cabinets, on index cards or possibly on wall charts.

An electronic system uses a computer. Paper may still be generated and stored in filing cabinets, but a great deal of work is done on the computer. The computer can also be used as a storage medium, which means that the filing cabinets can be dispensed with and, quite possibly, space needed by the company can be reduced.

Systems can also be a combination of manual and electronic. The most important thing is that they should be right for the task they are undertaking.

Computers are an integral part of modern life, and their use is likely to increase as they become easier to use, more compact and less expensive to purchase. The tourism industry was very quick to take them on board. A number of American airlines were at the cutting edge of the move towards computerization, and in the UK BEA and BOAC (the two companies which merged to become British Airways) were reliant on their own computers by the late 1960s. By the time BA emerged, computers were an essential airline tool. The computerization of major tour operators was led by Thomson Holidays, who encouraged travel agents to follow in their footsteps and embrace computerization.

The first organizations to computerize were the very large ones, which perhaps explains why some leisure organizations were slower to move towards electronic data processing and storage. Many leisure activities are carried out in centres which are quite small and independent and neither controlled nor greatly influenced by larger organizations within the same industry. This is not the case in the travel and tourism industry, where, for example, airlines and tour operators exert a great deal of influence on travel agents.

Computers can offer benefits to both leisure and tourism organizations. They can be used by both to perform many functions:

- To take bookings. No tourism organization can exist without taking reservations for its product and many leisure organizations also take reservations
- To process bookings. Once the booking is taken it must be passed on, perhaps to an airline, ferry company or hotel if it is a holiday booking, or to a swimming coach, golf professional, museum curator or restaurant manager if it is associated with the leisure industry

- To help keep accurate accounts
- To keep a record of staff rosters, when employees were off sick and when holidays are scheduled.

Computers are not always the answer, however, when small companies or simple tasks are involved and they are not without problems:

- It may be difficult to keep the data (information) held in the computer's memory secure from a determined hacker (somebody who gains access to a computer's files without permission)
- Hardware (the computer itself, printers, disks) can be very expensive, and there is such a variety available and so many aspects to consider – size of memory, operating speed, quality of print, etc. – that a certain level of expertise (which may not be available within the company and can be expensive to obtain from outside) is necessary just to choose the hardware
- Software (the programs which are put into a computer's memory to enable it to do something) which can be bought off the shelf may not do exactly what is needed, and a company could find itself changing its administration system to suit the software. Bespoke software (programs which are written specially for a company) is expensive and time-consuming to produce
- Staff may need training to use an electronic system
- Improvements to both hardware and software are being made so swiftly that both need to be upgraded regularly to keep abreast of technological advances
- The machinery must be maintained. Most organizations sign a maintenance contract with a company of hardware engineers. These can be expensive, especially if a call-out is required within an hour or two of anything going wrong with a computer; the swifter the guaranteed response time, the more expensive the contract.

These are just some of the negative points involved with computerized systems, which will be explored in greater depth later in this Unit.

Manual systems also have their drawbacks. Here are just a few:

- They can take up a great deal of space
- They may be time-consuming to use
- It can be easy to make mistakes
- Only one person can have access to a file at any time
- Files and charts can get lost or misplaced.

Designing a system requires a great deal of analysis, planning and good judgement. It is essential to know what is available in the market place and the costs involved. There is obviously no point in purchasing expensive computer equipment and providing staff with time-consuming and costly training if the company is small, the tasks simple and the equipment will be out of date and the company will have moved on and have different needs before the computer has paid its way. On the other hand, large companies which process huge amounts of information every day would be very short-sighted if they did not invest in up-to-date electronic equipment.

Leisure and tourism organizations and their administration needs

Routine needs

All organizations have some routine needs in common. Here are a few examples:

- Handling money received and money paid out
- Stock control of stationery, cleaning equipment, office furniture
- Staff movements (days off, illness, holidays, etc.)
- Personnel records (next of kin, references, previous employment, etc.).

There are other routine needs which, at first glance, appear to apply to some organizations more than others, but there are similarities between them:

- A travel agent may take holiday bookings, as does a tour operator, but do they have anything in common with a museum or country park?

  Yes. A leisure centre has a limited number of places available on a swimming course, so takes bookings on a 'first come, first served' basis.

  A museum may have a series of lectures for which people make reservations.

  The rangers in a country park may take bookings for wildlife days which they run for children during the holidays. Places are limited, as the rangers must each be responsible for no more than fifteen children.

  So all need a booking system, which is one type of administration system. The travel agent's and tour operator's systems may be more complex than those of the museum and the country park, but they all need one.

- A leisure centre may have a contract with a company which cleans the swimming pool on a regular basis.

  An art gallery will not have a swimming pool, but it may have an arrangement with a firm which cleans paintings or other works of art.

  A theme park needs to have the attractions inspected and repaired regularly.

In each of these cases a system will be in place to support contact with the contractors who undertake the work. They must be notified when work needs to be done, they must be paid, and arrangements have to be made for them to have access to the pool, the paintings or the attractions.

At first glance, the various organizations in the leisure and tourism industries may appear to have quite different routine administration needs, but in reality they have a lot in common.

Non-routine needs

The various sectors of the leisure and tourism industry have some non-routine administration needs in common with each other. Some examples are:

- Occasional reports on turnover (the amount of revenue taken by an organization in a set period), client's purchases, attendance, etc.

- A procedure to be followed if fire breaks out on the premises and a system which enables a record to be kept of what happened and what damage was caused and for a claim to be made to an insurance company
- An accident recording system in case a client or member of staff has an accident on the premises (this is considered in more depth in the Unit on Health and Safety)
- A system for dealing with theft from the premises.

There are also situations – often of the type which everybody hopes will never happen – which need to have a system in place, ready to support them if ever the need arises, which would be specific to each sector of the industry, although there can, again, be similarities between them:

- A tour operator may one day have to deal with a plane, train or coach crash or a hotel fire
- A swimmer may drown in a leisure centre pool
- An outward bound centre may take a group rock climbing and have an accident.

There must be systems in place in case any of these incidents occur – first in order that the incident itself can be dealt with caringly and efficiently, and secondly, because a great deal of information will need to be recorded and used at any inquiry resulting from the incident.

Do it well!

There is little point in recording information if it is not correct; in fact, incorrect information can cause immeasurable harm. Imagine if a clerk recorded the receipt of a cheque for £10,000 when only £1,000 had been collected. Many people would be given extra work trying to find out where the 'lost' money had gone and tempers would be frayed when the mistake was discovered.

When something is done well we say that it has a high level of quality, and 'quality' is something which is sought by the majority of companies in the UK today.

Quality

What is it?

Service industries in Britain are in the grip of a 'quality revolution'. What does this mean? Why has it happened? Why only service industries, why not all industries?

What is a service industry?

When you spend money on a service you do not buy an article which you can pick up and take away with you. You may get time in a swimming pool, a hotel bed or on an aircraft seat, but you do not purchase them, they do not become yours.

You may get advice from a sports coach or travel consultant, but they do not sell you something you can put in your pocket and take away with you. You may enjoy watching a film or play, you may learn a lot when visiting a museum or art gallery, but enjoyment and knowledge are not tangible, that is to say, you cannot touch them, they are not solid objects.

A service industry is, therefore, one which is concerned with selling intangible concepts such as time, advice, pleasure and knowledge rather than objects such as clothes, televisions and jewellery.

It is doubtful that any business would ever want to be known for producing an end product of substandard quality. This has meant that most manufacturing companies have concentrated their efforts on making sure that the products they produce are of a high quality, or at least of as high a quality as is possible in line with their purchase price. Manufacturing industries have tried to produce quality products for many years.

When there is a tangible product to be sold at the end of a manufacturing process it is easy for the customer to judge quality. It is equally simple for approval to be given to the product (if it comes up to the required standard) by the British Standards Institute (BSI). Most people are familiar with the 'kite mark' (Figure 5.1) which is shown

The mark of safety

Figure 5.1 The kite mark – any article which bears this mark can claim to have proved that it is made to a high standard

on goods which have been approved by the BSI – if you have never seen one, go into a shop which sells electrical goods and look at some of the 'white goods' (washing machines, tumble driers, refrigerators, etc.) which are on sale and look for the sticker with the 'kite mark' showing that it is approved by the BSI.

This approval shows that the goods have reached a required standard which was set by the BSI, not by the company which manufactured the goods. The vast majority of purchasers prefer to buy white goods which show the kite mark, as this gives them a guarantee of quality. It can be said that it increases customer confidence in the product.

Quality in service industries

In the late 1980s a system of approval was put in place which allowed the administration systems involved with services to customers to be given a quality mark. This differed completely from the kite mark for tangible goods, as the criteria for approval (the standards by which the system would be judged) were decided by the company seeking approval and not dictated to it by an outside organization. Any company which applies for recognition of the quality of its administration systems designs its own quality system to its own criteria. The criteria are called quality standards.

The proposed standards are considered by companies called accreditors, who work on behalf of the BSI or the International Standards Organization (ISO). Accreditors are companies which have been appointed by the BSI or the ISO to act on their behalf. They are authorized to visit companies, look at their quality proposals and make judgements on behalf of the BSI or the ISO. If the quality standards proposed by the company which is being inspected seem reasonable, the plan is accepted and the company must then prove that it can work to its own standards.

The quality marks

The two leading quality marks which are currently available are BS EN ISO 9000 (usually known simply as ISO 9000; this used to be called BS 5750) and BS 7750, a more recent introduction.

ISO 9000 is awarded to companies who have acceptable quality standards in respect of how they operate their systems. Examples of these quality standards are described in more detail a little later in this Element.

BS 7750 is awarded to companies who are aware of the impact that their operations may have on the environment and who take steps to ensure that they do as little damage to the environment as possible. In a service industry these steps may be as simple as fitting energy-saving light bulbs and efficient heat insulation or encouraging practices to reduce the amount of paper used.

What are quality standards?

Four examples of quality standards stated by a leisure centre might be:

1 To answer the telephone within six rings.
2 To answer all letters within forty-eight hours of receipt.
3 To have one male and one female attendant at the poolside at all times.
4 To have a member of the management team available during opening hours to deal with serious complaints.

Most of these are good standards and would certainly be accepted by the accreditor. However, if the leisure centre had said that it would answer all letters within four weeks of receipt, this would almost certainly have been questioned and not accepted. The fourth standard could be improved by either not using the word 'serious' or by being more specific; each member of staff could interpret 'serious' in a different way so it needs to be defined: complaints about health and safety, complaints about broken equipment, etc.

Task 5.4

This will provide evidence towards Element 5.1, PC 1 and Core Skill Communication 3.1.

Can you think of three quality standards which could be applied to the hire of equipment at the leisure centre?

Form a discussion group with about three of your fellow students and decide on a number of quality standards which you could apply to equipment hire. List them in order of importance. It is important that you all agree on the order.

It might help you to do this task if you think about what you would expect to happen if you had arranged to hire equipment, perhaps a squash racquet or an exercise bicycle, for a specific period of time at the leisure centre.

How does a company prove that it is working to its quality standards?

The accreditor who first looks at the system to decide whether it is acceptable would not only require details of the criteria but also information about how records were to be kept.

The telephone

It is all very well to say that the receptionist will always answer the telephone within six rings, but how do you prove that this has happened when the accreditor returns in a few months to check that your quality system is being adhered to? One method would be to instal a telephone monitoring system which records the number of times the telephone rings before it is answered.

Perhaps 'hard copy' can be taken each evening. Taking hard copy simply means copying what is on the electronic record and printing it out on paper. This can then be studied and analysed to determine whether the telephone was answered in accordance with the quality standard which the company itself has set and the accreditor, has accepted. The records can be kept ready for an inspection by the accreditor, but they also have a second function: they can be used by the management of the leisure centre to help them determine where action needs to be taken if they are not meeting their quality standards. Consider the following scenario: it will show you how useful one document (the hard copy or print-out from the telephone monitoring system) can be.

There may be three receptionists who cover the reception desk, where the telephone calls come into the building and visitors come for information, on set days and shifts – Alan, Barbara and Carol. When the manager studies the print-out, he may realize that Alan and Carol always answer within six rings but Barbara usually answers after eight rings but before ten. He can deduce a number of possibilities from this:

- Alan and Carol may ignore people who are at the reception desk in order to answer the telephone – he must investigate this possibility as it may be highlighting an area of deficiency in the quality procedures

- Alan and Carol may simply be very efficient and able to cope with the telephone and visitors – just what the manager wants
- Barbara may pay more attention to the people at the desk and allow the telephone to keep ringing – so she may meet quality standards where dealing with clients face-to-face are concerned but, in so doing, fails to meet them in respect of the telephone. If both cannot be done by one person, remedial action needs to be taken
- There may be more visitors on the days and shifts when Barbara works – extra staff may be needed
- Barbara may be unsure of what she is supposed to do – she may need some training.

The manager can use the system which records the number of times the telephone has rung to check that the quality standard is being met, but he can also use it to determine staff training needs, when extra staff may be needed, perhaps even when fewer staff are needed if the telephone is always answered on the first ring! When the accreditor pays a visit to inspect the records, he or she will not only want to know if everything is in order but, if it is not, what steps have been taken to rectify problems.

Response to letters

When a letter is received into an office, it is usually stamped with a receipt stamp which states the date on which the letter was received. The reply to the letter should state the date on which it is sent. It is usual to keep a copy of the letter on file in the office or, if it was prepared by word processor, it may be kept on disk. Either way, there will be proof of when the response was sent so, again, when the accreditor inspects the administration system it will be possible to determine whether or not the quality criterion in respect of response times was adhered to.

Staff presence

Duty rosters can be inspected to check that the third criterion was observed. These would give the names of the staff on duty, the area where they were allocated to work, when they took their breaks, what time they started their shift and what time they finished. It would even be possible to check that they had cover during break times (see Figure 5.2).

Management presence

Task 5.5

This will provide evidence towards Element 5.1, PC 1 and Core Skill Communication 3.3.

How would the quality auditor know if there had always been a member of the management team available to speak to people with complaints? How would he know if any complaints had been made?

Recording both staff presence and complaints can be done in a number of different ways. Try to think of at least two ways of recording each and produce written work to support your ideas.

You will get a clue about recording the management team's movements if you re-read the section about recording the staff's presence at the poolside. You may also be able to think of other ways of recording their presence in the building. Note them down in your answer to the task.

Records

Records are essential in any administrative system, and if quality standards are to be met it is essential that documentation, both for the administration system and the quality system, is kept up to date.

The quality audit

Without documentation it is impossible to carry out a quality audit (a periodic check which is carried out with the aim of detecting whether the published quality standard is being met). If the auditor (the person carrying out the check of the

Staff Roster for poolside attendants – MONDAY, 6 MAY 1996										
Staff name	10–11	11–12	12–13	13–14	14–15	15–16	16–17	17–18	18–19	19–20
David Jones	<--------	----------	------->	lunch	<--------	----------	--->brk	<---------	--->		
John Brown				<------->			<--->			<----	------->
Mary Smith	<--------	----------	--->lun	ch <-----	----------	-->brk	<-------	--------->		
Susan Green			<------	---->			<--->			<--------	-------->

Notes: please note any deviations from the plan, any problems encountered at the poolside and any action taken to remedy problems. Remember to note the time of problems and all subsequent actions.

This is one way of presenting a staff roster. The empty box at the bottom of the roster could be very important; it is essential that staff make notes as requested, as these can be used by management to check what action was taken over a problem. This is very important if a complaint is received or, even more importantly, if somebody has been injured.

These notes will also prove useful to the quality auditor when the audit is done.

Staff Roster for poolside attendants - MONDAY, 6 MAY 1996										
10–11	11–12	12–13	13–14	14–15	15–16	16–17	17–18	18–19	19–20	
<-- David	Jones ---	----------->	John B.	David ---	------------	--->J.B.	<David -	--> <J.B. -	----------->	
<--- Mary	Smith ---	-> <-Sue	--> <MS--	------------	--><SG>	<-- MS ---	----------->	<-- MS ---	----------->	

Notes : please note any deviations from the plan and state reasons why. Note any problems and action taken and give all timings.

This is another way of showing which staff are on duty. There are other ways in which the information could have been presented. There could be one very large plan which shows all areas of the building and all staff on duty.

Figure 5.2

documentation) discovers that a quality standard is not being met, a level of non-conformance will be issued.

There are three levels of non-conformance: low, medium and high. The auditor judges the level at which the breach has been made and will expect immediate action in all cases. Low and medium levels of non-conformance should be rectifiable immediately or within a short space of time; a high level of non-conformance may result in the quality certificate being withdrawn and will probably require major amendments to the quality system to be made.

The quality audit is itself essential, as nobody would know whether or not quality was being maintained unless an audit was carried out. People often have the impression that they are working to the quality standards, but when the audit is carried out shortfalls, which would have gone unrecognized without the audit, come to light.

Adoption of quality standards

The 1990s have seen many companies implementing quality standards, not only because they want to improve their administration systems and offer a high-quality service to their clients but also because they recognize that approval by the BSI or the ISO makes them appear more trustworthy in the eyes of the public.

Task 5.6

This task will provide you with evidence towards PC 5.1.1 and Core Skill Communication 3.2.

Write a list of reasons why companies want to be able to display that they have been awarded BS 7750 or ISO 9000 and briefly explain the benefits of accreditation.

The language of quality

There is one indisputable fact about quality management: there are many terms associated with it which are difficult for people who are not dealing with them every day to understand. Some of them are explained here. These explanations will help you when you tackle the task which will enable you to collect evidence towards the first performance criteria in this Element.

Investors in People – This is an area contained in ISO 9000. To be an investor in people a company must ensure that each person undertaking a task is trained to do that task. For example, a tourist information centre which employs a new switchboard operator must ensure that she is trained to work on the switchboard which it has in its office and not expect her to 'pick it up' as she goes along because she was familiar with a similar system in her previous employment. A company which wishes to be recognized as an investor in people must also provide employees with further training to enable them to advance within the company.

Quality procedures – These are the detailed descriptions of the steps which must be followed in order for a process to be completed to the given standard. For example, if the telephone is to be answered within six rings it is implicit within that standard that the switchboard operator must learn to count the rings and never allow more than six rings to occur before answering the telephone. There are further inherent suppositions within this procedure: the switchboard operator's job is simply to answer the telephone and pass the call on to the relevant person, not to engage in conversation; an existing call can be placed on hold in order that a new call can be answered within six rings. These items must all be identified within the quality procedure which refers to this standard.

Total Quality Management (TQM) ensures that attention is paid to quality at all stages of the business process, from designing a procedure through training people to undertake it to actually doing it. Not only is the procedure itself designed with quality in mind, but all aspects of the procedure and all the people involved with the procedure are considered. TQM means that everybody within an organization considers quality and strives to achieve it in everything they do.

Quality assurance is a concept which helps TQM to achieve its goal. It supports staff by providing them with what they need (systems, resources, etc.) to succeed in their aim of TQM.

Quality control – These are the day-to-day checks built into business processes to ensure that quality standards are maintained. The manager of the leisure centre may check the telephone print-out every day to ensure that the standard in respect of answering the telephone is met; he may go into the administration department and ask how many letters remain unanswered four days after receipt into the office; he may instruct his deputy to check the pool to ensure that there are both male and female attendants on duty at all times. These are the checks which enable quality to be controlled.

Quality circles are made up of a number of employees (between six and ten are average-size circles) who meet, with the management's agreement, to discuss ways in which quality can be improved. These workers, who are personally involved in the business processes, are often aware of quality shortcomings which management fail to spot. They may have authority to implement changes to the quality system themselves or they may make recommendations to management, who can then decide what action needs to be taken where quality needs to be improved.

Quality gap – This is the difference between what the provider of a service perceives as quality and what the customer perceives quality to be. A client returning from a holiday which has proved to be an absolute disaster will expect a swift response to a letter of complaint, certainly within a week. The tour operator may consider that it is giving a quality service if it replies within fourteen days. There is a gap between the thinking of the client and the thinking of the provider.

Quality and the law

There are no legal obligations on the service provider to ensure that the service is of good quality. There are many consumer laws which must be observed, but companies cannot be forced to answer the telephone swiftly or be polite and efficient in their dealings with the public. Those companies who have been investigated and are considered to have good enough quality standards to qualify them for ISO 9000 and environmental standards to give them recognition under BS 7750 will have the right to display the symbol removed if their standards fall below the required level.

Portfolio builder

Look back over the various tasks that you have been asked to do in the course of this Unit and make sure that you have written the answers to them all neatly and that you have not missed anything.

▪ Assignment 5.1 ▪

This will provide you with evidence towards Element 5.1, all PCs and Core Skills Communication 3.1, 3.2 and 3.3, Information Technology 3.1 and 3.3.

Scenario

You are a supervisor in the customer services department of a tour operator. It has recently become obvious that when complaints are received into your office they are not being dealt with as quickly as possible, and this is adding to your clients' annoyance.

Your manager has asked you to design a new system for handling customer complaints from receipt to first response. The company is committed to quality and you must apply quality standards to each stage of the process.

Write a report for your manager with your recommendations in respect of the new system and present this report at a meeting where the managers from a number of departments are present. Discuss the system with the other people present at the meeting and evaluate its potential for effectiveness.

Consider any suggestions which they make for improvement and, in the light of their suggestions and any second thoughts which you have had yourself, add a final section to the report stating where improvements could be made.

Element 5.2 Investigate and evaluate communication systems in the leisure and tourism industries

In the course of this Element we will answer the question, 'What is communication?' and look at the various methods by which it is achieved.

We will look at communications within leisure and tourism organizations and consider how good communications help an organization to run smoothly and efficiently and at some of the ways in which poor communications can harm an organization. By doing this, you will understand why good communications are very important to any organization.

You will become aware of various methods of communication, from the very simple to the very sophisticated, and you will be able to develop an understanding of the impact that the growth of information technology has had on communications.

The information in this Element, the tasks and the portfolio building exercise will help you to provide evidence towards the five performance criteria in Unit 5 Element 2.

What is communication?

Quite simply, it is passing information from one person (or people or organization) to another. All our senses can be used to receive messages, but the two mainly employed are:

- sound
    - spoken words
    - noises (e.g. Morse Code, fire alarm, ambulance siren)
- sight
    - written words
    - pictures (e.g. signs, photographs, film, graphics)
    - objects (e.g. traffic cones, life belt)
    - gestures (e.g. pointing, semaphore, body language)

See Figure 5.3.

A chef will use his sense of smell to receive a 'message' from food cooking in the oven and will test the message by using his sense of taste. A person who is visually handicapped will possibly use touch to read Braille writing, but the vast majority of messages are sent and received by sound and sight.

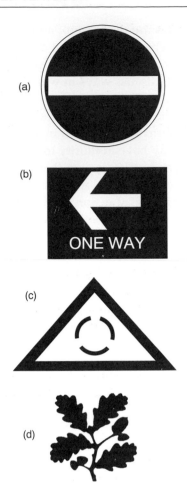

(a)

(b)

(c)

(d)

Figure 5.3 These are some common signs which communicate their message non-verbally. Do you know what they are telling you? The roads signs are well known to most people. If you saw the oak leaf being used as a road sign you would know that there is a National Trust Property nearby.

Oral and verbal messages

Two words which you will meet frequently when communication is being discussed are oral and verbal.

Oral means that something is spoken, not written.

Verbal means that words are involved – a verbal message contains words and can be spoken or written. It can be misleading to use the word 'verbal' on its own when talking about spoken communication; consider the following statements and explanations:

'He gave me a verbal message'.

This simply means that a message which contained words was given to the speaker. It does not give any indication as to whether the message was in writing or spoken, and there are no grounds for assuming that it was either one or the other.

'He gave me an oral message'.

We know from this statement that the message was spoken. It would be reasonable to assume that it contained words.

There are always exceptions to rules, however. The term 'verbal agreement' is one which is usually accepted as meaning an agreement which has not been written down.

The purpose communication serves in a leisure and tourism organization

Information, of one kind or another, is needed by everybody if they are to be able to do their jobs properly. This means that it must be passed between people inside the organization if the organization is to function efficiently (internal communication). Passing information requires people to communicate with each other in one of a number of ways, which we will look at in more detail as this Element progresses.

People inside the organization also need to communicate with people outside (external communication). The people outside the organization may be clients or they could be providers of goods or a service:

- They may supply a country park with fencing panels
- They may clean the swimming pool for a leisure centre
- They may sell stationery to an airline.

How would they know how many fencing panels were needed, when the pool needed cleaning or whether paper and envelopes were required if nobody had told them – to put it another way, if

nobody had communicated the information to them?

Communication systems

We looked at the meaning of the word 'system' in the previous Element. It has exactly the same meaning when applied in a communications situation. A system is a group of related elements which form a complex activity.

A communication system is made up of various methods of communication. It can be a combination of modern, electronic communication methods and traditional methods or it can be made up entirely of one or the other.

Types of communication

Communication can be broken down into types in a number of different ways. We will consider formal and informal communications in depth and then look at other ways of subdividing communication systems.

Formal communications

These are deliberate and planned methods of passing official information for which time has been made available to ensure that the message is worded correctly and contains relevant information. Formal communication is the type which is supported by communication systems which have been designed especially for the purpose.

When formal communication channels are used correctly, they assist in the smooth running of the organization, both internally and externally. A formal communication system may use one or more of the following.

Memos

These are usually fairly short messages which may be sent to one or more people. They are not as formal as a letter or report, but they are still a

```
                        MEMO
    To:      Andrew White              cc Mary Green
    From:    Alison Black
    Date:    25 September 1997
    Re:      Carhols' conference booking
             in the Marlborough Suite 22 December 1997

    Please note that the person dealing with the reservation
    on behalf of Carhols has changed. It is now being
    handled by Mary Green. All correspondence should be
    addressed to her. She is on the same telephone
    extension as George Grey, who was previously handling
    the booking.

                                         Alison
```

Figure 5.4   Example of a memo

formal communication channel. They have a fairly standard layout; sometimes they ask for a response, but sometimes they simply pass information on and do not require any reply.

Figure 5.4 gives an example of a memo. Study it before you read any further.

Alison, who sent the memo, should have kept a copy for herself so that she can prove that she communicated the piece of information to Andrew. CC means that a copy has been sent to Mary Green; this is a courtesy copy (hence the abbreviation cc). Alison is simply acting politely to let Mary know that the information has been passed to Andrew. Mary does not have to take any action herself as a result of receiving this memo.

Remember, this is a sample of what a memo can look like. Some companies will have their own standard layout, but this one is fairly typical.

Memos are usually used as internal documents, although they may be sent by an organization to a supplier or somebody doing some work for them. They should not be sent by an organization to its clients.

Electronic memos

Organizations which have invested in modern technology do not need to write their memos on paper and pass them around the office. They can be written on one computer terminal and transmitted to other terminals, to be read on screen rather than on paper.

This is part of the system known as electronic mail (e.mail) and it is helping organizations to reduce the excessive amount of paper which is a feature in most organizations. Paper is expensive, and a reduction in the amount of paper used means a corresponding reduction in costs.

Large organizations employ messengers to take memos and other mail around the building on a regular basis. The advent of electronic mail facilities means that the number of messengers can be reduced, again saving money.

Memos are useful means of communication, but they do have their problems:

- Some senders have the attitude that once the memo has been sent the contents are no longer their problem
- It can be an easy option to send a memo passing on a piece of work, rather than simply doing it
- Some memos do tend to get ignored or put at the bottom of a pile and then forgotten.

Proof of receipt

Most electronic mail systems are programmed so that when the recipient views the message on screen it is recorded in the computer's memory. The recipient cannot, therefore, claim that he has never seen the memo, which can happen with messages on paper. This makes electronic messages far more reliable than paper messages.

Letters

These are used externally, to clients and to other organizations. Letters are only used as a method of internal communication in a few circumstances, usually when a private and confidential matter is involved. Some examples are:

- Confirming promotion and a new salary
- A disciplinary letter, when an employee has contravened the organization's code of conduct
- Telling employees about a takeover or merger.

Information about the day-to-day running of the organization is more likely to be in the form of a memo.

Copies are kept of letters, either as hard copy or on disk.

Reports

These are formal or informal and may follow one of many layouts. Reports which need to be seen by a number of people are circulated. This can mean one of two things:

- A list of names will appear at the top of the report. When the first person on the list has read it, he signs his initials against his name and passes it on to the next person on the list (see Figure 5.5).
- A copy of the report is sent to each person who needs it.

Minutes of meetings

The minutes, or a record of what was said at a meeting, are written after a meeting from notes taken while it was in progress. They are usually circulated shortly after it finishes to help people remember what was said. The minutes of very formal meetings (board meetings, etc.) are read out at the next meeting, 'agreed' (anybody who

Minutes of the Meeting held at 19.00hrs, 26 October 1996, Allington Leisure Centre

Present: Mr T. Smith (Manager), Miss D. Day (Catering Manager), Mr F. Evans (Assistant Manager), Miss R. Lord (Outdoor Pursuits Adviser), Mr P. Graham (secretary)

Apologies for Absence were received from Councillor Lloyd (Leisure amenities Committee)

The attendees decided that as the meeting had been called to discuss one specific topic this would be the only item discussed.

Mr Smith outlined the problem: there has been a great deal of pilfering from both the changing rooms and the display counter in the coffee bar.

Miss Day suggested that the display in the coffee bar should have a glass top fitted. This would make it more secure and less tempting to opportunist pilfering. She had obtained three quotations; the cheapest was only £40. The meeting decided that Miss Day should proceed with this purchase.

Miss Lord asked if the pilfering was more noticeable at certain times. The question could not be answered. She then asked if the problem was more obvious in the male or female changing rooms. This could also not be answered. She then asked how many times thefts had been reported. There were still no figures available.

It was decided unanimously that the meeting should re-convene in three days' time when the figures had been extracted from the daily record sheet.

We agree that this is a true and accurate record of the meeting. Signed

T. Smith   D. Day   F. Evans   R. Lord   P. Graham

(secretary)

Figure 5.6 The minutes of this meeting have been recorded in a fairly standard format, all the people present have signed that they agree with the minutes

thinks that they were incorrect in any way has an opportunity to say so and discuss the discrepancy) and signed as being a true account of the previous meeting (see Figure 5.6).

Notice board

There are often a number of notice boards in any organization, especially the larger ones. Information which needs to be passed to a large number of people and which is not of a confidential nature can be put on the notice board.

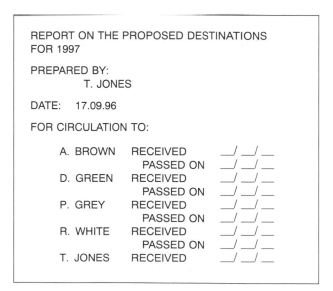

REPORT ON THE PROPOSED DESTINATIONS
FOR 1997

PREPARED BY:
    T. JONES

DATE: 17.09.96

FOR CIRCULATION TO:

A. BROWN	RECEIVED	__/__/__
	PASSED ON	__/__/__
D. GREEN	RECEIVED	__/__/__
	PASSED ON	__/__/__
P. GREY	RECEIVED	__/__/__
	PASSED ON	__/__/__
R. WHITE	RECEIVED	__/__/__
	PASSED ON	__/__/__
T. JONES	RECEIVED	__/__/__

Figure 5.5 The title page of a report which shows a circulation list

There are problems with notice boards, however. Here are a few of them:

- Not everybody reads the notices
- Notices may be removed or covered by mistake or maliciously
- Old notices may be left on the board. If this happens, people get tired of looking at the board and new notices get ignored
- Visually handicapped people are obviously disadvantaged by notice boards.

Public address systems

Loudspeakers tend to be used outside, at pop festivals, country fairs, motor rallies, etc.

Tannoy systems are used inside buildings, offices, railway stations, etc.

They are both forms of public address systems and are widely used in certain organizations. All airports used to use tannoy systems extensively, but some have now discontinued their use for announcements as they believe that people simply 'switch off' and do not listen to messages after a fairly short period of time.

Any messages given over a public address system obviously disadvantage people who have hearing problems.

Planned meetings

These can be internal:

- The weekly sales meeting
- A board meeting
- A departmental meeting, etc.

or they can involve suppliers and customers:

- Meeting representatives from BT to discuss a new telephone system
- Meeting the secretary and treasurer of a golf club to talk about a golfing holiday for the members, etc.

Presentations

Again, these can be used as an internal or external method of communication. Within the organization a presentation can be used to:

- Explain a new booking system
- Introduce new resorts which are to be featured in a holiday brochure
- Let employees know about expansion plans or the introduction of new technology, etc.

Externally they are often used as a sales tool:

- Perhaps the manager of a leisure centre would go along to a local social group and tell them about the facilities available at the leisure centre
- An art gallery's director may go into a college to tell the art students about a special exhibition which may be of interest to them.

Wording

Formal methods carry a message which has been carefully considered and which should give the receiver a clear and true representation of what the initiator intended the meaning to be.

Attention should be paid to the wording of formal, written communication, as there are many ways of saying the same thing but some ways can prompt a better reaction than others.

Imagine that you work in a travel agency which is usually closed on Saturday afternoon. The manager decides that during January and February, when there are lots of bookings being made and the agency is very busy, the shop will remain open until 5.00 p.m. on Saturday. She writes two drafts of the memo. Which do you think she should decide to use as the final copy: Figure 5.7 or Figure 5.8?

How did you feel when you read each of these memos? Which do you think would encourage a positive response from the travel clerks?

These two memos illustrate how different feelings can be evoked in a reader and show how care should always be taken over wording. It is very easy to fall into the trap of sounding officious rather than official in written communications, and people do not enjoy reading officious documents; in fact, they often provoke a swift, ill-considered and negative response when a

TO ALL STAFF

We are now entering one of our busiest periods. All staff will work until 5.00 p.m. on Saturday afternoon throughout January and February.

If it turns out that we are not as busy as I anticipate, we may be able to manage with reduced staffing levels.

Payment terms will be announced at a later date.

D. Smith, Manager
19 December 1995

Figure 5.7

TO ALL STAFF

I am delighted to be able to report that January and February look like being very busy months for us.

We expect quite an upswing in bookings and I need support from all of you so that the agency can handle the expected increase.

The shopping centre is busy until quite late every Saturday and I would like us to take advantage of this by remaining open until 5.00 p.m. every Saturday in January and February.

I would like all staff to work the first two weeks in January and we will make a decision about staffing levels for the remainder of the busy time once we have been able to make an informed judgement on the basis of bookings taken.

Staff may choose to take time off in lieu earlier in the week or overtime will be paid at the Standard rate.

If any member of staff has a previous commitment which cannot be altered (attendance at a wedding or similar), please bring this to my notice asap so that arrangement can be made for cover.

I know I can count on your support.

Donna Smith, 19 December 1995

Figure 5.8

well-thought-out, positive reaction was expected and needed.

Jargon

Did you notice something in the second memo which might not be understood by somebody who had not worked in an office environment? The abbreviation asap means 'as soon as possible'

and is widely used in offices, along with other abbreviations and quite a lot of jargon (specialized language which is used in a particular profession, trade or organization).

Jargon and abbreviations should only be used if you know that the person with whom you are communicating will know what they mean.

Task 5.7

This task will provide you with evidence towards PCs 5.2.4 and 5.2.5 and, if the discussion is observed by an assessor, towards Core Skill Communications 3.1

Go to a local organization which is involved in leisure or tourism and find out how it lets potential customers know what it has to offer. Make notes on what you see, perhaps even make drawings if this seems relevant.

Form a small discussion group with three of your colleagues to discuss and evaluate the information which you have collected. Look at the information from the position of the user, i.e. the potential customer. Suggest ways in which the communications could be improved.

Records

Formal communication is supported by systems and records are kept. Minutes are taken of meetings, copies of letters and reports are kept on file or on disk, presentations may be videotaped, at the very least all the figures announced and speeches made will be kept in writing. The records enable people to look back and check on the contents and ensure that no misunderstandings arise.

Informal communications

A great deal of informal communication is simply day-to-day conversations, 'Have the new ticket wallets arrived?', 'Would you like to look at these sales figures?', 'I thought you might be interested in this newspaper article about one of our competitors'.

Informal communications are not well planned and thought out; they often occur on the spur of the moment. However, without them an organization would not be able to survive, as they serve to pass information around an organization speedily. The delays necessary to formalize communications would be so costly that the organization would never get its work done.

Not only routine, day-to-day information is distributed informally. Sometimes official information which should really be subjected to distribution through formal channels finds its way into the informal system.

It is not unusual for informal communication channels to have a much stronger hold on a company than formal ones when it comes to distributing official, sometimes confidential, information. Unplanned opportunities are taken to pass information around an organization, and if the initiator has good official information which he passes to people who are allowed and need to know it, this can sometimes be a helpful method of communication. It is more relaxed than formal methods, and on occasions can lead to feedback from receivers who would be hesitant to speak in more formal situations.

Unfortunately, much of the information which finds its way into an informal communication channel is unofficial and not necessarily correct, or it may be official information which should have been kept confidential.

There are a number of informal communication channels which are used for distributing official information.

Impromptu meetings

A manager returning from a formal meeting may pass on to his staff immediately those contents of the meeting which are applicable to them. When all the relevant staff are involved in the impromptu meeting and care is taken to ensure that all the information passed is correct, relevant and not too sensitive to be passed on at once, this can be a useful method of communication.

Often, however, such impromptu meetings are less than helpful, especially when the source of the information has misunderstood what he has previously been told and then passes on his own misunderstandings to his staff. It is always advisable to think about information which has been received and check for validity before passing it on too hastily to a third party.

Another way in which the impromptu meeting can be harmful is when the manager has 'favourites' and only involves them in the impromptu meeting. They are left to pass the information on to the team members who were excluded. Not only does this provide another opportunity for misunderstanding to occur, but it also causes resentment from those team members who were excluded from the impromptu meeting.

People who are privy to confidential information sometimes find it hard to keep the details to themselves, and giving just a hint about information which would be better kept to themselves can have catastrophic consequences.

Case study

Paul was the reservations manager for a small tour operator. He was told, in confidence, that some of his staff were going to be made redundant as a result of the new computerized reservations system which was being installed.

He felt sympathy for his staff and brought one of the travel trade newspapers which contained lots of job adverts into the office with him. He then drew the attention of his staff to the jobs which were advertised. When they said that they were happy with the jobs they already had, heavy hints were dropped to them, 'Well, you never know what might happen ...'.

One evening after work, he was having a quiet pint in the company's local public house with a member of staff from another department. The landlord asked if it was true that the company was about to close down. He had heard rumours that staff were being told to look for alternative employment because the company was no longer sound.

Paul's friend was worried, so Paul told him the full story: that it was only his department which was losing half its staff because of the move towards computerization. Unfortunately, Paul had not recognized the woman next to him at the bar as he talked to his friend. He should have recognized her as she was the wife of one of Paul's reservations clerks. They had met at the Christmas party, so she recognized Paul and knew exactly which department was being discussed.

She rushed off home to give her husband, one of the biggest gossips in the company, the news. During the course of the evening he telephoned everybody else in the department and a number of other people as well.

Next morning, Paul arrived to find pickets at the entrance gates!

Paul's well-intentioned attempts to help his staff backfired, but there are even worse scenarios than this.

The grapevine

The means of informal communication which can cause endless problems is the grapevine. Fuelled by gossip, it can support rumours with or without any truth in them and can be extremely dangerous. The grapevine is able to flourish in organizations where information is not kept securely and roots easily where formal communication channels are limited and staff feel that they are kept in the dark by management.

- Some staff members think nothing of listening at doors and then passing on the information they have heard – or possibly misheard!

- Certain people will even stoop so low as to gain entrance to a manager's office when he is absent and go through the contents of his desk to look at papers (which should not have been left there) which will give them a clue about information which is supposed to be confidential. This information is then passed on to a close confidante, who passes it on again, and so it spreads around the organization. The documents may have been out of date or just an idea for further consideration, but once the contents have been leaked and become common knowledge they take the form of absolute fact, which may cause a great amount of trouble in the organization.

This is how rumours start and how companies can begin to suffer – at best with discontented staff, at worst with walk-outs and strikes or bad publicity.

During the Second World War there was a poster which read, 'Careless talk costs lives'. Its aim was to urge people not to chatter carelessly in front of people they did not know in case they were foreign agents. With just a little modification this message could be well used in any modern organization, 'Careless talk costs livelihoods'.

The need for clarity in communication

Communications should always be clearly expressed so that the intended meaning is easily understood. Imagine how confusing it could be if you requested directions from somebody who told you to turn left at the crossroads and you reached a public house called 'The Crossroads' located on a left turn but just beyond you could see a junction where four roads crossed, a real 'crossroads'. Which left turn would you take?

All written communications should be carefully studied before despatch and checked for possible double meanings or insufficiency of information which will cloud the intended meaning.

It is a good idea, before embarking on oral communication, to think out what is to be said and even write notes which can be followed so that nothing is forgotten. This is easily done in a formal and planned situation, but not so easy if you are suddenly presented with a customer who has a complaint. In a situation such as this, it is a good idea to take notes as the conversation progresses and to read the notes back to the customer at the end of the meeting to make sure that you have understood what the customer has said and vice versa.

However, there are some situations where this is impossible. In these cases notes should be made as soon as possible after the conversation while it is still fresh in your mind. There is no point trying to remember what was said six months after the conversation has taken place, as memory cannot always be relied on.

Task 5.8

This will provide you with evidence towards Element 5.2, PCs 1 and 2 and Core Skills Communication.

You are the manager of a leisure centre and you are arranging a treasure hunt for the members of the centre's social club. It will start quite late in the evening, after the centre has closed. You want all your staff to be involved with running the event on the actual evening, but you know that some of them have family commitments and that they will all be tired after a busy day at work. How would you tell them that their presence is required?

Describe the various methods which you could use to communicate the information and explain why you have decided in favour of the method you have chosen. Give details of the chosen method and explain how you are helped in your management role by the chosen method.

Receiving Information

Responsibility for ensuring that information is passed and received does not start and end with the initiator. The receiver must also accept some of the responsibility. Receiving information and processing it properly also has its problems, especially if the message was not absolutely clear in the first place.

It is important to listen when receiving an oral message. It is an amazing fact that many people can appear to listen to a message, make all the right noises in the right places, yet they have not heard a thing! As soon as the conversation is over, they take incorrect action because they have not really assimilated the content of the message. Taking notes and reading them back to the person who is giving the information to ensure that the content of the message has been received correctly is always a good idea.

Receivers should read and digest the contents of a written message before taking any action, and if there are any ambiguities or anything is unclear they should check it out before reacting to it.

Other ways of describing communication methods

So far we have looked at formal and informal communications and some ways to make them more effective. Communications can also be split into two-way and one-way communications.

Two-way communication

Communication can be two-way: that is, information passes from the initiator to the respondent and a reply is expected. Most two-way communication has the factor of immediacy: that is, information is given and an immediate response is made. Face-to-face conversations and telephone calls are examples of two-way communication where immediate response is possible. In these situations, misunderstandings or a double meaning contained within the communication can be questioned and clarified immediately and without too much effort.

There are a number of ways in which immediate two-way communication can take place – some within the organization (internally) and some making contact outside the organization (externally), some serving both internal and external purposes. Here are some examples of two-way communication and situations when the examples could be employed:

Telephone

These are very common pieces of equipment in many households and all organizations use them extensively between departments or people in the same department or to clients or suppliers. The telephone is a very popular, external communication tool and there are a great variety of telephone systems available.

In its simple form, it is used for making and receiving telephone calls, but more complex systems can offer many enhancements which are useful to leisure and tourism organizations. In addition to simple facilities which all business systems have – the ability to put the caller on hold (hold their call while another is taken), the ability to access a number of lines from the same handset, etc. – there are a number of enhancements available which do a lot to support the operation of any organization:

- *Call logging* keeps a list of all numbers called, which extension initiated the call and how long it lasted
- *Automatic call distribution* ensures that in organizations which have a large number of telephonists (e.g. tour operators with large reservations departments) incoming calls are distributed evenly among the telephonists
- *Conference calls* are possible on some sophisticated telephone systems. Instead of the usual type of telephone conversation where just two people talk to each other, a number of people can talk to each other at the same time. This is a very useful facility for large organizations, as different people can contribute to the conversation and it reduces the opportunity for misunderstandings as all the callers can hear what is being said – they do not have to rely on second-hand reports as they would if the call had only been between two

people who had to pass on the contents of the call after it was finished
- *Incoming call warning* – Some telephone systems will sound a warning 'beep' on the line if it is already in use when another caller tries to ring. The person speaking can then decide whether to hang up and take the next call. More sophisticated systems will allow users to move from one line to another with ease.

Mobile phones

The advent of the mobile phone has made it easier for people who are out of the office for long periods to keep in touch with what is going on back at the base, and the Global Systems Mobile Communications (GSM) network means that mobile phones on that network can even be taken overseas and used to keep in touch with UK-based organizations.

Telephone systems are now designed so that people who wear hearing aids can use them via a system known as a 'loop'.

Intercom

As telephone systems have increased the functions which they contain, intercoms have decreased in popularity, but they still do have some uses. A manager could have an intercom to his secretary's office; callers to a building may have to announce themselves into an intercom before the door is opened for them; hotels may provide intercom services for guests with babies so that parents who are in the restaurant can listen for sounds of the baby waking up. In this situation, the intercom is used as a one way communication system.

Mobile radio

These can be very useful in large buildings or areas where people have to move around and yet still keep in contact with a base or each other. They are used indoors in large exhibition halls and sports complexes and at outdoor events such as country shows and pop concerts. They are also used extensively at country houses with large gardens which are open to the public. They mainly support internal communications.

However, these methods of communication all present problems to people who have hearing difficulties. A great deal of research and work is being done to try to overcome some of the problems. The 'loop' system which was explained in the section above on telephones is becoming increasingly available, enabling people who would not otherwise be able to communicate by sound alone to do so.

These methods of two-way communication all lose a very important feature of communication. Can you name it?

When you are on the telephone, an intercom or a mobile radio, you cannot see the person with whom you are interacting. Therefore, you lose the visual aspect of communication. You cannot use body language (unconscious gestures, facial expressions and movements) as a means of picking up signals from the other person involved in the conversation. This can be quite a loss, as body language sometimes gives clues that a conversation has been misunderstood or even that a person who has agreed to do something has no intention of carrying out the act.

It is, however, no loss to people who are visually handicapped and cannot read body language even when facing somebody in conversation. They are disadvantaged when the following types of communication are used as they cannot see, or see well, what is happening. These types of two-way communications involve not only the spoken word to communicate a message but also body language.

Face-to-face

This is the most common type of two-way communication and the one in which virtually everybody in a leisure or tourism organization will participate, internally, with colleagues on a daily basis. Its external use can vary according to the type of organization.

A leisure centre, travel agent, tourist information centre and heritage centre are all visited by clients, and face-to-face communication with clients is a daily feature of their external communication systems. However, a business travel agent, tour operator and ferry booking office may do the vast majority of their business over the telephone and in writing; for them, face-to-face communication with clients is unusual.

There are numerous instances when face-to-face communication is employed:

- Interviews (with dissatisfied clients, in respect of employment, etc.)
- Meetings (board meetings, team meetings, to discuss client's needs, etc.)
- Discussions (solving problems, reviewing past events, etc.)
- Presentations (to prospective clients, to introduce new administration systems to staff, etc.)
- Training (computer training, management skills training sessions, etc.)
- Briefings (introducing staff to new equipment, extra resorts, new brochures, etc.)
- Reservations (booking office in concert hall, leisure centre, museum, holiday booking at travel agency, etc.)
- Coaching (swimming, golf, tennis, violin, painting, etc.).

Video conferencing

This facility is now available on very sophisticated telecommunication systems and is steadily increasing in popularity. Its current application is within and between businesses, but video phones will probably become a common feature in many households as the equipment becomes more affordable.

A video conference is similar to a conference call on the telephone, but a small screen allows the callers to see each other as they hold a conversation.

Communications which have a visual element are valuable to people who have hearing difficulties, especially those who 'speak' through the medium of sign language. They are also of use to people when the language barrier makes it impossible to make any sense out of a verbal conversation. Quite a lot of information can be imparted by gestures, showing pictures, pointing to signs, etc.

Interactive computer programs

This is an unusual method of two-way communication, as one of the 'people' involved is actually a computer. It could even be argued that it is not true communication, nor two-way, but there is definitely interaction between two parties, one human, one electronic.

Interactive computer programs are used internally for training purposes. Trainees can work their way, at their own speed, through a program which tells them what to do. It allows them to try an example and then tells them whether they have done it correctly or whether they need to try again. There are programs for many purposes: one to assist with keyboarding skills, one to help staff learn how to operate a Computerized Reservation System (CRS), one to teach people how to use all the facilities on an accounting package.

Externally, information packages which allow customers to access information on hotels, resorts, attractions, etc. are becoming increasingly popular as technology improves. The information packages are usually associated with touch screens – that is, screens which do not have keyboards but where the user touches the screen at specified places and the computer reacts by providing the requested information. Selected tourist information centres and some travel agents provide this facility.

Touch screens are also used in museums and art galleries. Visitors who are interested in a specific exhibit can press its number on the screen and information about the exhibit will appear. The user can then highlight a certain area of interest: the artist; the school of painting to which the

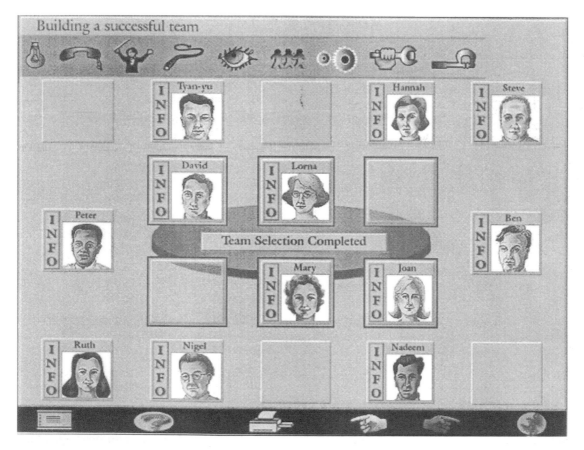

Figure 5.9 Example of interactive computer training

artist belonged; the artist's patron; the subject of the painting, etc., and further information will appear which is specific to the enquirer's interest.

Non-immediate two-way communication also known as one-way communication

There are usually grey areas (something which is not clear-cut with an absolute meaning) in any systems, and two-way communication falls into a grey area when it is subject to a time delay. A letter or memo may expect a response, but there will be a time gap between the letter being sent and the response being received.

One way of defining two-way communication is to state that there must be interaction between the sender and the receiver. If we accept that definition, then letters and memos cannot ever be regarded as being means of two-way communication systems, even if an answer is sent by return post.

The importance of clarity increases when there is a time delay, as it is not possible to immediately question what was meant by a statement.

Case study

Alan Dreyfus, an expert on early American art, planned a visit to the UK from February to April 1996. He advertised that he was free for lectures during that time and received a reply from an art group who wanted him to give them a talk on 4 March. Their letter said:

Dear Mr Dreyfus,

We would like to invite you to give a lecture to our group on 04.03.96. We are a small group which is not usually able to afford visiting speakers, but as your talks are free we can, at last, have a talk from somebody apart from one of our own members. This is a real treat for us.

Yours sincerely,

There are two misunderstandings in this brief case study. Can you spot them both?

One is fairly easy to identify. Alan Dreyfus should have said that he was *available* rather than *free* for lectures, this would have avoided the embarrassment of having to write back to the group to explain that he actually charged a fee. It would also have avoided the disappointment which the group would feel when they realized that they might not be able to afford to have a visit after all.

The other mistake is in the letter from the group. They asked him to visit on 04.03.96, which to anybody living in the UK means 4 March, as when we refer to a date by numbers we give day/month/year. To an American it means 3 April, as the first two numbers are reversed – in the United States the order for a date is month/day/year. The person who wrote the letter should have taken the trouble to write '4 March 1996' in full; this way there would not have been any opportunity for a misunderstanding to arise.

One-way communication

Communication can also be one-way. Information is given, but no response is expected. One-way communication is often subject to a time delay. A notice could be pinned on a board by a supervisor when no staff are present, so there is a delay between the information being given and received. There may be staff present and they may have a lot to say about the notice – perhaps it is telling them that the canteen will be closed for refurbishment for two weeks and no alternative arrangements will be made for them – but if the supervisor tells them he is not interested, the decision has been made and nothing the staff say can alter it. The communication could still be regarded as one-way.

Spoken messages can also be one-way. A speech made at an annual general meeting may not be designed to elicit any response from the people attending the meeting, so it is one-way communication. A message left on a telephone answering machine is a spoken message, but has to be a one-way communication as there is nobody to answer.

One-way communication is used both internally and externally. It is simply a way of communicating information which does not need a response.

Some methods of one-way communication are very common and are known to everybody:

- Oral
  - announcements
  - speeches
  - t.v. and radio statements, advertisements etc.
- Signs
  - directional signs inside and outside (fire exit, to the changing rooms, road signs, brown signs indicating tourist attractions, etc.)

  See Figure 5.10
- Notices
  - first aid information
  - fire procedures
  - advertising posters, etc.
- Written communication
  - memo
  - invoice
  - mail shot
  - itinerary, etc.

Written communication can be sent in traditional ways or using modern technology (fax, Internet, etc.). These will be considered in more depth later in the Element.

Some methods of one-way communication are associated with certain types of organizations, although they are used else where as well:

- *Display panels* – These are very common in art galleries, museums, craft centres, heritage centres, country parks, etc. They contain articles which need no explanation other than details such as period, materials, direction, etc.
- *Interpretation panels* – These are found in similar places to display panels and, at first glance, have a lot in common with them, but they explain what we are looking at, they interpret what we see.

  See Figure 5.11

One method which is increasing in application relies very heavily on electronic technology:

- *Computer-generated speech* – If you ring a mobile phone which is disconnected, a computer-generated voice will give you a message; on the London Underground the voice which tells you that the doors are closing is electronic; some cars are now fitted with 'voices' which tell you when you are over the speed limit; and there are many other occasions

Figure 5.10 These are probably two of the best-known non-verbal, one-way communication signs

Figure 5.11 Jodrell Bank Science Centre's Astronomy Hall has a number of interpretation panels which explain the displays and models

when computer-generated speech is used to communicate information to people.

Task 5.9

This will provide you with evidence towards Element 5.2 PC 2 and Core Skill Communication 3.2 and 3.3

You are the manager of a small leisure centre and the regular visitors have asked you to arrange a treasure hunt.

Design some posters, handouts, leaflets and advertisements which will present the information that:

1 Promotes the event.
2 Leads to the clues.
3 Announces the winner.

Describe some other methods of communication which you could have used to serve the same purposes.

Direction of information

There are a number of directions in which information can travel within any organization:

Vertical communication

This term is used to describe the downwards and upwards flow of information within an organization. We tend to think that vertical communication comes down from senior management to the more junior workers, but, in fact, it goes both ways.

Upwards vertical communication

Travel clerks, tour guides, lifeguards, etc. all need to pass on information which they receive to their immediate line managers (the person who is next in the line of seniority). They may then pass the information upwards again, and so it will continue to be passed upwards until it reaches a level where the information can be used and acted upon.

Case study

The tennis coach at the leisure centre was surprised that all his usually punctual students were late one day. He asked the last student if there was a reason. There was – all the parking spaces were taken up by cars belonging to residents at the hotel next door, which was having repairs done to its car park.

The coach told his supervisor of the situation. She told her manager and he arranged to have a sign erected saying that the car park was for visitors to the leisure centre only and any vehicles which should not be there would be wheel-clamped. This solved the problem immediately.

Downwards vertical communication

Information which comes down from the top, through various managers and onwards to junior

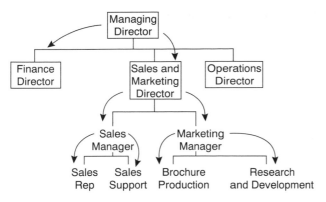

Figure 5.12 Information is cascaded from the top down, at each stage of its journey the receiver 'sieves' the information and cascades relevant information to the level below

staff, is referred to as being cascaded (Figure 5.12), as it flows down from the top, just like water cascading down a waterfall. Not all information which flows downwards is made available to all staff; some may only travel down a couple of levels, or even one, before the flow stops.

Horizontal (or lateral) communication

This is the flow which occurs constantly it takes place between people on the same level in the organization:

- A tour operator's reservations manager sends figures to the sales manager showing bookings taken each day
- The receptionist at a leisure centre rings through to the pool to let the supervisor know that a large number of people have arrived all at once, all wanting to have a swim
- A travel agency clerk rings the accounts department to check that a balance has been paid before he sends tickets out
- The museum curator rings the marketing department to ask if the posters advertising a new exhibition are ready.

Diagonal communication

This occurs when one person communicates with another, in a different department, who is junior or senior to him or her. It can be a difficult line to follow – supervisors and managers often become quite annoyed when somebody from another department comes into the one for which they are responsible and can be very touchy about their staff talking to other managers. There are times when a great deal of diplomacy is called for when following a diagonal communication line.

Technology and direct access to information

A great deal of internal communication is involved with accessing information which is needed on a daily basis, perhaps to make business judgements:

- A tour operator's sales manager would need to know how bookings were going for each departure date so that he would know which departures to advertise to make sure that he sold them. He would talk to the reservations manager and ask for statistics. Computerization has meant that he can now look at his own terminal and access the figures without speaking to the reservations manager.
- The manager of a farm park or heritage centre would like to know which items were selling well in the gift shop. He would have to talk to the staff in the gift shop and ask them to look at the shelves to check the stock to get an idea of which items were selling quickly. Now he can simply look at the stock control program on his own computer terminal and see at a glance what needs re-ordering quickly and what might have to be reduced as it is not selling well.
- The manager of a leisure centre would like to know how much is owed to the various companies which supply food for the vending machines and the small café which is part of the facilities offered on the complex. Before the centre was computerized he would have asked the accounts manager to go through invoices and add them up. Now the information is stored on computer, and he can access it via a terminal on his own desk.

This instant access to information means that each manager can get on with his job more easily and become more efficient. It also means that the people who would have previously provided them with the information can do other tasks, so they, and their departments, also become more efficient. There may even be an opportunity to reduce the number of staff needed in the department, thus cutting overheads and making the organization more profitable.

Communication systems and information technology

The advances in information technology over the last fifteen years or so have led to a complete re-working of the way in which many leisure and tourism organizations operate, which, in turn, leads to innovations in the communication systems and elsewhere.

Company structure

Information technology has changed the face of most organizations. The traditional structure of a company was like a pyramid, with a broad base of staff at the lowest level narrowing through various levels of supervisors, junior, middle and senior managers to the board with the managing director and chairman at the peak of the pyramid (Figure 5.13) The new technology has made it possible to dispense with a lot of supervisory, junior and even middle management posts. The need for staff at the base level has also been

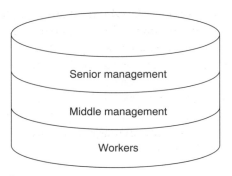

Figure 5.14 Modern organizations which have invested in information technology take on a flatter, more conical shape

reduced, and this has led to a flatter structure within organizations (Figure 5.14).

Reporting chains

The old, pyramidal structure of the company had long, vertical reporting chains. A base line clerk would report to a senior clerk, who reported to a clerical supervisor, and so it would go on, through many levels, until the managing director reported to the chairman.

The flatter structure has reduced the links in the reporting chain. In consequence, it has reduced the amount of time that was taken by employees at numerous levels reporting problems that they had discovered and what these were doing to the level above and has, consequently, contributed to making organizations more efficient.

Outsourcing

Some departments have been closed down, although the services which they provided continue to be needed, as outsourcing (which is also known as facilities management) has become a more economical proposition than undertaking all functions within the leisure and tourism organization. Outsourcing means that functions – usually those which are not specific to the organization's day-to-day business operation – are undertaken by other companies who have expertise in the area and the computer equipment and software packages to support it.

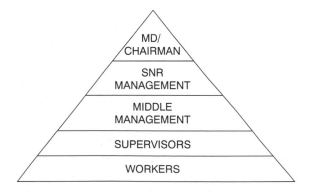

Figure 5.13 Traditionally organizations were described as having a pyramid structure with a few managers at the top and lots of workers at the bottom

An example of an area where outsourcing has become very common is in the management of payrolls. It requires quite a degree of expertise to work out the amount of national insurance contributions and income tax which each person on the payroll must pay, and it is sensible to outsource this function to a company which specializes in payroll management and has experts in the area.

The outsourcing company will handle payrolls for a number of organizations, so will be able to afford state-of-the-art (the most modern, up-to-date) software which will handle the task swiftly and accurately. The many organizations which use the outsourcer are unlikely to be able to afford such sophisticated software themselves.

Organizations which outsource some of the work which is not within the firm's own area of expertise are left with more time to concentrate on tasks which are central to the organization's own business. It also reduces the number of staff employed by the organization, and staff are a very costly commodity.

The new technology

We have already seen some ways in which technology has changed communication systems when we considered modern telephone systems. Video conferencing was only possible in the realms of science fiction films until quite recently, and mobile phones were very expensive and owned only by the very affluent and influential or for business purposes. Now they are inexpensive to purchase and reasonable to use, and many people have them for personal use.

The advances made in technology which uses a telephone line do, however, go further than telephones. This has been made possible by the invention of a piece of equipment called a modem.

Modems

Telephone lines are designed to carry the signals generated by voices, but computers generate a different type of signal.

A modem is a piece of equipment which will translate the computer signals so that non-voice messages can be sent down a telephone line.

This has been a major factor in the communications revolution, as it is now just as easy to transmit the written word to a distant location as it was to send a voice message ten years. All that is needed is a modem and one of a number of pieces of hardware, which are described below.

Fax machines

The original name for these machines was 'facsimile transceiver', which was made up of three words:

- facsimile = copy
- trans = transmit
- ceiver = receiver.

The word was soon shortened to fax, but the principle remains the same: it can make a copy and transmit it to a distant location or it can accept information and produce a copy where the information is received. It is a very useful piece of hardware which has made a lot of communications much quicker and reduced the risk of problems.

In 1980 a tour operator who wanted to send a rooming list to a hotel overseas would have to rely on one of four methods of delivery, all of which had their drawbacks:

- *The post*, which took some time and there was always a risk that the list could go astray before it reached its destination
- *The telex*, a machine which is now unfashionable and infrequently found. Telex machines were useful in their time, but fairly slow
- *The telephone* – This could be very expensive, especially when speaking to countries where the first language was not English, and some countries had rather poor telephone systems which were subject to interference and frequent loss of line

- *Personal delivery* – A member of staff travelling to a resort or a client would be entrusted with the rooming list for the next group of clients. These lists, like the ones which were posted, would go astray and then a new list would have to be drawn up and sent.

The advent of fax machines in the mid-1980s meant that a rooming list could be typed out and sent to the hotel with no worries about it getting lost and with minimal costs, especially if lists were sent overnight when cheap rate calls were available.

The early fax machines were large and very expensive, but they became popular so quickly that a great deal of research and development was done quickly and the size and cost reduced very rapidly.

Fax machines produce hard copy at the receiving end. This includes a header which gives the number of the sender and the time of receipt (Figure 5.15). This is very useful, but there is an even better way of sending a fax.

A computer with a fax modem

A computer which has a modem and a special card in the computer's mother board (the board inside the computer's processing unit which accepts cards that enable the computer to do different things) to allow it to receive fax messages goes a little further than a fax machine which can only receive hard copy. A fax received by a computer can be edited (altered) like any other document in the computer's memory.

Internet

The Internet is a means of communicating with people worldwide for business or pleasure. It originated in the USA as a support to the military,

Figure 5.15 Fax messages have standard 'headers' when they are received

its use was widened to allow academic institutions in the USA to access it and it is now available worldwide. It is sometimes known as the Information Superhighway – try to imagine roads crossing the world carrying information from one computer terminal to another, perhaps in the same country or perhaps on the other side of the world, and you will begin to understand what the Internet provides.

Anybody who has access to a computer with a modem is able to communicate with millions of other computers worldwide through an intermediary called an Internet provider or Internet gateway. The majority of Internet providers charge for the service which they provide, which enables owners of home computers or computers in an office to communicate with other computer users worldwide, but very large organizations have their own servers (the hardware and software needed to make Internet connections possible). This means that once they have purchased the hardware and software the calls cost nothing.

The Internet first became available for public use in the mid-1980s, but was under-utilized until the early 1990s. It is only just gaining in popularity in the UK. It has many uses, some of them business, some of them recreational, and its potential can still only be imagined.

It is, in itself, a leisure facility for many people who are interested in computers and in communicating with other users worldwide. The Internet incorporates a number of facilities, one of which is known as the Worldwide Web (often more simply known as 'the Web') which provides one of the most useful aspects of the Internet – it allows users to access an incredible amount of information on numerous topics. Many leisure and tourism organizations have 'web sites': these are places on the Internet where they can display information about their products and services (Figure 5.16).

It is possible, through the use of a search engine (there are a number of these, some with rather strange names, for example Webcrawler and

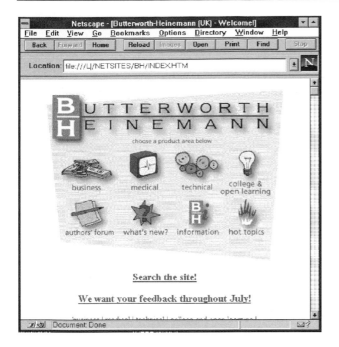

Figure 5.16 Introductory page on the Internet

Yahoo, others with names which indicate what they do, like Infoseek) to locate these web sites and also articles and information which will help you in your studies.

Much of the material written about the Internet claims that its use is free, but there are costs involved for users who have to access the Internet through a provider:

- Providers charge a monthly fee
- There is sometimes a connection fee and/or a usage fee each time the Internet is accessed
- The telephone line which enables the connections to be made is charged at exactly the same rate as would be charged for an ordinary voice call.

Usage of the Internet is not particularly widespread in business situations at the present time, but it is an area to watch. Its ability to help businesses has not yet been fully explored. However, is already providing some businesses with a very important communication system indeed, and many other organizations are certain to begin to use it in the future.

Task 5.10

This will provide you with evidence towards Element 5.2 PC 3 and Core Skill Information Technology 3.4.

Make an appointment to visit a local leisure or tourism organization which uses modern, electronic methods of communication. Ensure that there is somebody within the organization who remembers how communications were conducted before the new technology was introduced. Ask them to explain how the introduction of electronic technology has affected their communication systems.

Write up your findings as a brief report.

Reservations systems

Most organizations in the leisure and tourism industries take bookings of some kind:

- A leisure centre may take bookings for a series of swimming classes
- A museum invites an expert to give a talk to accompany an exhibition. Places are limited, so seat reservations must be made in advance
- A country house holds a series of concerts during the summer months. It takes advance reservations and sells any seats which are left over at the door.

All these organizations can be assisted by computer technology, but it is in the travel and tourism industry, where many organizations take tens of thousands of advance bookings a year, that advances in electronic technology and the invention of networks and installation of modems have been of immense value.

Networks

The early computers used in the leisure and tourism industries were known as stand-alone models. Each computer had its own memory and stored its own files. Computers might have been placed side by side on desks, but they could not 'talk' to each other.

The development of networks meant that the computers did not need large memories for storing software as this was held on a file server. This is another piece of hardware, separate from the desktop terminals, which holds operating and software packages. Each terminal can access the software from the file server and also send completed work back to the file server for storage. A user at another terminal can then access the work from the file server, unless it is password protected and the user does not have the correct password.

There are three types of network:

- *LAN or Local Area Network.* These are contained within a building or limited area. Most colleges (located on one site) now have their computers on a LAN. All the various software packages which the college provides can be accessed through the LAN, but only from the college itself – students cannot access the college LAN from their homes or offices where they undertake work experience and the college computers cannot 'talk' to computers on other networks.
- *MANs or Metropolitan Area Networks* are a more recent innovation. Colleges which have buildings on a number of sites in a town or city will still have all their computers networked, but the correct term to use in this situation is a metropolitan area network or MAN.
- *WAN or Wide Area Networks* are similar to LANs, but they link more than one organization and can cover the world.

The terms LAN, MAN and WAN are less used than when they were originally developed and all are now frequently referred to simply as 'networks', a trend which will probably continue into the future.

Travel organizations which take advance reservations by means of WAN and modem connections include:

- Ferry companies
- Airlines
- Tour operators
- Travel agents
- Car hire companies
- Hotels.

We all know what airlines, tour operators, ferry companies, travel agents, etc. are. Within the tourism industry two words are often used to describe them:

- **Principals** are organizations which actually own the facility which is being booked (airlines, ferry companies, hotels, etc.)
- **Suppliers** negotiate with principals, put a package of their goods together and supply these to the agent or customer. Tour operators are an example of suppliers.

The way these organizations conduct their business has changed dramatically since the advent of computers and they are now able to process bookings far more quickly than previously, with fewer mistakes, thus reducing many costs and leading to greater productivity. A brief look into the past will help you to understand how technology has changed the face of the reservation systems of most tourism organizations.

A brief history of reservations systems

The procedure from the client's side

When tourism first came within the reach of many people, just after the Second World War, most reservations were taken by agents who represented the tour operator, airline, etc. They took a booking from a client, made sure that he or she had also given a second and third choice of date, hotel, destination, etc. in case the first choice was not available, and then, usually, wrote to the principal or supplier. They also sent a deposit (a sum of money which the client could not usually get back if he or she decided not to travel) to hold the booking.

Clients could also write directly to the principal or supplier, but the client, like the agent, would have to wait for a reply to find out if he or she had been able to secure the holiday he or she wanted. It was not unusual for a couple of weeks to pass before the client heard whether or not he or she was going on the ferry, flight or holiday that he or she had requested.

Some airlines, shipping companies and tour operators had a free sale policy. This allowed agents to sell places on the flights, ships and tours without having to wait for a response to their enquiries. The agent would send a booking form to the airline or ferry company who would enter the booking onto the chart. When a date began to fill up, the free sale facility would be removed. Agents used to receive regular notices telling them they could no longer use free sale, but sometimes the notices would get lost in the post or would not be displayed prominently in the office so the free sale facility inevitably led to a number of overbookings.

The era of telephone reservations

Improvements in telephone systems meant that by the 1960s it was more common for the agent to telephone the principal or tour operator and check if the ferry or airline seat or holiday was available before sending the deposit to secure the booking.

Getting through to tour operators could be very difficult, especially when new brochures were released, as the number of lines in to the operators were limited and hundreds of agents would all be trying to get through at once. The lines would be jammed with calls, and travel agents and clients alike would become exasperated when they could only get the engaged tone for hours at a time.

When they finally got through, the holiday they wanted could already be full, but if it was available the booking would be held for a number of days so that it could not be re-sold to another client while the booking deposit was in the post, on its way to the principal.

The advent of computer bookings

By the late 1970s many travel agents who sold airline tickets had computers installed with a

modem and a software package which meant that they no longer had to use the telephone to make a voice call to make a reservation but could access the airline's computer from their own.

Shortly afterwards, major tour operators began to allow travel agents to access their computer systems, which meant that those travel agents who had installed modern computers and modems in their agencies could dispense with telephone reservations and make them via a computer link instead. This was speedier, more efficient and enabled far more work to be done, as, among other things, the time wasted on non-productive telephone calls was a thing of the past.

In the late 1970s travel agents with state-of-the-art computer technology were rare, but within ten years it became almost standard for all travel agents to have very modern equipment, and numerous bookings are now made via computer links with the larger tour operators every year. Until recently these bookings were all done by travel agents using their direct links into the tour operators' and airlines' computers, but it is now possible for clients with access to the Internet to make direct bookings with many companies without the need to use a travel agent as an intermediary.

The procedure from the principals' and operators' side

During the early years after the war, airlines, ferry companies and tour operators noted their reservations on manual booking charts. There were many types used: some were hung on walls, some stacked on racks – they all took up a lot of space, it was easy to make mistakes on them and they were extremely labour-intensive.

Airlines

The first big step away from the manual charting system was when airlines all over the world – the first tourism companies to take technology on board – began to set up their own Computerized

Reservations Systems (CRS). A CRS allowed all the information which had been contained on the manual charts to be entered into a computer. When CRSs were first used they contained details of each airline's own flights; these were quickly followed by details of flights operated by other airlines who worked closely with the original airline.

In the UK British European Airways (BEA, one of the two companies which joined forces to become British Airways (BA)) decided to adopt 'Beacon', a computerized booking system, in 1964.

British Overseas Air Corporation (BOAC, the company which joined with BEA) had its own system by 1968. This was known as Boadicea.

The system designed for BA, after BEA and BOAC amalgamated, was known as BABS (British Airways Booking System). This system made it a simple matter for travel agents and clients to telephone and make reservations very quickly, although there was a frequent tendency in the early days for the computer to go down (technology jargon for 'break down'), which could be very frustrating for agents and clients.

By the late 1970s agents with terminals in their own offices did not need to telephone (although they needed a telephone line and a modem); they could use their own terminal to access the airline's CRS and make a booking without speaking to an airline clerk.

The first CRS which agents could use themselves to book airline seats was called Travicom and this was later replaced by a number of other systems. The one which is used most extensively in the UK today is Galileo. There are others which are used for the same purposes but by different companies – Sabre and Amadeus are popular in the United States and Europe. They contain information about far more than just airline seat availability; an agent can make reservations for:

- Travel
- Hotels
- Self-drive or chauffeur-driven cars.

Clients can be provided with details about worldwide time bands and many other aspects of travel.

Of course, if the travel clerk preferred to telephone or if a client wished to make a reservation personally by talking to the airline's reservation clerk, this was still possible. In reality, however, most agents took to the new computerized systems with great enthusiasm and only made a telephone call when they had problems which they could not resolve on the computer.

Tour operators

The major tour operators were slower than the airlines to switch to electronic technology. The move was expensive, but as technology developed it became more attractive. Thomson Holidays led the way with their system known as TOPS, and by the mid-1980s all the major tour operators operated their own CRS, with access direct into their booking systems from travel agents' own terminals.

Other companies

Car hire companies, ferry operators, hotels and other tourism organizations developed their own CRSs during the late 1970s and 1980s. All major companies now work on computerized systems; it should, however, be remembered that some small operators continue to use manual charts even today.

Changes brought about by the introduction of computerized reservations systems

Clients who telephoned to make a reservation were only aware that it took less time to confirm availability than before computerization, but for the companies changes went much deeper than just speed.

Space

Manual charting systems required large numbers of staff and the space to house both charts and people. Reservation offices were noisy as clerks shouted requests to each other when they could not find the chart they wanted. When two clerks needed the same chart at the same time, it led to delays for the client on the telephone.

Computerization reduced the area needed, but it brought problems of its own.

The early computers were very large and had to be housed in specially prepared rooms with air conditioning and many safety precautions. In spite of this, however, they took up much less space than rooms full of reservations staff with manual charts. Office space is an expensive commodity, and if less is needed, overheads can be reduced dramatically.

Constant research into and development of electronic technology has meant that computers have reduced in size and are less temperamental than in the early days. Enormously powerful computers can now be housed in small areas and they do not need to have a specialized environment to prevent overheating etc.

Costs and efficiency

Manual charting systems can be very good indeed, and can even be better in some circumstances than a computerized system. It is more expensive to develop a computerized system than a manual one, and small companies or companies who only operate occasional tours may find it impossible to recover the costs of computerization. For them, there is no sense in investing huge sums of money in electronic equipment, but for the larger companies the opposite is the truth.

New skills and new situations

Reservations staff have had to be taught to use computers and, as with change in most situations, there is sometimes resistance to new methods. Changes need to be introduced very carefully, as staff become demotivated and worried that their jobs may disappear, often with good cause.

The old charting systems allowed staff to move around the reservations area to look for charts, but computerization has meant that they remain in their seats, in the same position, for hours at a time. This has led to eye strain, back problems and stiffness, and has encouraged the government to offer guidance, sometimes supported by legislation, about breaks, seating, lighting, desks, etc.

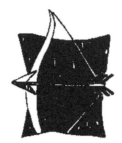

Task 5.11

This will provide you with evidence towards Element 5.2, PCs 2, 3, 4 and 5 and Core Skill Communications 3.2.

Go to an organization in the leisure sector (a leisure centre, heritage centre, cinema, hotel, restaurant, etc.) and find out how it takes advance reservations for one specific facility. A leisure centre may take advance bookings for the squash courts, a cinema for important dates and film premières, a hotel for special weekend breaks, etc.

Write a short report on the system you choose. Your report should include a section in which you evaluate the system you have investigated and make suggestions on how to improve it. If the system you investigate is a manual system, compare it with a CRS; if it is a computerized system, say how the same system could be operated manually.

Summary

It is impossible to review the wide range of communications systems and their applications which we have looked into in just a few words, so let us consider two of the most important aspects of communicating:

- *Clarity* – It is essential that communicators ensure that the message they send is the one which is intended. Written communications (letters, memos, etc.) should be planned and checked before being despatched; spoken messages should be carefully considered before being passed on so that there is no room for misinterpretation.

- *Suitability* – There is no point in choosing a communication system which is not suitable for the purpose. The landlord of a public house who is organizing a coach outing or the manager of a country estate who is booking places on a guided tour around the gardens have no need to spend vast sums of money on a CRS. On the other hand, a new airline, starting from scratch, would be unwise not to invest in the most advanced technology it could afford rather than start with a paper system, spend money developing that, and then have to spend additional cash developing electronic systems.

The future

There cannot be any doubt that the future will bring more advances in technology, both in ways we have not yet thought about and in making facilities which are already known to us but little used, perhaps because the technology is still too expensive, common facilities in all organizations. More and more individuals are purchasing computers for use at home, the number of people with access to the Internet is increasing at a dramatic rate and access to the Internet means access to travel information and the ability to make reservations with ease direct with airlines, tour operators and hotels.

In just a few years we may be *telling* computers what to do instead of typing instructions into a keyboard. We may even talk to our television sets and receive a confirmed holiday booking as we speak. Facilities which exist only in the realms of science fiction today may well be available for every leisure and tourism organization to use in the not too distant future.

Portfolio builder

Collect all the work from the tasks and put it into your portfolio. Make sure that you keep a record

of the PCs and the range within the PCs that you have covered.

▪ Assignment 5.2 ▪

This will provide evidence towards Element 5.2, PCs 1, 2, 3, 4 and 5 and Core Skills Communication 3.1, 3.2, 3.3 and 3.4 and Information Technology 3.2 and 3.3.

This assignment should ideally be undertaken by three or four students working together.

Scenario

You are partners in a company which organizes exhibitions and events. Your company has been approached by the local hospital, which is planning a summer fair to raise money towards the hospital's funds. The fair will take place in the hospital's extensive grounds.

The company would like you to take responsibility for all aspects of communication, from advertising the event to persuading people to take part to arranging signs in the grounds to direct people towards the various tents, events and facilities. You have been asked to base your plan on manual systems.

You must investigate the types of communication needed to support the event and then prepare a report for the hospital's management, explaining the communication channels which you have identified as being necessary to support the event. You should explain why you consider these communication channels to be necessary.

The report should also contain details of the ways in which these needs can be met using manual systems. Where electronic systems would give better results, recommend that the hospital consider these, justifying your recommendations.

You plan to give your report in person to the hospital management after a brief presentation. Prepare any graphics, tables or supporting images which you need for the presentation. Do a trial run of the presentation and consider what questions or doubts the hospital management committee may voice. Use these as a basis for evaluating the plan for the communication system and suggest where improvements could be made.

Element 5.3 Investigate and evaluate information processing systems in leisure and tourism organizations

We have already established that handling information is one of the main functions of any leisure and tourism organization. We are now going to delve a little more deeply into how some systems operate to support the storage, retrieval and use of data and information and why this is so important. To make the functions and purposes of information processing systems quite clear, we will consider some examples of systems in the context in which they are used.

We will consider both manual and electronic systems, but we will take a particularly good look at the main features of electronic technology and consider the various ways in which its advent has altered the way in which information is processed. You will be able to consider the examples given and conduct some research of your own which will enable you to evaluate how effective both manual and electronic systems are and how they could be improved.

Finally, we will look at the Data Protection Act. It has been necessary to pass legislation to stop information, which can now be stored, passed and used much more easily than at any previous time in the history of mankind, from being misused and harming or causing upset or embarrassment to individual people.

When does data become information?

The details which are initially collected and then recorded in an information processing system are known as data or raw data. The word 'raw' shows that nothing has been done to the data: it is unprocessed, it has not been worked on in any way within the current processing system. One piece of data is a datum, but we rarely hear the word used as a datum is such a small entity that it is not a lot of use on its own. We need an amount of data to be gathered before it can serve a useful purpose.

Once these facts and figures are processed they become information: they have had some additional meaning added to them to make them useful, or more useful than they previously were. This information can become raw data again if it is entered into a new processing system.

Case study

Alan Evans was the honorary (unpaid) manager of a village football club which played every Sunday during the football season. His son, Brian, helped him by keeping records: how many people attended each match, which players missed training sessions, etc.

Alan looked at the attendance figures (the raw data) one day. They showed that if the team were playing at home on the last Sunday of the month, the crowd watching was reduced from around forty people to only twenty. He asked his information processing system (his son) to work out why this should be. Fortunately, there was another piece of raw data held in his son's memory bank (his brain): on the last Sunday of every month a funfair visited the nearest small town.

Brian, in his capacity of information processing system, was able to put the two pieces of raw data together (there is a fall in numbers – there is a funfair in the local town) to become a piece of information: 'The crowd at the match is smaller because some of them visit the local funfair on the last Sunday of the month'.

The words 'data' and 'information' are frequently used interchangeably, but it is preferable to keep them separate and use them correctly: data is raw facts and figures which, when processed, produce information.

Functions of information processing systems

The simple story of Alan, Brian and the amateur football club has not only illustrated the fact that information is data which has been processed, but it also gives us a clue as to what an information processing system does. In short, it stores and keeps data ready for the time when it is needed and then provides it as information in the required format.

There are, therefore, three basic functions common to all systems, whether they are manual or electronic:

- Receipt of data
- Storage of data
- Provision of information.

As we have seen, there is one further function which is an integral part of information provision: the data which has been received needs to be processed so that information is provided in the way in which it is needed.

A very small tourist attraction, perhaps a privately owned museum, may simply put a tick on a dated page in a sales book each time a ticket is sold. Data has been received in the form of the tick and it has been stored on the page. At the end of the day the sales manager will ask how many people have bought tickets on that day. The ticks must be counted (the data processed) before the required information can be provided.

A larger facility which has invested in electronic technology will have a more sophisticated system, but the functions will be the same. Each time a visitor pays an entrance fee, the purchase will be recorded and stored electronically. At the end of the day the number of people who visited will be available at the touch of a button. Again, data has been entered, stored and then processed to produce information.

Let's take a closer look at each of the three basic functions.

Receiving data

All leisure and tourism organizations constantly receive facts and figures. These must be recorded ready for the time when they are needed. Recording this raw data in an electronic system is known as data inputting.

The way in which the data is received and recorded will, of course, depend on the information processing system which is used. Consider the following two examples:

- A social club which runs an annual outing to a theme park may set up a manual chart for the outing (Figure 5.17) and simply write the names of people who book in pencil, change it to ink when they have paid a deposit and put a red tick in the box when the balance is paid.
- A coach operator in a tourist area who runs ten trips a day throughout the summer season will benefit from a much more sophisticated system than this, probably one which involves a computerized booking system. (We should not, however, make the mistake of assuming that the coach operator could not operate without a computerized system. Manual systems were the

Coach departs from clubhouse at 0800				
Arrives Camelot 1000				
Return time at clubhouse 2000				
Pencil until deposit received, pen when deposit received,				
red tick when balance is paid				

				driver
b1	b2		a1	a2
b3	b4		a3	a4
b5	b6		a5	a6
b7	b8		a7	a8
b9	b10		a9	a10
b11	b12		a11	a12
b13	b14		a13	a14
b15	b16	b17	a15	a16

All seats in shaded section are smoking seats
No smoking in any other seats

Figure 5.17 A typical manual chart for a coach trip

only ones readily and economically available until the mid-1980s and hundreds of coach operators throughout the world managed very well, as many still do manage, with manual charts.)

Setting up the system

There are two stages to recording information. First, a decision must be taken on the physical system to be used, the information to be recorded and its format. In a manual situation this could utilize one of many techniques: index cards; wall charts; carousel charts; T charts; files, etc. (Figure 5.18). An electronic system is probably going to use an application known as a database. This allows information to be input and stored and then searched in different ways to produce the required information.

Secondly, specific information in respect of individual transactions has to be stored within the system. To illustrate this, let's take a closer look at the social club's annual trip to the theme park by doing this, we will be looking at a simple manual charting system.

Manual system: Inputting information stage 1 – Setting up the system

In the case of the social club's outing the database takes the form of a chart which is set out like the seating plan of the coach (Figure 5.17). There is a

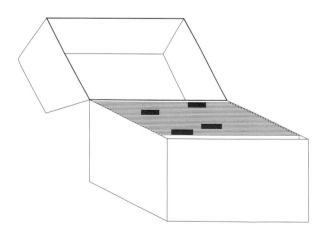

Figure 5.18 A simple card index system

space at the top of the chart for information which applies to the trip and everybody on it:

- They all leave at the same time
- They all leave from the same place
- They are all going to the same place
- They all return at the same time
- They all return to the same place.

There is also space for details of the coding system which the secretary has designed:

- An entry in pencil means a booking has been made but no money paid
- An entry in pen means a deposit has been paid
- A red tick means the balance has been paid.

There is then an individual space for each seat on the coach. As it is laid out exactly like the interior of the coach, it is easy to see at a glance which seat is beside a window, which are behind the driver, which are behind the guide. However, more information must be put into this manual database to ensure that people are given the seat they want:

- **Seat code** – On this chart all seats with 'A' in the code are behind the driver, all seats with 'B' are behind the guide
- **Smoking or non-smoking** – On this chart all seats in the shaded section are in the smoking area.

Inputting information stage 2 – Recording bookings

Each time a club member makes a booking the details must be recorded on the chart. Let's say that David Brown wants to make a booking for two seats behind the driver in the non-smoking area and Mary Stone wants a reservation behind the driver in the smoking section. Look at Figure 5.17 – you can easily see which seats are free and whether or not the two bookings can be accommodated as requested.

As it happens, both these bookings can be taken as the required seating is available. Information about the clients now has to be recorded. The social club secretary has decided that he wants to record the name of the person and a telephone number. This can be written into the space provided and in accordance with the coding system previously described.

Task 5.12

This will provide evidence towards Element 5.3 PCs 1 and 2 and Core Skill Communication 3.3 and Information Technology 3.3.

Look carefully at the system which has just been explained and decide if it could be improved by inputting more data at either the first or second stage. If you think it could be improved, say how and why. If you think that nothing could be done to improve the system, give your reasons.

When you have thought about this simple chart system which has been designed to take bookings on a coach, try to adapt it to reservations in other situations: a theatre, concert hall, aeroplane or other examples which you identify yourself. Design a chart, using the word-processing or desktop publishing facilities available at your college or school.

Write a brief summary of the functions and purposes which are served by these systems and describe what type of system this is.

Electronic system

The stages are exactly the same when recording information electronically, but obviously the equipment needed is far more complex than a chart with lines drawn on it and some information written on it.

An electronic system requires **hardware** (processing unit, monitor, keyboard, printer, disks, etc.) and an **application** or software package which can be loaded onto the computer to act rather like the piece of paper which can be drawn on and have information about clients written onto it.

The generic name (general name by which all such applications are known) for this piece of software is a database. Each company which produces a software package will give it a specific brand name by which it can be recognized.

Task 5.13

This will provide evidence towards Element 5.3 PC 5 and Core Skill Information Technology 3.4.

Write a list of the database packages which are available on your college or school system and then visit at least one shop and ask what other databases are available. Add these to your list.

Design an electronic counterpart of the manual chart which was used to record bookings on the coach. Compare the manual chart with the electronic version and evaluate the usefulness of each.

Clients' or members' details

The social club manager will need to keep details of his members' home addresses. He could do this with either a manual or an electronic system. If he uses the latter, it would have to comply with the terms of the Data Protection Act, which we consider in more detail later in this Element. However, as we have already decided that we are dealing with a fairly small club, it would be just as easy to keep the details on a manual, card index system.

This consists of a plastic box which holds cards, each of which has details of one member written on it. A set of index cards is inserted into the box so that members' details can be kept in alphabetical order (see Figure 5.18). This system deals admirably with membership lists for social clubs, and even works for small leisure and tourism organizations who wish to keep details of clients on a mailing list.

Financial information

Not all information which needs to be recorded by leisure and tourism organizations is about people. A great deal of information is required in respect of money taken or paid out.

It is essential that all financial records are kept accurately and up to date. Not only is this a legal requirement but also a business requirement, as businesses simply cannot function well without a reasonably accurate idea of their financial position.

A great deal of financial information needs to be recorded and stored. Not every organization has the same needs; the following list will give you an idea of some information which may need to be kept by a museum with a shop and café:

- Receipts from entrance fees
- Receipts from shop sales
- Receipts from food sales
- Receipts from equipment hire
- Payments for wages
- Payments for repairs
- Payments for rent, rates, heat, light, etc.
- Payments for purchases (stationery, furniture, carpets, etc.).

It is, again, possible to keep financial records with or without the aid of a computer. As in other situations, size is an important factor in the choice of system.

The majority of leisure and tourism facilities, especially those which handle thousands of pounds a week, will invest in the best electronic systems available to them. However, small, privately owned facilities which are run on a low budget (perhaps a museum with a souvenir shop which is only open from Easter to the end of September and does not have a large clientele) may decide that they have neither the money, expertise nor reason to purchase a computerized system to record all financial transactions. As computer equipment is reducing in price and more and more people are becoming **computer literate** (able to use computers with ease), the use of computers in even the smallest organizations will increase.

Storing data

This, as with data which is received (input), is usually a two-tier structure. To illustrate storage of information, we can look at the squash court booking system in a leisure centre.

Storing information stage 1 – The background details

In order to operate a system whereby squash courts can be booked, we must first know quite a lot of background information:

- How many courts there are
- At what times they are available for booking
- The duration of a booking
- When they must be left free for cleaning
- When any are damaged and awaiting repair.

Whatever system we decide to use, manual or electronic, this is the first information which must be stored in it.

Storing information stage 2 – The individual details

Once we have set up our manual system or electronic database, we can enter details of individual bookings for the squash courts. These can then be stored so that when a new booking is taken it is not taken on a court which is already booked or is awaiting repair or cleaning. The stored information can also be used at a later date for management purposes.

The link between inputting and storing

It is easy to see that there is an essential link between inputting and storing data. One task, inputting, leads inevitably to the other, storing. Data must be input before it can be stored and, once entered, storage is the virtually inevitable second step.

The only time that storage does not follow inevitably from inputting is when a deliberate action is taken to delete a record or destroy a file, or an accident occurs which leads to information being removed. This is more likely to happen with a manual system, where human error can have a great impact. A file can be mislaid or lost, and consequently the data which is being stored is lost with it.

Task 5.14

This will provide evidence towards Element 5.3 PC 1 and Core Skill Information Technology 3.4.

List some data which must be stored by a specific leisure and tourism organization and describe how you would store it, both manually and electronically. It will help if you visit an organization and ask how it stores its data currently and how it thinks it would store it if it were larger or smaller. You could consider any of the following:

- *A tour operator's reservations department*
- *A tour operator's overseas department*
- *A tour operator's agency sales department*
- *A travel agent's accounts department*
- *A travel agent's booking department*
- *A leisure centre's accounts department*
- *A leisure centre's booking department*
- *A museum or art gallery's exhibition department*
- *A museum or art gallery's accounts department*

or any other organization in the leisure and tourism sector.

Write a brief report outlining the main benefits and drawbacks of both the manual systems and electronic systems which you have studied.

Setting up storage systems

One of the main aspects which must be considered when setting up systems is the type of information which will eventually need to be provided. This is especially important with manual storage systems, which can prove very cumbersome to operate if the data is not stored in such a way that it can easily be retrieved in the required format.

Electronic databases do need some forethought when being set up, but they are designed to search for information in various ways, so the job of retrieving information electronically is usually much simpler than retrieving it manually, although manual systems can be very easy to operate when only limited information is required.

The scenario which follows highlights the differences between manual and electronic information retrieval.

Providing information

The final function of an information processing system is to provide information. There may be a further inherent step in this function – the distribution of information.

Consider the following scenario. We will look at how the travel agent can locate the information which he needs either with a manual system or with an electronic system.

Scenario

A travel agent decides to invite all his clients over the age of 21 who travelled to France within the last two years to attend a wine tasting of French wines.

An agent who is not computerized has quite a task on his hands!

There are many ways of storing files. This agent keeps his files in a filing cabinet in date order. When more than one client travels on the same date, each file for that date is placed in alphabetical order. The final destination does not play any part in the filing system.

The agent has established a number of criteria which need to be used in the search:

- Only clients travelling within the last two years need to be contacted
- Only clients who travelled to France need to be contacted
- Only clients over the age of 21 need to be contacted.

The first search criterion is quite simple to satisfy, as all files over two years old can be discounted. This is easily done, as files are kept in date order.

The second criterion calls for the file of every client who travelled within the last two years to be viewed, so that it can be established whether the client visited France. This is very time-consuming but, as destination is shown quite clearly at the top of the client's file, it is easy to spot which clients travelled to France.

The third criterion causes a real headache. The age of the client is recorded on a form inside the file, so when the file of a client who travelled to France is located it must be opened and the age of each person who travelled in the party must be checked.

In order that invitations can be sent, the clients' addresses must be transcribed onto a list, which the agent will keep as a master or control copy so that he knows who he has invited, and then typed onto envelopes which will contain the invitations.

The entire process is very time-consuming, and the agent probably wishes that he had invested in an electronic system. In this case, he would simply instruct the database to conduct a search for files which fitted the first two criteria, and people within individual files who fulfilled the final criterion.

His electronic system would then be instructed to make up a list of names and addresses and produce address labels which could be stuck onto the envelopes which contain the invitations. The entire process would require very little human input, and the list would very possibly be more accurate than the one produced by a member of staff for a number of reasons:

- The computer would not have become bored while compiling the list (one of the main reasons why people make mistakes when performing routine, unexciting tasks)
- The computer will not have been distracted, perhaps by a conversation between other members of staff, while searching through the files

- If the computer was 'asked' to do something else at the same time as it was looking through the files it could cope with this, whereas a human being might find he made mistakes through trying to do two jobs at once
- The computer would make automatic calculations, e.g. a client who was 19 when he travelled two years ago may be missed by the clerk who could unthinkingly discount him when she saw the age '19' on the booking form. The computer would automatically calculate that he is now 21 and ensure that an invitation is sent to him.

The computer's ability to be accurate is, of course, dependent on the accuracy of the information entered into it. This factor is summed up neatly in the word 'GIGO', which is an acronym (made up of the first letters) of the words Garbage In Garbage Out. In other words, if inaccurate information is put into the computer, then inaccurate information will automatically come out.

In the above scenario the information is distributed to clients in the form of an invitation to attend a wine tasting. Here are a few more examples of information based on data recorded and stored in an information processing system which may be distributed to clients:

- Invoices
- Itineraries (the 'timetable' which tells clients when to check into the airport, what time the flight departs, what time they arrive at their destination, where they travel each day of their holiday, etc.)
- Newsletters
- Advertising leaflets
- Notification of an amendment to a departure time.

Purposes of information processing systems

The primary purpose of an information processing system in a leisure or tourism organization is to assist in the running of the organization. It does this by processing the raw data which has been entered and stored within the system into meaningful information which is needed by various sectors within the organization.

The processed information can be used to provide:

- Customer service information
- Management information.

Manual information processing

In a manual system the processing is done by people who work for the organization. They may have certain tools at their disposal which help them with processing the data:

- An employee working with figures may use a calculator
- An accounts clerk preparing invoices may have a calculator and a typewriter.

Even in an organization which is mainly dependent on manual processing, there may be some elements of electronic technology:

- A secretary may use an electronic typewriter or even a word processor to prepare letters or mail shots
- When a number of copies are needed of the same letter, perhaps for a mail shot, a photocopier may be used to produce the copies or, if the secretary worked on a word processor with a printer attached, they could be produced on the electronic printer.

It would be unusual for any but the smallest manual systems, probably operated on a private basis by clubs or voluntary organizations, to be completely manual, without any assistance whatsoever from electronic technology, even if only a small, hand-held calculator.

Electronic processing systems

It is impossible for any electronic system to operate without some human intervention. Human input is needed when the system is first set up and at various stages throughout the processing stages. Although there has been a great deal of work undertaken with 'intelligent'

computers, no computer is sufficiently expert or intelligent to set up and operate an organization.

In order to understand the purposes of information systems we will look more closely at each of the purposes which have already been mentioned. We will consider them as they might appear in leisure and tourism organizations.

Customer service information

This is information which is made available to clients to improve the experience which they have with an organization.

The chart for the coach trip which we looked at earlier in this section gave all the information needed for people to be able to book the sort of seat they wanted: behind the driver or guide, smoking or non-smoking. This was essential information.

If the chart also showed clients where the coach's wheel arches were (which means limited leg room) or where the emergency exit was (which means additional leg room), it would also be providing customer service information. This additional information would allow clients to choose seats with added value to them – seats which would enhance their enjoyment of the trip.

A client who visits a travel agent may find it difficult to choose between two hotels which appear to be very similar in the tour operator's brochure. A travel agent who can provide additional information, either by using a manual information processing system (a book which tells him about the hotels) or an electronic one (a database which holds information on the hotels) is providing his client with customer service information which will help him to make the final choice in respect of destination. A simple piece of information – which of the two hotels provides a babysitting service or which has room service – may enable the client to choose the hotel which is the best one for him.

When making a booking for theatre seats there is some information which is essential: the cost of the seat, the time the performance begins. There is also information which is useful to clients: which seats have the best views, which are nearest to the fire exit, which are nearest to the bar. This is regarded as service information.

Task 5.15

This will provide you with evidence towards Element 5.3 PC 1.

Choose one of the following scenarios and write briefly what essential information you would need in the situation and what customer service information you would like to have.

Scenario 1

You are taking an elderly relative out for the day. She is fit, but cannot walk very far. You cannot decide whether to go to a local stately home or a special exhibition which is on at the art gallery. Your relative is quite happy to visit either. What customer service information could you request from each venue to help you in your choice?

Scenario 2

There are two sporting events taking place on the same day. You would like to attend both, but as they take place at the same time this is impossible. The cost of a ticket is the same for both and it will cost you about the same amount to travel to either of them. You want to decide which to attend based on information available to you. What would you like to know to make your final decision?

Management information

This is essential information within any organization. Management information, just like customer service information, is the result of putting raw data into a system, processing it and retrieving it in the required format.

A great deal of, but not all, management information is required for statutory financial reasons:

- VAT which a company needs to pay or reclaim must be calculated from the data which has been received
- The amount of company tax payable to the Treasury must be calculated
- Income tax payment must be calculated and payment made on behalf of staff on the PAYE (pay as you earn) tax scheme
- National Insurance payments must be made both on behalf of the company and on behalf of the staff

Other financial information may be required by management. This information helps in the tactical (day-to-day) and strategic (advance) planning for the organization:

- Is each department keeping to its set budgets?
- Are sales reaching targets?
- Does the organization take more money on some days of the week than others?

Other management information produced by an information processing system may be statistics, which allow a number of conclusions to be drawn and decisions made:

- Are some holiday dates proving more successful than others? If so, do the under-sold dates need to be re-advertised or reduced in price?
- Does the organization lose bookings at certain times because there are not enough staff to answer the telephones? If so, should more staff be recruited and trained to work at peak times?
- Are the saunas more popular than the jacuzzi and are the sunbeds used more than either of them? Should more sunbeds be installed?
- Are Japanese language tapes in audio systems becoming increasingly popular? Would it be sensible to invest in more Japanese language tapes?

The information processing system provides the basic information and it is then the job of a manager or a person with specific responsibilities to use this information to make an informed management decision.

Spreadsheets

Decisions involving any sort of numbers, money or statistics, can be helped by using a software package called a spreadsheet. The computers in your college or school will have at least one spreadsheet package loaded on them; among the most commonly used are Supercalc, Lotus and Excel. As with all software, it does not do anything which cannot be done manually, but it does it much more quickly.

Spreadsheets were originally designed for use in accounting situations, but are now used in any area where 'number crunching' is required. One of their main attractions to managers who need to make decisions based on figures is their ability to do 'what if' calculations quickly and accurately. Data is entered into the spreadsheet as either figures or formulae and then a figure is altered and the effect that this has on all the other figures on the spreadsheet is shown without delay.

Case study

Katy Smith is the manager of the very popular group 'The Hard Hitters', who are planning their next UK tour. They make a lot of money on the merchandise they sell: T-shirts, caps, etc. The group's popularity is firmly established, and they have decided to take advantage of the fact that three of the large cities where they are going to play have recently opened new venues which hold a lot more people than the previous concert halls.

Katy is easily able to calculate how many items of each type of merchandise she is going to need at the new venues. She inputs the size of the previous audiences and the number of each type of item sold and asks her spreadsheet to calculate:

'What if we play to an extra 1 200 people in Manchester, 700 in Birmingham and 950 in Bristol? How much extra stock will we need to order to satisfy the likely demand?'

She may then look at the figures from previous concerts in those towns and realize that not everybody buys something, so she can ask the spreadsheet to give her an answer to:

'What if only 92 per cent of the audience buy something in Manchester, 86 per cent in Birmingham and 94 per cent in Bristol?'

New figures will appear virtually instantaneously. She could have done the calculations with the help of a calculator, but this would have proved very time-consuming and she may have inadvertently made mistakes. She can be certain that the calculations done on the spreadsheet will be correct.

Displaying the information graphically

A feature of a modern spreadsheet is that the numbers produced can be displayed graphically in various ways. Pie charts, exploded pie charts, bar charts, line charts (Figure 5.19) can all be automatically generated by the spreadsheet software from numbers and information which it holds in its memory bank.

Some word processing packages are also able to produce graphic representations of numbers, but the numbers first have to be fed into them. Advanced word processors are able to do calculations, but they cannot compete with the versatility of a spreadsheet.

Choosing the right system

Any organization, particularly a commercial one, needs to think very seriously when setting up an information processing system. There is no doubt that electronic systems offer many advantages over manual systems, but an electronic system is not necessarily the right one in every situation. Let us first consider the advantages of an electronic system.

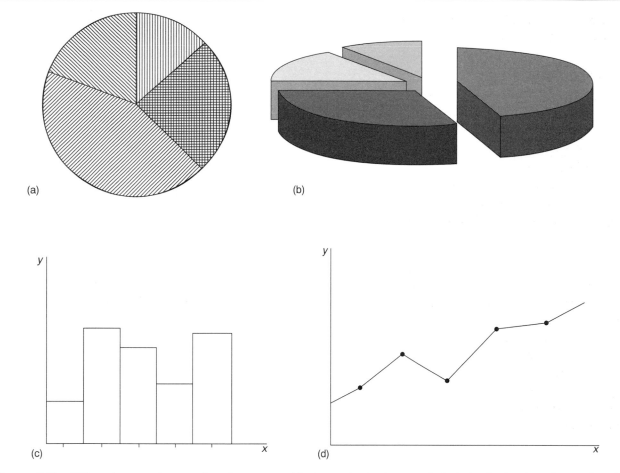

Figure 5.19   Different ways of presenting figures graphically: a pie chart, an exploded pie chart, a bar chart, a graph

Speed of access to information

Information can be accessed very quickly in an electronic system. A good system can do in seconds what a clerk could take hours, or even days, to do. We can say that **speed is improved** with electronic systems.

Speed of preparing information

An operations clerk working for a tour operator will have to make up manifests (lists of people who are travelling on a flight, coach or ferry) for the transport provider and rooming lists (names of the people travelling, the type of room they require, any special food requirements, etc.) for the hotels.

A clerk working with a manual system will have to work through files and charts, transcribe the

details, type them out and then despatch them to the transport and accommodation providers. If he has a fax at his disposal the despatch can be accomplished quite quickly, but the rest of the task is very time-consuming.

A completely electronic system would have been programmed to automatically process the data it held into the information needed, at the right time, and send the information via a modem into the computers belonging to the other companies.

Accuracy of information

The electronic system described above is not only much faster than a clerk working through manual records, it is also much more accurate, as the clerk may make mistakes through tiredness, boredom or sheer sloppiness.

Costs

The cost of setting up a system with this capability would be high, but the running costs would be low and, as fewer staff would be needed at an operational level, wage bills could be reduced. This is not guaranteed, however, as although operational level staff may be shed when an electronic system is installed, specialist computer staff may need to be employed.

Once electronic systems are installed, staff have different skill requirements from staff who have worked with manual systems. Current staff could be re-trained or specialist staff could be employed. Both cost more money as training must be paid for and specialist staff are more expensive to employ than clerical staff. Even if the work of three members of staff can be done by a computer, the one new specialist who needs to be employed to look after the computer may be more costly than the three clerks.

There is frequently a stage during automation when staff costs are very high indeed, as the clerical staff are still employed and specialist staff have been brought in to set up the new system; therefore, a greatly increased wage bill has to be paid for a period of time. However, as time progresses and the computer takes over more and more of the day-to-day clerical tasks, it is likely to become more cost-effective.

There are other costs apart from wage bills which can be reduced by automation. Modern computers can be very powerful and still be quite small and take up much less space than the equivalent number of staff. This means that the amount of office space needed can be reduced and overheads go down.

The fact that computers are more accurate than people means that costs are not incurred in rectifying mistakes. For example, a tour operator's ticketing clerk may have written and despatched 114 tickets with a departure time of 08.00 instead of 20.00. They would all have to be re-written and sent to the clients with an accompanying letter apologizing for the mistake and making it very clear that the flight departed in the evening, not the morning. Time is money, paper is money and postage is money – so the expense incurred by this one mistake would be quite high.

Reliability

Computers are more reliable than human beings in a number of ways:

- People are often ill or late for work, but a good computer system with a back-up electricity supply is very reliable indeed
- A computer will always do the same thing; it will not have the same 'blip' that the ticketing clerk above had. The clerk had probably written the tickets correctly for many weeks, and suddenly was confused by 8.00 a.m. and 8.00 p.m. The confusion resulted in costs being incurred and the company appearing inefficient. Once told that the departure time for the flight was 8.00 p.m. (20.00) the computer will, reliably, each week generate the correct time on the tickets.

Productivity

We have already considered the travel clerk sending invitations to the wine tasting and seen how much more quickly this can be accomplished by an electronic system. Computers are always more productive (do more in the same length of time) than people, if a computer is able to undertake the task in the first place.

Task 5.16

This will provide you with evidence towards Element 5.3, PC 3, 5 and 6 and Core Skill Communication 3.3 and Information Technology 3.4.

Visit a local leisure centre, health and fitness club, theatre or museum where computers have been installed. Establish how automation has altered the ways in which information processing now takes place. Write a brief report comparing the current situation with the pre-automated systems and evaluating the current system.

In your report, consider such aspects as costs, accuracy, productivity, etc. Recommend ways in which the current system could be improved.

The Data Protection Act

This Act was introduced in the UK in 1984. It is derived from the Council of Europe Convention for the Protection of Individuals, which was opened for signing in January 1981.

The Act sets out to offer protection to living individuals in respect of personal data about them which is held electronically. At the same time, it recognizes that people and organizations do have a right to process data. It is not concerned with data which is processed manually.

The Act is primarily concerned with data held in the UK, but also covers the transfer of data to other countries and has regulations which ensure that data can only be transferred outside the UK to countries which have similar protection for individuals.

The organizations which process data are known as **data users**. People who have personal information about them held on computer are known as **data subjects**.

The Data Protection Registrar

The Act is upheld by the Office of the Data Protection Registrar. This is a government-backed office which will intervene on behalf of data subjects if they are unhappy with a data user.

Who must register?

Virtually all organizations – certainly those which operate within the leisure and tourism industries – which process personal data electronically must register with the Registrar.

However, a few organizations are exempt from registering, notably those concerned with national security. There is some data usage which does not call for registration: for example, an organization which holds data only for calculating wages or one which keeps a mailing list consisting of nothing more than a name and address.

Computer bureaux

These are people or organizations who own computer facilities for use by other organizations. A computer bureau is not considered to be the owner of the data which is processed on its computer if it simply provides equipment and allows it to be used by a third party for processing data.

The Data Protection Principles

The Act consists of eight Data Protection Principles. The eighth, which is concerned with security, applies to all data users, but computer bureaux are exempt from the first seven principles. However, the organizations which use their facilities would have to observe all eight principles.

Rights of the individual

Data subjects have a number of rights under the Act. These are detailed in the Seventh Principle and, very briefly, consist of:

Access to information

> Any individual who wishes to see the information which is being held about him in a computer has the right to see it. He must make a written request to the data user and he may be asked to pay a fee, up to £10.

> The data subject would then be provided with the information held on him by that data user. This right is called subject's access, and a data subject who exercises this right can expect a response from the data user within forty days. If the response is not forthcoming, the Data Protection Registrar, or

even the courts, can be asked to intervene on behalf of the data subject.

There are certain cases where this right would not apply, for example if disclosure of the information is likely to make it easier for a crime to be committed.

Correction or deletion

A data subject who discovers that inaccurate data is being held on him may request that it is corrected or deleted. Again, the Registrar and the courts would intervene on his behalf in this situation.

Compensation

It has been possible, since 11 September 1984, for a data subject to seek compensation if damage has been caused by the loss, unauthorized destruction or unauthorized disclosure of personal data. The Registrar defines 'unauthorized' as meaning without the authority of the data user or computer bureau concerned. The damages claimed can include an amount for distress.

Since 10 May 1986 it has also been possible for a data subject to claim compensation for damage caused by inaccurate data. This claim can, again, include a claim for distress.

The right to complain to the Registrar

Any data subject who believes that there has been a breach of one of the principles or any other provision of the Act has a right to complain to the Registrar. If the complaint is upheld, he also has a right to expect the Registrar to take such steps as are warranted to rectify the situation.

Security

The Eighth Principle is concerned with security measures which must be taken by organizations holding personal data.

This principle makes it quite clear that any person or organization which holds personal data on individuals has a responsibility to ensure that it is kept securely. Measures must be taken to protect the data against deliberate unauthorized access, use, alteration, disclosure or destruction and also against accidental loss or destruction.

Organizations holding personal data should consider physical factors, such as controlling access to the data banks and taking precautions against fire or natural disaster to the building or room where the personal data is stored.

They should also consider the trustworthiness of their staff and have measures in place in case a member of staff breaches the trust placed in him or her. Organizations holding personal data should ensure that security measures, such as limited passwords, are built into their systems and that an audit trail (a record which allows actions to be traced to the person who performed them) is in place.

Task 5.17

This will provide you with evidence towards Element 5.3, PC 4 and Core Skill Communication 3.2.

The organization for which you work is changing from a manual system to a computer system. Write a report for your managing director outlining the contents of the Data Protection Act and stating what your company must do to comply with the Act.

▪ Assignment 5.3 ▪

This will provide you with evidence towards Element 5.3, PCs 1, 2, 3, 4, 5 and 6 and Core Skills Communication 3.1, 3.2, 3.3 and 3.4 and Information Technology 3.2, 3.3 and 3.4.

This is a whole class activity.

The class will debate the statement:

'Computerization in all leisure and tourism organizations is necessary and should be welcomed'.

Members of the class will speak on the various aspects of computerization. Each speaker will prepare a handout for the rest of the class on his or her particular topic. Every member of the group should be allocated a set period of time to speak on a particular topic or simply to give their views.

Students' speeches should all display evidence of research. Students must take notes on the content of the debate, which can be kept in their portfolios as evidence that they have understood the performance criteria.

DEVELOPING CUSTOMER SERVICE IN LEISURE AND TOURISM

We are all customers at one time or another, whether we are buying food or following a leisure pursuit, and, as a result, we have expectations about how we would like to be treated. This Unit explores customer service and applies it to leisure and tourism.

Element 6.1 Investigate customer service in leisure and tourism

In this Element we are going to look at:

- The types and components of customer service
- The importance of customer service.
- The importance of effective communication.
- The types of customers.
- An investigation into the provision given by the industry.

Types of customer service

We work within the service industry providing a service for our customers. The nature of our product is for leisure and entertainment and it is not necessary for people to survive. In other words, when obtaining services from our industry, people are spending their **disposable income**. Disposable income is the money we have left to spend on the extras in life after all the bills have been paid.

There are lots of competitors in the same market sector, and we have to provide a good product so that people will continue to come back to use the facilities, otherwise we will go out of business.

The way in which we are treated influences our perceptions of an organization. If a member of staff is rude and unhelpful, we will still have a bad impression of the organization even though it may be noted for the good product it offers. For example, if the assistant in a travel agency is rude to you while you are trying to book a holiday, you may decide to use another agency next time, or if someone in a heritage centre is unhelpful, you may not make a return visit.

The way in which we deal with customers is therefore very important, and that is why we are studying the subject. There are a lot of straight-forward and possibly obvious techniques that can be used, and it is important that we apply them.

Every employee in an organization has some responsibility to customer service, whether directly or indirectly.

Direct contact is fairly obvious. This would be given by employees who deal with customers. They are the point of contact between the customer and the organization. Sometimes these employees are called 'front of house' staff – examples would include people who work on reception desks or people who give information to customers, such as tour guides. They have an influence over the level of service or information provided. We have certain expectations of these employees.

However, other people in the organization also have responsibilities to customer service. We have all heard the term **backroom team**. These people may not have direct contact with customers on a daily basis – possibly they would deal with problems or less straightforward queries. An example would be a supervisor or manager who deals with the problems customers may have and who has the authority to make decisions on such issues as reimbursement (return of money) or compensation (an alternative product or service).

Support Staff also have a role to play. During their normal working day these employees may not have any contact with customers at all, but the standard of their work will influence customers' perceptions. Examples of these employees would be cleaners and maintenance people. If a cleaner did not work to a high standard, customers would complain if they found facilities dirty and untidy. There are examples where this could affect customers' health. If a kitchen was not cleaned properly, food poisoning bacteria may be able to reproduce to dangerous levels, so making customers ill. If a changing room was not clean, infections such as verrucas may be transmitted quite easily. If a tour bus was not maintained or serviced properly, the tour guide would have problems showing tourists around an area (unless they walked!).

Therefore everyone has a responsibility to customer service to a greater or lesser extent, and it is important that we all recognize that our contributions make a difference.

The components of customer service

What is customer service? You will probably already have ideas about what is involved and, as we have already mentioned, customers are important in the survival of leisure and tourism facilities. We are a 'people' business.

You may have heard someone describe themselves as a 'people' person, but what does this mean, and are you one?

Task 6.1

By completing this task it will lead to coverage of Element 6.1 PC 2, and Core Elements may include Communication Elements 3.1; 3.2; and 3.4.

Answer the following questions by ticking the appropriate column. Y = Yes, N = No, S = Sometimes. Answer the questions quickly and do not think too deeply about your answers.

Y N S

1 When communicating with others, do you do most of the talking?
2 Will you ask for help if you need it?
3 Are you usually punctual (on time) for appointments?
4 Do you have a quick temper?
5 Do you give praise to people as quickly as you find fault?
6 Do you try to make people like you?
7 Do you look at people when they are speaking to you?
8 Can you listen to other people without interrupting them?
9 If someone has bad manners, do you avoid them?
10 Are you easily demoralized?

Now score your answers as follows:-

Question 1 Score 1 for Y and 3 for N.
Question 2 Score 3 for Y and 1 for N.
Question 3 Score 3 for Y and 1 for N.
Question 4 Score 1 for Y and 3 for N.
Question 5 Score 3 for Y and 1 for N.
Question 6 Score 1 for Y and 3 for N.

Question 7 Score 3 for Y and 1 for N.
Question 8 Score 3 for Y and 1 for N.
Question 9 Score 1 for Y and 3 for N.
Question 10 Score 1 for Y and 3 for N.

Now total your score.

Out of a possible 30 marks, if you scored 25 or more you are probably a real 'people person'. 17–25: you are probably quite good at working with others. 10–17: you are not bad, but there is room for improvement. Below 10: you need to put a lot of effort into your 'people' skills!

This is not meant to be a scientific analysis of your skills, but merely a simple indication of how you might get on. However, by studying your answers and our outline, it may help to indicate where work is needed. Check your answers again and think what these responses mean about you. Again, our answers are only an indication.

1 When communicating with others, do you do most of the talking?
Listening skills are very important, and if you are talking most of the time, you cannot be listening very effectively. Listening is an important skill for a good communicator.

2 Will you ask for help if you need it?
Asking for help is not a sign of weakness, as some people may see it. In fact, it is an indication of strength, because you have enough confidence in yourself and others to admit that you do not have the necessary information and they do.

3 Are you usually punctual for appointments?
Being on time is important, as it shows concern for other people and their time, particularly if you need their help.

4 Do you have a quick temper?
If the answer was yes, this may indicate a lack of self-control and maturity. We all have to deal with situations that make us angry, but it is more difficult to resolve problems if you constantly lose your temper.

5 Do you give praise to people as quickly as you find fault?
We all like to be praised, and it is important to acknowledge a job well done. It is much easier to find fault. Good people practice giving praise.

6 Do you try to make people like you?
We all like to be liked. It is human nature, and certainly helps in all situations. However, if you try too hard, you may appear insincere and 'smarmy'. You do not need to like the people you work with and they do not need to like you, but if you are working in a pleasant atmosphere it is better.

7 Do you look at people when they are speaking to you?
This is an important aspect of non-verbal communication, which we will explore later on. However, looking at someone, apart from being good manners, can indicate things like interest and openness and honesty. It is not always easy to do!

8 Can you listen to other people without interrupting them?
Listening and hearing are two different skills, which, again, we will explore later. Do you really listen to what people are saying or do you want to speak? A people person is able to hear what is really being said.

9 If someone has bad manners, do you avoid them?
None of us like people with bad manners, but we should not avoid them. They may still have a valid complaint and, although it is difficult, they are entitled to as much of our time as someone who is polite. Why are they bad mannered?

10 Are you easily demoralized?
If you are demotivated and give up easily, if you cannot be bothered to look for and correct mistakes you have made, people may become fed up with you and decide you are not a good person to work with.

Customer service is about being a people person, and this Unit is designed to help you develop those skills.

Customers do not necessarily want to be awkward or to cause trouble and they do not want an unpleasant experience. They want to have their needs fulfilled, and satisfied customers will return to the organization.

The leisure and tourism business is highly competitive and, with such a range of provisions, customers can take their custom elsewhere.

Satisfied customers are also a good marketing tool. Word of mouth and personal recommendations are very important, as these people will tell their friends – the best form of advertising! However, the opposite is also true – dissatisfied customers will tell their friends and so influence potential customer's perceptions in an adverse way.

Good customer service policies make the customer feel important, influential and show them that their custom is important and valued.

All customers are individuals, and we must try to treat them as such. We can gain an awful lot of information by simply watching and listening, and many techniques can be used to find out what customers want, need and require. These include:

- Observing
- Listening
- Asking
- Monitoring.

Companies used to be afraid of asking customers what they wanted. This is gradually changing, although if you ask such a question, you should be prepared for an answer which may not always be what you are expecting. However, generally people will say whether they are receiving the service they want, as well as telling you if they are not happy.

Customers come from different areas. We usually think of them as being outside the structure of the organization – someone who comes into the facility to purchase a product. When you go to a fast-food outlet or a cinema you are an **external customer** because you are paying for the product and to use the facilities and you have the choice whether to go there again or not.

Internal customers may be colleagues who are also customers – they may work in another aspect of the company or in another location or outlet. They may have less choice over whether they will use the facility again or not, but they can still affect repeat business and can cause problems because they are unhelpful and demoralized. So colleagues are customers as well, and should be treated as well as people outside the organization.

Task 6.2

By completing this task it will contribute to coverage of Element 6.1 PC 1, and Core Elements may include Communication Elements 3.1; and 3.2.

In order to decide on the merits of a customer care policy, it is important to decide what should be included.

Make a list of the skills people could expect from you.

I have split this down into various areas.

- *Behaviour* – Customers expect sensible, calm and logical behaviour, so that problems can be resolved with understanding on both sides. If you are involved in supervising, your staff are your customers and they need treating in the same way.
- *Concern* – Sometimes people require sympathy and support of with their complaint or problem. Listening is a very important skill here, and it can help to remove some of the stress from the situation.
- *Reliability* – This is very important, and colleagues as well as customers need to be able to depend on you. Reliability is demonstrated by:
  - Keeping appointments/meetings
  - Doing what you say you will
  - Meeting deadlines
  - Working accurately
  - Not making promises you cannot keep
  - Passing on messages when necessary.

  If you are unreliable, it may damage your working relationships with colleagues and the public, which could result in the business being affected.
- *Good manners* – As with a lot of things, there are fashions even in what is considered good manners. What was appropriate thirty years ago may not be now. For example, a man is no

longer expected to give up his seat to a woman on a bus.

However, many small courtesies do make life run much more smoothly and make situations more pleasant for everyone.

Here is a list of things that we should all do, no matter who we are dealing with.

1 Always greet people – say 'hello', 'good morning', etc.
2 Smile at people.
3 Remember to say 'please' and 'thank you'.
4 Open doors for people.
5 Check behind you when you have gone through a door – do not let the door close in someone's face.
6 Offer to help people in difficulty – do not wait to be asked.
7 Pick things up for people when they drop them.
8 Call people by their names.
9 Get people's names right.

Apart from demonstrating certain skills in customer service, we also need to reassure our customers that they and their possessions are safe and secure. We have already dealt with the Health and Safety at Work Act in Unit 2, Human Resources. Legislation implies that we will take reasonable care to ensure the security of customers possessions, but also places responsibility on the customer not to take any avoidable risks with their possessions while in the building. For example, most of us are familiar with announcements in airports and train stations about not leaving luggage unattended and its treatment because it may trigger a bomb scare.

The importance of customer service

It is important for staff to put themselves in the customer's situation. How would you feel if you were ignored by staff or made to look small?

Impressions that are given by staff will influence what the customer thinks of the organization, and this applies whether they are internal or external customers. We need to bear in mind that it is we and our organization who depend on the customers and not the other way round.

We have already mentioned the importance of being 'people people' and having good manners, but we could still summarize some of the important aspects.

Here is a list of some of the ways in which we should react to customers.

● Look at customers in order to establish warmth, trust and interest
● Use the customer's name if possible
● Smile, say 'hello' and sound friendly and helpful
● Give the customer your full attention. Do not attempt to do two jobs at once, as neither will be done properly
● Be polite – customers will probably respond in a similar manner
● Offer to help. This can save time as you will find out what the problem is and hopefully solve it quickly.

It is important that a flexible customer service policy is developed by the organization. Traditionally, customers had to take or leave the level of service offered. Leisure and tourism is now far more diverse, with competition from other companies and limited customers. This means that staff and organizations have to be far more flexible.

Task 6.3

By completing this task it will lead to coverage of Element 6.1 PC 2, and Core Elements may include Communication Elements 3.1; 3.2; and 3.4.

Make a list of the important points that need to be considered when designing a customer service policy.

The following is a list of important points. However, it is by no means exhaustive, and you may have included aspects that I have not.

1 **Human relation skills** This requires knowledge of the customers, the organization for whom you are working, the facilities that can be provided, your roles and responsibilities and those of others to the organization and the customer.

2 **Service skills** This is where the customer and the organization meet. The product is unlikely to change very much, but customer requirements and those of the organization will, and at this point it can be an opportunity for things to go right or wrong. Hopefully, it will be the former.

3 **Customer satisfaction** Customers who are satisfied with the service will return, and hopefully encourage their friends to join them. However, we need to remember the influence of dissatisfied customers on their friends as well. Therefore, we need to treat customers with consideration, attention and understanding. Customers know what they want, so ask them!

4 **Contact** There are many opportunities for contact between ourselves and our customers. Some are obvious (such as reception desks), others less obvious (such as security staff). However, we should remember that every opportunity is one in which we can give a good (or bad) impression and demonstrate the policy in operation.

5 **Resolving queries** If a promise is made to contact someone with an answer, then this should be done. Again, the impressions can be improved even if a mistake has been made. People are far more approachable if the necessary apology is offered.

6 **Complaints** These are not necessarily all negative. They can be used as an opportunity to identify a poor procedure and so improve the service. You should listen, apologize, sympathize and suggest a course of action if the organization is at fault.

7 **Staff attitude and appearance** First impressions are very important. Research has shown that we form an impression of someone within the first fifteen seconds of a conversation. If these impressions are unfavourable, they are difficult to change, so that we may gain some customers but lose others. So the way staff look and behave are very important.

8 **Training** It is important that any staff who come into contact with customers are familiar with the customer service policy used and how to operate it.

If these basic principles are implemented, it should mean that we have satisfied customers who will return with repeat business, so retaining our client base. Through personal recommendation we will interest new customers, which will give a competitive advantage and an enhanced image of the organization.

Effective communication

What is communication, and do you communicate well? When asked this question, many people answer that it is speaking or talking with others and that of course they are good communicators.

To a certain extent we are all good communicators, as we have managed to make people understand what we want from a very early age, and this leads to patterns being established. However, communication is more than using language.

We mentioned communication in the Human Resources Unit, and you were introduced to a phrase in another language. Possibly the most important aspect of communication is understanding. I could talk to you or write to you as much as I liked, but if you did not understand me, there would be little point.

Task 6.4

By completing this task it will lead to coverage of Element 6.1 PC 3, and Core Elements may include Communication Element 3.1.

Ask four different people the meaning of the following words:

- *middle-aged*
- *soon*

- *truth*
- *honest*
- *morning*
- *winter*
- *entertainment*
- *encouragement*

You probably had many different answers given to this simple exercise, as we all see the world slightly differently because we are individuals and our opinions change due to experience and age.'

There have been many theories put forward to try to explain the communication process. Many of the early theorists thought of communication as a linear (straight line) process, but really communication is about exchange and feedback. It may be better, therefore, to think of communication as a circle, and the process is shown below.

1 **Intention of the sender** There must be some information that needs passing on to someone else – an acknowledgement, an instruction, an enquiry, whatever it is, there must be a message to transmit.

2 **Transmitting the message** When the information has been formulated in a way that is going to be understood, an appropriate method of communicating that message has to be found. For example, how would you let people know there was a fire?

3 **Receiving the message** No matter how important your communication, there is little point in carefully phrasing what you are going to say, then selecting the most appropriate method of saying it, if no-one is going to listen or pay attention. At this stage, the responsibility shifts from the sender to the receiver. We are quite selective about what we respond to. Think of a phone conversation you have had when there has been a lot of background noise. If the conversation is about something you are interested in, you will try to block out the background noise. Receiving information requires developing certain skills and sometimes may require you to 'read between the lines' to understand what people are really trying to communicate.

4 **Interpretation of the message** At this stage, it is a test of how well the message format has been interpreted. Again, one of the tasks in the Human Resources Unit asked you to answer some questions based on a piece of legislation. It was in English and you knew what the words meant individually, but problems probably arose because of the terminology used. We all have jargon that we use within our careers, and even people inside the organization will not necessarily understand what we are talking about. We also tend to abbreviate and use letters – almost like a code. When communicating, it is important that the person we are talking to also understands that code.

5 **Feedback** This tests whether the communication has been understood or not, and can be seen as communication in action. For example, if I asked you, 'Open the window, please' and you did it, my communication would have been successful and you would have given the necessary feedback.

Usually we choose between written and verbal communication. Written communications include letters, memoranda, newspapers, reports, questionnaires, etc. Often we choose to rely on these because there is less chance of misunderstanding. Language has a precise meaning, while non-verbal communication (body language) is open to misunderstandings.

There are many different types of verbal encounters, some of which we have already mentioned.

Task 6.5

By completing this task, it will lead to coverage of Element 6.1 PC 3, and Core Elements may include Communication Elements 3.1; 3.2; and 3.4

When meeting people in the following situations, what would be the first thing you would say?

1 Friends that you work with or see every day.

2 Your supervisor or teacher/lecturer.

3 The caretaker.

4 Someone looking lost.

5 A customer who has walked into your travel agency.

6 Someone you do not like, but have to work with.

Compare your answers with those of the rest of the group.

I expect that there were a variety of answers given, and it is unlikely that you would greet everyone in the same way.

Task 6.6

By completing this task it will lead to coverage of Element 6.1 PC 3, and Core Elements may include Communication Elements 3.1; 3.2; 3.4; and I.T. Elements 3.1; 3.2; and 3.3.

Compile a list of points for people to follow when answering the telephone.

Depending on the organization, there may already be a Code of Practice in operation to cover these procedures. Even if there is not, there are some simple rules that we can follow.

Answering a call

1 Give a greeting – 'good morning' (or afternoon). This is important to allow the caller to tune into your voice or accent (which we all have!) and it also allows time for the phone connection to be made properly.

2 Give a name or department or job title so that the caller will have an indication as to whether he or she is through to the right place. It also helps if he or she has to contact you again.

Making a call

1 Give a greeting.

2 Say who you are and where you are from.

3 Give an outline of what you want. Do not go into too much detail, as you may not be through to the right person.

When you have finished your conversation, it is also important that you both understand what the next step is, and always check that you understand. Therefore:

1 Repeat who is to do what next.

2 Check names, addresses and figures.

3 Say 'thank you' and 'goodbye'.

4 Do not slam the phone down!

The same basic rules of good manners apply to face-to-face communications. Even the most angry customer will tend to respond better if you smile and offer help. Simply changing our perceptions of people from being 'difficult people' to 'people with difficulties' means that we are then in a frame of mind to help them.

Things such as remaining calm and apologizing on behalf of your organization when a mistake has been made also helps. Finally, remember that you are there to represent the company, and an angry customer may react to you as being responsible for his or her problem. The comments will not be meant personally and should not be taken as such, no matter how hard this may be.

Written communications will be more formal and will often be referred to again. This particularly applies to changes in procedures, so the style adopted has to be appropriate. For letter writing and memos, the style has become less formal as the campaign for plain speaking and saying what we mean has gained support. However, it is still important to be polite and to be logical, whichever form of written communication takes place.

Non-verbal communications also play an important part in our exchange process.

Task 6.7

By completing this task it will lead to coverage of Element 6.1 PC 3, and Core Elements may include Communication Elements 3.2; and 3.3.

Look at the symbols in Figure 6.1 and write down what they mean.

These examples have very specific meanings and give direct information. Other examples of non-verbal communication are not so reliable when we interpret them.

We give out many signals, largely unconsciously, which can confirm or give doubt to our verbal reactions. These include:

- *Facial expressions* – examples include smiles, frowns, narrowed eyes (transmitting friendliness and approachability, confusion and anger)
- *Gestures* – The thumbs up sign, nodding the head shaking the head (signalling things going well, encouragement or disagreement)
- *Movements* – Finger tapping, pacing up and down (transmitting impatience and anxiety)
- *Physical contact* – Shaking hands, back slapping (signalling greeting and safety from threat and encouragement)
- *Positioning* – Keeping a respectful distance or looking over someone's shoulder (showing awareness of different status or a close working relationship)
- *Posture* – Standing upright, lounging, leaning forward (indicating alertness, self-confidence (or over-confidence), anxiety, etc.).

We have spent a great deal of time focusing on communications generally. Why? The answer is simple. If we do not communicate properly, we will not be able to provide the service our customers are looking for, and if we do not do that, then the organization will suffer.

First impressions of people are very important and, although we should not, we assess people on those impressions. Research has shown that an opinion is formed about all interview candidates within fifteen seconds of meeting them, which will obviously affect the interview. By their very nature, we only have one chance at first impressions and they are very important.

If the first contact with an organization is friendly and helpful, it will give a good impression. No-one expects staff to have all the answers, but they are expected to find out and give a reply. This is very important.

Communications will also be important to varying numbers of people. If a group of people asked you for information, communications would be complicated if they were foreign tourists who did not speak good English. Dealing with individuals is much easier because you can find out information from them, hopefully without someone interrupting.

Figure 6.1

Whichever group you are dealing with, questioning, and questioning techniques, are important to obtain all the facts.

Questions are divided into four different types:

1 **Open** Requires the respondent to answer more than 'yes' or 'no'. 'How can I help you?' gives an opening for a query or question to be raised.
2 **Closed** The respondent can simply answer 'yes' or 'no' such as 'Did you have a good journey?' No further answer is expected.
3 **Leading** This suggests an answer to the other person. 'Isn't the weather beautiful?' expects the reply 'yes'.
4 **Limiting** This allows for certain answers or preferences, such as 'Do you prefer tea or coffee?' It limits the choice for the individual.

Task 6.8

By completing this task, it will lead to coverage of Element 6.1 PC 3, and Core Elements may include Communication Elements 3.1; 3.2; 3.4; and I.T. Elements 3.1; 3.2; and 3.3.

Produce four questions in each of the four styles on either entertainment, sport or food and drink.

Listening to the answers you receive is also very important, and here are some guidelines to help.

1 Concentrate and show the talker you are paying attention.
2 Do not interrupt, particularly if the person is angry, as it will make the situation worse.
3 Do not assume – make sure you question properly so that you have all the facts.
4 Do not let your own prejudices and perceptions influence you. We all have our own prejudices – it is part of what makes us individuals – but be aware of them and do not let them affect your judgement.

Types of customers

Within your working life you are going to have to deal with a wide range of customers – people from outside the organization (external customers) and people from within the organization (internal customers). However, no matter where they come from, they are all people who require our services, so making them our customers.

Internal customers may include our colleagues, members of management, other staff teams, employees and departments. However, simply because they already work within the organization does not mean that they should be treated any differently, and it is important to ask yourself whether you treat people from within the organization as well as you treat those from outside it. Internal customers may have an idea of some of your problems, but that does not mean that they should be compromised on the level of service they can expect. In this situation the communication can still be fairly informal, but the level of service should not. It is important to remember that colleagues are customers as well.

Although internal customers work for the orgainzation, they may also fall into some of the categories of external customers.

As well as our customers being fairly 'standard' people, they may have some requirement that needs a special level of service. We can all be categorized into different areas depending on our age, cultural background and whether or not we have disabilities. Customers should be treated as individuals in respect of this classification, and appropriate skills should be demonstrated.

A youngster should be treated differently from an older person. However, simply because someone looks older does not mean that they are stupid, unable to understand or deaf. Also, they are not necessarily resistant to change. Nor do young people necessarily have no consideration for others, or are selfish and taking drugs. It is important to deal with the individual who is in front of you and find out the best way to help that person.

We have many foreign visitors to this country, and you may be involved in helping them. There is also a proportion of the population who find English difficult – your accent may also present problems. Here are some ideas to help you communicate with them, whether on the phone or in face-to-face conversations.

- Do not shout – they have problems understanding you, not hearing you!
- Speak slowly and carefully. Try to think of other words to use if they do not understand first time.
- Smile.
- Use gestures to demonstrate what you mean.
- Watch their eyes for understanding or lack of it.
- Do not use jargon or slang.
- Be patient.
- Listen and do not interrupt.
- Check your understanding of the situation by asking closed or limiting questions.
- Encourage them to talk by nodding and smiling. A smile can also be picked up on the phone.
- Do not correct their pronunciation or grammar.

Patience is very important, and remember, we are in the people business.

People may be disabled in many ways, and it is a mistake to treat all disabled people in the same way. Wherever possible, and if time allows, try to get to know the person, not the disability. Here are some useful do's and don'ts.

Do:

- Try to establish the problems in communication that the disability creates.
- Help when you know it is needed or when help is asked for.
- Speak slowly and clearly for deaf people and those who are hard of hearing.
- Look at people to check their understanding of the information.
- Remember that blind or partially sighted people may have to rely on you to describe things to them.

Do not:

- See the wheelchair and not the person. People in wheelchairs should not be patronized and they are certainly not stupid.

- Insist on giving help when it is not wanted or needed.
- Be afraid of disabled people or ignore them.

We have already said that you should see people as people with difficulties, not difficult people. The same applies to the disabled. They should be seen as people with difficulties or disabilities.

Portfolio builder

If you have completed these tasks you should have:

- An indication of your communication skills
- A list of contents for a customer care policy
- A list of points to be considered when designing a customer service policy
- Examples of different types of greetings for different situations
- A list of 'do's' and 'don'ts' for using the telephone
- A knowledge of the meaning of symbols
- A knowledge of questions asked in different styles.

▪ Assignment 6.1 ▪

By completing this assignment it will lead to coverage of Element 6.1 PCs 1, 2, 3, 4, and 5, and Core Elements may include Communication Elements 3.1; 3.2; 3.3; 3.4 and I.T. Elements 3.1; 3.2; 3.3; and 3.4.

Scenario

Good customer service can increase income through repeat business and through personal recommendation. If customers are not happy, they will go elsewhere. Customer service can be the key to the success of an organization within the people business.

Details

1 Produce a report that has two distinct sections.
2 Section 1 should deal with the theory that customer service is based upon. You should include information on the types and components of customer service, its importance in leisure and tourism organizations and the importance of effective communications. Include relevant examples.
3 Section 2 should be an investigation into the customer service policy of two organizations. One should be from the leisure and recreation industry and the other from the travel and tourism industry. You will need to establish the types and components of customer service in these organizations, the types of customers and the effectiveness of the communication used to support the customer service.

Element 6.2 Investigate sales and selling as part of customer service in leisure and tourism

Note: The selling aspect of any product or service is important, and you will also need to refer to the Marketing unit (Unit 3) which will give you further information.

This area actually looks at sales and selling as part of customer service. We are going to be reviewing the following areas:

- The functions and objectives of selling in customer service
- Sales techniques
- Duties, responsibilities and necessary qualities of sales staff
- The value of administration procedures
- Factors which make selling leisure and tourism products and services unique
- Investigating sales and selling in leisure and tourism.

The functions and objectives of selling in customer service

Why do we need to know about selling in customer service? After all, we are there to help our customers and provide a service for them. Very true – however, we also have a unique opportunity to promote and sell further goods and services to our customers. In today's competitive market we need to take advantage of the potential that is offered.

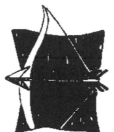

Task 6.9

By completing this task it will lead to coverage of Elements 6.2 PC 1, and Core Elements may include Communication Element 3.1.

Why do you think selling skills may be important for customer service staff? Try to think of some advantages that sales skills and information would have for the organization.

Apart from the obvious financial advantages to the organization, there are many others as well:

- *Providing product information* – In order to sell goods and services to customers, staff need to have a wide knowledge of the products and services offered by the company. This means that the member of staff can answer specific questions or queries that may arise and can quickly and efficiently deal with problems. Also, if certain areas are linked, such as customers enjoying a swim after their game of squash, other ideas and options are given to customers to enhance their enjoyment of the visit.
- *Maintaining good relations* – Having a good working knowledge of product information means that you will be better able to help customers more effectively and more quickly as well as giving a better impression of your skills and abilities. In giving a good impression about yourself and the organization, it means that you are also maintaining good relations with the public. We all like to be helped when we have queries that need answering, and if this is done by someone who is well informed as well

as being polite and helpful it enhances our opinion of the company.

- *A knowledge of sales techniques* can also be useful in helping with customers' complaints or operating a complaints procedure. A knowledge of the organization's procedure for dealing with complaints is important. No matter how hard we try, unfortunately things still sometimes go wrong, and it is always useful to have a set procedure to record and follow in order to resolve the problem. Again, if someone is angry, they want an answer now, so prompt treatment and finding a solution for the situation is always advisable, as it prevents an escalation.

When acting in a customer service function, you become the company (warts and all!) in the eyes of the customer. Helping to resolve problems, apart from being rewarding, also enhances the customer's image of the company.

These are some of the functions that customer service fulfils. In addition, there will also be objectives that the company would like to achieve through customer service skills.

Every organization has to be profitable, otherwise eventually it will cease to exist. So the financial incentive is very strong. Having once provided a service or product for customers, it will then be important to ensure that those people return to our organization rather than going to a competitor. Customers returning to use the facilities is called **repeat business**, and this can represent a large proportion of our market. By making sure that we retain repeat business, as well as encouraging new clients to the organization, we can hopefully manage to increase sales and so retain the company's market share, leading to profitability.

While ensuring that opportunities to sell goods and services are always taken, it is also very important that our customers are satisfied with the level of product offered. As already mentioned, we need to retain our customers to maintain our market share. If customers are not happy with what we are offering, they will look elsewhere

and take their custom where they feel most appreciated. It is part of our function, no matter which aspect of the organization we work in, to make our customers feel valued and wanted.

We have already mentioned that profitability is paramount in keeping the organization viable and successful. If we are able to retain customers as well as gain new customers, this means that profits for the organization will increase and that it will be easier to maintain the competitive edge that we would like over other providers within the area. Unfortunately, the company's success is measured by the profitability for owners or shareholders, so the financial incentive is very strong.

Sales techniques

The term 'quality service' is often used in reference to many aspects of selling.

Task 6.10

By completing this task it will lead to coverage of Element 6.2 PC 2, and Core Elements may include Communication Element 3.1.

Think of the last shop you went into to buy something. What do you remember about the sales person?

If the service was adequate, you probably will not remember very much. If the service was poor, you will remember and probably tell your friends, who will be influenced by your recommendation (or lack of it). Remember, word of mouth is a very powerful marketing tool and it can be either positive or negative for the company.

If you receive excellent service, you will remember that as well, although, human nature being what it is, we are more likely to grumble than to praise, so you are less likely to tell all your friends.

Customer service is about fulfilling customers' needs. **Quality** service is fulfilling these needs, whatever they are, whoever the person is *and* giving a little bit extra – the personal touch that is not in any of the textbooks.

Sales techniques can look very clinical and calculating on paper. They may also look very straightforward. However, things are very different when you are faced with a real-life experience and the customer has not read the script you have worked out for him or her in your head! The following points will help you overcome the difficult moments and help the customer to select the service or product he or she wishes to purchase.

1 **Preparing for the sales interview** When you first start a job, this may be the most difficult aspect to achieve. We gain knowledge through experience. Unfortunately, we tend to learn most from bad experiences and remember their lessons – learning the 'hard' way. When you first join a company, it is unlikely that you will know a tremendous amount about the products and services. The longer you are employed, the more knowledge you gain and will be able to apply or offer to the customer.

However, even when you are 'new' it is still important that you are well informed about the products and services your company can offer to the customer and that, if you are asked questions you cannot answer, you find out and in turn pass the information on to the client.

In addition to your product knowledge, the image and appearance you adopt is also important. Whether the company provides a uniform or you select your own clothes to wear, clean, well presented clothing helps enhance the image we give of ourselves and the organization. A cheerful smile can also help – people are less likely to reject your enquiry if you smile at them first, and it takes fewer face muscles to smile than it does to frown! It also makes *you* feel better.

2 **Approaching the customer** For some of us this may be difficult – some people are naturally shy. However, as we have already said, if you approach someone with a smile it helps to break the ice and prepare the way.

Task 6.11

By completing this task it will contribute to Element 6.2 PC 2, and Core Elements may include Communication Element 3.1.

You are employed in a tourist gift shop which also provides information. A group of customers have spent a long time looking at a certain leaflet. You decide to approach them to offer help.
What do you say to them?

We have all been in situations where we have been looking at something in a shop and the 'lurking' shop assistant decides to 'pounce'. Usually they ask 'Can I help?'

What sort of question is this? Open or closed?

If I am merely browsing, my reaction would be 'No, thank you'. The reply gives a further indication to the type of question. It is closed. It does not encourage me to give further information.

If I had been asked 'How can I help?', I would have had to give a longer answer – either 'I don't need any help yet, thank you', or 'Do you . . .?' or 'Can you . . .?', so that both assistant and customer have the opportunity to communicate.

So questioning techniques, listening techniques and non-verbal communication are very important.

We can quite easily tell when someone is angry and, by asking the right questions in the right manner, we can defuse the situation and genuinely help the customer with his or her problem.

3 Identifying needs When we first see people, we make certain assumptions about them simply on their image or appearance. This can be a dangerous trap to fall into and can lead to missed sales opportunities.

Task 6.12

By completing this task it will lead to coverage of Element 6.2 PC 2, and Core Elements may include Communication Element 3.1.

How would you identify the needs of your customer? What would you do?

We mention assumptions as being possible pitfalls, but they can also be necessary. If a child of 10 or 12 approached you for a pint of beer while you were serving behind the bar in the leisure centre, it would actually be illegal to sell it to them, and from their appearance you could probably assess them as being too young.

The questioning techniques that we mentioned when approaching the customer are also going to be important. From using open questions at this stage and *listening* to the answer, you will pick up a lot of information about the customer and his or her requirements.

Task 6.13

By completing this task it will lead to coverage of Element 6.2 PC 2, and Core Elements may include Communication Element 3.1.

If someone came into the leisure centre making enquiries about swimming lessons, what would you do?

Rather than just give out the times of lessons, it may be important to find out who they are, for it would be embarrassing for an adult to join a pre-school age group! Through successful questioning at this stage, you can save time by finding out about your customer's needs and expectations.

4 Sales negotiation Having found out about your customer's requirements, it is useful to check with him or her that you have all the necessary information. So tell them you are going to make sure that you have understood.

Once you have done this and you have the facts, you can then make your suggestions and justify them to the customer: 'I think this class would be better for your needs because . . .'.

5 Overcoming objections Once you have selected a product or a choice of products for your customer, he or she may then object. It is important to find out what those objections are and why they are a problem for the customer.

Very often money is a major factor. This could possibly be overcome by your company offering a regular payments scheme to help spread the cost of the item or service.

However, you need to make sure that the problem is money (as in the example above). If that was not the problem and you launched into methods of payment, you may offend the customer, lose the custom and waste your own time! Do not raise your own objections and create problems for yourself!

6 Handling complaints From time to time there will be complaints about the limitations or unsuitability of the product you are offering the customer for his or her requirements. Again, listening is very important here, and possibly checking your facts again.

Very often, the issue of competitors and their products is raised at this stage. Again, acknowledge what the customer is saying. If he or she mentions something that one of your competitors offers, acknowledge the argument but do not 'knock' the competitor's product. Simply explain the features that your product has and why that would be a better choice for the customer's requirements.

7 Closing the sale This is the part of the sale that many people shy away from. Having invested time, knowledge and a lot of 'people' skills into the communication process, it is easy to lose everything at this stage.

Many people leave the customer without closing the sale. However, it can be done without twisting the customer's arm! You simply need to change your style of questioning from open questions that invite replies to closed questions that require 'yes' or 'no' answers.

Here again you reiterate the information the customer has given, allowing him or her to add extra information if you have missed anything, and then you justify your choice of product by relating it back to the needs he or she has mentioned and confirmed to you. If people were unwilling to enter into a financial exchange for the product you are offering, they would have stopped the conversation before this stage.

Having successfully concluded your sale, most organizations will expect this information to be recorded in some way. As well as providing a receipt when an exchange of money takes place, it is important for the organization to monitor how successful certain aspects of its operations are and which aspects are the most popular.

Each company will have different methods of recording or reporting its sales. Whether it is computerized or paper-based, the administration aspect of any business is very important. This will be dealt with in greater detail later in this section.

In addition, such recording and logging of information can be used statistically to analyse time management skills. Time management is a very important part of any working day and time has to be used effectively. It is pointless pursuing a sale when people have expressed no interest and have not participated in the information exchange. Recognizing these situations is very important, as well as recognizing opportunities, and although it is something that develops with experience, it is an issue of which to be aware.

Duties and responsibilities

Whenever we obtain employment, there will be specific roles and duties that we are expected to fulfil. Usually this is stipulated in the contract of employment or other documents that may accompany the contract. However, there are also responsibilities that are implied when we commence work.

Having obtained employment, most of us want to do our best and succeed within the new role we have been given. We have expectations of the company and vice versa. The company expects loyalty and honest work from us and we are happy to give that.

Those of us who work within customer service will also have roles and responsibilities to perform. Ensuring high levels of customer satisfaction is one of the most important tasks facing businesses today. Unless we can retain the

---

Task 6.14

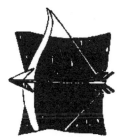

By completing this task it will lead to coverage of Element 6.2 PC 2, and Core Elements may include Communication Elements 3.1; 3.1; 3.3; and 3.4.

Work with someone in your group that you do not normally work with.

Pick one of the following situations about which you need information:

- *Tickets for a play*
- *A tour of a city*
- *Teaching someone to play tennis*
- *A tour of a historic property.*

Taking it in turns, one of you needs to be the customer and the other the sales person. Go through all the steps mentioned and advise your customer on the right choice of product for him/her in the circumstances.

loyalty of customers, we will not be able to retain their business and the long-term future of the company may be uncertain. Customer service and satisfaction is at the heart of retaining loyalty and it is everyone's responsibility. Again, individual companies will interpret this in different ways. However, it is important that we have an overview of procedures and practices.

Point of sales service deals with information, products and services that are paid for or dealt with there and then. For example, when a tourist buys a map at a tourist information centre and asks for local information, the assistant will probably be able to deal with the query immediately, or someone may want information about the cinema programme from the reception area of a leisure centre. Both these situations would give an immediate response to the enquiry, even if it does not always lead to an immediate sale of goods or services.

One of the functions of customer service is to give customers **assistance and information** that may eventually translate into a financial sale for the organization. A helpful attitude and showing care and attention to what we do are important; however, it is also essential that we have a good knowledge of the products and services that the organization offers.

As we have already mentioned, it is not always easy to obtain a working level of **product knowledge**, particularly when we first start a new job, but it is important that we take every opportunity to gain as much information as we can. Colleagues are usually helpful, but may be busy themselves, so again, timing of enquiries is important.

Many organizations offer a comprehensive **after-sales service** or products that complement each other. For example, a health and fitness programme designed to help people lose weight may be very popular, but how can people maintain the desired weight loss once it is achieved? Perhaps regular aerobics classes or swimming classes may help to maintain fitness as well as the weight loss. Other services offered by the organization should be reviewed and assessed as to where they interlink to increase customer satisfaction and the financial success of the organization.

So a working knowledge of all the products and services and how they complement each other is important.

When working on a cash desk or with payments, again individual company policies vary and you should be aware of the necessary procedures. However, whichever method of payment – cash, cheque or credit card – is accepted, some kind of receipt with the date and amount shown should be issued to the customer. This allows for statistical information to be produced and assessed and can be used to determine the most popular products and services. The production of a receipt also gives the customer certain rights and imposes responsibilities on the organization. The way in which refunds are carried out will, again, be at the organization's discretion, but facilities to do this should always be available and staff should be trained in the correct procedures.

The qualities of staff

In order to work well within any aspect of customer service there are qualities and traits that we should all possess.

- *Personality* – There are certain aspects of personality that all employers have a right to expect from their employees. Qualities such as honesty, reliability and loyalty, for example, are very important in every aspect of work. There are also those qualities that help particularly with customer service, such as enthusiasm, friendliness and being able to use initiative. Although many parts of customer service can be learned, qualities such as enthusiasm help the customer and help us to carry out the job successfully and to the best of our ability.
- *Knowledge* – is also very important. It falls under many headings, including knowledge of the industry and how it functions, of the organization and how it interprets the products and services it offers, of our own jobs and

where they 'fit in' and of the product we are offering to our customers. In addition to this specific information, we will also need to develop skills of judgement and assessment in different situations and we must remember to apply our standards consistently to try to give everyone the same standard of service.

The value of administration systems

Note: This information also links into Unit 5, Business Systems in Leisure and Tourism Industries.

What do we mean by the 'value' of administration systems? This is explained below.

Standardizing procedures is very important in any organization. It gives guidelines to staff as to how to deal with queries or problems so that everyone has a uniform practice. If this did not happen, I might devise one procedure for dealing with filing, for example, which may be totally different from the procedure you develop. If, for some reason, one of us was away and someone else needed information, they may spend a lot of time trying to retrieve that information, whereas if we had standardized methods, anyone who needed to access the information would be able to do so. So organizations need to operate in a uniform, recognized way so as to give a high standard of provision, no matter who is working for them.

Customers also benefit from good administration procedures. In this instance, they know that each time they visit an outlet, no matter who they deal with, they should expect the same level of service, with very few problems arising.

There are many different types of administration systems – as many systems as there are organizations. Records of transactions are a legal requirement, particularly for the Inland Revenue and VAT. If accurate and up-to-date paperwork is not kept, prosecution through the legal system can result. Records are very important to the

organization, and different companies will have their own standard records.

Generally there are computer-based systems or paper-based manual systems. We are going to review manual systems first.

Money transactions

Where cash is paid by customers for a service within a leisure or tourism facility, as well as being charged either to the customer or customer's account, there must be some form of book-keeping (a way of keeping financial records) to record these transactions.

The complexity of the system will vary, depending on the size of the organization and the amount of business that it has. Records need to be easily understood.

To give an overview of the business and all its different aspects, a summary book needs to be developed. It may go under many different titles, but basically it is used to record a breakdown of the total sales and their relevant methods of payment. Payments may also be subject to credit clearance, depending on the floor limit the company operates. This applies particularly to credit cards.

It is the cashier's main duty to receive payments – by cash, credit card, debit card, charge card and vouchers. Money may also arrive from other departments such as coffee bars, restaurants and vending machines. Details of the takings will be summarized on a departmental paying-in slip.

A receipt is required as proof of payment for all money received, whether from staff or customers – even if the payment is made by cheque.

Many organizations now use computerized systems, which save time and money. There are many different programmes available, and some organizations employ programmers to develop systems to the organization's specific requirements. If necessary, you will be instructed in their operation once you have joined the organization.

Other standard documentation includes booking forms, registering systems and ordering procedures.

Task 6.15

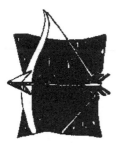

By completing this task it will lead to coverage of Element 6.2 PC 4, and Core Elements may include Communication Elements 3.1; 3.2; 3.3; 3.4; and I. T. Elements 3.1; 3.2; and 3.3.

Produce a standard booking form for either a leisure complex (you decide on the facilities it has) or a cinema multi-screen.
Try to think of all the information you may need. Whatever design you come up with, there are certain features you will need to include.

- *Facility (squash court, gym, etc.)*
- *Date*
- *Name*
- *Time*
- *Duration (how long for)*
- *Deposit*
- *Payment and method.*

For the cinema you may need different information, such as whether tickets have been issued or whether they are being collected and by whom.

Registering people into the facilities may also be important, not only for statistical purposes but also for safety reasons. For example, if a fire broke out, how would you know if the building was completely evacuated? Again, if customers are registering for accommodation, it is a legal requirement that they complete the registration form even if they are using an assumed name.

From these systems we are able to generate an awful lot of information about our customers.

Therefore, many companies make use of this to produce membership lists of names and addresses. These can then be used to send customers marketing information to encourage them to make more use of the facilities available to them.

Task 6.16

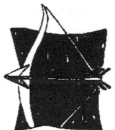

By completing this task it will lead to coverage of Element 6.2 PC 4, and Core Elements may include Communication Elements 3.1; 3.2; 3.3; and 3.4.

Visit a local leisure facility or tourism provider and try to establish the different documents and forms that they use.

Note: This may be slightly more difficult, as organizations can regard this as confidential information.

The unique nature of leisure and tourism

When we talk about leisure and tourism products we are referring to a unique experience.

Task 6.17

By completing this task it will lead to coverage of Elements 6.2 PC 5, and Core Elements may include Communication Elements 3.1; 3.2; and 3.4.

What are the differences between either a leisure or a tourism product and a CD/cassette?
Did you think this was rather silly? Did you find the task easy? What answers did you produce?

The point of this task is to illustrate that leisure and tourism are different from things that we usually spend our disposable income on.

- They are intangible products, which means that they are hard to characterize. You do not walk away with a product that you can use again (like you can with a CD/cassette) – it is an experience or a feeling that you may try to re-create, but you cannot put it into an album to look at again when you want to, like a photograph.
- There is an element of trust when buying a leisure/tourism product or service. This time the experience may not be as good as it was last time – or it may be better! There is an element of risk attached which we are going to pay for.
- Enjoyment is very hard to assess. What you enjoyed doing when you were younger, you may not necessarily enjoy now. What I enjoy doing may not interest you, so enjoyment of a pursuit is hard to quantify and put a price against.
- We have already explored customer expectations and satisfaction and have seen how these vary greatly between individuals.
- Service cannot be stored. A perception of the food provision in a hotel is only as good as the last meal. If an evening meal was wonderful, but breakfast was dreadful, we may not look forward to lunch because the last meal was bad. We carry such perceptions with us, and they do influence our decisions.

Portfolio builder

If you have completed these tasks, you should have:

- A list on the importance of sales skills to customer service staff
- Ideas on how to approach customers to offer help
- Ways to identify customer needs
- Experience in a 'selling' situation
- Knowledge of a booking form
- Examples of the documents used by the industry

▪ Assignment 6.2 ▪

By completing this assignment it will lead to coverage of Element 6.2 PCs 1, 2, 3, 4, 5 and 6, and Core Elements may include Communication Elements 3.1; 3.2; 3.3; 3.4; and I.T. Elements 3.1; 3.2; 3.3; and 3.4.

Scenario

Although sales and selling are a function of marketing, they are also an important part of the provision of customer service, and many of the sales and communication techniques are common to both selling and direct customer service.

Details

You should produce a brief report outlining the sales and selling aspect of customer service in one leisure or tourism organization. The report should:

- Explain the functions and objectives of selling
- Describe sales techniques
- Explain the duties, responsibilities and necessary qualities of sales staff in leisure and tourism organizations
- Explain the value of sales administration systems
- Explain what makes the selling of leisure/tourism products/services different.

Element 6.3 Analyse customer service quality for selected leisure and tourism organizations

Management of quality is an important part of the process of meeting internal and external customers' needs. It works alongside effective management and clear marketing strategies and needs a clear understanding of customers and the product or services that we provide.

In this Element we are going to:

- Review the assessment of the quality of customer service
- Appraise the customer service quality criteria
- Analyse the quality of customer service in leisure and tourism.
- Analyse the quality of customer service in related markets
- Suggest a basis for comparison.

Assessment of the quality of customer service

Some organizations believe that quality costs money, whereas in fact quality should be seen from the opposite viewpoint – that every quality failure costs money and that the cost is too high. From this perspective, quality becomes important within every task in the organization and also becomes everybody's responsibility.

When an organization works towards these standards and is committed to them, it is not only possible to achieve and maintain total quality, but customers are also educated to expect higher standards and becomes dissatisfied when they find that other organizations (i.e. the competitors) fail to meet your high standards.

Task 6.18

By completing this task it will lead to coverage of Element 6.3 PC 1, and Core Elements may include Communication Elements 3.1; 3.2; and 3.4.

Imagine yourself as a customer at a local sports centre or tourist information centre.
What criteria would you use to assess the level of customer care you have been given?
Make a list.
Does your list agree with the points I have made?

- *Reliability of service* – This is very important to all of us. If we make an enquiry or request information, we expect to be given reliable information so we can plan accordingly. We also expect to be treated with the same level of care and concern for our enquiry, no matter who actually deals with us. We need to assume that the quality of the personal contact will be the same, no matter how many enquiries we eventually have to make.
- *Availability* – We become very frustrated if the product or service is unavailable or if the person dealing with us is unable to give us the answers and is unwilling to find out. We actually want to be helped to make our purchase or reach our destination, and the availability of products and information is important.
- *Accessibility* – Closely linked to the availability of information is the accessibility of information. Imagine visiting a foreign country, unable to speak the language, and there is no information in English (if that is your first language) to help you. This is an example of how information may be inaccessible to you. If we take this a stage further, you may understand the language but may not be able to read it again excluding you from information. How would we deal with this in customer service? If someone looks as if they need help, ask them, but do not patronize them. They need help – they are not stupid. On a physical level, disabled people may be denied access to buildings because there are no facilities to help them. How would the customer service skills rate in this instance?
- *Health and safety* – Mentioning physical access to a building brings us to health and safety requirements. We have already reviewed the legislation in Unit 2 and seen the legal responsibilities, but do we have a right to expect a safe building in which to conduct our business? The answer is, of course, 'yes'. There are rights and obligations placed on organizations to ensure that the area is safe for staff and customers.
- *Staffing levels and service* – The number of customers that an organization has to deal with will vary considerably at different times of the day, let alone the year. It is always very

difficult to assess the usage of an organization by its customers; however, this has to be done. Generally we do not mind waiting our turn to be served (typically the British are very good at queuing!); however, there are limits. If customers are kept waiting for a long time, it is important that an apology is given. This will help to smooth any initial problems and hopefully allow you to attend to them more quickly rather than having to deal with complaints before getting to the main enquiry. Staffing levels are not your responsibility; however, the quality of service given is, and this should always be remembered.

- *Qualities of staff* – We have already dealt with this aspect in the previous Element; however, it is important that our appearance, behaviour, knowledge and judgement are the best they can be and that we supply answers in every situation to the best of our ability. We should also treat people as individuals, with individual needs and requirements.

- *Price and value for money* – However much we have to pay for goods and services, we like to feel that we have received value for money. What determines value for money is an individual assessment – what appears good value to me may not do so to you and vice versa. For example, do you like horror films? Do they really frighten you? Is this good fun? I do not like horror films and would not go to see one – so what is good value in this instance to you is not to me.

  However, customer service is one aspect of value for money. Someone who is pleasant, well informed and able to communicate as well as listen adds to the perceived value of the experience and hopefully does lead to value for money experiences.

- *Enjoyment of the experience* – This finally brings us to enjoyment of the experience. Who can place a value on this? Again, if we are looking at perceptions and placing enjoyment values against them, it is a totally individual experience.

  We have found that people are individuals and should be treated as such. However, a pleasant manner, with knowledge of the subject and a tidy appearance, can help in the realms of customer service and care.

Appraisal of the customer service quality criteria

We have already mentioned two different approaches to quality. The first, where quality is seen as being expensive, is called the Average Quality Level (or AQL). The second approach is where we try to achieve Total Quality Management (or TQM).

AQL is based on the idea that the market accepts that there are problems with the product and that these are within reasonable limits. In this instance, quality is monitored and managed at selected stages, from the start to the end of the products, and complaints are used to identify the sources of problems which may have caused defects. Sudden drops in quality should be investigated immediately to deal with any new or serious problem. However, two major problems have been identified: the impact of competition and the levels of customer satisfaction, which will vary greatly.

- *The impact of competition* – Quality may not be a problem until a competitor produces a reasonably priced product which exceeds the quality of existing products. As a result, the issue of quality becomes very important, and improvements to all existing products based on the idea of acceptable levels of quality can become difficult to introduce.
- *Levels of customer satisfaction* – When comparing approaches, one of the first things we realize is that quality does not cost the company, but failure does. When applying an AQL policy, there may be considerations that you have no information about.

  First, there is no way of knowing when dissatisfaction exists in the market about your product. A low level of quality relies on this being acceptable where there is no alternative to your product.

  Secondly, if quality is not that important, the cost of not getting the product right all the time is built into the AQL processes and systems.

TQM depends on various factors and will be influenced by the organization's management. It reflects the attitudes that:

- Everyone within the organization must be involved in the quality process
- Every detail is important
- Once the process has started, it cannot be stopped
- Quality must be maintained continuously and not just because standards need to be maintained.

So when management is developing a TQM process, it needs to cover the following:

- Staff training and development which shows a commitment to quality systems
- A clear understanding of the existing levels of quality in certain areas
- Responsibility for the problems, along with a willingness to improve and change situations
- Everyone playing their part to help in the responsibilities of TQM.

What does all this mean to customer service? To achieve TQM, we need to have clear goals as to the needs of our customers. Improvements in quality mean increasing benefits for the customer and giving higher levels of customer satisfaction. So perhaps we should ask our customers not only what they like about our product, but also how we could improve what we offer. This could be done through a questionnaire.

Task 6.19

By completing this task it will lead to coverage of Element 6.3 PC 2, and Core Elements may include Communication Elements 3.1; 3.2; 3.4; and I.T. Elements 3.1; 3.2; 3.3.

Design a questionnaire to find out about customer likes and dislikes on a certain issue within your school/college.

Try out the questionnaire either within your group or your year.

Did the questionnaire produce the answers you expected? If not, why not?

Once this type of policy has been introduced, there needs to be constant monitoring to ensure:

- *Quality* – Is the level of provision to the agreed standard?
- *Consistency* – Is the product always of at least that standard?
- *Timing* – Is the product always on time, at the right time, every time?
- *Satisfaction* – Does the product satisfy the customer's requirements every time?

We have now looked at the theory of TQM. Many organizations are now moving to adopt this policy and are introducing the idea in many ways. Often customers and their ideas are included within policy decisions.

Quality is assessed in many organizations through a process known as 'benchmarking'. This process sets standards of quality and service, and the organization's actual provision and performance are assessed against the aims.

Therefore, customer perceptions and expectations about our company and its provision of service are very important. Customer's ideas about what they want may vary greatly from what we think they want. Also, we may think that we are giving a certain standard or level of service or product, but our ideas may be very different from what the customers perceive they are getting.

Customers may not limit their spending power to our organization alone. They are likely to be aware of what the competition is offering and compare our provision with theirs. If our organization is found lacking, then the customer is likely to go to the competition. So involving customers and their ideas in this process is important.

The Quality of customer service in leisure and tourism organizations

Before we can analyse the standards of customer service that exist within our industry, it is important to find out what customers expect from us and what they would find acceptable.

Levels and standards are going to vary considerably because we all have ideas about what we consider to be good levels of service. So we need to obtain an overview of what people would expect.

We have already mentioned that questionnaires are useful as a means of generating information, but unless you go and ask people and help them to complete the questions, the chances are that not many people would volunteer information. Nevertheless, the exercise can be very useful in establishing our customers' perceptions of us and our product.

Task 6.20

By completing this task it will lead to coverage of Element 6.3 PC 3, and Core Elements may include Communication Element 3.1.

Can you find or think of any other ways of collecting information from customers?
How successful are they?

Having established what customers' perceptions of the organization are, we now need to find out how we rate against those ideas. We need to compare perceptions with reality! This can be a very productive process and can highlight areas within the organization that need attention.

What criteria should the organization be marked against as far as customer service is concerned? Obviously this is going to need to cover the areas that make up the customer service we offer.

- We need to look at how we *care for our customers'* whether they are internal or external to the organization. Do we treat customers with the same level of care even if we know that they are staff? What standards are we aiming for and do we achieve them? Are we polite, and do we always try to achieve a high standard?

- Do we actually manage to *meet our customers' needs*? Are we sure what those needs are? Is everyone the same? Should we treat them all the same or on an individual basis? How should we give information to them – should we vary the information?

- What is *customer satisfaction* for our customers? Do our customers 'put up' with the same service as everyone else, and should they have to? How do we know if our customers are satisfied – do we just assume they are until a problem arises?

- Do we *meet our customers' expectations*? Do the facilities look wonderful, but actually provide very little? Is the image good, but the product found to be lacking? Are we misleading our customers or underselling ourselves?

- Finally, *is the environment safe and secure* for our customers and their possessions? Are the customers free from threat when using the facilities we provide?

Customer service in related markets

Having established the type of service that we give our customers and what they think of it, we then need to establish what our competitors are producing to make sure that we are producing better. This does not necessarily mean copying ideas, but certainly improving our own service if this is necessary.

Task 6.21

By completing this task it will lead to coverage of Element 6.3 PC 4, and Core Elements may include Communication Elements 3.1; 3.2; and 3.4.

What do we mean by 'related markets'? Make a list of examples.

The term 'related markets' refers to the vast array of competitors that we may have within a given market. For example, within arts and entertainment there is a wide range of provision, from theatres to bingo halls and cinemas to art galleries. All have their own distinct product, but hopefully the customer service levels will be of a similar standard.

In the above example we have given a range of provision. Within whichever field we are operating, there will be direct competitors providing the same products as us. What do they do differently? Which aspects are we better at than they are? Could we learn anything from them?

As well as direct competitors, there are also other organizations in the same business as ourselves. They may be part of a larger organization and may be able to offer a slightly different product. Can we benefit from any of their ideas?

There may also be examples of organizations expanding into new areas for them but overlapping into our market. For example, larger hotels are now offering sports facilities to their guests as well as running a separate membership scheme for the facilities. One area of operation is supplementing and servicing another. Is this going to affect our business? Are we big enough to diversify?

Comparison of provision

Whatever our research uncovers, there will be areas of customer service that we provide particularly well and there will be areas that our competitors are good at. We need to look objectively at our own service, highlighting what we do well, as well as the areas that could be improved. We need to be honest – not too hard but not too lenient with our provision.

We then need to review the service our competitors give to the customer. Again, this needs to be objective. Perhaps they have higher funding levels for their customer service – do they make the most of their opportunities?

Recommendations should be based on the provision given by both organizations, with an assessment of the good practices and then suggestions as to how and where improvements could be made.

Conclusions

In this Element we have looked at the issue of quality and how to improve the quality of service we give to our customers. It is important that we know who our customers are, acknowledge their expectations and try to provide a service that fulfils those expectations.

Portfolio builder

If you have completed these tasks you should have:

- A list of criteria for assessing customer care
- A questionnaire and completed questionnaires about likes and dislikes
- Knowledge of different ways of collecting information
- A lot of examples of 'related markets'.

• Assignment 6.3 •

By completing this assignment it will lead to coverage of Element 6.3 PCs 1, 2, 3, 4, 5, 6, and Core Elements may include Communication Elements 3.1; 3.2; 3.3; 3.4; and I.T. Elements 3.1; 3.2; 3.3; and 3.4.

Scenario

This Element aims to introduce students to a method of assessing customer service quality. The theory is aimed at assisting an understanding of how to analyse the quality of customer service so that they can undertake the analysis themselves.

Details

1 You need to produce a presentation based on an analysis of customer service in a leisure or tourism organization.

2 The analysis should examine in detail the customer service quality criteria as well as the quality of service itself.

3 This should then be compared with our analysis based on an evaluation of the quality of customer service in related markets.

4 Recommendations for improvements to the customer service in the original organization should be made.

5 Notes should be produced for marking purposes.

Note: If you are involved in work placement during your course, this may provide a useful source of information. Also, any part-time work you may have within the industry may be useful for research purposes.

Element 6.4 Deliver and evaluate customer service in leisure and tourism organizations

This final Element in customer service is highly practical in nature. Obviously the main areas will be reiterated, but the main assessment is through application. Although students would benefit from actual situations in the industry, this is not always possible, so a certain amount of 'staging' and 'role-play' may also have to take place.

In this Element we are going to summarize the main points under specific headings, so that you will be aware of the areas you need to include. Much more detailed coverage is given in the previous Elements.

Customers

- Internal
- External
- Different age groups
- Different cultural backgrounds
- Groups or individuals with specific needs

Customer service situations

- Satisfied customers
- Dissatisfied customers
- Customers needing information
- Customers needing help with problems
- Customers needing sales help
- Customers needing advice.

Objectives of evaluation

- Customer satisfaction
- Repeat business
- Competitive advantage
- Attracting new customers.

Customer service quality criteria

- Reliability of service, health and safety
- Accessibility
- Availability
- Consistency
- Pricing
- Staffing levels
- Qualities of staff
- Value for money
- Enjoyment of the experience
- Provision for individual needs.

Delivery of customer service

- Prioritize customers' needs
- Use appropriate communication methods (with individuals or groups, remembering image, verbal and non-verbal techniques, etc.)
- Record necessary customer information (customer accounts, booking forms, membership lists, order processing, ticket issue).

▪ Assignment 6.4 ▪

By completing this assignment it will lead to coverage of Element 6.4 PCs 1, 2, 3, 4, 5 and 6, and Core Elements may include Communication Elements 3.1; 3.2; 3.3; 3.4; and I.T. Elements 3.1; 3.2; 3.3; and 3.4.

Scenario

Customer service is practical by nature. This assignment is designed to assess students within the practical situation, backed by notes and either witness statements or recordings. In addition to the role-play, a presentation should be given.

Details

1 EITHER
   (a) If you are already working within a customer service situation, ask a supervisor (after this has been agreed with your tutor) to watch you deal with three different situations selected from the list 'Customer service situations'.

   OR

   (b) Your tutor will have set up a 'role-play' situation for you. You will be dealing with three different customers from the 'Customer service situations' list earlier in the Element.

2 You should cover all the categories listed in 'Delivery of customer service'.

3 EITHER
   (a) Ask your supervisor to produce a witness statement of the situation and how you dealt with it and the outcome

   OR

   (b) Your tutor will produce a witness statement, stating how you dealt with the situation and the outcome, or possibly the interview will be recorded.

4 Give a presentation, which should:
   • Describe the evaluation's, objectives and the relevant customer service quality criteria for the three given customer service situations you have dealt with
   • Evaluate your own performance in the delivery of customer service
   • Compare your evaluation with that of your Supervisor or Tutor
   • Make recommendations as to where improvements could be made.

HEALTH, SAFETY AND SECURITY IN LEISURE AND TOURISM

Introduction

Health, safety and security issues are of vital importance to any organization. The provision of a healthy, safe, secure environment must be a high priority for any establishment. This is not only important for employees but also for clients.

The standards of health and safety across most organizations today is excellent. However, this has not always been the case, as throughout history workers have battled to improve the health and safety of their working environment e.g. Coalminers, Millworkers.

The diverse nature of leisure and tourism organizations means that different industries have their own specific requirements in terms of health and safety. These may include the following:

- *Arts and entertainment centres* – theatres, concert halls, galleries, arts centres, museums, bingo halls, race tracks, home-based entertainment and theme parks
- *Sports and physical activities* – sports centres, leisure centres, running tracks, sports stadia, gymnasia, fitness centres and swimming pools
- *Outdoor activities* – land-based, water-based, air-based and activity centres
- *Heritage centres* – historic sites, working and industrial museums and attractions
- *Play* – playing fields, playgrounds and play schemes

- *Catering and accommodation services* – food and drink services in leisure and recreation facilities, meeting rooms, hotel accommodation
- *Travel services* – airlines, rail, car hire companies and shipping
- *Tourism services* – national and regional tourist boards, tourist information centres, tourist attractions, guiding services, currency exchange, accommodation, catering and transport.

As has been shown by the range of facilities above, health, safety and security is an issue of importance to private, public and voluntary sectors.
It is an issue of consideration when any decision is taken within the leisure and tourism industry.

Element 7.1 Investigate health, safety and security in leisure and tourism

In this Element the following performance criteria will be covered:

1 Explain the importance of maintaining health, safety and security in leisure and tourism.

2 Explain how health, safety and security is ensured in leisure and tourism organizations.

3 Explain the purpose of laws and regulations (health, safety and security).

4 Describe appropriate sources of information about the key laws and regulations on health, safety and security.

5 Explain the relevance of the key laws and regulations on health, safety and security to different leisure and tourism organizations.

6 Prepare an induction booklet on health, safety and security in a selected leisure and tourism facility.

The importance of maintaining health, safety and security in leisure and tourism

Health, safety and security is of crucial importance to every leisure and tourism organization. Failure to respond to these issues can be extremely serious, and could lead to injuries and even the death of an employee or a client. Failure to provide a healthy, safe and secure environment can lead to prosecution and, in some cases, the organization being closed down.

All organizations should have a clear health, safety and security policy and clear guidelines for its implementation. Health, safety and security measures adopted by an organization will have an effect on the:

- Facility/organization itself
- Staff
- Customers
- Public relations
- Environment.

Health, safety and security issues should be central to the management of any organization's operations and the activities undertaken within the organization. A health, safety and security policy should be formulated and adopted. This will enable the organization to identify potentially hazardous situations before they cause injury to either staff or customers. This is particularly important with equipment which may have been damaged and, as a result, may pose a hazard. By undertaking routine regular health and safety

inspections of equipment an early warning of the problems arising will be highlighted and action can be taken.

Health, safety and security costs will need to be incorporated with the budgetary provision for the organization. Finance will be needed to meet the costs of:

- Staff induction/training
- Regular maintenance/inspections/remedial action
- Specialist equipment (e.g. clothing, etc.)
- Additional recruitment of staff.

Under the Health and Safety At Work Act 1974 (HASAWA), all employers and employees have a duty to act in a responsible manner. Staff must make sure that they take reasonable care to avoid injury both to themselves and to others by their work practices. They must co-operate with their employers to ensure that a safe environment is maintained for both staff and customers alike. Employers have a duty under this Act to provide equipment and premises which are not a risk to health. They are also required to provide training for all staff in issues involving health and safety.

All leisure and tourism organizations have a duty to provide a safe and secure environment for all those using their facilities, whether they are paying or non-paying clients. Management/employers have a duty to ensure that customers/visitors to their facility are not exposed to unnecessary risks and that measures are put in place to investigate and put right any hazardous situations which may arise.

Health, safety and security should take into consideration the needs of all users/customers of the facility. This may include people with special needs, for example, disabled people, young children and the elderly. Organizations should ensure that the safety of these groups are considered when, for example, emergency evacuation procedures are being formulated. The safety of the customer should be a high priority in any organization. Failure to ensure this could lead to injuries and prosecution of the organization concerned.

A serious breach of health, safety or security in a leisure or tourism organization/facility can have a serious effect on both the organization's image and visitor numbers. In this modern world of almost instant news reporting, a fatality at a particular tourist attraction or a disaster on a passenger ship will receive wide media coverage. It can take a considerable amount of time for organizations who have experienced these problems to regain customer confidence.

Green issues are becoming increasingly important within both the political agenda and the social conscience of the population. Leisure and tourism organizations should ensure that their operations are not causing problems within the local population (for example, noise pollution, traffic congestion/pollution, litter or disposal of toxic substances, etc.). Environmental issues are being given increasing importance when large-scale developments are being planned. It may be necessary for such organizations to undertake an environmental impact assessment (EIA) to demonstrate that they have investigated any potential environmental problems that their development may cause and propose measures that could be undertaken to overcome these problems.

Environmental Impact Assessment
This is an investigation undertaken by an organization to determine what effect its activity/development would have on the local environment.

Task 7.1

PC 1 – Core Skills
Communication 8.2

For a named leisure and tourism facility explain why maintaining health, safety and security is important. Detail operational practices which are undertaken to ensure that health, safety and security policies are put into operation in this facility.

How health, safety and security is ensured in leisure and tourism organizations

Health, safety and security is ensured in leisure and tourism organizations using both obligatory and voluntary measures.

Obligatory measures

There is a wide variety of health and safety legislation which imposes certain duties on leisure and tourism organizations. One of the main pieces of legislation is the HASAWA 1974.

In 1970 Barbara Castle, a member of the Labour Government at the time, asked Lord Robens to chair a commission which looked into safety at work. This committee reported that the law was too complex and technical and that its enforcement was virtually impossible. It concentrated too much on the workplace itself and paid little or no regard to visitors or the workforce. The recommendations which this commission put forward formed the basis of the HASAWA 1974.

There are four basic principles or objectives of the Act:

1 To maintain and improve standards of health, safety and welfare of people at work.
2 To protect persons other than persons at work.
3 To control the storage and use of explosive, highly flammable or otherwise dangerous substances.
4 To control the emission into the atmosphere of noxious or offensive substances from the premises.

Who is covered by the Act?

All 'persons at work', whether they are employers, employees or the self-employed. Many people who were not covered by previous legislation were included in this Act. For example, people employed in education, medicine, leisure and tourism industries and some parts of the transport industry were now protected by the Act.

Figure 7.1 Not only the water rises high

The HASAWA 1974 lays out general guidelines as to the duties of employer and employees.

Employers are required to display a poster (or distribute equivalent leaflets) entitled 'Health and Safety Law: What you should know' (available from HMSO) which gives information on the general requirements, duties, etc. under health and safety law. Contact details of the enforcing authority for the premises, the Health and Safety Executive (HSE) and the Employment Medical Advisory Service (EMAS) must be included.

Duties of employers

It is the duty of every employer to ensure, so far as is reasonably practicable, the health, safety and welfare at work of all employees. This duty is extended to non-employees (for example, contractors, members of the public, etc.) who are on the premises and who may be affected by the work being carried on.

In practical terms, this requires the employer to have regard for the following:

- The provision and maintenance of planned systems of work that are safe and without risk to health
- Arrangements for ensuring the safe use, handling, storage and transport of articles and substances which are inherently or potentially dangerous
- The provision of adequate information and training for all staff in matters relating to health and safety
- The maintenance of the workplace in a safe and risk-free condition and the provision of safe means of entrance and exit from the workplace

- The provision and maintenance of a safe and healthy working environment with adequate welfare facilities and arrangements

Duties of employees

Employees have a duty:

- To take reasonable care for the health and safety of themselves and other persons who may be affected by their acts or omissions at work
- To comply with all duties and co-operate with employers to ensure that the requirements of the HASAWA 1974 are performed
- Not to intentionally or recklessly interfere with or misuse anything provided in the interests of health, safety or welfare.

Powers of inspectors

Under the HASAWA 1974, inspectors who are appointed by the HSE or any other authority (for example, a local authority or a fire authority) have powers to:

- Enter premises at any reasonable time to enforce the conditions of the Act
- Be accompanied by a police or authorized officer and take any equipment they may need. They may also need to take photographs, measurements or recordings during their investigations
- Act and require any person to give assistance within their responsibility to allow the inspector to carry out necessary work.

Inspectors must produce their warrant of authority if requested to do so, and are required to give employers/employees information to keep them informed about issues likely to affect their health, safety and welfare.

Enforcement of the HASAWA 1974

If an inspector discovers a contravention of the HASAWA 1974 he or she can:

- Issue a prohibition (preventing use) notice, if there is a likely risk of serious personal injury, to stop the activity from taking place with resultant risk of injury, etc. until the necessary work or action specified in the notice has been

taken. This notice can be served on the person undertaking the activity or on a person in charge of it at the time the notice is served

- Issue an improvement notice, if there is a contravention of any of the relevant statutory provisions, to remedy the fault within the period stated in the notice, which must be at least 21 days
- prosecute any person contravening a relevant statutory provision instead of or in addition to sending a notice.

Contravention of health and safety legislation can lead to prosecution in a magistrate's court (or a sheriff's court in Scotland), or, in more serious cases, an indictment in a Crown court in England and Wales or a sheriff's court in Scotland.

There have been numerous prosecutions under the HASAWA 1974 in both leisure and tourism organizations. Swimming pools and the drowning of children have been the subject of many of these prosecutions, including *Portsmouth City Council v Holiday Inns* 1983. This was a civil suit for negligence when a child drowned. The alleged safety defects included:

- the cloudiness of the water made it very difficult to see the bottom of the pool
- Constant pool supervision was not provided
- Lifeguards were unable to see the whole of the pool
- The oxygen cylinder on the resuscitation equipment was almost empty.

Administration of the HASAWA 1974

- *The Health and Safety Commission (HSC)* – This has eight or nine members who are representatives of the CBI (Confederation of British Industry), the TUC (Trade Union Congress), local authorities, employers and employees. It is responsible for developing policies in the field of health and safety.
- *The Health and Safety Executive (HSE)* – this is a separate body, appointed by the Commission, which works in accordance with directions and guidance given by the HSC. The HSE provides an advisory service to industry and enforces

legal requirements where necessary. It also appoints HM Inspectors.

- *Employment Medical Advisory Service (EMAS)* – Acts as a medical branch of the HSC, giving advice to the Commission and to the various inspectorates.
- *Local authorities* – Under the Commission's guidance, local authorities are responsible for enforcing legislation in some areas of employment, including many areas covered by health and safety legislation. In general, these are 'non-industrial activities' and give local authorities the right to inspect and enforce the HASAWA 1974 with private commercial operators (for example, health clubs, etc.).

Within the workplace health and safety can be further ensured by safety committees being set up and safety representatives appointed. In this way, potential or existing hazards can be highlighted and action taken. Employees thus feel that problems which they may be experiencing are being given consideration and appropriate action taken. This will lead to a more secure and happier workforce.

Task 7.2

PC 2 and 3 Core Skills Communication 3.2; 3.3; 3.4

1 For a named facility produce a poster which summarizes in visual form the main points of the HASAWA 1974 as they relate to this particular workplace.

2 Explain why a poster of this nature–sited, for example, in a staff room–is of benefit to the health and safety procedures within the facility.

New European (EU) directives on health and safety

At the beginning of 1993 six sets of health and safety at work regulations came into force which apply to almost all kinds of work activities,

including leisure and tourism organizations. Like existing health and safety laws, they place duties on employers to protect:

- Employees
- Other people, e.g. members of the public who may be affected by the organization's work.

These UK regulations are needed to implement six European Union directives on health and safety at work. They form part of a modernization of many outdated laws and are a step on the road towards a Single European Market. Most of the duties in the regulations are not new, but make existing regulations clearer and easier to interpret.

The new regulations cover:

- Health and safety management
- Work equipment safety
- Manual handling of loads
- Workplace conditions
- Personal protective equipment
- Display screen equipment.

Health and safety management

The Management of Health and Safety at Work Regulations 1992 set out duties which apply to almost all work activities in the UK. These regulations encourage a more planned, systematic approach to health and safety management and make more specific the requirements laid down by the HASAWA 1974. These regulations require employers to assess the risks to the health and safety of employees and all those affected by activities within the workplace (e.g. clients, observers, etc.). Employers who have five or more employees are required to produce a risk assessment on the basis of their findings. It is a well known fact that in the majority of cases accidents do not just happen, but are frequently caused by various external factors. The aim of a risk assessment is to try to identify problem areas which, if left undetected with no action taken, could eventually lead to an accident.

Case study

A risk assessment was undertaken at Shelden's Leisure Centre. The door to the communal changing room within the swimming complex was examined, as there had been a number of minor accidents when lines of schoolchildren were entering and leaving the room. Although there was already a retarding mechanism fitted to the door which slowed down the closing process, it was decided that a 'finger safe' mechanism should be fitted to the door so that if any child put its finger inadvertently into the hinge, the finger would be carried clear of the hinge and thus no injury would be sustained.

Once an assessment has been undertaken it is the employer's/organization's responsibility to implement the measures highlighted in the risk assessment and to ensure that suitably qualified and experienced people are employed to interpret the risk assessment in measures and action.

Within these regulations employers are required to set up emergency procedures. These may cover such things as:

- Fire
- Accidents
- Illness
- Physical attack
- Bomb threats
- Breakdown of equipment.

The scale and extent of emergency procedures in an organization will depend on the size, scale, nature of the organization and the number of visitors, etc. it deals with on both routine occasions and during special events, where the capacity of the facility is at its maximum.

Emergency procedures should be practiced regularly by staff, as the best laid plans on paper can experience problems when they are actually put into operation. Staff should be so well briefed in emergency procedures that they slip into action with a minimum of fuss and time loss so that the situation can be dealt with both efficiently and effectively. Thus it is that as part of this Act employers are responsible for ensuring that their employees are provided with information on health and safety and that temporary workers are provided with health and safety information to meet their particular needs. Under this Act employers are further required to provide adequate training for their employees in health and safety. Many organizations have a member of staff who has as part of his or her duties the responsibility for the health and safety training of staff.

Some organizations require all their employees to take a health and safety course. Much of this training will be 'in-house' (i.e. under taken by the organization itself). However, when specialist training is required, for example, in electrical equipment, etc., staff will normally be sent to a specialist training centre.

Some organizations require all their employees to take regular written tests on health and safety within the organization to ensure that the training they have been given has been assimilated and understood.

Task 7.3

PC 2 Core Skills
Communication 3.1; 3.2; 3.4

For a selected leisure and tourism organization identify two different members of staff and report on the health and safety training they received as part of their job.

Work equipment safety

The Provision and Use of the Work Equipment Regulations (1984) have been designed to draw together all the legislation concerning work equipment. The regulations:

- Place general duties on employers
- List minimum requirements for work equipment to deal with selected hazards whatever the industry.

What is included in work equipment?

This includes everything from a simple screwdriver to large machines and plant systems: for example, a boiler room complex or a leisure centre or concert hall. Under these regulations employers are required to:

- Ensure that all equipment is suitable for its intended use
- Take into account the working conditions and hazards in the workplace when selecting equipment
- Make sure that all equipment is properly maintained
- Give adequate instruction, information and training
- Make sure that all equipment provided conforms with the EU product safety directions.

Specific requirements within these regulations cover, for example:

- Guards on specific equipment (e.g. with blades, etc.)
- Stability of equipment of scaffolding, towers, ladders, etc., in a theatre
- Use of warnings
- Use of markings.

Safety signs

The European Community has produced statutory regulations which require the standardization of safety signs throughout member states (Safety Signs Regulations 1980). All new safety signs must comply with and fall into four categories:

1 *Prohibition* – things which, for safety reasons, *must not* be done (e.g. No Smoking). A red circle with a red diagonal bar across it.

2 *Warning* – indicates a particular hazard (e.g. Danger – Wet Floor). A yellow triangle with appropriate picture.

3 *Mandatory* – something which, for safety reasons, *must* be done (e.g. Fasten Your Seat Belt). A blue disc with a white pictogram.

4 *Conditions of safety* – indicates the location of fire exits, first aid equipment, etc. A green square or rectangle with a white pictogram or legend on it.

Hazardous substances

The ever increasing use of chemicals in the workplace can pose a threat to health unless they are properly used in the full knowledge of their hazards. Substances should be detailed, marked and labelled.

Manual handling of loads

More days are lost at work through back problems and injuries caused by incorrect handling of loads than through any other injuries. Therefore it is of vital importance to ensure that employees involved in handling loads should take the utmost care and try to overcome this persistent problem. The Manual Handling Operation Regulations came into effect in 1993 and apply to any manual handling operations which may cause injury within the workplace.

Table 7.1

Characteristic properties of the substance	Classification and indication of general nature of risks	Symbol
A substance which, if inhaled or ingested or penetrates the skin, may involve serious or chronic health risks and even death	Toxic	
A substance which, if inhaled or ingested or penetrates the skin, may involve limited health risks	Harmful	
A substance which may, on contact with living tissues, destroy them	Corrosive	
A non-corrosive substance which, through immediate prolonged or repeated contact with the skin or mucous membrane, can cause inflammation	Irritant	
A substance which may become hot and catch fire in contact with air, or is gaseous and will ignite where there is any source of ignition	Highly Flammable	

Symbolic colours: Black on orange background.

Employers should:

- Avoid hazardous manual handling operations where reasonably practicable
- Adequately assess any hazardous operations which cannot be avoided
- Reduce the risk of injury so far as is reasonably practicable.

Workplace conditions

The Workplace (Health, Safety and Welfare) Regulations 1992 replace a large number of outdated laws (for example, the Offices, Shops and Railways Premises Act 1963), and as a result have made the whole area of workplace safety much more easily understood.

The regulations set general requirements in four broad areas:

1 The working environment (e.g. temperature, lighting, ventilation, etc.).
2 Safety (e.g. use of safety materials indoors, safety devices, safe passage of pedestrians).
3 Facilities (e.g. toilets, changing rooms, drinking water, etc.).
4 Housekeeping (e.g. maintenance, cleanliness, etc. of the workplace).

Personal protective equipment (PPE)

Under the Personal Protective Equipment at Work (PPE) Regulations 1992 all types of personal protective equipment (PPE) from gloves and goggles to lifejackets, safety harnesses and breathing apparatus are covered. Employers must supply this equipment free of charge to their employees.

These regulations require employers to:

- Provide PPE where risks to health and safety cannot be controlled adequately by other means
- Ensure that the PPE provided is suitable for the risk involved
- Maintain the PPE to acceptable standards and provide suitable storage accommodation
- Ensure that the PPE provided is used properly
- Ensure that employees are given appropriate training, information and instruction in the use, etc. of the PPE provided.

In addition to the employer's duties, employees have a duty to make proper use of the PPE supplied to them and to report any losses or defects immediately.

These regulations are focused more towards protection against physical risks than health risks. The Control of Substances Hazardous to Health Regulations 1988 (COSHH) cover these in more detail.

Display screen equipment

Under these regulations, which fall under the Personal Protective Equipment at Work Regulations 1992, people who habitually use display screen equipment as a significant part of their normal work will be protected against the risks associated with such work. These include physical, musculoskeletal problems, eye fatigue and mental stress. The protection offered by the regulations includes:

- An assessment and reduction of risks associated with work, workstations and the immediate environment around it. Any risks highlighted in this assessment must be reduced. So far as is reasonably practicable, to the lowest level possible
- Minimum workstation requirements – these include consideration of the actual equipment (keyboard, display screen, etc.), work environment and computer/user interface
- The planning of display screen equipment work so that users have regular breaks or changes of activity
- An entitlement for users to request and be provided with eye and eyesight tests. Corrective appliances (e.g. spectacles, etc). must be provided if they are found to be necessary for the display screen work (at the expense of the employer)
- Providing information and training for display screen equipment users.

Noise at Work Regulations 1989

Noise can be a problem in certain organizations within the leisure and tourism industry – for example, very loud discos, nightclubs, etc., or fun pools/swimming pools full of boisterous, noisy bathers. These regulations are extremely complex, and define levels of noise above which measures to counteract the noise should be taken (for example, the wearing of ear defenders). For safety reasons, in facilities where noise levels become very high an alternative method of communication with the public should be available if the PA system cannot be heard.

Data Protection Act 1984

Since May 1986 all organizations which hold personal data about individuals on automated systems have been required to register with the Data Protection Register and to comply with the Data Protection Act. In general, this means that information systems stored on computer fall within the Act, while manual systems do not. Indeed, because of this, some organizations choose to hold certain information in manual systems so that they do not come under the Act.

The Act encompasses eight principles which organizations should comply with and set a standard of good practice for all to work towards. Within the Act, individuals who have data stored on them have a range of rights in civil law, including:

- Rights of access to data
- Rights to compensation for unauthorized disclosure, loss or destruction of data
- Rights to compensation for inaccuracy
- Rights to apply to have any inaccuracies in the data rectified and, in certain circumstances, rights to have this information erased.

In the past, individuals suffered because of companies holding information to which they did not have access and which was inaccurate. There was often very little that individuals could do to rectify this situation, even though it may seriously affect their lives (for example, obtaining a mortgage, credit card, etc.). This new law addresses this type of problem.

Electricity at Work Regulations 1989

These extend previous legislation which focused on factories and building sites to cover all places of work, including leisure and tourism facilities. Managers of these organizations have to follow a precise programme of inspection/action to reduce the risks from electrical equipment, plant, etc. Inherent in this is specialized and up-to-date staff training and regular inspection of equipment, etc. to act as an early warning system for faults, and thus reduce the risk of an accident occurring.

The Control of Substances Hazardous to Health Regulations 1988 (COSHH)

These regulations supplement the employers' duties, as laid down by the HASAWA 1974, concerning the use of harmful substances. Under these regulations employers must assess the likely exposure to all hazardous substances and initiate control measures and monitoring procedures as

appropriate. The assessment, control and monitoring requirements must be carried out for every hazardous substance identified in the workplace. These cover any natural or artificial substance, whether solid, liquid or in the form of a gas or vapour. These substances may be classified as toxic, very toxic, harmful, irritant or corrosive.

There are many different chemicals used in leisure and tourism facilities. They are commonly used to:

- Treat swimming pool water
- Control vermin
- Mark pitches
- Clean and disinfect.

Task 7.4

PC 1, 2, 5 Core Skills Communications 3.1; 3.2; 3.4

Identify how the health and safety of bathers in a swimming pool is ensured. Highlight how chemicals are used within this process and how the COSHH Regulations are implemented.

The Reporting of Injuries, Diseases and Dangerous Occurrences Regulations (RIDDOR) 1985

These regulations require the person in control of the premises to notify the appropriate enforcing authority (local authority or HSE) in the event of a fatality, major injury or dangerous occurrence arising out of or in connection with work.

Reporting of accidents and dangerous occurrences

Fatal accidents, major injury, accidents and dangerous occurrences must be reported immediately by the quickest practicable means (normally the telephone) to the relevant enforcing authority. Following the initial notification, a written report on Form F2508 must be sent to the enforcing authority within seven days of the accident or dangerous occurrence.

Accidents causing more than three days' incapacity for work must also be reported using Form F2508 and sent to the enforcing authority within seven days of the accident. No immediate telephone notification is required.

Health and Safety (First Aid) Regulations 1981

The HASAWA 1974 places a duty on the employer to ensure, so far as is reasonably practicable, the health, safety and welfare at work of all employees. This duty obviously extends to the provision of first aid. This provision is specifically dealt with in the Health and Safety (First Aid) Regulations 1981. These regulations lay down the following three requirements:

1 The duty of the employer to provide first aid.
2 The duty of the employer to inform the employees of the arrangements made in connection with first aid.
3 The duty of a self-employed person to provide first aid equipment.

All accidents should be reported using an Accident Report Form. The following details should be noted:

- Name of injured person
- Address
- Telephone number
- Date of accident
- Location of accident
- Cause of accident
- Details of injuries
- Details of first aid given
- Name of hospital (if applicable)
- Treatment received.

Signature .... Date ....

In the case of accidents, injuries, etc. which come under the RADAR or RIDDOR Regulations, these should be reported as per the guidelines.

Consumer Protection Act 1987

Part III of the Act makes it a criminal offence for a person, in the course of any business, to give, by any means whatever, to any consumer an indication which is misleading as to the price at which any goods, services, accommodation or facilities are available.

A price is misleading if:

- It is, in fact, more than the price given
- It is described as being generally available, but is really only applicable in certain circumstances. For example, the coach fare from London to Rome is given as £80; however, in order to get a ticket at this price, the consumer has to be a student
- If the price includes other things for which an additional charge is, in fact, made. For example, the price of a holiday is given as '£150, which includes flight and self-catering accommodation. There will be a coach to transport you from the airport to your apartment'. Customers are not aware from this that there is an additional charge for the return transfer from the airport by coach.

Due to this Act, tour operators must pay particular care when setting price indications for their customers. An offence will be committed even if the price indication was innocent when it was set but subsequently becomes misleading. Tour operators must take all reasonable action to prevent consumers relying on the misleading price indication. They may therefore try to protect themselves by inserting warnings concerning extra charges, for example, airport charges and surcharges in their brochure. If warnings are inserted, this should be done in such a way that they are obvious to the consumer (not in small print at the end of the brochure so that the customer does not notice them).

Trades Description Act 1968

This Act protects customers against false descriptions by those who are selling or providing services. Any description given, for example, of a hotel, must be truthful at the time it is written. If the situation changes – for example, if the brochure states that the hotel is in a tranquil setting and a building site is then set up next door

A – Surcharges (Packages)

We reserve the right to change brochure prices before you book. After booking, the price of your holiday is only subject to surcharge on the following items: governmental action, increases in fares or transportation costs, including the cost of fuel and increase in dues, taxes or fees chargeable for services such as landing/embarkation/disembarkation. Even in this case, we will absorb an amount equivalent to 2% of the holiday price which excludes insurance premiums and any amendment charges. Only amounts in excess of this 2% will be surcharged. If this means paying more than 10% on the holiday price, you will be entitled to cancel your holiday with a full refund of all money paid except for any premium paid to us for holiday insurance and amendment charges. Should you decide to cancel because of this, you must exercise your right to do so within 14 days from the issue date printed on the invoice. No surcharge will be imposed within 30 days of your departure.

B – Our Liability (Packages)

(a) We accept responsibility, where you do not suffer personal injury, should any part of the holiday arrangements which you book with us not be supplied as described in this brochure and not be of a reasonable standard. In such a case, we will pay reasonable compensation.

(b) We also accept responsibility where you suffer death or personal injury as a result of an activity forming part of the holiday arrangements you book with us.

(c) Our acceptances of liability in (a) and (b) above do not apply where there has been no fault on our part or our suppliers and the cause of your unsatisfactory holiday arrangements, death or personal injury is (i) your own fault (ii) the actions of someone unconnected with your holiday which were unforeseeable or unavoidable or (iii) circumstances which neither we nor our suppliers could have avoided or anticipated even with the exercise of all due care. Further, our acceptance of liability is subject to assignment by you to us of all your rights against any agent, supplier or sub-contractor of ours.

(d) Our acceptances of liability and obligation to pay compensation pursuant to clauses (a) and (b) above are limited in two respects. First, in any case other than illness, personal injury or death, the compensation you will receive is limited to such an amount as is in our view reasonable taking into account all relevant circumstances. Second, the amount of compensation will be limited, in accordance with the amounts set out in international conventions. In the cases of air travel, road travel, sea travel or hotel accommodation, specific limitations are set out in the provisions of, respectively, the Warsaw Convention as amended by the Hague Protocol 1955, the 1961 Berne Convention, the 1974 Athens Convention, the 1973 Geneva Convention and the 1962 Paris Convention. We will supply you with copies of the Conventions upon request but please allow 28 days for delivery.

(e) If you suffer death, injury or illness arising out of activity which does not form part of the inclusive holiday arrangements made through us, we shall, at our discretion offer advice, guidance and assistance to help you in resolving any claim you may have against a third party, provided we are advised of the incident within 90 days of the occurrence. Where legal action is contemplated our authority must be obtained prior to commencement of proceedings and be subject to your undertaking to assign any costs recovered or any benefits received under an appropriate insurance policy to ourselves. Our costs in respect of the above on behalf of you and your party shall not exceed £5,000 in total.

C – Surcharges (Other Travel Arrangements)

Whilst every effort will be made to minimize the impact of surcharges, we reserve the right to pass on any cost increases similarly passed on to us by product providers or in the event of any governmental action. In the event of surcharges exceeding 10%, you will be given the opportunity to cancel and a full refund will be made, with the exception of insurance premiums and amendment charges.

In any event, subject to government intervention, no surcharges will be levied within 8 weeks of departure providing full payment has been received by us. For bookings made within eight weeks of departure, once full payment has been received, no surcharges will apply.

D – Our Liability (Other Travel Arrangements)

We act only as a booking agent and have no liability whatsoever for any aspect of the arrangements and, in particular, have no liability for any death, personal injury or loss of whatever nature you may suffer.

The contract and matters arising from it are governed by English Law and subject to the jurisdiction of the courts of England and Wales.

Figure 7.2   Example of surcharge notice in a brochure

to it – the operator must inform the customer of these changes.

Thus a duty is placed on owner and operators that they should not intend to deceive the consumer through their descriptions, etc. Therefore Tour operators have to be very careful in the descriptions they use within brochures and other promotional material.

Sale of Goods Act 1979

This act is particularly relevant to tour operators. It puts a duty on businesses/organizations/tour operators to take care when selecting all the elements which contribute to a package holiday. If they have given care and attention to the elements of the package when they put them together, they cannot be held responsible under the Act for the day-to-day running of the services they have contracted. However, some of the responsibilities within the Act take on a different complexion with the advent of the EU Package Travel Directive. The main aim of this directive, which came into force in 1993, is to give package holiday consumers more protection and access to compensation when problems occur with their holiday.

The duties placed on package organizers include:

- Providing clear terms of contract
- Giving information to customers as to who is responsible for the package holiday which they have booked – this clearly highlights responsibility/liability in the event of complaints, etc.
- Giving emergency contact telephone numbers
- Providing evidence of the organization's security against insolvency and details about insurance policies available
- Producing accurate promotional material
- Giving immediate notification, with reasons, of price increases which are permitted by the terms of the contract.

Food Hygiene Regulations/Food Safety Act 1990

These provides regulations for the hygienic preparation, handling and sale of foods intended for human consumption. These regulations lay down minimum requirements for both food handlers and food premises, with particular emphasis on temperature control for certain foods.

Employees handling open food, other than raw vegetables, intoxicating liquors or soft drinks, must wear suitable and clean clothing. Meat carriers must wear clean and washable neck and head coverings.

Food handlers must:

- Wash their hands after visiting the toilet
- Refrain from spitting
- Keep abrasions and open cuts covered with a suitable waterproof dressing (usually blue)

- Refrain from smoking while handling food or when in any room where there is open food present.

As soon as a person employed in the handling of food becomes aware that he or she is suffering from or carrying:

- Typhoid
- Paratyphoid fever
- Salmonella
- Amoebic/bacillary dysentery
- Any staphylococcal infection likely to cause food poisoning

he or she must advise the employer accordingly, who in turn must notify the appropriate Medical Officer of Health.

Since many leisure and tourism organizations are involved in the preparation and sale of food as either their main focus of business (e.g. restaurant) or a snack bar, they must ensure that all their food preparation, etc. complies with the regulations prescribed or face being fined or, in exceptional circumstances, being banned from serving food.

Fire Precautions Act 1971

The Fire Precautions Act 1971 has been supplemented for many leisure organizations by the Fire Safety and Safety of Places of Sport Act 1987.

One of the main requirements is that most leisure/tourism organizations have to apply for a Fire Certificate from the local fire authority. Within this, certain procedures within the organization have to be specified: these may include:

- Regular fire drills
- Fire safety training for employees
- Fire safety record keeping
- Setting maximum occupancy numbers
- Keeping means of escape clear, including fire exits, corridors, etc.

Most hotels, etc. have to apply for a Fire Certificate, depending on occupancy at different levels/floors. In the past, there have been several fatal hotel fires, and management within these organizations must ensure that all staff are fully trained in fire procedures and that all guests have instructions about what to do in the event of a fire, so that if a fire breaks out, the building can be evacuated as quickly as possible without any injuries being sustained.

The laws/regulations discussed in this Element form the main focus of almost all leisure and tourism organizations. However, this is by no means a definitive, exhaustive account of all relevant legislation. The following are also applicable to leisure and tourism facilities/services depending on the size, scale and nature of the organization. Reference should be made to these where necessary:

Occupiers' Liability Act 1984
Public Order Act 1986
Licensing Laws
Environmental Protection Act 1990
Employer's Liability (Compulsory Insurance) Act 1969
Clean Air Acts 1956 and 1968
Fire Safety and Safety of Places of Sport Act 1987
Factories Act 1961.

Health and safety is a dynamic issue which is constantly subject to change and amendment. Many laws are introduced as a direct response to an incident that occurs. A clear illustration of this is the Fire Safety and Safety of Places of Sport Act 1987, which was a direct response to the tragic fire which took the lives of fifty-six people at Bradford City Football Club in 1987.

In addition to compulsory measures as documented above, the health and safety and security of employees and customers is ensured through a variety of different voluntary measures which are often so routine and intrinsic to the operation of a facility that they become part of the overall operation of a facility, integral to the service being offered.

Voluntary measures

Codes of practice

These are, in essence, a set of rules governing a particular sport/facility or operation within the leisure and tourism industry. Many are voluntary, and form a reinforcement of good practice.

Like many laws, Codes of Practice are frequently established as a result of accidents or problems that may have occurred within a particular field. In the area of outdoor activities, there have been a number of accidents/incidents where, for example, parties (including children) have been mountain climbing without the correct equipment and suitably qualified guides, or potholing without the necessary equipment – just to cite two examples. This culminated in the horrific tragedy where several young people lost their lives off the Dorset coast while canoeing as part of an organized holiday. As a result of this, a voluntary Code of Practice was developed by the United Kingdom Activity Centre Advisory Committee (ACAC) which developed a code of principles and expectations for the provision of organized outdoor activity centres. It remains to be seen whether this code will be enough to improve the safety standards of this type of centre. The activities undertaken at many of these centres are so hazardous, with many children involved as participants, that safety should be of paramount importance. If the centres are slow to comply with the code, established legislation is sure to follow on such a sensitive issue as the safety of our children.

Maintenance

Any effective leisure and tourism organization will have within its management policy a highly developed, well organized and carefully documented maintenance programme. This can be instrumental in highlighting hazards or potential hazards and dealing with them before they cause an injury to staff or customers. If a regular maintenance programme is not adopted, the facility will start to look run-down and the image and reputation of the organization will suffer accordingly.

Sources of advice on health and safety issues

Health and safety is such a broad subject, covering so many different areas, that it is very difficult for an individual to be absolutely sure of all the legislation/regulations/codes, etc. covering their operation, event or service. Therefore, a sound knowledge of where help and advice on these matters can be obtained is vital for any organization. These sources include:

- HSE/regional offices
- Local authority
- Environmental Health Department/Building Control Department
- Professional bodies (e.g. ILAM)
- Sports Council
- Governing bodies
- Fire authority
- Professional consultant firms
- Training agencies offering health and safety qualifications
- Universities/colleges
- Citizens' Advice Bureau
- Law firms, solicitors, etc.

▪ Assignment 7.1 ▪

Element 7.1 PC 1, 2, 3, 4, 5, 6, 7 Core Skills, Communication 3.1; 3.2; 3.3; 3.4 I.T. 3.1; 3.2; 3.3; Application of Numbers

You are a trainee working for a health and safety consultancy firm trying to develop your knowledge in health, safety and security in leisure and tourism.

Task 1

Select four leisure and tourism organizations, two from leisure and recreation and two from travel and tourism. For each organization, explain the relevance of the key laws and regulations on health, safety and security for each organization/facility selected.

Task 2

You are the health and safety officer within a large theme/fun park which includes parks and gardens, an open air swimming pool and a variety of different rides. In addition to being the health and safety officer, you are also responsible for the health and safety training of all new employees. As part of this responsibility, you ensure that all new staff receive information and training on health, safety and security within the theme park. Produce an induction booklet for use within the theme park. You must include the following information:

- *The importance of maintaining health, safety and security*
- *How health, safety and security is ensured in the theme park*
- *The purpose/relevance of the main laws/regulations relating to the theme park operations*
- *Sources of help and advice which could be used to assist in health, safety and security issues.*

Element 7.2 Ensure the health and safety of a leisure and tourism event

In this Element we will be looking at how health and safety is ensured at a leisure and tourism event. The following performance criteria will be covered:

1 Identify health and safety hazards for a leisure and tourism event.
2 Evaluate health and safety standards in relation to all aspects of the event and summarize the findings.
3 Make proposals for realistic measures necessary to ensure health and safety of the event.
4 Ensure that the proposals are consistent with relevant legal and regulatory requirements.
5 Implement the proposals in the course of the event.

6 Describe the appropriate sources of expert help, information and advice used for reference.

Identify health and safety hazards for a leisure and tourism event

As we have seen in the first Element, the health and safety of any facility or special event is of the utmost importance. Although many leisure and tourism special events are temporary and are constructed for one particular occasion or series of performers – for example, a travelling circus, a roadshow or an outdoor musical festival or event – just as for a continuous service high standards of health and safety have to be implemented.

Accidents do happen at events – fortunately, most of these are only minor problems, for example, cuts, scratches, etc. It is an established fact that in many cases accidents do not just happen, but are actually caused through thoughtlessness or bad planning. As has been seen in Element 7.1, it is no longer good enough to simply respond to accidents that may occur: under the new EU directives on health and safety employers have a duty to carry out a risk assessment which should highlight any potential health and safety hazards and to implement measures necessary to reduce the risks identified. Obviously some of the hazards identified will be specific to the nature of the particular event. However, all events will share a 'core' of hazards which exist. These may include:

Problems with the fabric of the building

- Damaged floors
- Damaged steps on staircase
- Unsafe/inappropriate handrails
- Unsafe/damaged doors
- Inappropriate floor materials
- Insufficient/inappropriate heating
- Insufficient/inappropriate lighting
- Inadequate parking capacity/siting.

Problems with the equipment, fixtures and fittings, etc. within the building

- Obstructed gangways/corridors
- Blocked fire escapes
- Loose wires

- Problems with floor coverings (e.g. a carpet that may not have been fixed properly leads to people tripping over it)
- Inappropriate equipment stores
- Inappropriate siting of chemical store
- Broken/damaged equipment
- Ineffective use of signs
- Insufficient advice signs for dont's (e.g. depth signs at a pool)
- Inappropriate light fittings according to the nature of the activities undertaken (e.g. unguarded lights within a sports hall)

Problems with staff

- Staff who do not follow instructions given and 'cut corners' can be a potential hazard to customers
- Unsafe storage of equipment
- Lack of staff training
- Fatigue
- Lack of concentration
- Failure to report hazards observed
- Failure to wear specialized equipment provided
- Failure to follow laid-down safety procedures.

Problems with clients

- Dropping litter which other people could fall over and which could become a health hazard
- Failure to comply with safety signs for example, height restrictions or certain rides within theme parks, etc.
- Running in a swimming pool area, etc.
- Movement around the event/facility
- Inappropriate equipment
- Offensive/violent behaviour
- Larger than expected number of clients attending the event.

In addition to hazards occurring within these categories, other 'external' features may result in a hazardous situation at an event. This may include, for example:

- The weather
- Sea conditions
- Problems with animals (e.g., birds, foxes, squirrels, etc.) which may affect machinery and cause a hazard.

Task 7.5

*PC 1 and 2 + 3.
Communication 3.1; 3.2;
3.3; 3.4; 3.1; 3.3.*

*You are holding a special
event as part of your Leisure
and Tourism course. You
have been given the
choice of:*

- *Organizing a sports tournament in the sport of
  your choice for 14–16-year-olds within your
  locality*
- *Organizing a disco at the local church hall for
  14–16-year-olds within your locality.*

*Before the event, submit a word-processed report
in a group for your tutor, highlighting:*

- *The health and safety hazards of your event*
- *The probability of these hazards actually
  occurring and the severity of harm likely to
  result from these hazards.*

*Make realistic proposals which would help to
reduce the health and safety hazards you have
identified.*

Many minor accidents occur at most events
(e.g., cuts, bruises, etc.), and although they may be
reported within the organization itself they are
not publicized nationally. However, when major
accidents occur they are often a focus of national
concern and interest.

Task 7.6

*PC 4 and 6
Communication 3.4*

*On 12 October 1994, a Pink
Floyd concert held at Earls
Court, London was cancelled
due to the incident which
occurred. Read the articles
'Stand collapses at concert'*
and 'Standing up for safety' and answer the
following questions:

1 *Describe briefly what happened.*
2 *How many people were injured? What was the
  nature of their injuries?*
3 *There had been a recent inspection of this
  stand. Who made it?*
4 *Guidelines exist which are intended to ensure
  that satisfactory safety standards are adhered to
  at this type of event.*
   - *Give the title of these guidelines*
   - *Give the name by which they are commonly
     known.*
5 *State whether true or false: These guidelines
  only cover outdoor events of this nature. Indoor
  events of this nature are not covered by these
  guidelines.*
6 *What was the aim of this code?*
7 *Which organization carried out an inspection of
  the stand after this accident?*

*The final paragraph of 'Standing up for safety'
highlights that an employer or employee found to
be personally liable for errors which occur as a
result of their negligence and which subsequently
result in an accident. State under which law these
people could be prosecuted.*

Fortunately, at this event there were no fatalities.
However, this is not always the case: the
Hillsborough disaster in 1989 resulted in the death
of 96 football supporters. When the accident was
reviewed, one of the main causes of the problems
was attributed to the late arrival of fans due to
delays on the motorway, the over crowding of
fans entering one particular section of the ground
and the failure of measures to open surrounding
fences quickly enough.

As a result of this incident, various measures were
adopted to improve the safety at such events.

Task 7.7

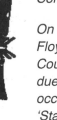

*PC 3 Communication
3.1; 3.2; 3.3; 3.4*

*In a group, research
the measures that were
introduced in response to
this disaster. You could
consult:*

STAND COLLAPSES AT CONCERT

Around 30 people were taken to hospital last week after a temporary stand collapsed at the Earls Court Exhibition Centre during a Pink Floyd concert.

The 20ft high stand, which had been erected by Arena Seating, had been cleared for use by the local authority's safety inspectors the previous morning.

The stand, which was supported by scaffolding, was holding 1,200 fans who triggered the collapse when they stood up to welcome the band on stage.

Victims said the whole stand tilted forward throwing some people 20–30ft to the ground, and then caved in like a concertina.

"We have used Arena Seating at Earls Court and Olympia many, many times in the past," said halls managing director Doug Littlejohns. "We are completely mystified as to why this accident happened."

The Health and Safety Executive is carrying out an inspection of the stand.

The incident took place on the same night as Channel 4 screened a *Dispatches* documentary on safety in stands at public events, particularly football matches. The exposé showed flaws at Premiership and Football League clubs despite the recommendations on safety made after the Bradford fire in 1985 and the Hillsborough disaster in 1989.

Standing up for safety

Stadium and arena operators are awaiting the results of the inquiry into the collapse of a section of a temporary stand at Earls Court on 12 October. Thirty-six people were taken to hospital with shock, bruising, and in the most severe cases, back injuries. All have now been released.

The collapse occurred at the beginning of a Pink Floyd concert as the crowd stood to welcome the band. The 20ft high stand, which was holding around 1,200 people, had been cleared for use by the Royal Borough of Kensington and Chelsea's safety inspectors the night before. The concert was cancelled and held on 17 October.

Accident like this, which occur in spite of stands having passed current inspections, are an operator's worst nightmare. They have a detrimental effect on all events and also a dangerous habit of becoming confused in the public's mind with every other incident which has occurred in a public space, giving an impression that the industry is inherently unsafe. This is obviously the last thing the stadia and arenas market needs, as it battles to keep the volume of business up in the face of rising costs and pressurized profit margins. While the market awaits the outcome of the investigation into the cause of the accident, the issue of safety in leisure settings is being reviewed by a number of operators and councils.

There is still some confusion in the market about the standards required by the licensing body for both indoor and outdoor events, and also about the guidelines which exist to ensure satisfactory safety standards are adhered to. The publication of the *Guide to Health,*

Safety and Welfare at Pop Concerts and Similar Events, more commonly known as the 'Pop Code', in 1993 was intended to standardize the safety requirements under which events are operated and to lead to a consistency of enforcement approach across the country.

There are still operators who believe that the pop code only applied to outdoor events when it does, in fact, cover both indoor and outdoor events in the finest detail. The code was published by the Health and Safety Commission, the Home Office and the Scottish Office following extensive consultation and thorough reviews of a wide range of events from large outdoor concerts to smaller indoor gatherings. This information was used to develop the document which is exhaustive in its coverage of the safety issues involved with staging any public event.

The aim of the pop code was to create a document which could be used by both the operators of events and the inspectors, creating a collaborative approach to improving standards and ensuring that requirements were clearly set out in black and white.

One thing which is sometimes overlooked in these circumstances is the fact that individual managers are personally liable for errors which occur as a result of their negligence and which subsequently result in an accident. Such actions are brought through the criminal courts, meaning that custodial sentences are a possibility for the most serious misdemeanor. Individuals are not protected from the law by their status as employees, meaning that they have every incentive to ensure that safety measures are adhered to scrupulously.

Liz Terry, Editor

Figure 7.3 Two articles from *Leisure Opportunities*, 21 October 1994 (Copyright of Dicestar 93, tel: 01462 431385)

Match began -then all Hell let loose

Officers stood by chatting while trail policeman almost disppeared under sea of surging supporters

'POLICE MUST BEAR BRUNT'

Mercy mission by the carers

MP calls for 'full penetrating Inquiry'

Merseyside soccer giants join together in emotional tribute

Fans were trampled underfoot

THE GATES OF DEATH

Figure 7.4 Headlines on Hillsborough

- *Parents, etc.*
- *Local football clubs*
- *FA*
- *HSE.*
- *Articles from news papers*
- *PFA*

Although health and safety hazards can be assessed for potential risk, there are times when the unexpected action of an individual can raise problems of health and safety for others – for example, when a man suddenly ran out onto the racecourse at Ascot, endangering not only himself but also the jockeys and horses. Although detailed planning is carried out for such events, it must be remembered that it should also take place for the unexpected. This may include:

- Demonstrations
- Streaking
- Deliberate sabotage
- Mistakes made by an official.

High Court judge to head National fiasco probe

Jockey club official tells of 'profound regret' over National

The joke's gone too far

Racing chiefs act after Aintree chaos

<u>One simple fact evaded the starter...</u>

<u>Horses and riders are not machines</u>

Figure 7.5 Headlines on the Grand National

At the 1994 Grand National at Aintree the whole focus of the meeting was thrown into disarray.

Task 7.8

PC 3 Communication 3.1; 3.2; 3.3; 3.4

Produce a brief report on the incident which occurred. In a group, produce recommendations to prevent a repeat of this incident in the future.

Measures taken to ensure health and safety

Safety

Implementing legislation

As we have seen in Element 7.1, the legislation, regulations and codes of practice which cover leisure and tourism events and facilities are diverse and cover many different areas of operation. All organizations should be familiar with the legislation applicable to their organization and implement it accordingly. As this is such a broad field which is of the utmost importance, any organization would be well advised to seek help and advice on health and safety issues.

Sources of help and advice on health and safety

As was shown in Element 7.1, there are many different sources of help and advice available to leisure and tourism managers. These include:

- The HSE
- Local authority
  - Environmental Health Department (EHO)
  - Building Control Department
- Local fire authority
- Professional organizations
- Governing bodies
- Private consultancy firms
- The Citizens' Advice Bureau (CAB)
- Solicitors

Staff training

A responsible, efficient management team will have staff training as a high priority. Staff should receive training appropriate to the position they hold. For example, a receptionist at the leisure centre would not necessarily need to be trained in water-based life-saving skills, but may need to be able to treat clients with first aid needs.

All staff, even seasonal or temporary employee's, should receive health and safety training as part of their induction programme. There should also be regular updating where new practices are applicable. All staff should be well versed in emergency evacuation procedures, etc., so that in the case of an emergency they are able to respond calmly and efficiently.

Staff working in a hazardous situation should receive the necessary training and, if appropriate, personal protective equipment (PPE) relevant to the work undertaken.

Regular maintenance

A detailed, efficient routine maintenance programme will contribute significantly to reduce the health and safety hazards within an event. This is useful, as it operates an early warning system of problems that may occur (e.g., faults with machines, which, if left unattended, could result in a hazardous situation for both employees and clients).

Risk assessment inspections

Under new EU directives it is no longer good enough to react to problems or hazards as they occur (see Element 7.1). Organizations must now try to anticipate problems which may occur by undertaking risk assessment and implementing corrective measures.

Corrective maintenance

If a client or an employee experiences a problem with equipment or a fitting, etc. in the course of the event, this should be reported to the manager who should take steps to rectify the problem. If the maintenance cannot be undertaken immediately, the equipment should be withdrawn from use until such time as it is put right. If the equipment cannot be removed, a large notice should be attached to it advising clients that it is *not* to be used.

Customers with special needs

The fabric and equipment within the facility/event should be assessed to ensure the health and safety of customers with special needs. These could include:

- The elderly
- The disabled
- The very young
- Mothers/fathers with babies or young children
- People with special needs.

Measures taken to try to ensure the health and safety of this group may include some or all of the following:

- Disabled parking
- Parent and child parking
- Disabled toilets
- Specialized equipment for the disabled relative to the activity to be undertaken
- Lifts
- Low-level reception/phones, etc.
- Highchairs, etc.
- Safe, secure, hygienic changing areas
- Child/baby feeding areas
- Safe ramps.

Special Facilities.

We hope the following information will assist your movement around the site and enable you to visit every attraction. Should you need any further assistance please do not hesitate to contact any member of staff.

TOILETS

Disabled facilities are situated in the following areas:
New York Street
Exhibition Hall, upper level
Stables Restaurant, Grape Street
Deerstalker Pub, Baker Street

LIFTS

A lift is situated inside the New York De Vere Hotel, for access to upper level.

SHOWS

There is disabled access to all shows on site, as follows:-

UFO Zone:	Via entrance ramp on Grape Street.
MotionMaster:	Although this attraction cannot be ridden by disabled guests, the film may be viewed from a stationary position.
The Sooty Show:	In New York Projections, disabled access via ramp.
House of Commons/ 3D Show:	Via lift in entrance of De Vere Hotel, up to Exhibition Hall.
Sound Effects Show/ Make-Up Show:	Situated on ground level.

Access Coronation Street via lift in New York De Vere Hotel and through Baker Street set.

EXIT

When you are ready to leave the grounds please make your way to the main entrance gate, which will be opened for you.

BABY CHANGING

New York Street
Stables Restaurant, Grape Street
Rovers Return Pub

TELEPHONES

New York Street
Coronation Street
Rovers Return Pub

PHOTOGRAPHY

Photography of the Tour is encouraged. Free camera hire courtesy of Kodak is available from Laughing Stock on New York Street. Films are sold in all our shops.

Figure 7.6 Special facilities

Some organizations produce information about special facilities for clients as part of their literature (See Figure 7.6).

Emergency procedures

All leisure and tourism organizations should have prescribed emergency procedures which are clearly written and understood by all employees. Furthermore, appropriate signage relevant to these procedures should be displayed as and when appropriate. Emergency procedures may include some of the following:

- Major accidents
- Heart attacks, etc.
- Bomb threats
- Suspicious packages
- violence/attacks on staff
- Fire
- Equipment failure
- Gas leaks, etc.

Finance

All responsible organizations will ensure that they budget for health and safety wisely within their overall allocation of funds. Budgeting may include provision for:

- Remedial emergency action on equipment
- Training of staff
- New equipment
- Response to new health and safety initiatives.

Case study

A new fun/leisure park was opened at Meretown. This consisted of a main fun pool with wave action, a smaller splash area, a jacuzzi and two flumes with access in steps and a waiting area.

The following were some of the measures taken to ensure the health and safety of bathers:

Poolside

- Glass doors – stickers on them so that they could be clearly seen

- Barriers to prevent diving, jumping in
- Depth markers
- Signs advice to bathers
- Lifeguards (number appropriate to facility, etc.)
- Flashing yellow warning light=waves in motion
- First aid signs
- Emergency exit signs
- Increased number of lifeguards on duty during wave action
- Chief lifeguard/radio contact with flume and reception and controlling movement of other lifeguards to ensure concentration, etc.
- Non-slippery surfaces.

Flume

- CCTV monitors people coming out of flume
- Member of staff with radio control watches people enter and exit flume using CCTV. Able to summon immediate aid if required
- This member of staff supervises clients waiting and entering flumes, ensures that they are orderly and follow the red/green lights which show that the next client may enter the flume
- The stairs leading up to the flume are shallow and non-slip
- The exit to the flume is in a trough of water which slows bathers down and stops their progress in a safe, controlled manner
- All bathers are out of the exit trough when the next person enters the flume.

Figure 7.7 Pictures of the pool

▪ Assignment 7.2 ▪

PC 1, 2, 3, 4, 5, 6 Core Skills
Communication
3.1, 3.2, 3.3, 3.4
I.T. 3.1, 3.2, 3.3, 3.4

As part of your Advanced Leisure and Tourism course you have been asked to participate in the organization and staging of an event. While you are participating in this event, ask a colleague or a member of staff to:

- Observe the way you ensured the health and safety of the event. This may be through:
  - equipment you used
  - dealing with signage
  - dealing with clients
  - responding to situations as they occur, etc.

  Ask this person to record their observations and comment on your ability/effectiveness to ensure the health and safety of this event.

- As you undertake the planning and implementation of the event, keep a working notebook of the health and safety hazards you identify as part of your chosen event.

- Detail the measures you take to overcome these hazards and the processes/procedures you put in place (e.g. evacuation procedures, accident reporting, etc.). Remember that the measures you propose for ensuring the health and safety of this event should be realistic and consistent with relevant legal and regulatory requirements.

- Evaluate these hazards in terms of:
  - the probability of these hazards occurring
  - the severity of harm likely to be caused by the hazards.

- Describe the source you have used or possibly could use. Refer to your tutor for help and advice on health and safety issues for a similar type of event.

- Produce your work in a suitably word-processed format.

Element 7.3 Ensure the security of a leisure and tourism event

In this Element the following performance criteria will be covered:

1 Identify security hazards for a leisure and tourism event.

2 Evaluate security hazards in relation to all aspects of the event and summarize the findings.

3 Make proposals for realistic measures necessary to ensure the security of the event.

4 Ensure that the proposals are consistent with relevant legal and regulatory requirements.

5 Implement the proposals in the course of the event.

6 Describe the appropriate sources of expert help, information and advice used for reference.

The need for security

Security is an issue which is high on both the social and political agenda. People want to be able to conduct their lives without the fear of theft, violence, etc. impinging on them. Realistically, many people nowadays have adapted their lifestyle to try to reduce these threats by adopting certain measures which help to make them feel more secure in their daily lives. These measures may include:

- Carrying personal alarms

- Installing burglar alarms and other security devices in their homes (e.g. window locks, etc.).

- Installing, car alarms

- Carrying a minimum of cash and relying on credit/debit cards, etc. for transactions

- Taking care when outside the home – for example avoiding, where possible, walking alone after dark (people may decide to walk with a friend or take a taxi).

It is not only the threat of theft which is a feature of people's lives, but the increasing use of violence which we are seeing in certain youth cultures within the UK. This may include, for example, carrying knives or other offensive weapons. It is against this background that managers within the leisure and tourism industry are forced to operate.

Security hazards in leisure and tourism

As we have seen, the leisure and tourism manager has to operate in a society where crime, particularly juvenile crime, is becoming an increasing threat. Customers visiting any leisure and tourism event or facility want to be able to feel confident that both they and their personal possessions are safe and secure for the duration of their visit.

Managers within leisure and tourism events/facilities have a legal and moral duty to ensure that everything possible is done in order to reduce potential hazards to their clients. These hazards may include:

- Violence
- Theft
- Fraud
- Sabotage
- Damage to property, equipment, etc.

Violence

As we have seen, there has been an upsurge in the use of violence, particularly within the juvenile population. Many sectors of the leisure and tourism industry have to deal with large groups of young people intent on having a good time. In addition to this, their behaviour may be affected by the consumption of or over-indulgence in alcohol or other substances. This may result in a more aggressive manner being adopted and problems occurring (e.g. fights, etc.).

Theft

The possibility of theft is always prevalent in leisure and tourism organizations. This may include:

- Theft of information: for example, on security, financial or marketing issues

- Theft of personal possessions of both clients and staff
- Theft of stock or equipment. Many organizations find that it is not theft by the general public which is their major problem, but theft by their own staff of stock, equipment, etc.
- Theft of cash – this could be through a direct attack on staff, inefficient handling and storage of cash, or dishonesty of staff
- Theft of organizational equipment.

Fraud

This may include such things as passing forged currency, stolen cheques, credit cards, etc.

Sabotage

This is wilful damage or destruction of property for political or economic reasons. There are events within the leisure and tourism industry which are at particular risk of sabotage – for example, the organizers of the Grand National have to include within their security plan measures to combat saboteurs. These may be animal activists who wish to interfere with the event, maintaining that this particular event is cruel to the horses taking part.

Other acts of sabotage may include acts of terrorism, with tourist attractions, airports, etc. being a popular target.

Damage to property, equipment, etc

This may include accidental damage to property on equipment, deliberate damage to property and criminal damage to property.

The extent to which any leisure and tourism facility or event is subject to this range of hazards will depend on its size, scale, nature, location and the security measures it adopts. A small, local church fete is far less likely to experience these problems than, for example, a large city centre pop concert.

Task 7.9

PC 1 & 2 Core Skills
Communication 3.1; 3.2; 3.4

From the list below,
select one event:

- *A local charity football match*
- *A firework display in a local park*
- *An all-night dance marathon at a local nightclub.*

Identify the security hazards of this event and evaluate these hazards in terms of:

- *The probability of hazards occurring*
- *The type of likely loss*
- *The level of likely loss.*

Ensuring safety in leisure and tourism

As we have seen, leisure and tourism events/facilities have numerous security hazards. It is the responsibility of the organization to manage its event/facility to ensure that these hazards are reduced to a minimum by the security measures it adopts within its operational practices, equipment, purchases, etc.

Violence

This can be reduced in a number of ways. For example, nowadays most young people are searched on entering a nightclub for offensive weapons or illegal substances. This measure will help to reduce the occurrence of violent attacks. Nearly all leisure and tourism organizations employ security staff on both the entrance/exit to the facility and within the facility itself. This helps staff to monitor their clients closely and to take speedy action if a problem suddenly erupts.

In addition to security staff, many organizations monitor their operation and the behaviour of clients both inside and outside the facility by the use of close circuit television (CCTV) cameras.

Theft

Organizations should adopt measures to try to ensure the security of their clients' and employees' personal possessions. Measures adopted may include some of the following:

- Use of lockers
- Secure/staffed storage areas (e.g. cloakrooms)
- Use of safes/deposit boxes
- Use of electric keys
- Notices warning of dangers of theft
- CCTV monitoring.

An organization may do as much as it can to ensure the safety of its clients'/employees' personal possessions. However, it is also the duty of the individual to act in a sensible, responsible manner and to make the task of the thief difficult. Far too often, people enjoying themselves and relaxing in a pleasant atmosphere forget the need for security of their personal possessions and fall victim to the attentions of the opportunist thief!

Theft may also be a problem within an organization itself, with stock, equipment/cash, etc., mysteriously disappearing. Theft by staff is a common problem within organizations, and measures to overcome this include:

- Efficient stock control
- Efficient storage systems
- CCTV
- Spot checks
- Staff areas, storage, etc. outside the 'controlled area'
- Rules about not carrying cash, etc. inside the 'controlled area'
- Warning notices, etc. in staff areas.

Car parking

This is a critical area in practically all leisure and tourism organizations. People want to be able to park their cars in the knowledge that they will be there when they return. Organizations which do not institute measures to try to ensure the security of customers' cars risk a serious loss of custom if theft of cars becomes a regular occurrence. Measures adopted to ensure the security of car parks include:

- Effective security lighting
- CCTV surveillance
- Regular security patrols.

Fraud

This is becoming an increasing problem with the greater use of credit cards, etc. Furthermore, organizations have to make sure that the money they accept is not itself forged. Measures adopted to overcome these problems may include:

Dealing with credit cards

1 Check that the card is designated as acceptable by the organization.
2 Check expiry date
3 Check that name/signature matches that on the card.
4 Check credit limit.
5 Obtain authorization if applicable.
6 Ensure that all data (e.g. cost, etc.) is correctly entered onto the payment slip.

Dealing with cheques

1 Ensure that all details entered on the cheque are correct (e.g. date).
2 Ensure that the amount of the cheque figures and numbers tally and do not exceed the limit on the cheque guarantee card.
3 Make sure that the client signs the cheque in front of the member of staff taking the payment.
4 Ensure that the signature on the cheque matches the signature on the card.
5 Make sure that the cheque guarantee card has not expired.

Dealing with forged notes

Due to the large numbers of forged notes in circulation, most organizations have installed special equipment which will detect fake notes. This may include:

- Special till guards which can highlight forged notes
- Special machines
- Forgery pens.

Staff must be alert to this menace, because if forged notes are accepted a great deal of potential revenue is lost to the organization.

Sabotage

This is often very difficult to combat, as it frequently happens very quickly and unexpectedly. Measures which an organization may adopt to try to combat sabotage may include:

- Police surveillance
- CCTV
- Increased number of stewards
- More secure fences/boundaries
- Extra vigilance by staff.

Organizations should incorporate into their contingency plans the threat from terrorists. Simple measures which can make the terrorist's job more difficult to achieve include:

- A responsive reception
- A tidy work area makes it very difficult to conceal an explosive or fire-raising device
- Staff should always be alert
- Staff should make eye contact with customers. Potential terrorists may feel less confident if they feel they have been 'noticed' by staff
- People dealing with telephone calls should be trained in how to deal with bomb threats
- CCTV.

Damage to property, equipment, etc.

Damage to property, equipment, etc. has been an increasing problem in the leisure and tourism industry over recent years. One of the major problems is acts of vandalism. Organizations have responded to try to overcome this problem by:

- The use of CCTV
- More durable design of equipment
- The use of special surfaces (for example, those which are difficult to write on.)

- Fitting security locks to doors and windows
- Employing security personnel
- Fitting intruder alarms
- Prompt action to rectify faults
- Security lights
- Design of building
- Restricted access to specific areas (e.g. PIN access to staff areas, etc.).

Case study

Dovedale Borough Council had a problem with its leisure centres. They were designed with corridors that had many areas where youths could loiter without being seen by the reception staff or staff on duty within the activity areas. These youths were causing a great deal of damage to the centre. The response of the centre was to instal CCTV and to employ extra attendants to patrol the corridors to spot these offenders.

When a new leisure centre was to be built in the town, the council wrote to the Sports Council to ask for advice on the design of the centre to improve security and reduce the problems they were experiencing elsewhere.

The Sports Council replied by suggesting that the council build a SASH (Standard Approach to Sports Hall) sports centre which was designed to be relatively low-cost, energy-efficient, and easily supervised.

- Pricing strategies
- Employee details
- Financial status of the organization
- Personal information about clients
- Client lists.

Organizations must ensure that this information is kept secure. Most organizations do this nowadays by using computer storage methods, with sensitive information being restricted to certain users, for example with access via an individual password. Organizations are advised to make 'back-up files' of the data stored on computer, for example using floppy disks. These should be securely locked away, and could be used if problems are experienced through computer viruses, etc.

It should be remembered that under the Data Protection Act (see Element 7.1) customers are entitled to see any information held about them on computer.

Legal and regulatory requirements to enhance the security of customers in leisure and tourism organizations/events

We have looked at the regulatory/legal aspects of security in Element 7.1. These included:

- The Trades Description Act 1968
- The Fire Precautions Act 1971
- The Sale of Goods Act 1979
- The EU Package Travel Directive 1993
- The Health and Safety at Work Act 1974 and new EU Directives on Health and Safety 1993.

Other Acts which assist in ensuring the security of customers and employees include:

- The Public Health Act 1936 – an enabling Act giving local authorities wide powers, including advising and specifying means of escape from buildings
- The Fire Services Act 1947 – this allows the fire services to advise on fire prevention
- The Licensing Act 1964 and the Gaming Act 1968 – these both give fire authorities the power to object to the removal of a licence on safety grounds
- The Private Place of Entertainment (Licensing Act) 1967.

Sources of information, help and advice on security in leisure and tourism

Help and advice are available from a number of different sources. These include:

- Fire authorities
- HSE
- Company safety committees
- Company safety officers
- Private security consultancy firms
- Environmental Health Department
- Local council Trading Standards Department
- Police crime prevention officers
- Security specialist equipment suppliers
- Professional bodies (e.g. ILAM).

As we have already seen in this Unit, the health, safety and security of both customers and staff are of vital importance to any leisure and tourism organization. How this is managed and ensured affects:

- The enjoyment of the user
- The morale of the staff
- The image of the organization itself.

Health, safety and security issues should be central to any new innovations or developments introduced into any organization.

▪ Assignment 7.3 ▪

PC 1, 2, 3, 4, 5, 6.
Communications
3.1; 3.2; 3.3; 3.4;
I.T. 3.1; 3.2; 3.3; 3.4;
Application of Nos. 3.1

As part of your GNVQ Advanced Course, you will undertake the planning and organization of an event.

Task 1

Ask a colleague or teacher/tutor to record, by means of a video camera or notes, how you assist in ensuring the security of this event. This may include some of the following:

- *Handling of cash/payments*
- *Dealing with goods*
- *Ensuring the safety of staff/clients' possessions*
- *Controlling the entrance/exit to the event.*

Task 2

Produce detailed notes on the security hazards posed by your chosen event. You should:

- *Identify the security hazards*
- *Evaluate them in terms of:*

  – *the probability of hazards occurring*
  – *the type of likely loss*
  – *the level of likely loss*

- *Make proposals for realistic measures which could be adopted to ensure the security of the event. These proposals should be consistent with the relevant legal and regulatory requirements*
- *Describe the sources of help and advice used to ensure security at this event.*

Produce your work in a suitably word-processed format.

EVENT MANAGEMENT IN LEISURE AND TOURISM

Element 8.1 Propose options and select a feasible event

Introduction

As part of your Advanced Level course you will be required to take responsibility for running an event as part of a team. As you progress through the Unit, you will gain an understanding of:

- The reasons why events are undertaken
- Their main characteristics
- The need for detailed planning
- How teams operate
- The need for review and evaluation.

An event is something which includes a range of different activities which have significant requirements for planning resources and evaluation.

Events are special occasions which are different from the routine activities of our daily lives. They are highlights which often linger for many years in the memories of the participants. Reminiscences of these events are often tinged with nostalgia. Problems that may have occurred at an event can lose this importance with the passage of time and are often recalled as a memory or as being memorable. The problems have faded into the overall memory of the event itself.

In this Element we will look at:

1 The distinctive characteristics of events
2 Objectives of events
3 Options which will achieve objectives
4 Realistic estimates of resources required
5 Realistic costs/benefits for the proposed option
6 Justification of the proposed option
7 Procedures at meetings.

Events play a significant part in all our lives. They are something which people look forward to with anticipation and, in most cases, expectations of having an enjoyable experience. Many events, for example the Grand National, attract large numbers of visitors to both the event itself and the area, and hence form an important aspect of the leisure and tourism industry.

Events are staged by all sectors of the leisure and tourism industry, including the public, private and voluntary sectors. They have the ability to lift an individual or an organization out of its usual routine and, as a result, can have a major effect on the participants – for example, someone attending a golf competition may be inspired to take up the sport themselves, thus embarking upon a whole new lifestyle! Or an organization, may generate new members by staging an exhibition match between two professional players.

When we think about events, large, major events immediately come to mind, for example, Wimbledon or the FA Cup Final. However, the nature of events that take place within the leisure and tourism industry are extremely diverse – for example, a regatta at a local sailing club, a five-a-side competition held at a local leisure

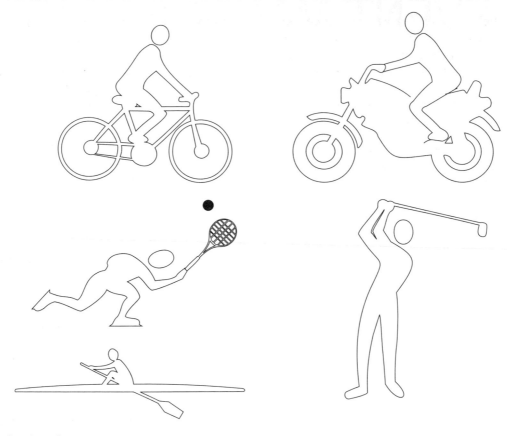

Figure 8.1 Overlay of events

centre, or the Rugby League Cup Final. They can be focused within a specific locality, for example, a village/scheme fete, they could be regional (e.g. a country show), national (e.g. the FA Cup Final) or international (e.g. The Olympics).

Although all these events share a basic organizational structure – for example, they all need to be carefully planned – although obviously the scope of these activities will vary according to the scale of the event. In addition to sharing features of organizational structure, events have the same distinctive characteristics.

Characteristics of events

- Perceived as something special
- Usually 'one off' or different from usual routine or programme
- Enable organizers to achieve their objectives
- Have set deadlines/schedules
- Need co-ordination

- May have a theme or mark a particular date or occasion
- Usually involve a group of people working as a team
- Involve a number of different officers (e.g. co-ordinator, treasurer, etc.)
- Require special allocation of resources
- Are usually undertaken in addition to or alongside usual duties
- Usually a relatively short-term completion
- Provide opportunities for enjoyment by the public
- Provide opportunities for the public to fill their leisure time in a variety of different ways.

Many leisure and tourism events arise due to a specific need of the industry. For example, the Blackpool Illuminations are a special event held every year to encourage tourists to visit Blackpool just at the time when traditionally visitor numbers to this type of seaside resort are significantly declining due to the onset of autumn and children returning to their new school year. This event has the bonus of extending the season of visitors to the resort into the autumn and attracts visitors who would not have visited this area at this time of year.

The leisure and tourism industry often has a want or prescribed objective when staging an event.

An objective is a short-term goal or target. For example, an objective of a Women in Sport event at a local leisure centre may be to increase the number of female clients using the centre.

Objectives of the event could include some of the following:

- Promotion of a worthwhile cause
- Making a profit
- Increased take-up
- Heightened awareness/interest in an organization's products/services
- Improve teamwork of staff
- Morale building
- Promotion of an organization
- Customers' enjoyment
- Promotion of an organization's image
- Benefits to the community
- Unifying staff in an organization.

Whatever objectives are set, they should be:

- Specific
- Measurable
- Achievable
- Realistic
- Time constrained

Task 8.1

A hotel in a popular seaside resort is holding a Murder Mystery Theme weekend. List the objectives it may have for this event.

In the event that you are planning as a group, you may find that you are not tied to prescribed objectives but are free to set them yourselves as part of your work in this Unit.

Once objectives have been set, a brainstorming session giving ideas of possible events which could fulfil these objectives can be undertaken. Some ideas/suggestions will be rejected immediately by the team as they may only appeal to a very limited group or they may be too ambitious. The following issues may be considered at this stage:

- What are the objectives of the event?
- Is there a suitable venue?
- Have we got the necessary finance that will be required to stage this event?

Once the more unrealistic ideas have been rejected, the remaining suggestions should be considered by undertaking a feasibility study to determine which, if any, event should be carried forward.

Feasibility study
This is an objective study to explore the viability and practicality of proposals that have been put forward as ideas for an event.

When commencing a feasibility study, many large organizations will employ an external consultant. However, in smaller organizations this task usually falls to an existing member/s of staff. The feasibility study should be an objective investigation into the capability of the organization/group in running the event in terms of both financial and operational considerations.

Detailed forecasts should be made as to the cost of staging the event and the projected income it will generate.

As much detail as possible regarding the event should be given for consideration within the study. This may include some or all of the following:

- The aims and objectives of the event
- Details about the nature of the event
- The perceived costs/benefits to the organization
- The timescales/schedules

- The implications for resources (staff, finance, time, equipment)
- Possible problems and solutions
- Health, safety and security issues
- Promotional details
- Forecasts.

On the basis of the findings of the feasibility study, a decision then has to be taken as to which event, if any, will be carried forward into the planning stage. If the event is staged within an organization, it is usually the senior management team who will take the decision as to whether or not an event is to proceed. Within a college situation, it would fall to the event planning committee to decide which event would be adopted.

Successful events require thorough and careful planning. For most events, there are many different tasks that need to be undertaken in order for the event to go ahead. It is, therefore, usual for an event planning committee to be set up to organize the proposed event. This team will have specific responsibilities – for example, usually a treasurer is appointed to manage the event's financial resources. Most importantly, a co-ordinator or team leader is elected by the committee to be the dynamo behind the rest of the group.

Roles and responsibilities will be looked at in more detail later in the Unit. However, it must be emphasized that how well the committee works together can either make or break an event. The committee should be supportive of each other and it is vital that a good communication network between members is established. Furthermore, in working as a team they should be working towards the same goal. This is one reason why setting clear objectives is so important, so that all members can know and understand exactly what it is that they are trying to achieve. Thus, fractionating and 'splinter' groups can be avoided.

Once the committee has been set up and the feasibility study completed, it is very important for all committee members to fully understand exactly why one particular option for staging the event has been selected over another. They should all be cognizant of not only the objectives of the event

but also the resources required, the cost/benefit forecasts and the constraints on the proposed event. In this way, individuals should be able to appreciate the scale of the task ahead of them and how different pieces make up the whole picture.

Whatever event is to be organized, a great deal of hard work, determination and often ingenuity are required to steer the idea through the planning stage to the execution of the event itself. One of the major problems that any event can face is one of resources. All necessary resources required to stage an event should be estimated as accurately as possible. The following could be included:

- Finance
- Personnel
- Health and safety issues
- Location/premises
- Environmental issues
- Disruption to other activities/programmes.

All events, whatever their size, will need some degree of financial support. The extent of this will obviously be affected by the scale and nature of the event itself. Financial support can be obtained from a variety of different sources: for example, sponsorship from local firms, help from local and central government. Once the necessary financial resources have been obtained, it is very important that they are monitored and documented so that an account can be produced to the event planning team as required. As events are frequently undertaken by leisure and tourism organizations in addition to their usual activities, careful financial planning is vital so that resources are not overstretched.

Most events need a variety of different skills/expertise in order for all aspects of the event to be managed successfully. Therefore, staff will need a variety of different qualities, with careful selection to ensure that all necessary skills are covered. In many events staged by the voluntary sector most contributions are made by unpaid volunteers, whereas large private sector events are almost exclusively staffed by paid personnel. Many of these could be employed for a short term, specifically for the staging of the event. All staff are part of a team and should be made to feel some sort of ownership for the event. This will increase morale and foster a team spirit.

Health, safety and security is an issue that requires careful attention in every event, no matter what its size. In addition to statutory requirements, organizers should remember that they have a duty of care to both staff and visitors. There are a number of specific laws and legal regulations which organizers should be mindful of: these are covered in Unit 7, Health, Safety and Security. However, it is always advisable to err on the side of caution and seek help and advice on this issue so that arrangements can be checked and any problems highlighted, with the necessary action taken. Sources of help and advice could be obtained from some of the following:

Professional associations

- Governing bodies
- Sports Council
- Emergency services
- Insurance companies
- Solicitors
- Health & Safety Executive
- Environmental Health Officer
- Accountants
- Security firms
- Special Event-running firms

Most events, however small, will need some provision for first aid. Often St John's Ambulance or the Red Cross are willing to provide volunteers who will staff first aid posts. However, when a large event is being planned it is advisable to contact the emergency services to give details of the event, with anticipated numbers attending and details concerning access, etc., in case an emergency arises which needs a prompt, efficient response.

The location/venue of an event should be thoroughly investigated for its suitability for the event for which it is required: for example, it should meet health and safety regulations, fire etc., and should be able to cater for anticipated numbers. It is not just the venue itself which needs to be considered but also other external factors – for example, adequacy of car parking. In addition to this, how the event affects the local

environment should be planned for. Will there be a disturbance to the local community through noise? Will litter left after the event be promptly and efficiently cleared up? Will members of the community be given sufficient advance warning of road closures or temporary parking restrictions that may be put into operation during the staging of the event?

Task 8.2

As has been stated, many leisure and tourism events are undertaken alongside the normal activities/programme of the organization; therefore, the event will almost certainly lead to some disruption of usual routines. It is important that this factor is anticipated and planned for to minimize the disruption both to the organization and to regular clients.

Whatever event is to be staged, the estimated costs and benefits to the organization/group should be carefully calculated. It is very important that a budget is set for the event, with each cost centre (e.g. advertising/marketing) being set its own budget within the overall financial resources available. If overspending occurs, this could seriously damage the predicted income and profit made from the event.

Many events will try to offset some or all of the cost of staging the event through, for example, sponsorship or advertising. At the Los Angeles Olympics the organizers were so effective at attracting financial backing through selling the television rights, etc. that the games were not the financial burden that they had proved to be in previous years.

Income can be supplemented through a variety of different sources prior to the event:

- Television/radio rights
- Sponsorship
- Donations

- Selling advertising space
- Grants (e.g. from local authority)
- Sale of merchandise (e.g. T-shirts, mugs, etc.).

All these factors need to be considered when analysing the finances of the event. As has been illustrated, not all events aim to make a profit; however, all events should include within their organizational structure a clear, concise, accurate record of all income received and expenses incurred. Most events, whatever their nature, will try to minimize expenditure and maximize income. Most events will have a clear picture of their break-even point.

Break-Even Point

This is the point where income covers all costs incurred. After this point a profit is made.

Task 8.3

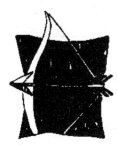

A photographic society is holding a Christmas function. The cost involved in organizing this event includes:

Room hire	*£ 50*
Catering	*£600*
Disco	*£100*
Printing	*£ 40*
Miscellaneous	*£ 50*

comfortably hold 200 people. Tickets have been priced at £15.00 each.

1 How many tickets need to be sold to reach the break-even point?
2 What profit would be made if all 200 tickets were sold?
3 Suggest one way that income could be increased by a fund-raising activity on the night itself.
4 Suggest what possible benefits this type of event may have for the photographic society.

Just as there are a number of different sources from which income can be gained prior to the event, there are also a number of different sources of income during the event which organizers may use to supplement the income from the main focus of the event. These may include some or all of the following:

- Income from raffles/competitions
- Car parking fees
- Sale of food and drink
- Sale of programmes
- Sale of merchandise such as T-shirts, mugs, badges, etc.
- Income from concerns. For example, at a school fair an ice-cream van is allowed to come onto the field in return for a payment to the event.

Obviously it is not enough just to consider the sources of income for the event, as any event will incur a variety of different costs which need to be incorporated into the financial overview of the event.

Costs that need to be considered could include the following:

- Hire of equipment/services, e.g. large events often need to have extra toilets
- Lighting and PA
- Radio communications systems for the key personnel
- Entertainment
- Staff costs
  - Salaries
  - Specialist training
  - Recruitment
  - Facilities for staff only
- Advertising and promotion costs
- VIP costs (hospitality may need overnight accommodation, etc.)
- Printing costs
- Security costs
- Signage
- Health and safety measures
- Bank charges
- Hidden costs (e.g. telephone, postage).

This is not an exhaustive list of costs, but illustrates the diverse nature of costs that are incurred within the event.

In addition to financial costs and benefits, other benefits to an organization include such things as:

- Heightened awareness of the facility/services by the public
- If the event is successful, it can mean a positive reinforcement of the organization's image within the community/region, etc.
- It can increase staff morale as their routine activities may have been interrupted, making their work more interesting/unify the organization.
- It can increase take-up of certain activities. For example, if a centre has a keep-fit exhibition this may result in more clients taking up these classes in subsequent weeks.
- If the event has been staged to raise money for a good cause, e.g. to build a new playground for local children, it will ultimately have real benefit for the local community, providing a safe, stimulating environment for local youngsters. It can also lead to better provision of facilities, with profit made being ploughed back into the facility, or improve the range or quality of existing provisions.

When looking at the feasibility of staging the event, the constraints must be clearly considered.

Constraints are something that will put limitations on the event or problems that the event may incur. As they are looked at, solutions to problems raised can be implemented. Examples of constraints could include legal aspects – for example, a group may wish to hold a local fund-raising social event in a church hall. If alcohol is to be sold, a liquor licence must be obtained. Other legal aspects may include such things as fire safety.

Some larger events may need to consider certain legal requirements such as contracts of hire or employment, franchise arrangements, insurance agreements, licensing of buildings, performing rights or copyright. It is always advisable to seek professional legal advice or consult specialist publications rather than attempt to muddle through.

Other events may have particular problems concerning health and safety due to the nature of the event. Motor racing has had to review its procedures/safety mechanisms for spectators due to accidents which have resulted in injury to spectators and course personnel. All organizers of events, whatever their nature, have a duty of care to their clients and staff to provide a safe environment.

All events need to consider security factors. At some events it is very difficult to keep unpaid spectators out due to the nature of the premises/environment used. For example, if an event is held in a local park it can be difficult to keep casual visitors outside the boundaries of the

Figure 8.2 Motor racing

event itself. This constraint on the event may be such that an alternative location is investigated.

The security of clients and staff for example, in terms of physical threat or danger to personal belongings (e.g., cars, etc.), must be considered. If a client experiences problems at an event in terms of rowdy, disruptive behaviour or theft, etc., it is unlikely that he or she would find the event itself enjoyable. Permission to stage some events – for example, pop concerts – have been refused on this basis, as there may have been problems with drug trafficking, theft and disruptive behaviour at events in previous years. Although this has an effect on the clients, it can also have an effect on the local community, as trouble can spill over into the surrounding area. This can lead to objections from local residents who do not want their lives disrupted, and this can therefore lead to organizers being refused a licence to stage the event.

Other problems that may arise include, for example, a lack of expertise of staff in a critical area. This may be overcome by staff training or by bringing in new personnel with the necessary expertise.

As has been shown, the problems that can arise and which can cause serious headaches for event organizers are many and varied. The types of constraints described are by no means exhaustive, but have been set out to illustrate how problems can have a marked effect on event organization to the extent that they may cause the nature of the event to be modified or, in some cases, cancelled completely.

Once all the aspects of the event have been documented, if a decision is to be made from a wide variety of options available it is important that this decision is reached after discussion of all the different options between members of the event organizing committee. It would be absolute folly to make a decision on the nature of the event to be undertaken without a full and frank discussion being undertaken. The reason for this is that if you want the team to be committed to the event this is far more likely if they have been involved in the decision process. Furthermore, each individual will consider the alternatives from a slightly different perspective. This can lead to

some members seeing advantages/disadvantages that others may not have perceived.

The discussion about the event option to be selected should be undertaken within a formal meeting structure. The formality of meetings varies according to their nature and purpose and can also vary in their degree of formality. Types of meeting can include:

- Working party meeting
- Sub-committee meetings
- Buzz groups
- Brainstorming session meetings
- Informal meetings
- Full committee meetings.

For the purposes of the Unit we will focus on a formal committee meeting.

Within an event organizing committee various roles or appointments of key positions will be made. These will be looked at in detail within subsequent Units; however, one member of the committee will act as chair or chairperson.

All meetings are governed by rules. Sometimes these are in the form of laws decreed by Acts of Parliament, sometimes in the form of company regulations lodged with the Registrar of Companies and others, in the case of voluntary societies, take the form of a constitution. Even in informal meetings where no written rules exist, there will often be a set of conventions or unspoken rules.

In any committee it is important to maintain accurate records of the meetings held, discussions which have taken place and decisions taken. These can then be referred to in the future if a dispute or query over a particular decision arises.

Such documentation could include:
- Notice of meeting
- Minutes of last meeting
- Agenda items
- Formal proposals Correspondence
- Reports (e.g. financial reports, written reports).

Prior to the meeting, members of the committee will be sent notice of the date, time and venue of the meeting. They will also be given the opportunity to submit items for the agenda and may be asked to submit reports for the consideration of the committee, for example, a financial report.

An agenda is a very important part of the meeting structure. As well as providing an early warning to help members to prepare themselves for topics to be covered, it can also act as a running order or schedule for the meeting itself. A skilled chairperson will ensure that the agenda is followed without red herrings taking up time and wasting effort. Furthermore, careful thought may be given to the position of an item on the agenda. Frequently, routine business/issues are completed before controversial issues which need lengthy debate are raised. The chairperson will know where best to site the items on the agenda.

Once the meeting takes place, it generally takes the following form:

1 Apologies for absence – The secretary records the 'apologies' sent in advance by a member unable to attend the meeting.
2 Minutes of last meeting – Here the chairperson will ask members of the committee who have normally received a copy of the minutes beforehand whether they represent a true record of the previous meeting. He will then sign them.
3 Matters arising – These are issues that have arisen or action that may have been taken as a result of the last or previous meeting.
4 Ordinary business – This will include new issues to be discussed at this meeting.
5 Any other business – This may include items which members may wish to raise that have not been submitted on the agenda but need consideration before the next meeting.
6 Date, time and venue of the next meeting.

During the meeting the chairperson takes a leading role. People wishing to speak should normally indicate this to the chair, who will invite them to comment at the appropriate time. This role of the chairperson is very important – if he or she is not careful, issues can be debated between a small group within the committee, and the committee can become fractionalized. The chairperson must ensure that all members have equal opportunities to express their opinions and that this is done in a reasonable manner. The chairperson can

be instrumental in avoiding major confrontations or 'slanging matches' between members by the way in which the debate is managed.

During the meeting minutes are usually taken by the secretary. These are the written record of a meeting. Producing minutes of a meeting is probably the most demanding task allocated to the secretary or his/her representative. As the discussion takes place, the secretary makes an accurate record of the business of the meeting. This will not be a word for word account; however, comments are ascribed to particular members and the secretary has to sift through all the dialogue and report the important observations and decisions. No-one would thank the secretary for reporting word for word an argument that may have erupted within the meeting. The secretary must also remember that these minutes will be closely examined before the next meeting by other members who will be quick to criticize inaccuracies noted.

Minutes are very important to an organization or an event planning committee as they are an on-going reference for decisions and resolutions taken. A decision made which is later disputed can easily be checked by looking back at the minutes where the issue was discussed and a decision made – it is very difficult to argue with a record that is written down rather than someone's vague recollection. This written record of decisions made democratically also avoids a unilateral decision by the chairperson or a subsection of the committee.

In some organizations, the minutes produced record only the decisions that have been reached and an account of how these came about or the discussion that took place. These are **resolution** minutes. On the other hand, an organization or committee may wish to record the discussion which led up to a decision taking place in the minutes. This will include the key points of contributions made in the discussion. These are referred to as **narrative** minutes.

It is becoming quite common practice for the outcomes of the meeting or action to be taken to be summarized at the end of the minutes, indicating who is to take the action and a target date set. This makes it clear to members whether he/she is required to undertake a particular action and the timescale in which it is to be completed.

Task 8.4

PC 7

Hold a meeting in your group to discuss the ideas that have been put forward for your event. Take minutes of the meeting and word-process them in a standard format.

In this Element we have looked at how ideas for events are carefully considered for their feasibility. In the next Element we will look at how events are planned as a team.

▪ Assignment 8.1 ▪

PC 1, 2, 3, 4, 5, 6, 7, 8.

You are a member of an Advanced Leisure and Tourism group which has been set the task of organizing an event. The group forms an event organization committee.

Task 1

Produce a report for this committee, explaining in general terms the distinctive characteristics of an event and detailing the objectives you wish to meet when staging this event.

You have now been asked to research what type of events could be held which would meet the objectives which have been set.

Task 2

Propose and produce a presentation for the general committee, suggesting three event options which will meet the selected objectives. Your proposals should include:

- *Realistic estimates of cost*
- *Benefits*
- *Resource implications*
- *Constraints.*

Task 3

You should indicate to the committee which of the three events is the most favoured option. In addition to your presentation, you should submit a paper to all members of the committee, summarizing the reasons for selecting this particular option.

Task 4

Once the options have been presented and the report considered, they should be discussed at a formal committee meeting, using a formal meeting procedure with relevant documentation produced.

Element 8.2 Planning an event as a team

In this Element we will look at:

1 How targets are set for an event.

2 Key factors which should be incorporated into an event plan.

3 A planning flow chart.

4 Allocation of resources.

5 Contingency plans.

6 Roles within an event team.

7 How to work with others.

8 A team plan for an event.

In the previous Element the way in which ideas for an event are analysed and adopted have been considered in detail. In this Element we will consider how the event is carried through into the planning phase. How this phase fits into the overall process of event organization can be seen in Figure 8.3.

One of the first tasks of any event planning committee is to set the targets they wish to achieve in staging and planning this event. As has been illustrated, nearly all events are the result of teamwork. Therefore, it is important to make the team feel that they are part of the decision-making process so that their commitment and drive are fully behind the work to be undertaken.

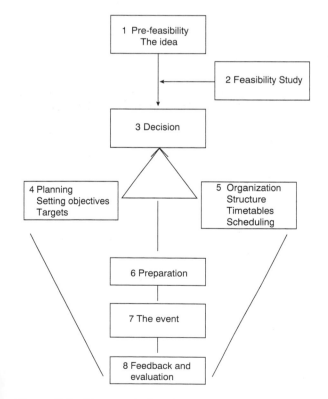

Figure 8.3 The event planning process

Furthermore, if the team is involved in the setting of targets for the event it will be much easier for everyone to remember their main purpose and will thus avoid people going off on a tangent and 'doing their own thing'.

Targets can be divided into two main sections: those to be achieved by an individual or group and those to be achieved by the team overall. For example, a member of a planning committee responsible for public relations may have been set the target of obtaining sponsorship for the event from a local/national company according to the nature/scale of the event. Some events could not be staged if this type of target were not met. The London Marathon depends heavily on the sponsorship it obtains for its very existence. It is by this means that the event manages to cover its costs each year.

Other targets which may be set for the overall team may include such factors as number of people participating in the event and amount of profit made by the event.

Like objectives, targets should be clearly set and should be able to be specific, measurable, achievable, realistic and time constrained (SMART). The responsibility for these targets should be clearly assigned, with everyone involved understanding the extent of their responsibilities. The importance of these targets will be seen when the evaluation of the event is being planned, as the extent to which the predetermined targets have been met will be assessed and reviewed.

Inherent in these targets will be the key factors of the event. These must be outlined in advance, with planning covering all the factors that have been incorporated into the plan. These would include such things as:

● *Anticipated income* – As was seen in Element 8.1, income for an event can come from a variety of sources. However, by calculating the anticipated income from all sources and the costs/outgoings of the event, the overall economic position of the event can be clearly understood. This should give an indication as to whether the event will run at a loss, break even or make a profit.

Obviously, as most of us have discovered at one time or another, the best laid plans can at times go wrong. The anticipated income of an event can be drastically affected by the weather. Organizers should prepare contingencies for these problems within their overall event strategy.

- *Promotion of the event* – It is very important to publicize the staging of an event well in advance of the actual date. This will enable people to fit the event into their calendar. The date of the event should be carefully selected so that it does not clash with popular major events – for example, the FA Cup Final or the Grand National – as this could have a serious effect on attendances. It is obviously very difficult to avoid all events clashing within a locality; however, the date should be planned carefully to maximize the attendance.

The promotion of an event will depend on the budget that it has been set. Many events have a very low budget, particularly small, local events. This type of event often relies on local avenues for promoting the event, for example, posters in shop windows, etc. Other means of advertising an event could use: fliers, adverts on buses, local/national radio; local newspapers, national newspapers; magazines; specialist journals; television; billboards.

early stage in the planning process. Some resources may need to be hired, for example, such things as public address systems, marquees, CCTV and toilets. It is important that these vital resources are booked well in advance to ensure that they are available on the day.

All items that have been booked from hire companies should be carefully documented. Anything booked over the telephone should be confirmed in writing. This documentation should be filed carefully at the time of hire, so that if there is a problem the arrangements made can be easily verified. The cost of these resources should be included in the expenditure of the event. Obviously some events will not have the necessary budget to fund a high rental cost, but this will be affected by the anticipated income of the event.

Other resources will include staff or human resources. If the event is in a leisure/tourism facility, there may be a ready 'pool' of staff available. However, even in these circumstances the orientation may have to 'bring in' certain skills to supplement those of their staff, for example, marketing skills. Other events may appoint personnel just for the life of the event plan, with more staff being brought in towards the event itself. Other smaller, more local events often rely on an army of voluntary helpers who all have different skills and expertise to contribute towards the organization of the event.

Task 8.5

PC 4

Morchester Races have a regular race meeting each year. They have decided to stage an extra meeting. Where would they advertise? Give reasons for your choice and costs, etc.

- *Resources required and their sources* – The team should draw up a comprehensive list of resources required to stage the event at a very

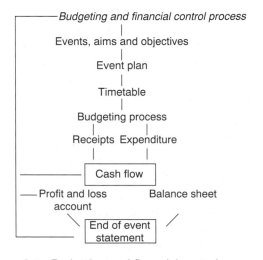

Figure 8.4 Budgeting and financial control process

Voluntary organizations can be a very useful source of help in an event – for example, the Red Cross and St John's Ambulance will often provide first aid assistance. Other areas where assistance is often given is from organizations such as Cubs/Scouts, Guides, etc. These organizations have a large pool of helpers and have been used, for example, to clear up litter after an event, with a small donation being made to the organization in question.

Financial resources are an important aspect of any event. Income could be obtained from a variety of different sources:

- Bank loan
- Education authority
- Sponsorship
- Local/National Sports Council, etc., working within a budget
- Fund-raising, etc. donations
- Advertising
- Prince's Trust
- Lottery.

The available financial resources should be allocated as they are required, with different sub-committees controlling them: for example, a catering sub-committee would be allocated a budget and would work within the financial parameters set. An example of how the financial resources could be managed within an event is given in Figure 8.5.

- *Health and safety* – Even the smallest event will have to adhere to the health and safety regulations which must be considered in the overall event plan. The organizers must consider the health and safety not only of visitors/clients but also of the staff. The following legislation may need to be covered within the overall plan:

- The Health & Safety at Work Act 1974
- Health & Safety (First Aid) Regulations 1981
- The Supply of Goods & Services Act 1982
- The Safety of Sports Grounds Act 1975
- The Derelict Land Act 1982
- The Countryside Act 1968
- The Betting, Gaming & Lotteries Act 1965
- The Licencing Act 1964
- The Fire Precautions Act 1971

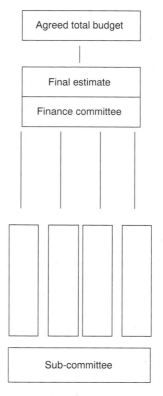

Figure 8.5 Budget formation

- The Fair Trading Act 1973
- The Occupiers Liability Acts 1957 and 1984
- The Employers Liability Act 1960 (Compulsory Insurance)
- The Employment Protection Act 1978
- The Defective Premises Act 1978
- The Consumer Safety Act 1978.

Over the last few decades there has been a significant increase in the amount of legislation relating to employees and customers, agents and health and safety. As these are very complex areas, it is advisable to seek advice when staging an event.

Insurance is another factor which needs to be considered, and a reputable insurance broker can give good advice on insurance for safety matters, etc., as well as other crises, for example, cancellation due to bad weather.

There are other things to consider, including performing rights, negligence, liquor licensing, catering rules, public entertainment, copyright and fire regulations. These will have some effect on all events, no matter what their size.

- *Security* is an ever increasing issue in leisure and tourism, and must be planned in minute detail if the event is to be a success. Security issues include:

  - Security of people (staff/clients, etc.)
  - Security of property
  - Security of money
  - Security of information.

  If an event is to function well, security of access in and out of the event should be closely monitored. There are some events – for example, pop concerts – where participants wish to enter and leave the main area many times within the day. Procedures such as tagging may be used, whereby a band is put on a person's wrist with a locking mechanism on it which cannot be opened without the band being cut. This type of security device is a quick, easy, efficient and effective method of controlling the movement of people in and out of the event. Another device, as used at Disneyland, Paris, is to stamp the hand of the client as he or she leaves. These stamps are sometimes visible, but in the case of Disneyland, Paris can only be seen when the hand is placed beneath an ultra-violet light. One great advantage of not being able to see the stamp is that visitors do not have to spend time after the event scrubbing the mark away!

When a team meets to plan an event, it must incorporate into its plan all the critical features of the planning process leading up to the event itself and the post-event administration and management.

A planning flow chart will help to highlight where different aspects of the planning process fit into the overall picture of the event plan. All members should be made aware of key dates and targets which should be achieved in order for the event plan to progress smoothly. Sometimes a delay in one aspect of planning can result in a backlog for other activities. A critical pathway within the overall plan charts clearly deadlines, action and dates. Anything outside this pathway could have consequences for the staging of the event (key steps through the event).

Task 8.6

PC 3

Make a list of the critical features of your chosen event. Chart these features against the time working up to the event so that the sequence and target dates of these tasks are very clearly illustrated.

We considered the nature of targets at the beginning of this Element. Target dates should be discussed at length within the planning committee. Setting unrealistic targets will help no-one and can result in an event having to be cancelled if not enough preparation time has been allocated. If one target is not met, it can have repercussions on other targets which form a sequence in a chain of events.

As part of the overall plan, provision should be made for contingencies.

Contingencies are solutions that you prepare in advance for problems which may arise. These may include emergencies such as:

- *Fire*
- *Illness/heart attacks*
- *Accidents*
- *Lost children.*

A plan should be carefully formulated for these occurrences, with all the team members being

Figure 8.6 Planning flow chart

briefed on the details of what if . . . . It would also help if, during the rehearsal for the event, the team is expected to respond to some simulated emergency so that the plan can be tried out. It is surprising, when something is actually acted out, how many problems can come to light that the theory had not covered. By having a 'dry run', problems can be overcome and solutions found.

Task 8.7

PC 5 & 6

The issue of lost children is very sensitive. With your team, formulate a policy to deal with lost children and supply briefing notes for staff who may have to respond to this situation from the perspective of:

- *Finding the child*
- *Dealing with the parents.*

Other contingency plans for non-emergency situations should be planned for. These may include such factors as:

- Traffic congestion
- Car parking problems
- Overcrowding in toilets
- Electricity
- Long queues at entrances
- Late arrival of celebrities.

In the next Element we will be looking at roles in greater detail. However, the event plan should include how the roles within the event are to be allocated, how different roles inter-relate and show the structure of the team, drawn up with lines of authority and reporting procedures clearly laid down as illustrated in Figure 8.7.

All members of the event planning team should be very clear about these reporting procedures and lines of authority, so that they know who they are to report to and where the lines of authority are drawn.

```
              Reporting structures
          5-a-side football competition
                   Co-ordinator
Secretary                        Treasurer
                          Publicity Officer
Participating
teams
                  Referees
Players
```

Figure 8.7 Lines of authority: reporting structure

As we have shown in Element 8.1, most events are the result of teamwork, with all members of the team working together for a common goal, using a wide range of skills and expertise effectively. We will see how a team works in more detail in the next Element. Within a team all roles work together to achieve a common goal, and the responsibilities and duties of team members will also be looked at in detail in the next Element.

Finally within the event plan, the team should plan how the event is to be evaluated. The evaluation process should include all the stages of the planning phase, from pre-feasibility to evaluation and feedback, as shown in Figure 8.8.

The style of evaluation will depend upon the nature of the event. There is much to be learned by reflecting on the work that has been undertaken. An evaluation report form could be adopted, using a similar format to the event evaluation list as shown in Figure 8.9.

▪ Assignment 8.2 ▪

PC 8, 2, 1, 2, 3, 4, 5, 6, 7, 8.

You are part of a GNVQ Advanced Leisure and Tourism group which has decided to stage one of the following:

- A celebrity football match in aid of charity
- A weekend of activities for underprivileged children
- A sports competition
- A party for senior citizens.

Task	Who?	With whom	When	Equipment	Other comments

Figure 8.8 An event action list

Subject:	TASK			
TASK WHO	ON TIME Yes/No	PROBLEMS ENCOUNTERED	COMMENTS	FUTURE

Figure 8.9 An event evaluation list

Task 1

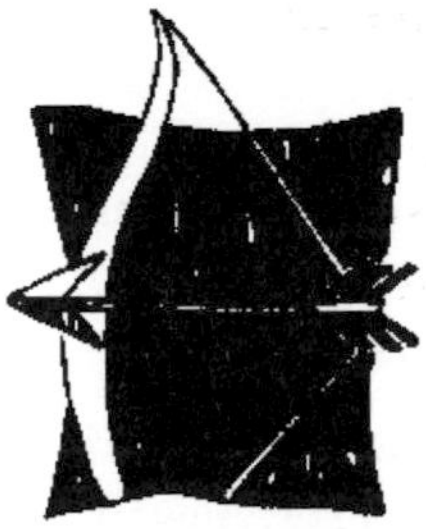

Produce a team plan for your chosen event, including targets, key factors, a planning flow chart, resources, contingency plans, role allocation, briefing and an evaluation process.

Task 2

Plan a method of observation of your contribution to the team plan. Record and present your observations in an appropriate format.

This does not give an exhaustive list of evaluation criteria, but could be expanded/adjusted as required. The evaluation process can be useful in a leisure and tourism organization as it may identify staff development and training needs. If this issue is handled sensitively, it can be a good morale-building exercise. However, if the evaluation process is used solely for 'back-biting' recriminations and settling old scores, then it will not be a useful mechanism and will prove a disincentive for people to become involved in event organization in the future.

In this Element we have looked at how the team plans the staging of an event. In the next Element we will look at how individuals' contributions/roles interact to produce the team effort in planning an event.

Element 8.3 Participate in the running of the team event

In the first two Elements of this Unit we have looked at how events are organized from the proposal stage to the formulation of an event plan. In this Element we will look at how individuals/groups participate in the running of a team event. In so doing, the following performance criteria will be covered:

1 Contribute to the team event according to the role briefing.

2 Make own contribution to the event, with due regard for health, safety and security.

3 Co-operate effectively with others during the event to ensure that it goes according to plan.

4 Recognize and respond effectively to any disruptions during the event.

5 Keep a log of own contribution to the team event.

Within a team event there are usually a number of different roles which need to be undertaken. Larger events may have a hierarchical management structure, with senior management, middle management and employees/volunteers/ support staff within the overall structure and with lines of authority and responsibility falling within this structure. Most large events will normally have an organizing committee which works in co-operation with the event co-ordinator. Small, local events are at times left to one individual to manage the whole event single-handed. However, more frequently a small committee is set up to ensure that decisions are taken in a fair and democratic manner. The number on the committee will depend on the size of the event and the number of people who are willing to become involved. Some committees will consist of only three officers:

- The chairperson/co-ordinator
- The secretary
- The treasurer.

Others will include a more comprehensive list of officers and may include sub-committees, for example, a finance sub-committee. This allows for work to be spread out and shared between a number of people so that one person is not overwhelmed by the magnitude of the task that faces him or her. In addition to the three officers listed above, many events include:

- A publicity officer
- A catering officer
- A facility officer.

Each officer has his or her own responsibilities within the overall team event management.

Co-ordinator

- Overview of the event
- Liaison with other members of the team
- Ensuring that all jobs are completed
- Ensuring that deadlines are met
- Raises problems, helps to find solutions
- Chairs event committee meetings
- Ensures equal opportunity of contribution at meetings
- Keeps order at meetings
- Ensures that agenda is covered
- May instigate use of a casting vote to decide an issue.

Administrator

- Deals with correspondence/letters, etc.
- Produces minutes of committee meetings and circulates to all members prior to the next meeting
- Assists other committee members with administrative procedures
- Sets up administration systems.

Treasurer

- Oversees all financial transactions
- Records financial transactions
- Holds cheque book (if one exists)
- Setting up a secure system of using the money available, e.g. designating two people – one of whom may be the treasurer – who are jointly responsible for signing and authorizing payments
- Produces an income/expenditure account, with receipts, etc. clearly documented
- Designs procedures for the secure holding of income before, during and after the event
- Ensures that the team meets the budget set.

Publicity officer

- Promotes the event
- Organizes promotional materials (adverts, leaflets, etc.) according to the scale of the event
- Liaises with outside agencies, e.g. local newspaper companies, radio stations, etc.
- Organizes press coverage of the event, e.g. arrangements could be made for a photographer from the local paper to attend.

Catering officer

- Provides hospitality services for the guests, staff and VIPs
- Orders all food/drink/catering equipment
- Responsible for hygiene
- Organizes catering team members
- Oversees preparation of food and drink, etc.

- Oversees clearing-up operation during and after the event.

Facility officer

- Finds and organizes the venue
- Organizes specialist equipment for the event, e.g. PA system
- Organizes security arrangements
- Organizes parking arrangements
- Organizes toilet facilities
- Obtains and displays appropriate signs
- Ensures adequate access into and around the building.

Each officer within the team should be clear on his or her position and responsibilities within the overall event plan. They should all have a clear understanding of the aims, objectives and targets both of the team and of their particular responsibilities within this.

Task 8.8

PC 1

A group of leisure and tourism students is planning a Christmas party at a local venue. Prepare a briefing for the role of the facility officer in this event. Demonstrate how the responsibilities/tasks involved in this position are organized and scheduled. Use the Event action list and Schedule for individual officers to help you in this task.

Many of the contingency plans within an event will be made by the whole team. However, within certain roles staff may be responsible for formulating contingency plans for their particular field of operations. This would be discussed with the rest of the event planning team, as contingencies made may impinge on other areas.

Role	Weeks before an event						After event	
TASKS	8	6	4	2	1	E	1	2

Figure 8.10 Schedule for individual officers

Task 8.9

PC 1 & 2

A safety officer at a firework display has been asked, as part of his role, to produce a contingency plan in the event of:

- *Minor burns*
- *Major burns.*

Describe the contingencies that this officer may plan.

All personnel, within their role briefing, should have a clearly designated responsibility for specific resources. If this is not organized effectively, resources at an event have a tendency to disappear. By giving clear lines of responsibility, this problem can be avoided. Resources which individuals may be responsible for may include the following:

- Financial resources (e.g. they may have been set a budget to work within)
- Human resources (e.g. they may have a team of staff working under their direction)
- Physical resources (e.g. they may be responsible for goods for sale or specialist equipment which has been hired).

In addition to individual briefings, the co-ordinator should ensure that all staff are briefed on a number of different issues fundamental to the success of the event. These may include:

- Customer care
- Health, safety and security issues
- Communication networks
- Keeping to published times.

Customer care

The importance of good customer care should be emphasized to all staff involved in the event. If staff are attentive and helpful to clients, this will add to the positive experience. Attention should be given to the needs of disabled customers.

Health, safety and security issues

All staff should be briefed on this issue from the perspective of themselves, colleagues, customers, the facility, information, the environment (e.g. litter, noise, pollution). If clients do not feel that they are in a safe, secure environment, their enjoyment of the event will be seriously affected.

In addition to health, safety and security being an issue which should be part of the overall event plan, each individual has his or her own contribution to make to ensure that this plan is adhered to and that safety practices, etc. which have been formulated are strictly followed. The actions of one member of the team who does not follow the health and safety guidelines may have a direct effect on other colleagues by:

- Putting them in danger when they are providing assistance
- Making their working environment unsafe.

Individuals are responsible for following health and safety guidelines in keeping with their individual role. If they are dealing with chemicals or substances hazardous to health, they should follow the handling instructions very carefully and wear the appropriate protective equipment which has been provided for them by the event organizers.

The actions of individuals may not only affect colleagues, as has been described above, but may result in a health and safety problem for both customers and the facility. Therefore, the importance of individual actions should be clearly appreciated by each officer within the event, and responsibility for this should not be taken lightly.

Officers within an event will also have responsibility for security issues. This may include relatively straightforward actions – for example, keeping watch over entrances/exits and goods on a stall – or may be more complex – for example, ensuring the confidentiality of information within an event. The marketing manager of a tourist attraction staging a particular event would be very careful to keep the information on attendances and success of promotional campaigns from its competitors, and systems would need to be established to ensure that all information stored was secure and remained confidential.

Communication

All staff involved in an event should be briefed on how communication between staff during an event will be established. Nowadays, with modern technology, mobile phones or two-way radio systems are frequently used at larger events. Not all personnel would have access to these, but

they would be made aware of their nearest communication point to minimize delay in an emergency.

Keeping to published times

Keep all times within the event running to schedule. If activities within the overall event are allowed to overrun their allotted time, this will have a domino effect on all other timings within the event – visitors may arrange their own schedule around the publicized times, and problems can occur if these go drastically wrong.

All personnel within the event planning team should have a clear overview of the resources for which they are responsible.

As has been shown, most successful events are the results of effective teamwork, with detailed and thorough planning being undertaken. It is important that all members of the team co-operate effectively with each other to ensure that everything goes according to the plan which they have devised. All members must have a clear knowledge and understanding of its reasons for existence:

- Objectives
- Targets
- Planning process
- Lines of authority
- Communication networks
- Resources
- Contingency plans
- Individual/team role allocations
- The evaluation/monitoring of the event to be undertaken.

All team members must be clear as to:

- *What* is to be done
- *How* it is to be done
- *When* it is to be done
- *Where* it is to be done
- *Why* it is to be done.

The most important person within the team is the team leader. This person will be of vital importance in ensuring that all the team work together as a unit and that everyone is kept up-to-date with events as they occur. He or she will be an important source of support, help and guidance. A good team leader usually means a good team and a successful event. A weak team leader frequently leads to failure.

Even in the most carefully planned events disruptions can occur. These may be caused by:

- Deviations from the team plan
- Emergencies, e.g. fire and accidents occurring
- The weather
- Unexpected numbers of customers/participants
- A section of the crowd/visitors, etc.

Problems may occur within the team plan. For example, there may be:

- Illness of a key member of staff
- Failure to have a vital piece of equipment delivered to schedule
- Late arrival of a VIP.

All these factors would cause a disruption to the team plan, which would need to be modified to encompass the problem which has occurred.

An emergency situation may suddenly break out – for example, a fire may start, a person may collapse or have an accident. Although these incidents may have been covered within the contingency plans of the event, they will nevertheless lead to disruption, with all the commotion that this type of emergency involves.

The weather is an age-old problem, and the nature of the British climate is so changeable that an event can commence in full sunshine and suddenly a heavy downpour occurs or a storm may break out. This will have a severe disruptive effect on any event which is staged outdoors, with people scurrying to find shelter and to go indoors out of the rain. This in itself can cause problems and disruption to indoor facilities/services, with overcrowding, etc. becoming a problem.

Disruption can occur as a result of the number of visitors at an event being much higher or lower than expected. When numbers of visitors far exceed anticipated numbers, major problems can occur in pressure on space, services and facilities.

Organizers should keep a careful record of numbers entering an event to ensure that the number of entries does not cause a safety problem. Once the maximum number has been reached, for safety reasons no more people should be admitted until others have left.

Many events suffer disruption due to the behaviour of certain sections of the crowd. These may involve individuals (for example, a person streaking at a major sporting event) or groups (for example, animal rights' groups demonstrating at the Grand National).

Although disruptions can be planned for within the contingency plan, it is very difficult to cover all possible reactions of a large number of people attending an event. Some surprises are bound to occur from time to time.

Task 8.10

PC 4

As an event planning team you are organizing a disco for a local youth club. Describe the disruptions that may occur at your event and detail the action you would take in response.

During an event, many of the tasks an individual undertakes can be forgotten with all the general activity that is undertaken. It is helpful to record your contribution to an event by keeping a daily or weekly log of the work that has been undertaken by both:

- The individual member of the team acting alone
- An individual acting as part of a group.

If all team members keep this type of log, the contributions and development of the event can be clearly charted. This log should include both the processes undertaken in planning the event and the actual content of work undertaken. This would include:

- Process:
  - Schedule
  - Progress mapping
  - Revisions
  - Summary
- Content
  - Record of own contribution
  - Record of team's contribution
  - Adherence to the role briefing
  - How health, safety and security were maintained
  - Co-operation with others
  - Adherence to the plan
  - How many disruptions were dealt with.

Case study

A simple, local event organizer's timetable

1 As planning begins eight to six weeks before the event, the following should be undertaken:
   - Obtain/book necessary venue and facilities
   - Confirm the booking made for all items listed above
   - Produce an event plan
   - Obtain necessary support (staffing/volunteers, etc.)
   - Send information about the event to all possible interested parties and personnel. If competitions are to be held within the event, entry details, forms, etc. should be given so that participants can organize their entries, etc.
   - Ensure that all essential specialist equipment is available for the event
   - Schedule the purchase of any awards which may be needed (e.g. trophies, medals, etc.).

2 Two to three weeks before the event, the organizer/co-ordinator should:

   - Contact the media about event arrangements

   - Organize event security
   - Plan for increment/security of crowd
   - Arrange for all paperwork necessary for the day of the event to be completed (e.g. programmes)
   - Check with staff that all are clear on their roles and responsibilities on the day itself
   - Go over all arrangements and make sure that all aspects have been covered.

3 During the last week before the event, the co-ordinator should:

   - Make sure that all final arrangements have been completed
   - Arrange for necessary signs to be delivered
   - Arrange for signs to be erected on the day.

4 On the day of the event, the co-ordinator should:

   - Run a final check to make sure that everything is in order and everyone is ready to go
   - Hold a briefing meeting with all key personnel to confirm readiness and to deal with last-minute alterations and problems
   - During the event, make contact with personnel – support as necessary
   - Deal with problems that may arise.

5 Immediately after the event, the co-ordinator should:

   - Ensure that a press release has been prepared and sent to the local paper
   - Check that all thank you letters have been prepared
   - Remind the financial officer to chase up accounts and pay any bills outstanding.

6 Within one to four weeks, all necessary final reports should be completed:

   - Reports to participants
   - Organizers
   - Official personnel
   - Sponsors/supporters
   - A final event financial report
   - Recommendations for future events.

Task 8.11

PC 5

You are the co-ordinator at the local event detailed above.

Produce a log detailing:

- *Your contribution*
- *The team's contribution.*

You should build upon the case study and include all relevant details in your log on aspects of process and content.

Once all the contributions have been made in the planning of the event, a full review and evaluation of all stages of the event should be undertaken. This will be covered in the extent section of this Unit.

▪ Assignment 8.3 ▪

PC, 1, 2, 3, 4, 5

As part of your GNVQ Advanced Leisure and Tourism course, you are participating in the staging of an event.

Task 1

Keep a log of your own and the rest of the team's contributions to this event.

You should include in this log:

- *Process*
  - *Schedules*
- *Progress mapping*
- *Revisions*
- *Summary*

- *Content*
  - *Record of own contribution*
  - *Record of team's contribution*
  - *Adherence to the role briefing*
  - *Health and safety issues*
  - *Co-operation with others*
  - *Adherence to the plan*
  - *Management of disruptions.*

Task 2

Present a record of observation of your contribution to the team event. The record should reinforce the content of your log.

This could be achieved through:

- *Video evidence*
- *Minutes of meetings*
- *Witness testimony*
- *Tutor/student reviews.*

Element 8.4 Evaluate individual team and event performance

In this Element we will be covering the following criteria:

1 Agree with the team the evaluation criteria for the event.
2 Agree with the team and follow the evaluation process
3 Gather evaluation feedback from appropriate sources
4 Provide clear and constructive evaluation feedback to other team members on their performance
5 Respond constructively to evaluation feedback from others on own performance.
6 Identify factors which affected individual, team and event performance and explain why.

7 Formally present the overall findings of the team evaluation and suggestions for improvements in staging similar events in the future.

Evaluation is a vitally important aspect of the event planning process. Evaluation is not carried out solely at the end of the event, but is an on-going process throughout each phase of the planning both before, during and after the event.

As has been shown in previous Elements of this Unit, when the event is being planned the need for evaluation should be considered. Objectives with clear evaluation criteria should be laid down so that everyone is aware of what is being evaluated and how this is to be achieved. Evaluation criteria would include such things as, remember objectives (SMART).

If objectives have been clearly stated in this manner, it will be a relatively straightforward task to determine whether or not they have been met. As we have seen, some objectives are set for individuals, some for the event planning team and others for the event itself. Each of these needs to be considered carefully within their respective contexts.

Within the overall planning process of the event schedules and targets are carefully planned so that all necessary tasks are completed within the optimum timescale leading up to the event. If these targets, etc. are not met and tasks start to 'back up', this could lead to the event being postponed or cancelled.

Some targets may be cumulative, i.e. one task may depend on a number of others being completed before that particular task can be undertaken. These targets should be monitored closely throughout the event so that help and remedial action can be taken promptly before problems build up and cause friction between team members.

Accuracy of anticipated income

The anticipated income will have been estimated in the planning stages. As part of the evaluation process, the team should consider the financial statement produced after the event to determine whether the anticipated income was predicted fairly well or was well below or above expectations. If actual income was well below that anticipated, this will have a significant effect on whether the event is to be staged in the future.

Promotion of the event

This should be considered to determine the effectiveness of the methods used to promote the event (were the adverts placed at the right time, in the right place, etc.). Some events fail due to a problem with the promotion of the event. The media/locality used may be ill advised or the timing may have been wrong – too far in advance of the event or not far enough. Promotion is vital to the event, as even if all the planning has gone to schedule, if no-one turns up for the event it will be a failure.

It is important to receive feedback from visitors/clients to an event as to where they found out about the event (e.g. the local paper, posters, etc.). By doing this, we can determine which media is the most cost-effective in terms of numbers responding and lessons can be learned for future events. This information could be included in a feedback questionnaire which you may decide to give to clients at your event.

Resources

Did you obtain all the necessary resources required to stage the event? Was there a problem with any of these? If so, what was it and how could this be improved upon in the future? In terms of human resources, the event may have highlighted areas where staff need training. If this is undertaken, it will result in a positive effect for the individual, the organization and any future events which may be planned.

A review and evaluation of the providers of resources should also be undertaken:

- Were the resources of the standard required?
- Delivered on time?

- Maintained as necessary?
- Back-up resources available in the event of breakdown?
- Were any hire charges competitive?
- Did they meet the needs they were intended to cover?

In addition, the financial efficiency of resources should be considered within the overall income of the event. The following could be looked at:

- Staff costs : Total event income
- Operating costs : Total event income

Providers of services

In the event, certain services may have been provided by external agencies. The team needs to consider the quality and efficiency of the service offered. This should also be looked at in terms of relative cost within the overall income of the event.

Task 8.12

Core Skill

The cost of services at a 10-km. Family Run organized by a local authority leisure and tourism department was £1,500. The total income for the event was £10,000. Express this as:

- *A percentage of total income*
- *A ratio of total income.*

Health, safety and security measures

The team should review the measures taken within the event to determine whether there were any particular problem areas that came to light. A record of accidents/injuries/security problems at the event should have been made, in addition to any action taken. The team may find that they can learn from this.

Case study

An exhibition was organized by a tourist information centre, as part of a County Show, to promote local tourist attractions/services. Most of the exhibits were in a marquee, but one was housed in a small trailer which had very bright fluorescent strip lights.

When the event was reviewed, the first aid providers commented on the unusually high incidence of visitors requesting paracetamol for headaches. The only common factor between the headache sufferers was that they had all recently been into the TIC trailer to see the display.

As a result of this, the event team looked at the lighting used within the trailer to try to find out if any problems could be detected. They found that the covers on the fluorescent strip lights had not been cleaned for some time and were full of dust. This was distorting the light being emitted. All lights were subsequently cleaned, and at the next exhibition the incidence of headaches was minimal.

The security of the event should be reviewed, and problem areas discussed. Customers need to feel that they and their belongings are secure when they attend an event, otherwise this will seriously affect their enjoyment of the event itself.

Did the team adhere to the planning flow chart (Figure 8.6)? Was this planning flow chart used by individuals and the team? Was it helpful, beneficial and informative? Did any aspects of this cause a problem, or were there any weak links?

Contingency plans

- Were all contingencies covered?
- Were any contingency plans put into operation during the event?
- Were they successful?
- Did any problems occur for which a contingency plan had not been made?
- Lessons learned for future events.

All these evaluation criteria should be considered carefully and a reporting procedure should be established for this information to be collected.

PC 1

Design a proforma or a series of proformas which could be used to record reports on criteria to be used in the evaluation of an event.

Once the evaluation criteria and reporting documents have been set up, formal reports can be sent to the organizing committee, evaluating different criteria within the overall event. The evaluation process may vary in its methodology. There will be formal and informal evaluation.

Formal evaluation will be received in the form of a report from a variety of different parties, for example, individuals, teams, customers, sponsors, providers of services, etc. This formal evaluation may be contributed to by letters received from the public, which may be letters of complaint or congratulations.

Informal evaluation will take place through observation:

- Is the event going well?
- Is the attendance good?
- Are staff responding favourably?
- Do people seem to be enjoying themselves?

Informal feedback will also be received by staff from customers' comments – these could be reported, as applicable.

Feedback should be obtained from as many different sources as possible. These may include:

- Customers
- The team
- Staff
- External agencies
- Providers of services
- Sponsors (if applicable).

An evaluation questionnaire designed for each of the different parties listed above would prove useful in collection of evaluation data. However, sometimes relatively simple methods may be used as an alternative – for example, a comments book strategically placed for feedback to be obtained. The method adopted will obviously be affected by the scale of the event, the resources available and future plans for restaging the event.

PC 3

Design a questionnaire to be used to gain feedback from clients at an event. State the nature of the event, where these questionnaires would be sited and how distribution and completion would be organized.

As well as feedback on the event, evaluation of individual and team performance should be undertaken. Evaluation can be obtained from individuals' own assessment of their performance. This may include 'back-up' evidence (for example, from customer comments, etc.) to reinforce their own assessment. Individuals will not only be expected to undertake self-assessments, but will also be involved in assessment of their colleagues and the rest of the team.

As team members will be evaluating each other, it is important to remember that feedback given to colleagues should not be seized upon to score points or to settle old rivalries. Feedback given should be clear, concise and constructive. Any member of a team needs to learn both to give and receive feedback on his or her performance. This may involve learning things about oneself that may come as a surprise. A good team will realize the necessity of support for other members both when things are going well and when an individual is having problems coping with the feedback he or she is being given. It is often difficult for people to respond constructively when what is seen as criticism is levelled at them. This is sometimes seen when complaints are made by customers to members of staff about themselves. The way they deal with this will depend upon their confidence, maturity and professionalism. A good staff/team member should be able to accept criticism/feedback from a variety of sources and respond in a constructive manner.

An individual/team's performance may be affected by a number of different factors. These may include:

- Strengths of the team were effectively used
- Strengths of the team were not used in the appropriate area
- Staff did not have the necessary expertise for the job allocated
- Insufficient briefing to staff
- Weakness in communication systems
- Weakness in lines of command
- Weakness in reporting systems.

The individual/team may have been constrained in their performance due to issues beyond their control, for example:

- Legal requirements
- Health and safety issues
- Security issues
- Financial resources
- Physical resources
- Human resources
- Environmental problems (e.g. weather)

- Disruption to other activities which may be taking place.

Task 8.15

PC 6

At a school summer fete the person responsible for the catering arrangements spent £100 on cold drinks, £200 on ice-cream and £30 on tea, coffee and milk. All the tea and coffee was used, but only £20 was taken on cold drinks and £10 pounds on ice-cream. Give an explanation of why this might have happened and suggest a contingency plan that could be put into operation at a future event of this nature.

Once the evaluation process of the event has been undertaken, recommendations for future improvements can be made. These may include improvements to:

- Individual performance
- Team performance
- Factors pertaining to the event itself
- The event plan
- The evaluation process.

Once the evaluation process has been completed and recommendations made, it is important for the team to review their experiences in a positive, constructive, informal atmosphere. Within an event team, people have been working closely together and lasting friendships have been forged. The experiences gained often form a topic of conversation for many years to come, with amusing incidents being related many times over. The all-prevailing message that is often conveyed is, 'It was hard work, but a very enjoyable, rewarding experience'.

▪ Assignment 8.4 ▪

PC 1, 2, 3, 4, 5, 6, 7

You have staged an event within your leisure and tourism group.

Contribute to a team presentation, detailing the evaluation findings and suggesting improvements if this event was to be restaged.

Take part in a discussion with the rest of the event planning team. In this discussion you will cover the following topics:

- Evaluation criteria
- Evaluation process to be adopted
- Gathering/exchanging feedback
- Factors which affected individual and team performance.

This discussion should be recorded by:

- Taking minutes of the meeting
- Reporting on your contribution
- Asking another colleague or a tutor to observe your contribution
- Making a video recording of the discussion.

INDEX